CONCEPTS OF CALIFORNIA CRIMINAL LAW

by

Dr. George T. Payton

Emeritus
Administration of Justice Department
Evergreen Valley College

Formerly Sergeant
San Jose Police Department

and

Dr. James E. Guffey

Department Chair
Administration of Justice
Porterville College

Illustrated by

Tom F. Macris
San Jose Police Artist, Retired
P.O. Box 270
San Jose, California 95103

2000

Published by
Criminal Justice Services
P.O. Box 21115
San Jose, California 95151

Other Books by the Author

Patrol Operations and Enforcement Tactics
(with Sergeant Michel Amaral)

Peace Officer's Guide to Criminal Law
(with Dr. James E. Guffey)

Peace Officer's Promotion Manual

Typesetting and Technical Assistance
Vera A. Nazarov

Table of Contents

CHAPTER I   A Brief History Of Criminal Law In Western Civilization

1.0:0   **Introduction** 5

1.1:0   **The Development of Law** 5
     1.1:1   Family Rules of Order 5
     1.1:2   The Customs and Taboos of Small Groups 6
     1.1:3   Written Laws, Codes, and Ordinances of Larger Societies 6
     1.1:4   What Makes a Good Law? 7
     1.1:5   Laws of Ancient and Newer Civilizations and Their Effect on American Law 7

1.2:0   **Babylon** 7
     1.2:1   King Hammurabi 8
     1.2:2   The Code of Hammurabi 8
     1.2:3   Samples of Laws from the Code of Hammurabi 9
     1.2:4   Babylonian Legal Concepts In Use Today in the United States 10

1.3:0   **Egypt** 10
     1.3:1   The Egyptian Courts 11
     1.3:2   Selected Egyptian Laws 12
     1.3:3   Importance of Egyptian Law to the United States 12

1.4:0   **Israel** 12
     1.4:1   The Mosaic Code 13
     1.4:2   Moses the Lawgiver 13
     1.4:3   Examples of Mosaic Law 13
     1.4:4   The Talmud 14
     1.4:5   Ezra 14

1.5:0   **Greece** 15
     1.5:1   The Draconian Code 15
     1.5:2   The Code of Solon 15
     1.5:3   The Great Court Of Areopagus 16

1.6:0   **Rome** 17
     1.6:1   The Law of the Twelve Tables 17
     1.6:2   Examples of Laws from the Law of the Twelve Tables 17
     1.6:3   The Judices 17
     1.6:4   The Justinian Code 17
     1.6:5   Role of the Church in Preserving Roman Law 18
     1.6:6   The Fall of Rome and the End of Roman Law in Favor of Feudal Law 18

1.7:0   **Europe** 18
     1.7:1   Common Law of the Feudal Kingdoms 19
     1.7:2   Charlemagne's Capitularies 19
     1.7:3   Spain 19
     1.7:4   Las Siete Partidas 20
     1.7:5   The Code Napoleon 20

1.8:0   **England** 20
     1.8:1   The Common Law of England 21
     1.8:2   Trials in England 21
     1.8:3   The Magna Charta (the Great Charter) 22
     1.8:4   The Habeas Corpus Amendment Act 22
     1.8:5   English Jurists of Note 23

1.8:6   The Reform Act of 1832 and the Rules of Equity 23
1.8:7   Precedence (*Stare Decisis*) 24

1.9:0   The United States 24
1.9:1   The Pre-Revolution Colonies..24
1.9:2   English Mismanagement of the Colonies...........................26
1.9:3   The Declaration of Rights...26
1.9:4   The Revolution 26
1.9:5   The Declaration of Independence 26
1.9:6   Victory for the Colonies 28
1.9:7   Law in Post-Revolutionary Times 28
1.9:8   The States' Rights Concept in Our Early History 28

Chapter I Study Questions..33

CHAPTER II   Constitutional Law in the United States and Provisions for the Making and Administration of Law

2.0:0   The United States Constitution In Development........................39

2.1:0   The United States Constitution As It Deals With the Administration of Justice 39

2.2:0   The Amendments to the Constitution As They Deal With the Administration of Justice 42
2.2:1   The Bill of Rights 42
2.2:2   Amendment 1..42
2.2:3   Amendment 2..45
2.2:4   Amendment 4..46
2.2:5   Amendment 5..47
2.2:6   Amendment 6..50
2.2:7   Amendment 7..52
2.2:8   Amendment 8..52
2.2:9   Amendment 9..53
2.2:10 Amendment 10..54
2.2:11 Amendment 14..54

2.3:0   General and Specific Sources of Law 56
2.3:1   United States Constitution 57
2.3:2   State Constitutions 57
2.3:3   Federal Legislature (Congress) 57
2.3:4   State Legislatures 58
2.3:5   Counties, Cities, and Towns 58
2.3:6   Appellate Court Decisions 58
2.3:7   Historical and Cultural Background of the People 58
2.3:8   Executive Agency Rules 59

2.4:0   Police Power And Its Limits 60

2.5:0   The Model Penal Code..60

2.6:0   How Laws Are Made...60
2.6:1   The Legislature and Terminology.......................................60
2.6:2   Procedures Involved in the Making of a New Law 61
2.6:3   Through the State Legislature 61
2.6:4   Through a Referendum 64
2.6:5   Through an Initiative 64
2.6:6   Discussion 64

Chapter II Study Questions 69

CHAPTER III   Legal Research and Methodology

3.0:0   Ramifications of Legal Research 75

3.1:0   Judicial Review...75
    3.1:1   The Judiciary Act of 1789...75
    3.1:2   John Marshall and "Marbury v. Madison" 75
    3.1:3   Judicial Review of Lower Court Decisions 76

3.2:0   Precedent (*Stare Decisis*)...76
    3.2:1   Basis For Appeal...79
    3.2:2   Case Law and Its Uses...79
    3.2:3   Decisions of the Higher Courts..79

3.3:0   Case Law and Case Citations...79

3.4:0   The Use of the Law Library 80

3.5:0   The Legal Brief and Its Outline 95
    3.5:1   Writing a Case Brief...95
    3.5:2   Parts of the Case Brief...95
    3.5:3   Sample Case Briefs 96

3.6:0   Attorney General Opinions 97
    3.6:1   Weight and Effect of Attorney General Opinions 97
    3.6:2   Types of Opinions..98

Chapter III Study Questions...99

CHAPTER IV   General Aspects of Criminal Law

4.0:0   The Adversary System In American Law...103
    4.0:1   The Function of the Judge in the Adversary System 103
    4.0:2   The Ethics of Defending Guilty Persons 104
    4.0:3   Other Systems...104
    4.0:4   The Juvenile Court System 104
    4.0:5   The Claimed Injustice of Inadequate Counsel for the Poor....................105
    4.0:6   Plea Bargaining...105

4.1:0   The Purpose of Criminal Law...106

4.2:0   Rules Controlling the Language and Construction of Penal Statutes...................108
    4.2:1   Rules Controlling When Laws Are Considered To Be In Effect................110
    4.2:2   Interpretation of How the Law Is Written..111

4.3:0   Rules Controlling the Conviction of Criminal Acts 114

4.4:0   Legal Requirements For Citizen Action When Crimes Occur 116

4.5:0   The Meaning Of Terms Used In Penal Code Statute...116

Chapter IV Study Questions..121

CHAPTER V   Classification of Offenses and Punishment

5.0:0   **Classification of Offenses By Type of Law: Criminal and Civil** 127
      5.0:1   Major Differences Between Civil and Criminal Law 127

5.1:0   **Classification of Offenses By Seriousness: Mala In Se and Mala Prohibita** 127

5.2:0   **Classification of Offenses By Purpose: Substantive and Procedural** 128

5.3:0   **Classification of Offenses By Punishment: Felonies and Misdemeanors** 128

5.4:0   **Public Offenses** 129

5.5:0   **The Classification of Crimes By Punishment** 129

5.6:0   **Systems of Law: Statutory and Common Law** 130

5.7:0   **Punishment: Types of Sentencing and Special Penalties** 130
      5.7:1   Sentencing 130
      5.7:2   Types of Sentencing 131

5.8:0   **Lesser Offenses and Lesser Degrees of Crime** 132

5.9:0   **Crimes Without Victims** 133

Chapter V Study Questions 135

CHAPTER VI   Components Needed For a Criminal Offense

6.0:0   **Definition of Crime** 139

6.1:0   **Parts or Elements Needed To Constitute a Crime** 139

6.2:0   **Criminal Conduct** 139

6.3:0   **The Mental Element** 142
      6.3:1   Types of Criminal Intent 143

6.4:0   **Malice** 145

6.5:0   **Motive** 146

6.6:0   **Criminal Negligence and Recklessness** 147
      6.6:1   Discussion Of Elements Normally Involved In Negligence 147
      6.6:2   A Proper Standard of Conduct 148
      6.6:3   A Breach or Violation of that Standard of Conduct 148
      6.6:4   A Chain of Causation Exists Between the Original Act and the Final Result 148
      6.6:5   Some Harm or Injury Results from the Negligence 149
      6.6:6   Example of Negligence By Applying Five Elements 149
      6.6:7   Recklessness 150
      6.6:8   Degrees of Care or Responsibility Between Classification of Criminal Offenses 150

6.7:0   **Presumed Knowledge Offenses** 150
      6.7:1   Strict Liability Crimes 150
      6.7:2   Justification for Strict or Absolute Liability Crimes 150
      6.7:3   Responsibility Under Strict Liability Offenses 151
      6.7:4   Strict Liability and Responsibility Under the Principal-Agent Rule 152

6.8:0   **Presumptive Laws** 152

6.9:0   **The Joint Relationship Between the Act (Conduct) and Intent (Mental Part)** 153

6.10:0 The Cause-and-Effect Relationship and the Doctrine of Proximate Cause...........153
    6.10:1 Causation 153
    6.10:2 Types of Causation 154
    6.10:3 Elements Needed for Criminal Causation................................154
    6.10:4 Contributing Factors In Causation 155
    6.10:5 Considerations In Applying the Doctrine of Proximate Cause........156
    6.10:6 The Difference Between the Physical Cause and the Proximate Cause 157
    6.10:7 Improbability of Outcome As It Affects Rules of Causation........157

Chapter VI Study Questions..161

CHAPTER VII Parties To Criminal Acts

7.0:0 Parties To a Crime In California...167
    7.1:0 Acts Committed Outside State 167

7.1:1 Who Is a Principal In California 167
    7.1:2 Advantages of the California System of Parties to a Crime 167

7.2:0 Who Is an Accessory In California...171
    7.2:1 Accessory After the Fact (After the Crime).............................171

7.3:0 Compounding a Crime..173

7.4:0 Who Is an Accomplice In California 174

7.5:0 Corroboration and the Accomplice 174

7.6:0 Parties To a Crime Under Common Law 175

Chapter VII Study Questions..179

CHAPTER VIII The Inchoate Offenses

8.0:0 Introduction To Inchoate Offenses.......................................185

8.1:0 Solicitation..185
    8.1:1 Elements of Soliciting..186
    8.1:2 The Dangers of Soliciting 187
    8.1:3 Merging and Soliciting 187
    8.1:4 Soliciting as Entrapment..187
    8.1:5 Corroboration for Soliciting...187

8.2:0 Conspiracy 188
    8.2:1 Dangers of Conspiracy...188
    8.2:2 Definition and Elements of Conspiracy 189
    8.2:3 Criticism of Conspiracy Laws 192
    8.2:4 Conspiracy and the Federal Government...................................192
    8.2:5 The Partnership Aspects of Conspiracy and Liability 193
    8.2:6 Withdrawal from a Conspiracy...194
    8.2:7 Proof of the Conspiracy 194
    8.3:8 The Scope of the Conspiracy 194
    8.2:9 Model Penal Code..195
    8.2:10 Proposed Federal Criminal Code 196

8.3:0   **Attempts To Commit a Crime**..196
    8.3:1   The Law on Attempts in California..196
    8.3:2   The Elements of an Attempt..197
    8.3:3   Two Classes of Attempt..197
    8.3:4   Discussion of the Elements..197
    8.3:5   Abandonment of the Attempt...201

Chapter VIII Study Questions...205

CHAPTER IX   Defenses Against Criminal Prosecution

9.0:0   **Introduction** 211

9.1:0   **Common Law Defenses**..211

9.2:0   **California Defenses Listed Under Section 26 of the Penal Code** 212

9.3:0   **Defenses Involving Mental Impairment or Diminished Capacity** 212
    9.3:1   Infancy 212
    9.3:2   Idiocy 213
    9.3:3   The Insanity Defense In California..214
    9.3:4   Persons Unconscious of the Act 216

9.4:0   **Defenses Based On Constitutional protection, Statutory Provision or Legal Rules** 217
    9.4:1   Former Jeopardy 217
    9.4:3   Entrapment as a Defense...218
    9.4:4   Statute of Limitations...219
    9.4:5   Immunity as a Defense..220
    9.4:7   Consent as a Defense 221
    9.4:8   Status as a Defense...221
    9.4:9   Self-Defense...221
    9.4:10 Legislative Intent (Spirit of the Law)...222

9.5:0   **Defenses Based On Lack of Intent or Criminal Negligence** 222
    9.5:1   Mistake of Fact 222
    9.5:2   Accident and Misfortune...222
    9.5:3   Innocent Agents 222
    9.5:4   Acts Under Force, Threat or Duress 223

9.6:0   **Other Defenses**...223
    9.6:1   Necessity as a Defense..223
    9.6:2   Physical Impossibility...224
    9.6:3   Corporations and Partnerships 225

9.7:0   **Illegal or Untenable Defenses** 225
    9.7:1   Custom and Matters of Honor as Defenses.......................................225
    9.7:2   Religion as a Defense..225
    9.7:3   Alibi as a Defense 225
    9.7:4   Irresistible Impulse (Uncontrollable impulse) 226
    9.7:5   Moral Insanity and Emotional Insanity 226
    9.7:6   Homosexuality or Sexual Deviance..226
    9.7:7   Contributory Negligence...226

Chapter IX Study Questions...229

CHAPTER X   Common Crimes and Their Elements

10.0:0 Homicide In General..235
    10.0:1 Elements of Homicide 235
    10.0:2 Breakdown of Homicide in California...236

10.1:0 Unlawful Homicide...236
    10.1:1 Murder (187 PC)..236
    10.1:2 First Degree Murder...236
    10.1:3 Second Degree Murder 237

10.2:0 Lawful Homicide 240
    10.2:1 Excusable Homicide (195 PC)..240
    10.2:2 Justifiable Homicide (197 PC)..240

10.3:0 Kidnapping (207 & 209 PC) 244
    10.3:1 Regular Kidnapping (207 PC) (Simple Kidnapping) 244
    10.3:2 Ransom Kidnapping (209 PC) (Little Lindbergh Law).................245

10.4:0 Assault (240 PC) 245

10.5:0 Battery (242 PC) 246

10.6:0 Assault With A Deadly Weapon (245 PC) 246
    10.6:1 Definition of Deadly Weapon..246
    10.6:2 Assault With a Deadly Weapon on Certain Classes of Workers ...247

10.7:0 Rape (261 PC) 247
    10.7:1 Rape In General 247
    10.7:2 Rape Of Spouse (262 PC)..250
    10.7:3 Unlawful Intercourse (261.5 PC)...250

10.8:0 Robbery (211 PC) 250
    10.8:1 The Elements of Robbery 250
    10.8:2 Degrees Of Robbery (there are two)..252
    10.8:3 Robbery of a Pharmacy..252
    10.8:4 Robbery and Extortion 252

10.9:0 Extortion (518 PC) 252

10.10:0 Disturbing the Peace (415 PC) 253

10.11:0 Burglary (459 PC) 253
    10.11:2 Shoplifting as Burglary..255
    10.11:3 Degrees of Burglary (460 PC)...255

10.12:0 Theft (484 PC)...255
    10.12:1 Degrees Of Theft (486 PC)...256
    10.12:2 Grand Theft (487 PC)..256
    10.12:3 Other Grand Theft Classifications 256
    10.12:4 Petty Theft (488 PC)...257

10.13:0 Vandalism (594 PC)..257

Chapter X Study Questions 261

CHAPTER XI   Title 15 of the California Code of Regulations – Corrections

11.0:0   **Introduction** 265

11.1:0   **Rules and Regulations of the Director of Corrections** 265
     11.1:1   Article 1 – Behavior..265
     11.1:2   Article 3.5 – Credits 265
     11.1:3   Article 8 – Appeals 266

11.2:0   **Inmate Resources** 267
     11.2:1   Article 4 – Mail...267
     11.2:2   Article 7 – Visiting 267

11.3:0   **Inmate Activities**...267
     11.3:1   Article 3 – Inmate Councils, Committees and Activity Groups. 267

11.4:0   **General Institution Regulations**..267
     11.4:1   Article 1 – Public Information and Community Relations. 267
     11.4:2   Article 2 – Security 267
     11.4:3   Article 7 – Administrative Segregation 268
     11.4:4   Article 10 – Classification 270

11.5:0   **Chapter 1 – Offenses By Prisoners** 270
     115:1   Assaults With Deadly Weapon by Life Prisoner (4500 PC).......................270
     11.5:2   Assaults With a Deadly Weapon by Prisoner Not Serving Life (4501 PC) 270
     11.5:3   Battery by Gassing by Prison Inmate (4501.1 PC)....................................270
     11.5:4   Battery Upon a Person Who is Not a Prisoner (4501.5 PC)........................270
     11.5:5   Possession of Deadly Weapons by Prisoner (4502 PC)..............................271
     11.5:6   Holding a Hostage Within a Prison (4503 PC) 271

11.6:0   **Chapter 2 – Escapes and Rescues** 271
     11.6:1   Escape or Attempt to Escape From Prison (4530 PC)................................271
     11.6:2   Escape or Attempted Escape from County or City Correctional Facility (4532 PC) 271
     11.6:3   Officers Aiding Escape (4533 PC) 272
     11.6:4   Assisting Escape or Attempted Escape by Prisoner
               Whose Parole is Revoked (4534 PC)..272
     11.6:5   Carrying Article Useful for Escape Into Prison or Jail (4535 PC) 272
     11.6:6   Escape by Mentally Disordered Sex Offender (4536 PC)...........................272
     11.6:7   Notification of Law Enforcement:
               Escape From Secure Detention Facility (4537 PC) 272
     11.6:8   Rescue or Attempted Rescue (4550 PC) 272

11.7:0   **Chapter 3 – Unauthorized Communications With Prisoners** 273
     11.7:1   Taking From or Bringing in Letters to Prisons (4570 PC) 273
     11.7:2   Unauthorized Communication With a Prisoner in Transport (4570.1 PC)......273
     11.7:3   Using False Identification to Secure Admission to Prison or Camp (4570.5 PC)......273
     11.7:4   Unauthorized Entry on Prison or Jail Grounds by an Ex-Convict (4571 PC) 273
     11.7:5   Smuggling Controlled Substances Into Prison or Jail (4573 PC)...................273
     11.7:6   Bringing Drugs or Alcoholic Beverages Into Penal Institutions or Jails (4573.5 PC) 273
     11.7:7   Possession of Controlled Substances Where Prisoners are Kept (4573.6 PC)..................274
     11.7:8   Possession of Alcoholic Beverages, Drugs etc. in Prison, Camp or Jail (4573.8 PC).....274
     11.7:9   Selling, Furnishing, Controlled Substances in Prison, Camp or Jail (4573.9 PC)..........274
     11.7:10   Smuggling Firearms, Deadly Weapons, or Tear Gas Into a Prison or Jail (4574 PC).....274
     11.7:11   Damaging or Injuring a Prison or Jail (4600 PC) 274

Chapter XI Study Questions..275

CHAPTER XII   Corrections, the Courts, and Inmate Rights

12.1:0   Introduction 281

12.2:0   Inmates and Litigation 282
   12.2:1   The Civil Rights Act 282

12.3:0   Access To the Courts 283

12.4:0   Inmate Freedoms and Institutional Security 283

12.5:0   The Bill of Rights and Inmate Rights 284
   12.5:1   The First Amendment: Religion, Mail, Publications, Visiting, and Expression 284
   12.5:2   The Fourth Amendment: Searches and Seizures within the Institution...........................285
   12.5:3   The Eighth Amendment and Cruel and Unusual Punishment 286
   12.5:4   The Fourteenth Amendment: Due Process and Equal Protection................................288

12.6:0   Suicide 289
   12.6:1   Liability Theories: Why Inmates Must Be Protected From Themselves........................289
   12.6:2   Categories of Factual Allegations 290

12.7:0   Legal Aspects of the Use of Force 290
   12.7:1   When Can Force Be Justified?..290
   12.7:2   Deadly Force 290
   12.7:3   Excessive Force 290
   12.7:4   Restraints 290
   12.7:5   Documentation of Excessive Force 291

12.8:0   The Americans With Disabilities Act (ADA) 291

Chapter XII Study Questions 295

Topical Index..297

Penal Code Sections Referenced in the Body of the Text..317

Case Citations Referenced in the Body of the Text 321

ABOUT THE AUTHORS

Dr. George T. Payton is a former Patrol Sergeant with the San José Police Department. He has a B.A. and M.A. from San José State University and an Ed.D. from the University of Southern California in Los Angeles.

When he left the police department to become Department Chair at a local college, Dr. Payton transferred to the San José Police Reserves in order to keep abreast of new developments in the field; he is a Lieutenant in that organization. He also organized the first Regional Criminal Justice Training Academy in Santa Clara County and established the first Campus Police at San José City College.

Dr. Payton is a veteran of two wars. He served first in the U.S. Navy and was later commissioned in the U.S. Military Police. He has written books in the area of California Criminal Law, Criminal Investigation, Patrol Operations, and Police Supervision. He has also written articles for several law enforcement journals. His biographies are listed in *Leaders in Law Enforcement, Who's Who in Law Enforcement*, and *Outstanding Educators*. Dr. Payton has also received the Outstanding Criminal Justice Educator's Award. He recently retired after twenty-seven years with Evergreen Valley College.

Dr. James E. Guffey is a former police officer, investigator and evidence technician for the City of Oakland Police Department (13 years). He has a B.S. Degree in Industrial Relations, an M.A. In Police Science from Sam Houston State University, and a Ph.D. In Public Administration from Golden Gate University.

Dr. Guffey is currently the Director of the Public Safety Division at Porterville College. In this position, he coordinates both the academic and vocational courses for law enforcement, corrections and fire technology. He was previously a Professor of Criminal Justice Administration at the California State University, Hayward.

Dr. Guffey is a retired Lieutenant Colonel (USAR) with 29 years of service to his country. During his U.S. Army career, he taught military science at the University of California at Davis, the Combined Arms & Services Staff School at Fort Leavenworth, Kansas, and was an adjunct instructor at the United States Military Academy at West Point, N.Y. Dr. Guffey has had numerous articles published in various law enforcement journals.

CONCEPTS OF CALIFORNIA CRIMINAL LAW

CHAPTER I

A BRIEF HISTORY OF CRIMINAL LAW IN WESTERN CIVILIZATION

1.0   **INTRODUCTION**
1.1   **DEVELOPMENT OF LAW**
1.2   **BABYLON**
1.3   **EGYPT**
1.4   **ISRAEL**
1.5   **GREECE**
1.6   **ROME**
1.7   **EUROPE**
1.8   **ENGLAND**
1.9   **UNITED STATES**

1.0:0   INTRODUCTION

Some students may feel that they have had their fill of history. To many it is something of the past, and they are only interested in the present and the future. There is, however, a definite purpose in covering the history of criminal law in western civilizations. That purpose is to gain an understanding of our present-day law. Thomas Paine, the American political theorist and writer, stated:

> It is by tracing things to their origins that we learn to understand them, and it is by keeping that line and that origin always in view that we never forget them.

Because man is not perfect, there has been a need for law throughout recorded history. Laws consist of rules of conduct that a society enforces to protect the rights of its individual members.

Laws are also made by a society so that it may function properly and preserve itself. No society, large or small, can function without laws. History shows us very clearly that there is a relationship between the greatness of a civilization and the quality of the laws of that civilization.

It seems that there is always someone who will complain about even the most just of laws. It has always been this way, and will probably always remain so. It is for just this reason that we must have laws. Man must be protected from the selfish acts of other members of his society. If it is left up to the individual to decide what is right or wrong in the law, then we are in serious trouble. There are always some who will be able to justify to themselves any act, including murder.

Let us take traffic laws, for example. Probably more people in our society complain about the enforcement of traffic laws than any other type of law. Yet if we were to completely abolish the traffic laws, or fail to enforce them, we would be taking our lives in our hands each time we drove our automobiles on the streets. You would never know whether a car coming from a side street would stop at the stop sign, or drive through it and hit your car because the driver didn't see you. Traffic officers can readily testify that a common statement made during the investigation of an accident is "I don't know where he came from. I looked both ways and he wasn't there."

Even with our traffic laws being enforced, the United States has more people killed or injured on its' highways in just one year than it has had soldiers killed or injured in over ten years of war in Viet Nam. You can imagine what it would be like without traffic laws.

1.1:0   THE DEVELOPMENT OF LAW

Laws and their enforcement are as old as humanity. Recorded history is filled with references to both the existence and the violation of law.

The Bible tells us that even before the creation, there were angels who refused to obey the law of God and were punished by being banished from Heaven. Humanity's very history begins with the violation of God's commandments, when Adam and Eve disobeyed a commandment not to eat the fruit from the forbidden tree. The violation of law continued when Cain murdered his brother, Abel. Today we see no sign that people have changed in any way.

There seem to be three major stages of development pertaining to law. This closely parallels the development of society from small family units to large civilizations.

1.1:1   Family Rules of Order

In order for the smallest family to function properly, there must be some system of rules of conduct or order. Even in the caveman family, if there were not some form of order, there would undoubtedly be arguments and fights over who would get the most to eat, or who was allowed to sleep closest to the fire, or who must stand guard in the middle of the night. There is also the necessity for someone to assume responsibility and to carry out the enforcement of the rules. Even in animal families this order is maintained to a certain degree by one of the animal parents.

In the fourth century BC, Aristotle, the famous Greek philosopher, noted, when commenting on the nature of man: "For man, when perfected, is the best of animals, but, when separated from law and justice, he is the worst of all."

Fig. I–1:   Aristotle Teaching

Aristotle went on to say that when man is governed by intelligence and by virtue, he functions very well, but when he lacks virtue, "He is the most unholy and the most savage of animals, and the most full of lust and gluttony." It was his feeling that if men join together to form a society, that they must, of necessity, have some form of law and a system for the administration of justice.

The rules for family order were unwritten, and were usually enforced by a parent. These rules were made by the elders of the family who, through years of experience, had arrived at a system of right and wrong. They would then enforce these rules on the younger members of the family for their own preservation and safety as well as for the betterment and proper functioning of the family as a unit.

1.1:2   The Customs and Taboos of Small Groups

As small families joined together with other small families for protection and general welfare, problems arose. The rules of one family would often contradict the rules of another family, resulting in friction. In order for these small groups to function, there had to be developed rules that applied to all families in the group. This resulted in the beginnings of government, and in the development of laws designed for that particular group.

For the most part, these laws were unwritten and took the form of customs (some times called "mores" — pronounced "more-aze") and taboos. Although it is sometimes common for the terms "taboos" and "mores" to be used with the same meaning, taboos usually have a religious or supernatural association, and are of a negative nature. Mores are social customs.

Often the purpose of the taboos was to protect the young members of the group and at the same time teach them obedience. Today some parents might tell their children not to go out of the house at night because of the "bogeyman," when the real purpose is just to keep the children in the house for their own protection.

The primitives would tell their children not to eat certain fruits or not to go into certain parts of the jungle because it was taboo. The real reason was that the fruit was poison, and that the particular part of the jungle that was forbidden had quicksand If someone violated the taboo and died from poisoning, or sank into the quicksand, the elders would tell the people that the violators died because they had disobeyed the taboo and angered the gods. This would result in the people becoming more obedient to all laws.

Mores are more often associated with the interpersonal relations between members of a group. The rules are most often positive in nature. Rather than say that you cannot eat certain foods, mores would tell the people that they must feed the elderly persons in their group when they can no longer work, or that the women must do the cooking for the men.

The enforcement of mores was accomplished through the acceptance or rejection of a person by the members of his social group. In small societies, this is a very effective means of enforcement because people always need the approval of those close to them. Even the juvenile delinquent, who violates the rules of society and is rejected by it, has the approval of his fellow delinquents.

1.1:3   Written Laws, Codes, and Ordinances of Larger Societies

As small groups increased in numbers of people, and as others joined small groups for the purposes of mutual protection and general betterment, there arose the need for newer and more complicated laws. As a society grows, its members acquire more property and material possessions than it had before, and the group often becomes involved in trade and commerce with other groups or societies. All of this in turn develops the need for new laws pertaining to the control and protection of property.

Some of the earliest known laws pertain to the enforcement of tariff and smuggling regulations in the Mid-East. They were the result of increased population and trade between different societies.

Because these new laws were more complex and detailed, it became necessary that they be written down so that people would not have to memorize so much. It also prevented misunderstandings in the actual wording of the laws. The law was there on tablets for all members of that society to see. There also arose the need for special people who could interpret these laws for individual situations or when there were extenuating circumstances. Thus the legal profession was born — judges were selected to hear all sides of the matter and decide if the law was truly violated. These first laws were inscribed on clay tablets as well as stone.

In the case of taboos, symbols and markers were often used to indicate the rule or the areas that were taboo. This allowed primitive peoples, who could not read, to easily learn the taboo symbols. These symbols would be similar to the "skull and crossbones" found today on bottles that contain poison, or the new non-verbal traffic and informational signs becoming so common. Below are samples of the new non verbal informational symbols.

Fig. I–4:   Modern Non-Verbal Directions

1.1:4   What Makes a Good Law?

There will undoubtedly always be argument concerning the conditions that make certain laws good and others bad. There are some basic considerations that can be used to evaluate a law as being just and lasting. The three most common are:
(1) It does the Most Good
(2) For the Most People
(3) Over the Longest Period of Time

To be enduring, laws must be more than simple rules of conduct. They must have a purpose that serves the common good of the people who live under them. Laws that are passed without the cooperation of the people, or without considering their rights and needs, are seldom effective. If the people do not accept a law, it would take one police officer for each citizen to make sure that the law was obeyed, This, of course, is impossible. Unfortunately, when laws are passed that people do not accept, the people not only violate those particular laws, they also develop a "law breaking" attitude that can carry over into other areas of law. The Prohibition law of the 1920's is an example. People do not have to like a law to accept it. If they realize it is necessary for the functioning of the society in which they live, they can accept it as necessary.

1.1:5   Laws of Ancient and Newer Civilizations and Their Effect on American Law

A short review of the laws of ancient civilizations will reveal how they all affected each other, and in turn affected the laws of the United States. In this review, only the western civilizations that have affected us will be covered. It should be understood that when ancient civilizations are discussed, we can only cover those civilizations of which we are aware. Hidden under the desert sands or fathoms below the surface of the Mediterranean, could very easily lie evidence of a civilization that would surpass all of those now known to history.

For example, in December of 1976, archaeologists from Rome University discovered the royal palace of Ebla, an ancient kingdom that extended from the Red Sea north to what is now Turkey and east to Mesopotamia. Thirteen feet below the surface they discovered the royal library con-

taining 15,000 clay tablets. These give detailed information concerning the life of this civilization from 2400 to 2250 BC. In 2250 BC. King Naram-Sin of Mesopotamia conquered Ebla and burned the royal palace. The fire did not, however, destroy the clay tablets. Preliminary examinations show that the tablets contain much information about the early Hebrews; as one member of the team stated, "It is as if we had ignored that Rome had existed and suddenly find out about it and the Roman Empire." Although it will take time for all the tablets to be translated, archaeologists believe they will soon discover even more libraries of clay tablets.

Below is a chart listing different civilizations. The arrows in the chart show the effect, directly or indirectly, of certain civilizations on others.

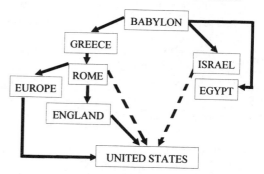

Fig. I–2:   The effect of civilizations on each other.

1.2:0   BABYLON

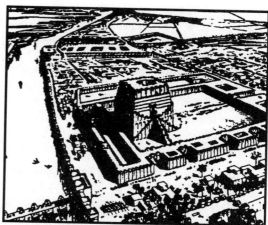

Fig. I–3:   Babylon

The most famous civilization in the area of Mesopotamia and Phoenicia was the kingdom of Babylon. It has been referred to as the "first seat of human existence."[1] It was here that the day was divided into twenty-four hours, and the hour into sixty minutes, and the minute into sixty seconds.[2] When Babylon was conquered, its enemies tore down almost everything and even plowed salt into the fields so that crops would not grow there. Because of this desolation, evidence of major laws of Babylon was not located for thousands of years. Reasoning would indicate that such a civilization must have had a major system of law. As Morris commented,

> A highly civilized community without an adequate system of law is as much an impossibility as would be a well disciplined army without a leader."[3]

Historians and archaeologists have found written references from civilizations such as Egypt and Greece that praised the laws of the Babylonians, but they could find but very few concrete samples of those laws. It was not until 1901 that a French archaeologist discovered the basement storeroom of one of the generals who had helped conquer Babylon. It was located in Susa, the ancient city of the Persian kings.

In it were prizes of war that he had brought back from conquered cities. Among the finds were three large pieces of black diorite, which, when pieced together, contained the famous law referred to by the ancients as the Laws of Hammurabi. Later it was called the Code of Hammurabi.

1.2:1   King Hammurabi

King Hammurabi was the sixth King of the First Dynasty of Babylon.[4] He reigned for about 55 years, around 2100 BC. (Although the records refer to important happenings, such as wars and floods, and mention the names of other rulers, historians can only estimate the date, because the records are inexact in this regard.)

King Hammurabi was noted for his military leadership and his desire to have honesty in his government. Unfortunately, when he was away fighting wars, his civil servants did not always follow his dictates. He also championed those who were less fortunate such as the widow and orphan. His law specifically mentioned them.

1.2:2   The Code Of Hammurabi

The Code of Hammurabi (also called the Judgment of Righteousness) was written on a seven foot, four in#h tall piece of black diorite, and contained 282 laws, but about 99 of them were not readable. Someone had purposely chipped them off the stone.[5] The type of writing in this code was cuneiform, which was the form of writing of the Babylonians. This writing was formed by symbols made from the imprint of a chisel, when it was held at different angles and positions. Since the Babylonians did considerable writing on clay tablets, this type of writing was easily accomplished by pressing a sharp flat instrument such as a chisel into the wet clay at different angles.[6] Later, when the Egyptians invented paper and ink, a more modern form of writing was developed. Below are samples of the cuneiform writing of the Babylonians.

Fig. I–5:   Cuneiform Writing

The Code of Hammurabi is now located in the Louvre Museum in Paris. However, a reproduction of that code is also located at the Rosicrucian Museum in San Jose, California.

The Code has a very long beginning that explains why it was written. Parts of the beginning are listed below.[7]

> "...at that time, Anu and Bel called me, Hammurabi, the exalted prince, the worshiper of the gods, to cause justice to prevail in the land, to destroy the wicked and evil, to prevent the strong from oppressing the weak, to go forth like the sun over the Black Head People, to enlighten the land and to further the welfare of the people — who helps his people in time of need, who establishes in security their property in Babylon, who made justice prevail and who ruled the race with right. When Marduk sent me to rule the people and to bring help to the country, I established law and justice in the land and promoted the welfare of the people."

(The Black Head people were residents of Babylon)[8]

On the top of the stone is a picture of King Hammurabi standing before the Sun-God Shamash Some believe that it is a picture of Hammurabi receiving the laws from this god, but the code states that Hammurabi developed these laws himself. (In most mythologies, the Sun-God is the God of Justice.)

Fig. I–6:   Code of Hammurabi

The Code of Hammurabi is the oldest known major set of laws. These are not the first laws known to man. Archaeologists have discovered even older laws in the same general area, but they were just a small number of clay tablets from local areas. However, some of them were the same laws as those in the Code of Hammurabi, so he must have borrowed some of his laws from those already existing in the region. The importance of the laws of Babylon to us today is that the laws of the United States have been greatly affected by the Old Testament, and these laws were in turn affected by the laws of the Babylonians. Since the ancient Hebrews were neighbors of the Babylonians, it would be natural for them to borrow the laws they felt were appropriate. When the Code of Hammurabi was first discovered in 1901, it was a great shock to some people to find that some of the laws in the Old Testament were the same as those found in the Code.

The Code of Hammurabi, like the laws of the ancient Israelites, was basically an "eye for an eye" type of code. This is called the Lex Talionis, or the law of retaliation. Like the ancient Hebrews, there was no law punishing murder. It was left up to the members of the family to seek justice (or vengeance).

Lying must have been a common thing, because many of the laws were concerned with perjury. Because of this, all contracts had to have witnesses. The Code is a victim-oriented law and requires that a person who has committed an offense against another be required to pay the victim many times the loss that the victim suffered. This is called the Law of Multiple Retribution. Usually the law required a retribution of three or four times the value or damage done. However, it did go much higher sometimes. Some of the laws list five times, ten times, twelve times and thirty times the loss.[9] If the person committing the crime could not pay the judgment, he or his family were sold into temporary slavery until the debt was paid off. The law was generally administered by the priesthood and the court was often held in the temple.[10] This aided the practice of swearing oaths before the gods when testifying.

There are some records that refer to "witnesses" who were used during trials in Babylonian times, and indicate that they were a form of jury made up of judges.[11]

The law was very protective of the crime victim. If a man's house was broken into and money was taken, the victim could be given the money from the government treasury if the victim would make an official report and then go to the temple and swear before the gods that the money was taken. If, however, it was found that he had lied, his head was cut off. The law was both protective and severe.[12]

California is the first legal jurisdiction since Babylon to enact victim oriented reimbursement. Our law enables the state to reimburse a crime victim for injury or loss. Since then, other states and countries have followed this example. We also have the "Good Samaritan" laws which reimburse loss when a citizen suffers that loss as a result of assisting a peace officer or in some way assisting the law.

1.2:3   Samples of Laws from the Code Of Hammurabi

There were many laws for the control of alcohol. If a bar owner did not fill a customer's cup to the top, his punishment was that he be drowned. Apparently they had problems with priestesses and wine. The Code forbade any priestess from either owning a wine shop or drinking wine.[13]

The Code provided for many different types of punishment; some of them were unusual. For example, persons caught in the act of adultery were bound with rope in the sexual position and then thrown into the river to drown.[14] They also branded the foreheads of criminals with a symbol representing the crime committed. Incest was punishable by being burned to death if it was between mother and son. If it involved father and daughter, the father was banished from the land.[15]

Other examples of punishment mentioned in the Code of Hammurabi were: Having the tongue cut out; eyes torn out; breasts cut off; bones broken; teeth knocked out; ears cut off; children slain, and a series of lashes with a cowhide whip.[16]

In the United States we feel that we have been very progressive concerning juvenile laws and the treatment of juveniles. We were the first in modern history to have special courts, and to institute special laws, for juveniles. Two thousand years before the birth of Christ, the Babylonians had juvenile laws that allowed the state to take children away from unfit homes and put them into proper foster homes. They also had a juvenile court system with special judges to handle the cases.

Most of the Code dealt with wage and price control. The government was very protective of its people. It set down exactly what wage would be given for each type of job, and what price would be charged for a bushel of wheat or for the building of a boat according to its length. The Babylonians feared inflation.

Hammurabi ended his laws with a long statement which again explained that the purpose of the law was to give the land "stable support and a pure government," and "that the strong might not oppose the weak, and that justice should be given to the orphan and the widow in Babylon." He finished the Code by placing a curse on anyone who changed this law after he died. The curse was a long one in which he appealed to each of the many Babylonian gods. The translation of this appeal amounted to three pages.

1.2:4   Babylonian Legal Concepts In Use Today in the United States

Although much of the law of the Babylonians might seem strange, and sometimes a little harsh, there are some concepts that have found their way into present law. Some of these are: separate courts for juveniles; written contracts; the legality of witnesses; the swearing of oaths before God; homesteading; and inheritance rights.

1.3:0   EGYPT

Because Egypt was close to Babylon, there were exchanges between the countries in the form of trade and war. Egyptian leaders respected the laws of Babylon, but felt their own law was better suited to their people. Egypt was known throughout the ancient world as the "Seat of wisdom." The Acts of the Apostles (Ch. vii: 22) states that Moses was instructed in the "wisdom of the Egyptians."

Punishment

Egyptian law was rather mild regarding punishments for criminal offenses, and even though they had the death penalty, it was easily commuted to a prison sentence or some type of forced labor.[17] It should be remembered, however, that the Egyptians allowed slavery, and had different laws for citizens and for slaves.

There was a tendency to favor immediate punishment, as opposed to long jail sentences. This is especially true for minor offenses. Rather than being sent to jail for a minor offense, the offender was usually beaten with a stick called a "bastinado" and released to nurse his wounds and think about what he had done.

Truth and justice were highly regarded by the ancient Egyptians, so crimes involving falsehood by oath were severely punished.

If a person observed a crime in progress, and was physically able to prevent it, but did nothing, he received a number of lashes and was not given food for three days and nights. This type of law is similar to that for the Angles and Saxons in later times.

For minor offenses it was common to assign a person to the mines to do hard labor or to be assigned to some type of public works project. The number of days was based on the type of crime.

If a parent killed his or her child, they had to carry the child tied to them in an embrace for a period of three days. The killing of a parent was punishable by being lacerated with sharpened reeds, then thrown on a pile of thorns and burned.

For the crime of adultery, a woman had her nose cut off. The man received 1,000 blows with the bastinado. A pregnant woman sentenced to death was not executed until after the baby was born. This prevented harm to an innocent party, the baby. Persons of high status were not beaten with the common bastinado. A special iron club was used. Since it did more damage, the privilege of rank in this case would be questionable. Hanging was a common form of capital punishment, but for crimes involving forgery or counterfeiting, the hands were cut off. Idleness was a crime.

On the lower levels, the police were called "Medjay." Although they were civilians, they were under military officers.[18] They not only handled the initial investigation of crime, but also the trial and punishment for minor offenses. Figure I–7 shows ancient Egyptian policemen administering punishment for petty theft.

Fig. I–8:   Egyptian policemen administering punishment for petty theft.

On the higher levels, the professions of law, medicine and religion were all lumped together and administered by the Egyptian priests, who were the ruling class.

The ancient Egyptians were basically a religious and law-abiding people. They held strong beliefs that after death there would be a judgment. In this judgment, the gods would place a person's heart on one side of a scale, and either the feather of Maat or a statue of Maat on the other side. A person's after-life destiny was determined by the way in which his heart weighed up against justice. Figure I–8 shows this process. This was a common theme on tomb walls.

The early Egyptian system of law was based on the concept of "precedent," developed and codified over time through custom, usage and prior decisions of learned judges. The laws of England and the United States are based on precedent.

The earliest known lawgiver was Menes, the first ruler of the Old Kingdom (approximately 3400 BC). There are a few written comments about his law, but not much of it has been recorded.[19]

Fig. I–7:   Weighing one's heart against the feather of justice.

1.3:1   The Egyptian Courts

The courts were well-respected in the ancient world. They received praise from Solomon. The Great Court of Areopagus in Athens was considered one of the world's best courts, yet the Roman historian, Deodorus, praised the Egyptian courts as being equal. Solon, one of the world's greatest lawgivers, spent considerable time in Egypt studying its laws and court system before writing his own great code of laws.

The presiding judge of the court wore a medallion of the god Maat on a chain around his neck. It contained precious stones. When the court decided which party had won the case, he would go to that person and touch his or her forehead with the medallion.

Trials were often held in the temple, as were the Babylonian trials.[20] Each province or "Nome" contained local judges, and a great central court composed of thirty judges, ten from each of the three major districts.[21] If an Egyptian citizen wanted to take a case to court, there were no costs. The administration of justice was free. The courts did recognize the danger of hearsay evidence, or statements that have been repeated by persons other than the one who originally made it. They knew that a person could rarely repeat a conversation in exactly the same way that it was first spoken so they were one of the first systems to exclude such statements from a trial.[22] The Egyptians also knew that a smooth-talking attorney could influence the decision of the court, so they did not allow closing arguments during a trial. The case was based on the presentation of written evidence and even testimony was written.[23]

Maat, the God of Justice

Law, to the Egyptians, was both civil and religious. They had a special god for justice. Her name was Maat. She always wore an ostrich feather in her headband. The feather later became a symbol for justice, and became a part of the flag for Egyptian police officers. Our statue of justice is blindfolded. Older paintings of Maat showed her eyes as empty circles—an indication of being blind. It would be reasonable to assume that the ancient Egyptians also saw justice as blind. The word "Maat" also implied the entire concept of justice and was often used in its place.

Fig. I–9: God of Justice: Maat.

When young men went through a rite of initiation, they entered a temple dedicated to Maat. Around the walls of the temple were forty-two gods each of whom represented one of the forty-two basic laws. To show themselves worthy of initiation they would make the following proclamation:

I know Thee and am attuned with Thee and Thy two and forty Laws which exist with thee in the Chamber of Maat.

In truth have I come into Thine attunement, and I have brought Maat in my mind and soul.

I have destroyed wickedness for Thee.

I have not done evil to mankind.

I have not oppressed the members of my family.

I have not wrought evil in the place of truth and right.

I have had no intimacy with worthless men.

I have not demanded first consideration.

I have not decreed that excessive labor should be performed for me.

I have not brought forward my name for exaltation to honors.

I have not defrauded the oppressed of property.

I have made no man suffer hunger.

I have made no one to weep.

I have caused no pain to be inflicted upon man or animal.

I have not defrauded the Temples of their oblations.

I have not diminished from the bushel.

I have not encroached upon the fields of others.

I have not filched away land.

I have not added to the weights of the scales to cheat the seller.

I have not misread the pointer of the scales to cheat the buyer.

I have not kept the milk from the mouths of children.

I have not turned back the water at the time when it should flow.

I have not extinguished the flame when it should burn.

I have not repulsed God in His manifestations.

Therefore, evil shall not befall me in this world, because I know the laws of God.

1.3:2   Selected Egyptian Laws

The husband and wife were considered to be equal, but the wife was often the head of the household and all property was inherited through her, and not the husband. Women had control of their own property and estates, and did not lose possession through marriage as happens in most other civilizations.[24] The law allowed the practice of polygamy (having more than one wife or husband). Divorce and incest (sexual relations with close relatives) was allowed, although seldom practiced by the average Egyptian. Cleopatra did marry her younger brother for a while. The reason for these types of law was that the Egyptian gods practiced these particular acts, and therefore it was OK for the people to do the same.[25]

1.3:3   Importance of Egyptian Law to the United States

The real importance of the laws of ancient Egypt to American law is that Moses was raised in the house of the Pharaoh, and was well trained in Egyptian law before he wrote his Mosaic Code. This Code had a very great effect upon the laws of the United States as well as other western cultures.

Because we know so little about ancient Egyptian law, we cannot trace this law to the law of Moses, but it defies common sense to believe that all his legal training would not have an effect in the later development of law for his own people. It should also be remembered that the Hebrews lived in Egypt for a considerable time before Moses led them out. During this time, they lived and worked under Egyptian law. It was a part of their lives.

1.4:0   ISRAEL

The ancient Israelites have had a great effect upon the laws of the United States through the Old Testament which contains the Mosaic Code. Nearly all of our founding fathers were Christians, and for some reason they seemed more oriented toward the Old Testament than the New Testament. The law of the ancient Israelites became the basis for the moral code of western civilization.

1.4:1　The Mosaic Code

Most of the law of the ancient Israelites is contained in the Five Books of Moses. The Greeks called it the Pentateuch, but in Hebrew it is called the Torah. It is contained in the first five books of the Old Testament, which are Genesis, Exodus, Leviticus, Numbers and Deuteronomy.

The Code was written during the forty years the Israelites roamed the wilderness.[26] Moses did not write all the law himself, but relied on the help of Joshua, Ezekiel and other leaders who knew more about Hebrew culture and religious practices than did Moses, who was raised as an Egyptian.

1.4:2　Moses the Lawgiver

Fig. I–10:　Moses the Lawgiver

Many people think of Moses as an itinerant religious leader who received the Ten Commandments on a mountain top amid thunder and lightning, or they think of him leading his people through the Red Sea with hordes of Egyptian chariots chasing them. In reality, Moses was exceptionally well-trained in law and leadership. He was raised in the house of the Pharoah where law was developed and taught. Since Egypt was a major, highly developed civilization at that time, and was respected by other countries for its laws and wisdom, it can safely be stated that Moses was as well-trained in law as any man could be at that time in history. Today, Moses is considered one of the world's greatest law givers. Michelangelo, the famous artist, was asked to sculpt a statue of Moses. The pose and title he selected after much research was "The Lawgiver," which depicted Moses in a contemplative mood with a law book in his hand.

When Michelangelo sculpted the statue of Moses, he placed two horns protruding from his head. This was due to an early misinterpretation of the language in the Bible. The Bible states that, when Moses descended the mountain with the second set of tablets, "The skin of his face shone." The word "shone" was translated into "Horn" and was interpreted as stating that he had horns when he descended. Later biblical scholars have corrected this error.

The name "Moses" is Egyptian, not Hebrew. The name was given to him by the Pharaoh's daughter. It comes from the Egyptian word "Mose" which means "is born."

1.4:3　Examples of Mosaic Law

Hebrew law allowed slavery, but looked upon slaves as human beings with certain rights. Many laws dealt with the proper treatment of slaves and the inheritance rights of the children of slaves. The "Sabbatical Year" was instituted in this law. Each seventh year, those who were put into slavery because of debt or crime were released.[27] Later, when the Romans conquered Greece and brought back its intellectuals and artists as slave teachers for the Roman children, they released the slaves for one year after they had been slaves for seven years. Today, those in the teaching profession still carry on this tradition with the "sabbatical leave" in which they can be given a year off after seven years of teaching service. It is expected that this time will be used to improve themselves as teachers.

It is interesting that the Babylonians had a term Sabattu, which meant the last day of their seven-day week. Another aspect of the "Sabbatical Year" was that the fields were left idle each seventh year so the land would not be exhausted. It is probably a practice they learned from the Egyptians, who were concerned about soil conservation.[28] This practice is also mentioned in the Old Testament in Leviticus 25: 1-7,

> Six years shall you sow your field — but
> in the seventh year there shall be a Sab-
> bath of solemn rest for the land, a Sabbath
> to the Lord.

It is quite likely that the releasing of slaves at this time might be based on the fact that with the fields being idle, there was no work for the slaves who normally worked in the fields.

The Mosaic Code was exceptionally strict regarding sex offenses. Most of them were punishable by death. However, the law also stated that no person could be found guilty of a capital offense without two or more witnesses to the crime charged (Numbers XXXV:30). If a man was careful, he could avoid the death penalty for his sexual offenses. If the transgressor was a woman, the story was a little different, as the village women often took the law into their own hands and stoned the suspect to death without a trial. Today, as a general rule, countries with a Judeo-Christian culture have the strictest sex laws of any in the world.[29]

Like the Code of Hammurabi, the law was Lex Talionis, or the law of retaliation. The law demanded "an eye for an eye." However, although the law stated punishment would be based on "an eye for an eye," it was not always carried out—just as in California today, a defendant is rarely sent to state prison for the maximum sentence listed in the Penal Code. Future generations may look at today's Penal Code and draw the conclusion from the punishments listed that all persons found guilty of that offense received the listed punishment. In ancient times, the families of the person committing the crime would try to mediate the punishment by offering compensation to the victim or his family, and try to "settle the matter out of court." The crime of murder was actually handled solely by the victim's family, and not the authorities. The only law in the matter pertained to not providing sanctuary for a murderer when he was pursued by the victim's relatives.[30] The law allowed divorce rather freely[31] and did not prohibit the practice of polygamy (having more than one wife) which was a common practice in ancient times.[32]

It was the first law to apply equally to both citizens and aliens.[33] This was based on a verse in the Old Testament that solicited the Israelites to treat strangers with kindness because they, above all other peoples, had spent much time as strangers in other lands. Leviticus 24:22 states: "Let there be equal judgment among you, whether he be a stranger, or a native." Deuteronomy 1:16 states: "Hear them and judge that which is just: whether he be one of your country or a stranger." Leviticus 19:33 states: "When a stranger sojourns with you in your land, you shall not do him wrong. The stranger who sojourns with you shall be to you as the native among you, and you shall love him as yourself; for you were strangers in the land of Egypt." However, it was illegal to charge interest on a loan to a fellow Israelite, but not to an alien.

As with the Code of Hammurabi, "Multiple Retribution" was a common form of punishment. If a thief stole two pieces of silver from another and was caught and convicted, he would have to pay the victim three or four times that amount. If he could not pay the judgment, he was sold into temporary slavery until the debt was paid off, just as in Babylon.[34] This legal concept carried over into the time of Christ. An example can be found in the Book of Luke, Chapter XIX, 1:10:

> And Zacchaeus stood and said to Jesus, "Behold Lord, the half of my goods I give to the poor; and if I have defrauded anyone of anything, I restore it fourfold."

Even today in the California Penal Code we can find this concept in 496(4), where it requires a person who has received stolen property and has lost or destroyed the property, to pay the victim threefold the loss. There is also a section in the California Military and Veteran's Code, section 393, in which it states that if charges are brought against a National Guardsman for some act while he is on call-up duty, and the charges are found to be not true, the Guardsman can recover three times his cost from the person initiating the action.

1.4:4   The Talmud

The Talmud is a commentary on Mosaic Law, written sometime between the second and sixth centuries AD. It illustrates the law by examples and involves considerable philosophical discussion.[35]

1.4:5   Ezra

Ezra was also an important Israelite law-giver. In 458 BC, he was given authority over all Jewish religious matters. Like Moses, he received his legal training in foreign lands. He was well-trained in law under the Persians, and was therefore qualified to modify the work of Moses to suit later times. Many scholars believe that Ezra really wrote Deuteronomy ("second law" in Greek). Deuteronomy modified the law to better suit a republican form of government, and also caused a revival in the study of law. Schools were established for the training of lawyers, who were called "scribes."[36]

1.5:0   GREECE

The ancient Greeks had two important centers: Sparta and Athens. Sparta was the center for the development of athletics and the military; Athens was the center of culture and law. Although there were many lawmakers in ancient Greece, only the two most prominent will be discussed: Draco and Solon.

1.5:1   The Draconian Code (621 BC)

The first Greek lawmaker of any note was Draco. He was basically a good man, but he was a strict theorist. He felt that the violation of the law was more important than the type of offense. His feeling was that if a person lived in a society, he gained certain advantages that he would not have if he lived alone. If he profited by living in a society, then he owed something to that society. Draco felt that he owed the society complete obedience to its laws, for without laws there would be no society. A society cannot function without law.

As a result of this philosophy, the punishment that Draco established for theft was the same as that for murder. His law, the Draconian Code, was so strict that even today we use the term "Draconian" when we are referring to a particular law that we feel is overly strict.

When Draco was once asked why his punishments were so severe even for minor crimes, he replied that the smallest crimes, in his opinion, deserve death, and he could find no more severe punishment for the more serious crimes.[37]

His laws were so strict, that they became unworkable. Judges were reluctant to find a person guilty of a minor theft when the punishment could be death. As a result, very few persons were charged with or convicted of crimes. A law that doesn't work is as bad as no law at all.

In desperation, the Greek leaders turned to a very wise legislator by the name of Solon.

1.5:2   The Code of Solon

Solon (639-559 BC) was an Athenian lawgiver, poet, and social reformer. He was the Archon (Director—like a mayor) of Athens in 594. He was asked by the Greek leaders to develop a law by which to govern the people. Solon knew quite a bit about law since he had spent considerable time in Egypt studying their law.[38] He also had a good understanding of people. He knew that each legislator would want to have some say in either making the law, or in changing it to suit his particular interest or that of his friends. In California today, very few proposed laws are passed just as they were originally proposed. They are usually amended to please certain groups and organizations. (This is not necessarily a bad thing) Because of his understanding of human nature, Solon made a contract with the other legislators that if they tried to change the law in any way within ten years, they would have to give the government their own weight in gold. Because they wanted a new law so badly, they made the agreement. They agreed, however, because they were sure they would be able to pressure Solon to alter the law himself.

Fig. I–11:   Solon, the Archon of Athens.

Solon knew what they were thinking, but had a plan to outsmart them. He spent years developing the new law, and when he was finished, he caught the next ship leaving Greece, and went into voluntary exile so that no one could pressure him into making changes.

The Code of Solon was a good law, and after the people had lived under it for a few years, they accepted it without wanting to make major changes. Solon was later asked if his law was the best law he could devise; he replied that it was not. He did state, however, that it was the best law that the people would accept.[39] This shows that he was wise and understood human nature.

Solon, along with Moses, is considered one of history's great lawgivers. The greatness of his law is shown by the fact that when the Greeks were conquered by the Romans, not only did the Romans allow the Greeks to keep their law, they copied some of it themselves. It is said that imitation is the highest form of flattery.

The Code of Solon was inscribed on brass tablets and placed in the marketplace so that everyone could see it when they shopped.[40] Because the Greeks placed such a high value on culture, and because Solon was a poet, the Code was written in verse. It was basically a very humane law.[41]

Although none of the original brass tablets have survived, and there is not a complete set of the laws on record anywhere, we do know some of the individual laws because they have been found in other documents.

Examples of laws:
- Multiple retribution for crimes against property.
- Idleness was a crime.[42]
- Prostitution was allowed.
- Divorce was allowed.
- Adultery was severely punished.
- Polygamy outlawed for the first time in a major law.[43]
- Concept of "statute of limitations" existed.[44]
- First traffic laws against women instituted. (Women chariot drivers could not drive at night without a servant carrying a torch at least 50 feet in front of the chariot.)[45]

Although not a part of the Code of Solon, there was a Greek law that if a person was obnoxious to his fellow citizens, and 6,000 of them so voted, he could be banished from Greece for up to ten years. This was done by writing the name of the person on a clay tablet, and turning it in to the proper authority. There are cases on record of this happening.[46] It was probably politically motivated, for in those times there were no means of mass communication, so a person would have to be pretty obnoxious to offend 6,000 people.

1.5:3   The Great Court Of Areopagus

To touch on Greek law, we must also mention the Great Court of Areopagus. This was the shining light of Greek jurisprudence. It was located on the Hill of Mars, northwest of the Acropolis in Athens. The exact origin is unknown. It is known to have preceded Solon by some seven hundred years. Greek Mythology suggests that it was started by the gods, and that it precedes Greek history. The court consisted of many judges, depending upon the importance of the case before it. It usually had anywhere from nine to fifty judges. They were appointed for life just as our justices of the Supreme Court. In the trial of Socrates, there were three hundred judges because the case was considered to be so important.

Fig. I–12:   Court of Areopagus.

The decisions of this court were so just, that foreign states would send cases to it for a hearing. Like the Code of Solon, the Great Court of Areopagus remained long after the fall of Greece.[47] The apostle Paul was taken before the Court of Areopagus to explain the new doctrine that he was teaching. In Acts 17:19-34, it states that when he did talk to the court that he converted a judge. This is but one reflection of how highly the Roman conquerors thought of this court.[48]

Because the judges for this court were appointed for life, they were not concerned about pleasing important people in their decisions. The court was held at night and in the open. It was felt that this would better serve the interest of justice. If it were held in the open where anyone could listen in on the proceedings, there would be nothing to hide. It was held at night so that the judges, who being human, would not rule against the defendant just because he reminded a judge of his no-good brother-in-law. At night the judges would not be able to see the facial features of the defendants, and they would be in a better position to judge them on evidence and testimony alone.

1.6:0   ROME

It has been said by many historians that the Roman Empire owed its long existence, not to the superiority of its armed legions, but to the justice of its system of law. Too often we think of Rome when the Empire was about to fall, or we think of some of the atrocities practiced by the Romans against the Christians, and judge the whole empire by those incidents

Roman law was basically a just law. This was especially true of the Justinian Code. It allowed for individual rights and property ownership. Although there were many Roman lawmakers, only two laws will be covered in this chapter.

1.6:1   The Law of the Twelve Tables

The Law of the Twelve Tables originally contained just ten tables. Later it was found that two more tables were needed to adequately cover the law. These laws were written around 450 BC. They were inscribed on tablets made of brass and hung on the wall of the Temple of Jupiter.[50] Since these laws followed the writing of the Code of Solon, it can be assumed that the idea of writing the laws on tablets of brass and placing them where everyone could see them was copied from the Greeks.

The Law of the Twelve Tables was not so much a specific code as it was a series of legal "maxims" (rules of conduct). The Greek, Hermodorus, was a great contributor to the compiling of this law, yet it was not a Greek law. It was a putting together of all the existing laws that had been part of the Roman law up to that time. There were some similarities between this law and the Code of Hammurabi.[51] Most of it had an origin in earlier laws.[52]

Before the Law of the Twelve Tables, the law was basically religious in nature, and was unwritten. The interpretation of the law was up to the priests who were members of the patricians, or upper ruling class. The leaders or rulers of Rome, in later times, were nearly all lawyers.

The Law of the Twelve Tables set up a system of law that was the same for both classes of Romans, the Patricians and the Plebes (or common People). It applied to all Roman citizens, but not to slaves.

1.6:2   Examples of Laws from the Law of the Twelve Tables

The law demanded multiple retribution, as did other ancient civilizations. For example, the punishment for theft was two times the value of what was taken. However, if the property was stolen during the night, the punishment was death.[53]

Although it followed the Lex Talionis concept, the defendant was often given a choice of paying damages or suffering the same injury as the victim.[54] The law placed heavy responsibilities on debtors. If a man could not pay his debts, his creditor could seize him and bind him, and keep him under a form of arrest, provided that the prisoner be given one pound of bread each day. If the debtor did not then pay his debt, he was paraded in the market place for three days and it was announced to everyone the amount of money that he owed. If he still did not pay his debt, he was either put to death or sold into slavery "beyond the Tiber."[55]

The Law of the Twelve Tables gave the father of the family supreme authority over the other members of the family. In some cases it allowed the victim of a crime to decide the punishment for the defendant after conviction. Unfortunately, this promoted the "vendetta." If the punishment was too severe, the members of the defendant's family would take revenge against the victim or his family. If a four-legged animal caused damage to any property, the victim was given the animal.[56] A judge who accepted a bribe was put to death.[57] Arsonists were burned alive.[58]

1.6:3   The Judices

The Romans had somewhat of a jury system made up of judges. The word Judice means judge. The Judices would weigh evidence and then decide the issues in a trial. They were selected by the Praetor of Rome and then put on a list for call-up like our present juries,

At one time there were about 4,000 Judices available throughout Rome. They were selected for each trial in numbers usually not exceeding nine persons. In the trial they acted in the function of both judges and juries When the trial was over, they were released and put back on the waiting list.

1.6:4   The Justinian Code

In the sixth century AD, Emperor Justinian gathered together ten noted jurists under the leadership of a famous judge, Tribonianus (the name is sometimes given as Tribonian). He commissioned them with the task of collecting and systematizing the existing Roman law.

They were also to resolve some of the major problems of law at that time. This task took ten years to complete. When it was completed in 529 AD, Justinian had the commission develop from it an updated set of written laws that were called the Corpus Juris Civilis (Body of Civil Law). This was later also referred to as the Justinian Code. It comprised one of the largest and best codes in the history of law. Not only did the Justinian Code last long after the reign of Emperor Justinian, it became the basis for the laws of many other nations, including many nations far in the future.

Fig. I–13: Justinian

1.6:5   Role of the Church in Preserving Roman Law

The Christian Church has come under much criticism for becoming so political and powerful throughout the Middle Ages, and also because of the special privilege of trying its own members in the Ecclesiastical Courts, rather than the harsh and severe courts that were in existence during feudalism and under early common law. Yet from a historical view of jurisprudence (the science and philosophy of law), it was the Church that not only preserved and further developed Roman law in the Ecclesiastical Courts (Church courts), but later started the first university law school at the end of the Dark Ages. This could not have been accomplished if the Church did not have the political power to maintain its own legal identity. It is just possible that, without the Church, Roman law might have been lost. As it was, only one complete set of the Justinian Code could be found by the Church when it founded the School of Law at the University of Bologna in the Eleventh Century.

A contributing factor to the relationship between the Barbarians and the Church was the superstitious nature of the Barbarians. By this time, the Church had developed a considerable and colorful pomp and ceremony in their worship, and this caused the superstitious Barbarians to keep a respectful and healthy distance for fear of curses being placed on them. Later the Barbarians were converted to Christianity, further increasing the power of the Church.

1.6:6   The Fall of Rome and the End of Roman Law in Favor of Feudal Law

When the Barbarians in the north of Europe suffered a problem of overpopulation, and the Romans in the south became weak from within, the Barbarian "hordes" moved to the south, defeating the Romans and taking over most of Europe.

The period of feudalism began in Europe, and the people began living in a period known as the Dark Ages. Because the feudal kings were so strict and severe, and the people had no rights, there was no need for just Roman law. As a result, a new form of feudal law replaced Roman law. It was a law that was unwritten and was based on the idea that "might makes right." The law was whatever the feudal lord said it was just because he was the lord.

1.7:0   EUROPE

Before Europe became part of the Roman Empire, a form of common law existed that had its origin in the tribal laws of the various small communities. Upon becoming a part of the Roman Empire, however, Europeans were obliged to adopt Roman law. When the Roman Empire collapsed under the might of the Barbarians, Europe became a collection of feudal kingdoms. This occurred around 476 AD. Each military leader in effect "staked a claim" of territory, usually based on natural boundaries such as rivers, mountains, and valleys. The Barbarians were a tough and brutal people who were raised under difficult conditions. They therefore became difficult leaders to serve. When the Barbarians established their feudal kingdoms, the people became "serfs" and lived a life worse than slavery. They had no rights and were not allowed to own property. They themselves were treated as the property of the feudal lord. This was carried to such extremes that if a woman serf was to be married, the lord could spend the first night with her if he wanted to, since she was his property. It is easy to understand why this period in history is referred to as the Dark Ages.

Because Roman law was just and recognized the rights of the individual, it had no place in feudal Europe. Yet any large group of people under one jurisdiction needs some form of law. The law that developed is called European common law.

1.7:1 Common Law of the Feudal Kingdoms

Common law is an unwritten law formed solely by usage and by the customs developed in a particular area over time. If a person in power punishes a subject for an offense that he feels is wrong, and he continues to punish his subjects for this act, it soon becomes known throughout the area that this act is a crime, and that a common punishment will follow a conviction for that act. It should be remembered that the Barbarians were not educated, and could seldom read or write, least of all develop and interpret a series of laws.

The only rule of court procedure was common sense reasoning. A suspect was taken before the feudal lord, if the kingdom was small, or before one of his judges if the kingdom was large. The testimony was presented and the evidence observed. Two decisions were then reached: The first one pertained to guilt or innocence, and the second decision concerned punishment. In difficult cases, the feudal lord would seek advice from his council. They in turn would try to find some other case that was similar in order to follow precedent. If there was no local case, they might look to neighboring kingdoms for cases.

If the crime charged was that of stealing a pig, and the feudal lord decided to cut off one of the defendant's fingers, chances are that he would give the same punishment the next time a similar case came before him. Soon everyone in his kingdom would know that the stealing of a pig would cost the thief one of his fingers. It did not have to be written down. Everyone knew the punishment from past cases. The crime and punishment then becomes part of the common law of that kingdom from common usage or practice. The law may never be written in a book of law, but it is known and usually accepted by the people.

Since it is legally difficult to prepare a defense for a crime if that crime is not written down in a law book somewhere, and there are no examples and explanations of that crime in other law books, early European common law was not a very just law for the common man. Things did, however, improve in time. When the feudal kingdoms were first established, the rulers were fresh from the harsh military life. An old Roman writer once remarked that "Amid the clash of arms the laws are silent."[59] In time, the rulers tended to mellow and their children became more civilized. Another development was the gradual unification through war of several kingdoms. When a feudal kingdom became quite large, the feudal lord could not administer the law himself, so he appointed judges to do this for him. With several judges, a system had to be developed to ensure uniformity. It is usually at this point that the law becomes more just.

Common law differs from statutory law in that statutory law is written in a book of law as legal statutes. It is usually voted on by a legislature, but not in all cases. Many ancient laws were written down but were not voted upon. They were developed by rulers and passed down to the people.

1.7:2 Charlemagne's Capitularies

Fig. I–14: Charlemagne.

It was inevitable that eventually some leader would unify Europe through force of arms and then develop one major law for that new kingdom. At the end of the ninth century, Charlemagne had conquered and reunited most of Europe. Still there was no single law. In an effort to solve this problem, he began to issue from his court a series of Capitularies (or little laws) that he hoped would serve as a guide to the individual jurisdictions regarding what legal directions to follow. Because the territory that he had united was made up of many nations with many types of differing laws, he felt the one common tie between all the peoples was religion. Because of this, Charlemagne made an agreement with the Pope to be crowned Holy Roman Emperor. This served to further cement his position as ruler, and aided the acceptance of his Capitularies. Although Charlemagne's Capitularies are not considered great law, they did prepare the way for the return of Roman law.

1.7:3 Spain

After the fall of the Roman Empire, Spain was conquered by the Visigoths who were later driven out by the Moors, a nomadic people from North Africa. Christian re-conquest of Spain began in the eleventh century, but the Moors were not completely driven out until 1492.[60]

In the eleventh century the city of Bologna in Italy formed the first European university and assembled the Justinian Code into one body. The specialty of the university was law, specifically Roman law. Anyone who wished to study law at a university had no choice but to study Roman law.[61]

1.7:4 Las Siete Partidas

When Spain began driving the Moors from their country, they also knitted themselves into a powerful nation and needed a new national law. Those selected to develop this law in the thirteenth century were graduates of the University of Bologna law school. The law that they developed was, therefore, based on the Justinian code.

The new law was broken down into seven parts and called the Law of the Seven Parts, or "Las Siete Partidas." It was a much shortened version of the Justinian Code.

This law is important to us in the Western hemisphere because, shortly after its development, Spain became a great power and expanded its colonial empire. As a result, about half the countries in South America, Mexico and the southwestern part of what is now the United States, including California, were under this law, and the laws of most Latin countries are to this day based on it.

1.7:5 The Code Napoleon

Fig. I–15: Napoleon

After the French Revolution, French leaders began to seek a new law that would be a compromise between the Germanic law of the north of France and the Roman type law of the southern and eastern parts of France.

Although Cambaceres, a famous French jurist, had started the groundwork of such an endeavor before the revolution, under the direction of Napoleon Bonaparte, the work was completed between the period 1800 and 1804, and referred to as the Code Napoleon.[62] It has been called the model of condensation and brevity. Unfortunately, its brevity has left open a lot of room for interpretation that the Justinian Code eliminated. It was,

however, much better written than the Justinian Code. Because of its brevity, the code had to be changed and expanded later for easier application.

It is noteworthy that, after Napoleon's defeat, all the countries that caused his overthrow (except England) adopted the Code Napoleon (or a revision of it) as their law. When Japan broke the chains of its ancient feudalism, it also used the Code Napoleon as a model for its new law.[63]

In the United States, the French territory of Louisiana was under the Code Napoleon. The title breakdown of this Code is quite similar to the various codes that we have in California today.

Of the Latin American countries that did not adopt the law of Las Siete Partidas, most of them adopted the Code Napoleon.

Napoleon is quoted as stating, "My true glory is not in having won forty battles: Waterloo will blot out the memory of those victories — but nothing can blot out my Civil Code. That will live forever."[64]

1.8:0 ENGLAND

Since the United States began as an English colony, and our legal system has its roots in English law, it is important to know something of the basics of this law. To cover the subject in depth would take the space of at least one chapter, so only a brief outline of this material will be presented.

Because England was invaded by many conquerors throughout its history, it has been subjected to the laws of many different cultures. Around the fifth century AD, after the Romans had left, England was invaded by the Anglo-Saxons. This term really covers two Germanic speaking peoples: the Angles and the Saxons.[65] They brought with them a system of law that made each person responsible for the acts of his neighbor. The "Frankpledge" was a system of dividing a community into "Tithings" or groups of ten persons, and each was responsible for the criminal acts of other members of the group.

Another similar system was the "Hue and Cry." This was basically a Saxon practice which lasted for many centuries. When a person committed a crime, or a felon escaped, and it was discovered, an alarm was sounded by blowing a horn. When others heard the alarm, they raised a cry, sounded their horns, and by law had to lay aside their work and join in the immediate pursuit of the criminal. If any able-bodied man failed to take up the pursuit, he was considered to have taken the side of the escaping person and would be liable to arrest and punishment.[66]

Fig. I–19: Hue and Cry.

The early history of England was one of many small kingdoms under different forms of law. The general form of law was common law as in Europe. It was noted for being harsh and oppressive. It was not until the seventh century that the first known English code was written. King Aethelbert wrote it under the influence of the Justinian Code.

In the ninth century, Alfred the Great rewrote the law, but added very little. In the eleventh century, Canute again rewrote the law and consolidated it. Also in the eleventh century, Edward the Confessor compiled the Law of Edward the Confessor, but it was not new. It amounted to the same laws that were already in existence.

1.8:1   The Common Law of England

Fig. I–16: Norman soldiers of William the Conqueror.

In 1066, when William the Conqueror invaded England, the law varied from county to county because each Sheriff controlled the individual county courts. William established royal control over the local courts in an attempt to make the law "common" to all of England. He accepted the law of crimes that were the same in all areas or that were crimes "by common understanding," and these crimes became known as the "common Law Crimes." He had his representatives go from court to court and record the decisions of the various judges, and then distributed the decisions to all the courts. This resulted in judges relying on the decisions of other judges which was later called Stare Decisis. It resulted in the law finding a more common ground on a national level. Later, new laws

were added by either the King or Parliament when it came into existence. This over all system of law became known as English Common Law.

1.8:2   Trials in England

Fig. I–17: Early English Judge.

Before the coming of the Normans, the Anglo-Saxons used a system called "Compurgation" in which the person who could bring the most witnesses to swear, not to the facts in the case, but that they believed he told the truth, would win the case.

When the Normans came into power, they brought with them the old feudal "Trial by Duel," in which the winner of the duel won the case. "Champions" could be used by those involved in the trial.[67]

Trial by Jury

Fig. I–18: A "John Bull" jury.

In the twelfth century, trial by jury was developed in England. At first it was not very workable. The members of the jury were selected by the sheriff, and were people whom he felt would favor the Crown. The sheriff was also allowed to starve the members of the jury if they did not come to a decision. He could also punish them for making a wrong decision. This rule was due to the fear that jury members would always side with the accused. A "wrong decision" was determined by retrying the case with a jury of Knights. If they felt that the decision was wrong, the sheriff could take action against the first jury.[68] It took a long time for the jury system in England to look anything like the jury of today. The juries were usually made up of conservative, upper-class gentlemen. They were referred to as "John Bull" juries because they were usually in favor of prosecution.

In the thirteenth century, Edward I, known as the "English Justinian," completely revised and brought up to date the English law. This was also the beginning of a system of professionally trained lawyers. In the fourteenth century the Inns of Court was formed, where English lawyers were trained as apprentices. This was done in the form of a medieval guild.[69]

1.8:3   The Magna Charta (the Great Charter)

Fig. I–20:   Seal of the Magna Charta

One of the greatest steps forward in the English people's struggle for freedom occurred in the thirteenth century: the signing of the Magna Charta.

In 1215 AD, at Runnymede, King John was forced by the barons, under the leadership of Stephen Langton, Archbishop of Canterbury, to sign the Magna Charta. It was prepared in advance by Langton, who held the degree of Doctor of Laws from the University of Bologna. The Church became involved because it suffered as much under King John as did the Barons.[70]

The Magna Charta is viewed as the founding stone of English freedom, and a document which greatly influenced the founding fathers of the United States. In reality, it gave certain rights to "freemen" a term which did not include the ordinary Englishman. King John, and later monarchs, made a habit of ignoring the Charter when it suited them, so the process of freedom for the English common man was one of slow progress.

Fig. I–21:   King John signing the Magna Charta.

The importance of the Magna Charta was the introduction of a new philosophy of government and law for the English. It stated that the people should have some say in the running of their government, and a people who live under a system of law should have some say in its formation.

Before this time, every major law in western civilization was developed by the leaders. The people had no input concerning these laws. Even though some of them were based on local customs, these customs were developed by local leaders.

Code of Hammurabi	Mosaic Code	Code of Solon	Justinian Code	Code Napoleon	Magna Charta
↓	↓	↓	↓	↓	↑
PEOPLE	PEOPLE	PEOPLE	PEOPLE	PEOPLE	PEOPLE

1.8:4   The Habeas Corpus Amendment Act

Next to the Magna Charta, the Habeas Corpus Act of 1679 is of utmost importance. For centuries, it was the custom in England, as in other European countries, to send spies throughout the country to find evidence of treason and rebellion. They would then turn in a list of names to the Crown, and these persons would be arrested and thrown into prison without charges, some never to be seen again. They could also be legally tortured in order to obtain a confession. It was based on the belief that innocence could overcome all and that God would protect the innocent.

Fig. I–23: Obtaining a "confession" on the rack.

Until the Second World War, this concept of freedom from unjust imprisonment was used mostly in English speaking countries. Even today, many countries allow the imprisonment of a suspect until the prosecutor feels that his case is ready.

The Habeas Corpus Act in effect states that cause must be shown why a certain person is being held in police or state custody. The authorities must show the judge who issued the writ that a crime was, in fact, committed, and that there is some evidence to indicate the suspect is the one who committed it. The evidence does not have to be so strong that it proves the suspect's guilt. The purpose of the writ is to prevent a person from being thrown into jail with no justification whatsoever, except that someone doesn't like him.

The concept of habeas corpus was developed in the latter part of the sixteenth century. When it was first used, it was often circumvented by the authorities who would deny that the person was actually in custody. After the Habeas Corpus Act was passed in 1679, severe penalties were imposed on any judge who refused to issue a writ when warranted. It also applied to any officer or jailer who refused to comply with the writ.

1.8:5 English Jurists of Note

As time passed, there arose a great need for English common law to be written down and properly interpreted for easier application. In the seventeenth and eighteenth century two famous jurists filled this need.

(A) **Sir Edward Coke** (1552–1634) A great English jurist who became Solicitor General and speaker of the House of Commons. He became Attorney General in 1593. He was a severe prosecutor, yet he promoted personal liberty and was involved in the writing of the important Petition of Right (1628) involving freedom of speech.[71]

(B) **Sir William Blackstone** (1728–1780) He wrote the "Commentaries on the Law of England" between 1765 and 1769. He became very influential in English law, and has long been used as "the" authority on English common law. Lord Avonmore once stated that Blackstone "gave to the law the air of a science. He found it a skeleton and clothed it with life, colour and complexion."[72] Because American law has its roots in English law, it is a rare student of law who does not spend considerable time reading Blackstone.

1.8:6 The Reform Act of 1832 and the Rules of Equity

The beginning of the nineteenth century in England was one of unprecedented harshness in the punishment of criminal offenders. It was a time when Common Law could not be used to resolve all the newly developing legal problems that were arising. Punishment was thought to be the answer to rising crime. Over 200 offenses were punishable by hanging. This included the stealing of a loaf of bread worth twelvepence.[73] The law made no differentiation between men, women or children in regard to capital punishment, and mass hangings occurred in all groups. In fact, it was a form of public entertainment, and especially engraved tickets were sold for both the trials and the hangings. Despite this, it was a time of legal awareness. It became very obvious that something had to be done to relieve the muscle-bound restrictions of common law in solving the more complicated legal cases before the courts.

Fig. I–22: Women being hung at Newgate Prison.

The answer was the Reform Act of 1832. This laid the groundwork for the Rules of Equity. The Rules of Equity are rules that allow a court to use Roman law when English common law is either unsatisfactory or would simply not apply to the case being tried. The Reform Act also established the Parliaments of the People of England which gave the people the power to control Parliament. This was a great step on the road to justice and freedom for the English people.[74]

1.8:7 Precedence (*Stare Decisis*)

One of the principles on which the common law of England developed was that of using very strict precedence in making legal decisions. If a judge could find a previous decision similar to the one which he was deliberating, he would follow the prior decision. This is an English principle that we have followed to a great extent, but not as strictly. It does create uniformity, and gives attorneys some established legal basis on which to prepare their cases.

1.9:0 THE UNITED STATES

The legal history of the United States has been affected by many things. First would be the multicultural background of the people in the various parts of the country. In the Northeast, the Puritans enacted very strict behavioral laws, and even burned "witches." In the South and Southwest, the Spanish and Mexican influence prevailed for quite a long time. In the large territory of Louisiana, the Code Napoleon was the existing law.

To understand the variety and multiplicity of law in the United States, one must first understand something of its historical and political development. Parts of the North American continent at one time belonged to various European nations. Even when the United States became independent, it was based on a "States' Rights" concept where there was no strong national government; each state was independent to do almost as it pleased. The early colonists, say from Virginia, often looked upon themselves as being Virginians rather than Americans. They had a feeling of local independence.

1.9:1 The Pre-Revolution Colonies

In the year 1606, King James I granted the Virginia Company a charter to settle on a peninsula in the James River on the American east coast. In 1607, it became the first permanent English settlement in America. They called the settlement Jamestown. Although the settlers had a rough time surviving, in 1619 they were allowed to form a house of burgesses. Since the members were elected, it became the first representative assembly in the New World. Because of their form of government, they did not have to suffer the strict religious laws of the later arriving Puritans..

Among the colonists coming to America were the Pilgrims. They came in hopes of finding religious freedom. The Puritans had received a corporation charter in England, and under this business corporation, formed the Massachusetts Bay Colony. Since the Puritans were very conservative, the colony turned out to be a dictatorial theocracy.[75] (A theocracy is a government run by religious leaders claiming to rule by divine authority.)[76] The Old Testament became their constitution. The laws were quoted verbatim from the Mosaic Code. The first governor, John Winthrop, called democracy "the worst of all forms of government."[77]

Fig. I–24: Punishment in the early colonies
Courtesy: *Ye Olden Times*

Any form of criticism was considered "heresy," and severe and cruel punishment was the result of any criticism of the leadership. Some members were even charged with violating the Fifth Commandment as a result of their criticism since the established authorities of the colony were considered to be the "father and mother" of its members.[78]

The Capitall Lawes of New-England, as they stand now in force in the Common-Wealth.
BY THE COURT
In the Years 1641. 1642.
Capitall Lawes, Established within the Jurisdiction of Massachusets.

1. *If any man after legall conviction, shall have or worship any other God, but the Lord God, he shall be put to death. Deut. 13. 6, &c. and 17.2 &c Exodus 22.20.*

2. *If any man or woman be a Witch, that is, hath or consulteth with a familiar spirit, they shall be put to death. Exod.22.15. Lev.20.27. Deut.18.10,11.*

3. *If any person shall blaspheme the Name of God the Father, Sonne, or Holy Ghost, with direct, expresse, presumptuous, or high-handed blasphemy, or shall curse God in like manner, he shall be put to death. Lev.24.15,16.*

4. *If any person shall commit any willfull murder, which is manslaughter, commited upon premeditated malice, hatred, or cruelty, not in a mans' necessary and just defence, nor by meer casualtie, against his will; he shall be put to death. Exod.21.12,13,14. Num.35.30,31.*

5. *If any person slayeth another suddenly in his anger, or cruelty of passion, he shall be put to death. Num.35.20,21. Lev.24.17.*

6. *If any person shall slay another through guile, either by poysonings, or other such divilish practice; he shall be put to death. Exod.21.14.*

7. *If a man or woman shall lye with any beast, or bruit creature, by carnall copulation, they shall surely be put to death; and the beast shall be slaine, and buried. Lev.20.15,16.*

8. *If a man lyeth with mankind, as he lyeth with a woman, both of them have committed abomination, they both shall surely be put to death. Lev.20.13.*

9. *If any person committeth adultery with a married, or espoused wife, the Adulterer, and the Adulteresse, shall surely be put to death. Lev.20.10. and 18.20. Deut.22.23,24.*

10. *If any man shall unlawfully have carnall copulation with any woman-childe under ten yeares old, either with, or without her consent, he shall be put to death.*

11. *If any man shall forcibly, and without consent, ravish any maid or woman that is lawfully married or contracted, he shall be put to death. Deut.22.25,&c.*

12. *If any man shall ravish any maid or single woman (committing carnal copulation with her by force, against her will) that is above the age of ten yeares; he shall be either punished with death, or with some other grievous punishment, according to circumstances, at the discretion of the Judges : and this Law to continue till the Court take further order.*

13. *If any man stealeth a man, or mankinde, he shall surely be put to death. Exod.21.16.*

14. *If any man rise up by false witnesse wittingly, and of purpose to take away any man's life, he shall be put to death. Deut.19.16,18,19.*

15. *If any man shall conspire, or attempt any invasion, insurrection, or publick rebellion against our Common-Wealth, or shall indeavor to surprise any Towne or Townes, Fort or Forts therein or shall treacherously, or perfidously attempt the alteration and subversion of our frame of pollicy, or government fundamentally, he shall be put to death. Num.16.2. Sam.3. & 18. & 20.*

Per exemplar incre, Nowel, Secret.

Fig. I–25:   Capital laws of New England, 1641–1642.

Those who came to America to escape persecution became severe in their persecution of others. Church membership was necessary for citizenship. Quakers and Baptists suffered imprisonment, torture and untold atrocities at the hands of the Puritan leaders. Citizens had no rights, only duties. There were fifteen crimes for which the death penalty was meted out.[79] It is interesting to note that the Puritans (greatly influenced by Oliver Cromwell who considered Christmas a Catholic plot and objected to the remnants of pagan traditions it contained) in 1659 made the celebration of Christmas a crime in Massachusetts.

Roger Williams suggested that there should be a separation of church and state and that the land was illegally taken from the Indians. He was banished from Massachusetts and went to a new area and founded the Colony of Rhode island and Providence Plantations.

In 1684, the Charter of Massachusetts Bay was revoked by the Crown and all of New England was put under one governor. This took the dictatorial power away from the Puritan leaders and led to a somewhat more democratic government for the people. (See example of laws on page 25)

1.9:2 English Mismanagement of the Colonies

Generally speaking, laws in the colonies were just, but were often administered in an unfair manner. Special acts were passed allowing British business concerns to exploit the colonies. Sometimes trial by jury was denied. The problems of religious fanaticism were now replaced by mismanagement and mistreatment by the English government in its dealings with the colonists. The colonists were not afforded the rights and privileges of English citizens. They were unjustly taxed and allowed no representation in Parliament which passed legislation prejudicial against the colonies. Trade barriers were overly restrictive. A series of laws known as the Intolerable Acts caused such indignation, they sowed the seeds of revolution. Writs of Assistance or general search warrants were issued with such frequency that it amounted to harassment.[80]

Many young leaders in the colonies had been affected by the philosophical ideals of democracy, and were quite vocal in voicing those thoughts. Patrick Henry was accused of treason because he contended that "government is based upon a contract between the people and the sovereign which cannot be violated." Even so, most of the colonists were not anti-British. Although many were upset at the unfair administration of the colonies, they believed the matter could be resolved and favored neither war nor separation, feeling that a redress of grievances sent to the Crown would solve the problem. Some, however, took action.

1.9:3 The Declaration of Rights

In 1774, the Continental Congress at Philadelphia wrote a Declaration of Rights, setting forth what it felt were legitimate complaints. The main issues were:

(1) The colonists' ancestors were entitled to all rights, liberties and immunities of free and natural born subjects in England.
(2) Descendants are, therefore, entitled to the same rights.
(3) Colonists are not represented in Parliament.
(4) Colonists are entitled to English common law, and to be tried by a jury of their peers.
(5) Colonists are being denied the rights granted them by royal charter.
(6) Colonists have a right to peaceably assemble to discuss grievances and petition for redress.

Parliament responded to this Declaration of Rights with further restrictions. The stage was set for war.[81]

1.9:4 The Revolution

Blood was shed in Vermont on March 13, 1775, and the battles of Concord and Lexington took place on April 19, 1775. The Revolutionary War had begun.

1.9:5 The Declaration of Independence

After the battles of Concord and Lexington, a Second Continental Congress assembled in Philadelphia in May 1775. This Congress established a committee to draft a Declaration of Independence. Thomas Jefferson was appointed to set it down in writing, but Franklin and Adams made a number of changes in his drafts.

The Declaration was based on the concept that all men were created equal and that their creator had endowed them with certain inalienable rights. It also declared that governments were established to protect and guarantee these rights, and not to deny them. Their idea became one of the cornerstones of American Constitutional law.

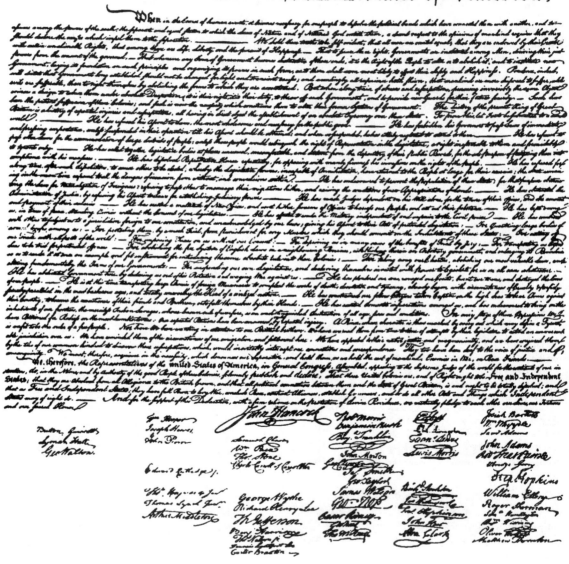

Fig. I–26:   The Declaration of Independence.

Franklin had long been an advocate of independence and of strong unity among the colonies. His symbol of a snake cut in pieces was an effort to promote unity among the colonies.

Fig. I–28:   Benjamin Franklin's warning symbol.

Of the fifty-six members who signed the Declaration of Independence, twenty-five of them were lawyers.[82] Jefferson was well educated and well read in the philosophy of freedom and democracy, and he strongly believed in those principles.

The Declaration of Independence, although a political document, is really one of the cornerstones of American constitutional law. It laid down the basis, not only for our government, but our legal system as well. Although not a new philosophy, it firmly established the theory of equality and basic human rights. Another writer who influenced the early thought of colonial law was Thomas Paine, who, in "The Rights of Man," wrote that "All the great laws of society are laws of nature."

1.9:6   Victory for the Colonies

With the surrender of Cornwallis, a new chapter began in American history.

BE IT REMEMBERED!

THAT on the 17th of October, 1781, Lieutenant-General Earl CORNWALLIS, with above Five thousand British Troops, surrendered themselves Prisoners of War to his Excellency Gen. GEORGE WASHINGTON, Commander in Chief of the allied Forces of France and America.

LAUS DEO!

1.9:7   Law in Post-Revolutionary Times

Some wonder why the colonists kept English common law as their own law after they separated from England. It should be understood that the colonists did not dislike English law in its entirety; their complaint was that the law was used improperly against them and they were denied their rights as English citizens under it. As mentioned earlier, almost half the men who signed the Declaration of Independence were lawyers, and their legal background was solidly based on the concepts of English common law. It is only natural, therefore, that

the basic operational law in the new states of the Union would be English common law, with some modifications to suit the special philosophical differences of the people living there. It should also be remembered that most of the leaders were more conservative than many people believe.

1.9:8   The States' Rights Concept in Our Early History

Critics of American law often complain that it lacks national uniformity; they are certainly right. To understand this, it is important to cover the concept of "States' Rights." The colonists were very leery of a strong, centrally controlled government. They wanted their independence as states and not as a new American nation. The various colonies would have never agreed to anything else.

The very term "United States" indicates groups of individual states united together, and not one single country. Because of this, the development of law, even though it naturally started out as being English common law, was to take different directions in different states. The only limits established were those set down in the Constitution.

Each state retained its own sovereignty, and the Articles of Confederation, which established a confederation of states in 1781, created the loosest form of control over the states. Until the United States Constitution established a system of federal government in 1789, Congress had little power, and was, in fact, in a state of chaos.

The Articles didn't even establish provisions for an executive (President) because they feared that he might somehow become another king. Since the Congress had no provisions for financial support due to the strong feeling the colonists had against taxation, congress had to print its own money which was looked upon as being worthless.

Fig. I–27:   Worthless Continental money.

Independent Judiciary

American law is not American. We inherited a vast majority of it from the English. There is one area of law that is strictly our own, however. That is the concept of an "Independent Judiciary."

Although the Romans talked about it, the United States was the first country to put it into operation. Our forefathers were very aware of the problems that resulted from the courts being controlled by the government rulers. In an effort to further protect citizens from a possibly oppressive executive branch of government, they made the judiciary an independent branch.

It soon became obvious that the United States could not function with such a weak central government, and many political leaders like Washington and Hamilton began pushing for more power and central control for the federal government. Their efforts eventually resulted in the United States Constitution. The next chapter will cover Constitutional law.

REFERENCES FOR CHAPTER 1

(1)   M.F. Morris, The History of the Development of Law, John Byrne & Co., Washington, D.C., p. 53.

(2)   Ibid.,p.52.

(3)   Ibid.,p.54.

(4)   Chilperic Edwards, The Hammurabi Code, Kennikat Press, New York, p. 16, pp. 82-83.

(5)   Ibid.,p.5.

(6)   Ibid.,p.9.

(7)   Ibid.,p.23.

(8)   Ibid.,p.29.

(9)   Ibid.,p.85.

(10) Ibid.,p.161.

(11) M.F. Morris, The History of the Development of Law, p. 57

(12) Chilperic Edwards, The Hammurabi Code, p. 31.

(13) Ibid., p. 42.

(14) Ibid., p. 46.

(15) Ibid., p. 51.

(16) Ibid., p. 61.

(17) M.F. Morris, The History of the Development of Law, p. 72.

(18) John Wilkinson, The Ancient Egyptians, Vol. III, John Murray Publ. London, 1878, p. 61.

(19) Columbia-Viking Desk Encyclopedia, Viking Press, New York

(20) M.F. Morris, The History of the Development of Law, p. 68.

(21) Ibid.,p. 29.

(22) Ibid.,p. 36.

(23) Ibid.,p. 67.

(24) Ibid.,p. 69.

(25) Ibid.,p. 70.

(26) Ibid.,p. 71.

(27) Ibid.,p. 71.

(28) Walter Abbott, Arthur Gilbert, Rolfe Hunt et. al. The Bible Reader, Bruce Books, New York, p. 126.

(29) M.F. Morris, The History of the Development of Law, pp. 39-40.

(30) Chilperic Edwards, The Hammurabi Code, p. 109.

(31) M.F. Morris, The History of the Development of Law, p. 34.

(32-50) Ibid., pp.34-160.

(51) Chilperic Edwards, The Hammurabi Code, pp. 93-95.

(52) M.F. Morris, The History of the Development of Law, p. 160.

(53) Ibid., p. 162.

(54) Chilperic Edwards, The Hammurabi Code, p. 104.

(55) Ibid.,p. 93.

(56) Ibid.,p. 94.

(57) Ibid.,p. 95.

(58) Ibid.,pp. 96, 99.

(59) M.F. Morris, The History of the Development of Law, p. 201.

(60) Columbia-Viking Desk Encyclopedia, Viking Press, New York.

(61) Ibid.,

(62) Rene A. Wormser, The Story of the Law, Simon & Schuster, New York, p. 219.

(63) M.F. Morris, The History of the Development of Law, p. 242.

(64) Frances McNamara, 2000 Famous Legal Quotations, Aqueduct Books, New York.

(65) Columbia-Viking Desk Encyclopedia, Viking Press, New York,

(66) George T. Payton, Patrol Operations, Legal Book, Los Angeles, pp. 37-38.

(67) Rene A. Wormser, The Story of the Law, p. 240.

(68) Ibid.,p. 245.

(69) Ibid.,pp. 259, 260.

(70) Ibid.,p. 250.

(71) Columbia-Viking Desk Encyclopedia, Viking Press, New York.

(72) Frances McNamara, 2,000 Famous Legal Quotations, p. 53.

(73) M.F. Morris, The History of the Development of Law, p. 119.

(74) Ibid., p. 291

(75) Rene A. Wormser, The Story of the Law, p. 307.

(76) David Guralnik, Webster's New World Dictionary, Popular Library, New York.

(77-83) Rene A. Wormser, The Story of the Law, p. 308.

(78) Ibid.,pp 310, 313, 320, 324, 325, 333.

STUDY QUESTIONS

CHAPTER I

(1)   The code of Hammurabi was the first major set of laws known to mankind.   T or F

(2)   The laws of the Babylonians have had an effect on the United States through the fact that the ancient Hebrews lived next to the Babylonians, and later incorporated some of those laws into the laws found in the Old Testament.   T or F

(3)   The law of the ancient Babylonians was written in:

    (A) ✓ Cuneiform   (B) ____ Hieroglyphics
    (C) ____ Roman numerals   (D) ____ Aramaic

(4)   The Code Of Hammurabi was an "eye for an eye" type of law.   T or F

(5)   The Code of Hammurabi was a law that was very protective of its people.   T or F

(6)   The Code of Hammurabi required "multiple retribution."   T or F

(7)   Criminals who couldn't pay fines in Babylon were sold into slavery until the debt was paid.   T or F

(8)   Egyptian law has affected the United States indirectly because Moses was raised in Egypt and trained in Egyptian law before he wrote his own code.   *MOSEIC LAW*   T or F

(9)   The ancient Egyptians allowed the practice of incest and polygamy.   T or F

(10)   The Egyptian priests were also doctors and lawyers.   T or F

(11)   The ancient Egyptians charged high fees for taking a case to court.   *It's a SERVICE*   T or F

(12)   At one time, Cleopatra was married to her brother.   T or F

(13)   The ancient Egyptians did not allow closing arguments in their courts.   T or F

(14)   The ancient Hebrew law demanded multiple retribution.   T or F

(15)   The legal term for the "eye for an eye" type of punishment was:

    (A) ____ Maximus Lege   (B) ✓ Lex Talionis
    (C) ____ Lex Multimum   (D) ____ Lege Siempre

(16)   Moses is often referred to as the "great law giver."   *10 Commandments*   T or F

(17)   The sex laws of the ancient Hebrews are some of the world's strictest.   T or F

(18)   The Mosaic Code is found in:

    (A) ____ First five books of old testament   (B) ____ Pentateuch
    (C) ____ Torah   (D) ✓ All of these

(19)   The Draconian Code failed because the punishment for its laws was too mild.   T or F

(20)   The Code of Solon lasted about five years.   *CENTURIES*   T or F

(21)   There were many changes in the Code of Solon after the first year.   T or F

(22)   The Code of Solon outlawed polygamy.   T or F

(23)   The Code of Solon contained the first known laws against women drivers.   T or F

(24)   The Code of Solon was written on brass tablets and placed in the marketplace for citizens to see.   T or F

(25) The Code of Solon allowed prostitution.   T or F

(26) Athens was the center of Greek law in ancient times.   T or F

(27) Solon and Moses are considered to be the two greatest law-givers in recorded history.   T or F

(28) The Great Court of Areopagus had four judges to hear its cases.   T or F

(29) The Great Court of Areopagus lasted long after the fall of Greece.   T or F

(30) The Great Court of Areopagus was held at night and in the open. *CAN'T SEE FACE FOR FAIRNESS*   T or F

(31) Judges in the Great Court of Areopagus were appointed for life.   T or F

(32) The Law of the Twelve Tables was written on tablets of brass like the Code of Solon, but they   T or F
      were placed in the temple rather than the market.

(33) Before The Law of the Twelve Tables, Roman law was a series of unwritten religious laws.   T or F

(34) The Law of The Twelve Tables demanded "multiple retribution."   T or F

(35) The Law of the Twelve Tables contained "Lex Talionis" laws.   T or F

(36) There was no death penalty in the Law of the Twelve Tables.   T or F

(37) In later times, Roman leaders were, for the most part, lawyers.   T or F

(38) The Justinian Code was also called the Corpus Juris Civilis.   T or F

(39) The Justinian Code became the basis for most of the western laws after the dark ages were   T or F
      over.

(40) The Romans had a system of judges who acted as a jury. they were called:

          (A) _____ Leges   (B) ✓ _____ Judices
          (C) _____ Pax Leges   (D) _____ Judicators

(41) During the dark ages, Roman law was preserved by the Christian church in their ecclesiasti-   T or F
      cal courts.

(42) In the dark ages, the law of the feudal kings was extremely severe.   T or F

(43) The common law of Europe in the dark ages was developed by custom and usage, and at first   T or F
      was not written down.

(44) The first law school since ancient times was established at the University of Bologna in the   T or F
      eleventh century.

(45) Charlemagne's capitularies were a series of small or little laws.   T or F

(46) The Spanish law, Las Siete Partidas, was based on the Justinian Code.   T or F

(47) Las Siete Partidas is the basis for much South American law.   T or F

(48) The Code Napoleon was a brief set of laws that was based on the Justinian Code.   T or F

(49) The Code Napoleon was at one time used on the North American continent.   T or F

(50) All of the countries that helped defeat Napoleon, except England, later adopted the Code Na-   T or F
      poleon as the basis for their law.

(51) In early England, all citizens were required to pursue a suspected criminal or be punished.
      This system was called the:

          (A) _____ Watch and ward   (B) _____ Knights Templar
          (C) ✓ _____ Hue and cry   (D) _____ Stare Decisis

(52)   The criminal law in early England was unified into a common system that was called "common law crimes." This was done by taking power away from the Sheriffs and establishing royal control. The ruler who accomplished this was:

    (A) ____King Henry   (B) ____Albert the Great
    (C) ____Canute   (D) _✓_William the Conqueror

(53)   The system of establishing truth in court by the number of witnesses a defendant could get to swear in his favor was called:

    (A) _✓_Compurgation   (B) ____Perjury
    (C) ____Consternation   (D) ____Factualization

(54)   Trial by jury originally came from the French.   T or F

(55)   The Magna Charta brought about a new philosophy in law, that the people have a right to some say in the laws under which they live.   T or F

(56)   Early English Anglo-Saxon law could make a person responsible for the crimes of his neighbor.   T or F

(57)   The Habeas Corpus Act was an English law meaning that a body must be produced in a murder case, or there could be no conviction.   T or **F**

(58)   Blackstone was a famous English jurist who interpreted English common law.   T or F

(59)   The rules of equity allowed English judges to use Roman law if they could not resolve the case with English common law.   T or F

(60)   The Latin term meaning precedence is:

    (A) ____Precedorum   X(B) _✓_Stare Decisis
    (C) ____Leges Precio   (D) ____Corpus Delicti

(61)   The American system of an "independent judiciary" is not new. The French also used it in the 1700s.   T or **F**

(62)   The development of American law over the last 200 years has been a slow movement away from English common law back to the concepts of Roman law.   **T** or F

(63)   The first colony in Massachusetts was called a "theocracy." It means:

    (A) ____Dictatorship   (B) _✓_Government Under God
    (C) ____Democratic Government   (D) ____Colony

(64)   When the colonies gained their independence, they dropped English law.   T or **F**

(65)   After independence, each state developed their own law. this was based on the American concept of:

    (A) _✓_States Rights   (B) ____Colony Law
    (C) ____Legislation   (D) ____Jurisprudence

CHAPTER II

CONSTITUTIONAL LAW IN THE UNITED STATES AND PROVISIONS FOR THE MAKING AND ADMINISTRATION OF LAW

2.0   THE UNITED STATES CONSTITUTION IN DEVELOPMENT
2.1   THE UNITED STATES CONSTITUTION AS IT DEALS WITH THE ADMINISTRATION OF JUSTICE
2.2   THE AMENDMENTS OF THE CONSTITUTION AS THEY DEAL WITH THE ADMINISTRATION OF JUSTICE
2.3   GENERAL AND SPECIFIC SOURCES OF LAW
2.4   POLICE POWER AND ITS LIMITS
2.5   THE MODEL PENAL CODE
2.6   HOW LAWS ARE MADE

2.0:0 THE UNITED STATES CONSTITUTION IN DEVELOPMENT

When the Continental Congress adopted the Declaration of Independence, the next step was to develop some type of Constitution. Under the direction and guidance of Benjamin Franklin, the Articles of Confederation were developed. It was a difficult task because the colonists were very sensitive toward a "Big Brother" type of government. The Articles were debated for sixteen months and finally adopted in 1777. Ratification by the states did not come until 1781.[1] Because the colonists were so concerned about states' rights, the Articles of Confederation were little more than a "paper" agreement to unify. There were no provisions for a President, or for financial support of the federal government. Washington and Hamilton were quite disappointed in the weak central government, and the ineffectiveness of the Articles. Hamilton became a great moving force toward constitutional reform and a stronger central government. He was admitted to the bar when he was twenty-five, but was a mature thinker and had great leadership qualities. Hamilton once said of law:

> It will be of little avail to the people that the laws are made by men of their own choice if the laws be so voluminous that they cannot be read, or so incoherent that they cannot be understood.[2]

The key to revising the Articles of Confederation into a workable Constitution was compromise. No official records were kept, and the sessions were held in secret behind locked doors. In this way the delegates were able to approach the problems in a more direct manner without worrying about their constituents. Benjamin Franklin, although eighty-one-years-old, was the great mediator due to the respect the delegates held for him.

Although the convention had been called to amend or revise the Articles of Confederation, it soon became evident that the only solution was an entirely new Constitution. The delegates sought help in the writings of famous English political philosophers, and because compromise was essential, the delegates accepted a republic as opposed to a monarchy or democracy.[3] The major compromise was the structure of Congress. A system of checks and balances was established. There was to be an upper House with membership based equally among the states, but representation in the lower House was to be proportionate to population. This overcame the fear of small states that states with larger populations would control Congress.

The issues that were most easily settled were:

(1) Separate executive, legislative and judicial branches of government. This would make the United States the first country to have an independent judiciary. The Romans discussed it, but we were the first to put it into practice;

(2) Congress would have the power to tax;

(3) Congress would regulate foreign and domestic commerce; and

(4) Congress would issue bills, and control the currency for the nation. It created a strong Executive, but made him subject to impeachment and trial by the Houses of Congress.[4]

Before work started on the Constitution, the Convention made the provision that the Constitution would become effective upon a vote of two-thirds of the states. If it were not for that provision, it is doubtful that the Constitution would have been ratified. As it was, the process of ratification was a battle with many hot tempers flaring. The Federalist Papers, written by Alexander Hamilton, James Madison, and John Jay in 1788, had a great effect in persuading delegates to vote for ratification.

2.1:0 THE UNITED STATES CONSTITUTION AS IT DEALS WITH THE ADMINISTRATION OF JUSTICE

William F. Weld, governor of the Commonwealth of Massachusetts, once stated:

> Government has no role more important than protecting the safety of its citizens. If we are not free to walk our streets in safety, no other freedoms really matter. Those rights that frame the foundation of our system of government—the rights of life, liberty and the pursuit of happiness —are secure only within secure communities. This is the essence of the social compact.

Because there was so much controversy in accepting the Constitution, many compromises had to be made. There was very little in the Constitution that dealt with the rights so well stated in the Declaration of Independence. Wormser believes that the delegates felt that the state constitutions would cover this area, but he also felt that delegates were so exhausted that they might have presumed the existence of certain rights which were by no means clearly stated.[5]

The following are sections from the United States Constitution that have a direct bearing upon the Administration of Justice:

Article 1

This article establishes the legislative branch of Government as the lawmaking, branch. It is to be called Congress, is divided into two houses. They are the Senate and the House of Representatives. The purpose for this vision was to enable each house to keep a check on the other and to correct possible mistakes made by the other house. This separation of powers is referred to as the system of checks and balances.

Sect. 6 This section protects members of Congress from arrest on the way to, during, and returning from a session in the legislature. This does not apply to cases of treason, felonies, or a breach of the peace. The purpose of this section is to guard against a Congressman's being arrested in order to prevent him from voting on an important issue that may be decided by a very close vote.

Sect. 7 This section gives the President ten days in which either to sign a new law or to veto it. If he fails to sign the law within ten days, it automatically becomes law. It also allows Congress to overcome the President's veto by a vote of two-thirds of both Houses. This further helps the system of "checks and balances."

Sect. 8 Allows Congress to set up federal courts lower than the Supreme Court. These are the Court of Appeals and the District Courts.

Sect. 9 Provides for the Writ of Habeas Corpus to protect people from unwarranted arrest except in times of war or rebellion.

This section also protects a citizen from the legislature passing Bills of Attainder (a trial by the legislative branch of government) and Ex Post Facto laws (Laws passed after the crime has been committed in order to arrest or charge a person with committing the crime when he committed it before it was illegal).

Article 2

This article sets up the Executive branch of government. (The police are considered to be under this branch of government, and are sometimes referred to in certain laws as "Executive Officers" —E.g., 'Bribery of an executive officer'.)

Sect. 2 Gives the President the power to grant reprieves and pardons for crimes, and the right to nominate Supreme Court Justices. This is a most important power. Our founding fathers wanted to assure independence for the judicial system, but it is doubtful they realized how powerful the Supreme Court would become. The Supreme Court is not supposed to make law, only interpret law and the Constitution. Today, it actually makes law through its interpretations. Because of this, the political makeup of the court greatly affects the administration of justice in the United States.

Presidents who have an opportunity to nominate a Supreme Court Justice will usually choose persons whose political thinking is similar to their own. If (through death, age, or illness) vacancies occur on the Supreme Court, new members can often change the court's whole approach since its decisions are based on a simple majority.

For example, the famous Miranda Decision handed down by the predominantly liberal "Warren" court, which so greatly affected the administration of justice in the United States, would not have been reversed by the present, more conservative, court.

The President does not need approval to grant pardons. President Ford used this power to grant a pardon to ex-President Nixon.

If the President wishes to nominate a person for a vacancy on the Supreme Court, he must obtain approval of the Senate by a simple majority.

Sect. 3 This section gives the President both a great responsibility and great power. It makes the President responsible for seeing that the laws are faithfully executed. It also gives him the right to appoint subordinate officers to carry out executive duties for him. If President Nixon were to be put on trial for the Watergate cover-up, it would undoubtedly be for violation of the responsibility of seeing that the laws are faithfully executed.

Article 3

Establishes the Judicial branch of government as a special and separate branch of government answerable to neither the executive nor legislative branches for its decisions.

Many legal writers feel that the "Independent Judiciary" is the shining light in American jurisprudence, the one distinct legal difference in American law as compared to all other law.

This article establishes the Supreme Court, to which members are appointed for life, as long as they are able to properly carry out their duties. It allows Congress to establish such lower federal courts as are needed to handle the cases involving the Constitution and federal laws. It gives the Supreme Court the power to review the decisions of the lower courts when they are appealed. It also guarantees citizens the right to Trial by Jury, and in the same state where the alleged crime was committed. It should be remembered that during the last period of the colonial days, the English would, at times, arrest a person and take him back to England for the trial and in that way separate him from his loved ones and trusted counsel.

It also eliminates the English legal concept of "Corruption of Blood" so that the children or family of a convicted person cannot be punished through loss of inherited property that was seized by the Crown upon conviction, or by taking away the rights of the children of a convicted felon.

Article 4

Establishes the Laws of Reciprocity between states. Because each state has its own set of laws that differ in many ways, it is necessary that some system of reciprocity be established to allow one state to accept the laws of the other state. For example, if you were to drive from California to New York, you would be driving in many different states, but you would not have a driver's license for each of those states. Under the laws of Reciprocity, each state allows an out-of-state driver to use the license of his own state for a short while. It also allows one state to honor the birth and death certificates and court decisions of other states.

If Willie Wart were convicted of a felony in Virginia, and then came to California, he would be classed as an ex-felon in California even though he was not convicted in a California court. In the same manner, a medical specialist can come to California from another state and perform an operation even though he does not have a license to practice medicine in California. His license to practice in the other state is recognized the same as the driver's license, and is accepted in California for a limited amount of time.

Sect. 2 Established Rules of Extradition between the states. This is accomplished by the Governor of the state wanting the criminal to petition the Governor of the state where the criminal is held or located. The Governor of the state holding the wanted criminal must agree before the criminal can be returned. Although it applies to all types of crimes, from a practical sense, a Governor will not go to all the trouble for a misdemeanor.

There have been cases in California where the Governor has refused extradition because he felt that extradition would not serve the interest of justice. For example, a man was arrested in Georgia for a crime that would be considered a misdemeanor in California, with a very minor punishment. In Georgia, the man was sentenced to a "Chain Gang," but after a year escaped. He came to California and led an exemplary life in Los Angeles for fifteen years, was married and had several children. In making an application, his name was run on a computer and it was discovered that he was wanted for escape in Georgia. The Governor of Georgia filed extradition papers, but the Governor of California, after investigation, refused extradition because it would not serve the interest of justice.

Sect. 4 This section guarantees each state a republican form of government. The Constitution does not state what a "republican" form of government is, but from the writings of the founding fathers at the time it was written, the definition is accepted as including three conditions:[6]

(1) The power of government is set forth and limited by a constitution.

(2) The power of government lies with the people.

(3) Laws are made by elected representatives of the people.

If there were to be a major earthquake in California, and the Governor called up the National Guard and established martial law until the disaster was properly handled, this would be a legal procedure. It would be needed for the immediate health, protection and safety of the people of the state.

However, if, after the emergency, the Governor decided that he liked being in complete control of the state and took advantage of the situation to establish a dictatorship, the Constitution would protect the citizens of California from this predicament. If the Governor refused to re-establish a republican form of government for the state, the President would use the armed forces of the United States to enforce the Constitution.

Article 5

Gives Congress the right to propose amendments to the Constitution by a two-thirds vote of both houses. It allows the amendment to become ratified (or legal) when the legislatures of three-fourths of the states agree to it.

Another way of proposing amendments is through a national convention called by Congress at the request of two-thirds of the state legislatures. Another way to ratify an amendment is through a special convention in three-fourths of the states. The quickest way is through Congress by the first procedure listed.

This article is most important. It gives life to the Constitution. It stops the Constitution from becoming a lifeless document, one "cast in concrete" that can never change. Our forefathers knew that it would be necessary in the future to make certain changes to fit circumstances. This makes revolution unnecessary. The people can change the government and the Constitution without bloodshed. They also knew that a quickly changed law is not always a good law, so they made sure that if the Constitution was amended, it could only be done with the approval of a very large majority of the people. When people complain that laws cannot be changed, they are really saying they cannot be changed quickly enough to suit them. It may be that they are the only ones wanting the change.

Article 6

This article establishes the rule of preemption in order to prevent a conflict in law between the different levels of government. In essence it means that a legislative body of a lesser form of government cannot pass a law that contradicts the law that has already been passed by a higher form of government.

The order of precedence is:[7]
(1) United States Constitution
(2) Federal Law (passed by Congress)
(3) State Constitutions
(4) State Law (passed by state legislature)
(5) Local Law (passed by city councils and county boards of supervisors; also town councils)

Preemption is sometimes a difficult concept to deal with. The order of preemption is firmly established as far as the order of precedence is concerned. The problem occurs in determining exactly what areas of law have been preempted by the higher jurisdiction.

2.2:0 THE AMENDMENTS TO THE CONSTITUTION AS THEY DEAL WITH THE ADMINISTRATION OF JUSTICE

When considering the spirit of the Declaration of Independence, and its promotion of basic human rights, the Constitution is certainly lacking in that spirit. The leaders of this country at the time were well aware of this deficiency, and it was an area in which many of them were concerned. Some of them wanted amendments added to the Constitution even before it was ratified. As a result, within two years, ten amendments were developed and called the Bill of Rights. These amendments are called the Bill of Rights because they deal with the basic human rights that were mentioned in the Declaration of Independence.

In covering this topic, only those amendments will be discussed that have an important bearing upon the administration of justice.

2.2:1 The Bill of Rights

The first ten amendments to the United States Constitution are referred to as the Bill of Rights because the writers of the Constitution used these amendments to compensate for the lack of stated rights in the Constitution as first ratified.

Waiver of Rights

Any person who is of sound mind may waive any of the following rights provided that person is not under duress to do so.

2.2:2 Amendment 1

Congress shall make no law respecting an establishment of religion, or prohibiting the free exercise thereof; or abridging the freedom of speech, or of the press, or the right of the people peaceably to assemble, and to petition the government for a redress of grievances.

(a) Congress shall make no law respecting an establishment of religion.

The purpose of this amendment was to correct some of the problems that had occurred when European governments had established a church-state relationship.

Whenever the state chose one particular church, there was invariably persecution of other religions. A good example of this in America was the Puritan theocracy in Massachusetts. The various Supreme Courts in our history have handed down many decisions regarding this section of the first amendment. There are many who feel that it has almost amounted to a persecution of some churches, but it was usually the prevention of public funds in any way being used for religious purposes.

It would be interesting to see the reaction of the authors of the Bill of Rights to the Supreme Court decision to prohibit Christmas plays in public schools. Our founding fathers were very religious persons, although some of them did not always practice their faith strictly. An example of their philosophy on religion can be found in George Washington's Farewell Address.

...and let us with caution indulge the supposition that morality can be maintained without religion...reason and experience both forbid us to expect that national morality can prevail in exclusion of religious principle.

(b) Congress shall make no law prohibiting the free exercise of religion.

Some examples of this would be:
(1) A person claiming that he is part Indian, and that the use of Peyote (a hallucinogenic drug) is part of his religion. Therefore, the narcotic laws violate his rights under the first amendment.
(2) A person marrying more than one woman at a time and claiming that his religion permits bigamy.
(3) The killing of a person and the excuse of the killer that he belongs to an ancient Inca religion which permits human sacrifice to the gods when things are going badly.
(4) The headstrong evangelist who is annoying or pestering people in an effort to "save their souls." He feels that the police have no business stopping him when he is engaged in such an important religious matter.

The key to these situations is whether the individual is violating the rights of some other person in order to achieve his or her own religious rights. This can also include harm to the society in general, or even harm to the person who is claiming this religious right.

One of the saddest types of cases involving this particular right are parents who belong to a religion that does not believe in doctors or medical help. They can be very sincere in their belief, and when one of their children is seriously injured, they violate 270 of the Penal Code by refusing to provide medical care for their child when they are able to do so. There seems to be no easy answer to this type of situation. If discovered in time by some outsider, a judge of the Juvenile Court can be contacted (even over the phone) and he can legally make the child a ward of the court under section 300 of the Welfare and Institutions Code. When this is done, the judge can authorize medical care.

(c) Freedom of Speech

There are limitations on freedom of speech. Freedom of speech is really freedom of expression. Even then there are limitations. This right does not excuse offenses of libel or slander. If you say to a friend, "I believe that Lilly Liverwart is a prostitute," this statement is protected under freedom of speech because it expresses a personal belief and is stated as such. On the other hand, if you were to say to your friend, "Did you know that Lilly Liverwart is a prostitute," you have stated a "fact," not an opinion, and could therefore be guilty of slander. Persons cannot say anything they want and have it excused under the First Amendment; especially if it violates a law (for example, making an obscene phone call, or yelling in the middle of the night, while drunk, and waking up all the neighbors). This is an example of disturbing the peace, and is not excused under the First Amendment right of freedom of speech. Even in cases that are not criminal violations, the right can be restricted. In

1919, Chief Justice Oliver Wendell Holmes stated: "Even the most stringent protection of free speech would not protect a man in falsely shouting fire in a theater and causing a panic."[8]

The same case established the Clear and Present Danger Doctrine in which Chief Justice Holmes stated that the rights under the First Amendment can change according to the circumstances. If the words spoken cause a "clear and present danger" they would not come under this protection. The same words spoken another time under different circumstances would receive First Amendment protection. He stated:

> The question in every case is whether the words are used in such circumstances and are of such a nature as to create a clear and present danger that will bring about the substantive evil that Congress has a right to prevent. When a nation is at war, many things that might be said in time of peace are such a hindrance to its effort that their utterance will not be endured.

It was the intent of the writers of the Bill of Rights to allow free expression by the individual. Without that, democracy could not long survive.

(d) Freedom of the Press

It has been said that freedom of the press applies only to those who own one. This particular freedom is essential to maintaining a democracy, yet it presents an unlimited opportunity for power among those who own or control forms of mass media. In 1887, Lord Acton made the famous statement, "Power tends to corrupt, and absolute power corrupts absolutely."[9] When the art of printing and its potential uses began to be understood, King Henry VIII felt that it was necessary to take absolute control of it.[10] John Adams recognized the problem of freedom of the press when he stated:

> Philosophers, theologians, legislators, politicians and moralists will find that the regulation of the press is the most difficult, dangerous and important problem they have to resolve. Mankind cannot now be governed without it, nor at Present with it.[11]

Now that we have some hindsight, there is no doubt that the "Watergate" situation would not have come to light without freedom of the press. For good or for bad, it is a most powerful media.

In recent years serious problems have developed between the judicial branch of government and the press. It really amounts to a conflict of rights; on the one hand, freedom of the press, and on the other, the right to a fair trial. Under freedom of the press, does a newspaper reporter have the right to publish information that will in any way prejudice a defendant's right to a fair trial? Does a newspaper have the right to publish anything regardless of the consequences? Like all other rights, the right of freedom of the press also carries with it responsibilities. It amounts to finding a happy medium. When the press makes an effort to police itself, that balance can be obtained.

Another problem that has developed recently is the right of grand juries to force a reporter to reveal sources of information. Representatives of the news media state that if they have to reveal their sources of confidential information, they will no longer receive this information. In 1972, in Branzburg v. Hayes, the high court, in a five to four vote, rejected the argument that secrecy of news sources is essential to a free press. They stated that reporters must testify and reveal the contents of their notebooks before grand juries.

(e) Freedom of Radio and Television

It is doubtful whether the founding fathers could have conceived of such devices as radio and television. Yet, on a theoretical basis, they are protected the same as the printed press. There is a major difference, however. That difference is that neither radio or television is printed on private stocks of paper, but transmitted over public airwaves, and are, therefore, regulated by the FCC (Federal Communications Commission), an executive agency of the United States government. This is a very powerful agency, and through its power, it gives the executive branch of government a lot of leverage in controlling or curtailing "freedom of radio and television."

Just before "Watergate," President Nixon had radio and television "running scared." With some support from the high court regarding more equal and fair reporting of politics, the threat of having their licenses revoked was ever present. The answer to this problem is even more difficult than that of freedom of the press. Article 2 of the Constitution gives our President more power than the head of any other democratic form of government.

(f) The right of people peaceably to assemble

The key word to this sentence is "peaceably." This is also a right that is essential if a democracy is to be maintained, The problem today is that often an assembly will be planned with the intent that it will be peaceful, but later the group becomes emotional as the result of some speaker or leader, and then they change their objective from peaceful to violent. The purpose of the law on "Unlawful Assembly" is to prevent such an assembly from becoming a riot.

A major problem for enforcement officers is dealing with groups that claim their purpose for assembly is lawful and peaceful when their actual purpose is to infringe upon the rights of others in an effort to obtain their own personal objectives. Strikers will often get "carried away" with their personal objectives and misuse their right to peaceful picketing by blocking the free passage of other persons in effort to harass. Enforcement officers are sometimes required to maintain constant surveillance in order to protect the rights of others during strikes.

Recent events have revealed how militant groups have used the right to assemble as a means of obstructing the free passage of streets and sidewalks. An example of this would be the picketing of abortion clinics by anti-abortionists. When this is done skillfully, it can serve their purpose of harassment, yet be difficult to prove in court.

One of the methods of controlling demonstrations is through the use of ordinances requiring parade permits. This is a touchy matter, and can in some cases amount to an infringement upon First Amendment rights. This is especially true if the ordinance appears to be directed toward one particular group or organization. The key to the valid exercise of police power in matters of this type is whether the regulation is reasonable. It must also be shown that the public interest is sufficiently strong to justify legislation that curtails First Amendment protection.[12] As with the other rights, a balance must be sought between individual rights and public protection.

(g) To petition the government for a redress of grievances

This was already a right under English law before the revolution, but it was denied the colonists when they tried to resolve the problems between the Crown and themselves in this manner. The concern of the colonists was shown in the wording of the Declaration of Independence:

> In every stage of these oppressions we have petitioned for redress in the most humble terms; our repeated petitions have been answered by repeated injury.

If this right had been allowed to the colonists, it is possible that the U.S. would still be an English colony today. The difficult part of this right is that, unlike criminal matters where the defendant is provided with an attorney, it could become costly to the individual to initiate a petition through legal counsel. If the grievance is one of great importance, there are organizations that would undoubtedly support such a petition with their greater financial resources.

2.2:3   Amendment 2

A well regulated militia being necessary to the security of a free state, the right of the people to keep and bear arms shall not be infringed.

There is much misunderstanding about this amendment. It should be read very closely. The legislative intent should also be considered in view of the conditions at the time the amendment was written. In the Declaration of Independence, the authors complained to the Crown that they were being denied the right as colonies to bear arms which was necessary for their own defense. The first part of this amendment refers to a militia. This is a state militia or what today we call a National Guard. In colonial times, the people were subjected to attacks by unfriendly Indians, and the colonial or state militias were a means of protection. The word "people" is also important. Some interpret it as meaning individual persons, while others see it as meaning the people as a whole or as a state.

Unfortunately, this amendment has become a "political football" as the "right to bear arms" becomes more and more an emotional issue. Those of conservative politics have taken the side that this amendment allows the individual complete authority to possess guns without restriction. On the other hand, those who are more liberal maintain that the amendment does not give the individual citizen the right to possess guns, and that because of the great number of murders and other crimes committed with guns, that these weapons should be taken away from citizens. The National Rifle Association is the major lobby organization supporting the "right to bear arms," and the promoter of bumper stickers that say, "When guns are outlawed, only outlaws will have guns."

(a) Supreme Court Decisions Regarding the Second Amendment

In the Supreme Court case U.S. v. Cruikshank,[13] the court stated that the Second Amendment does not grant the right to bear arms; it merely means that the right of the states to regulate this shall not be infringed upon by Congress. Later, the high court further affirmed this philosophy when they declared, in U. S. v. Miller,[14] that a "sawed off shotgun" had no reasonable relation to the preservation of a well-regulated militia and that possession of such a weapon was not within the meaning of that amendment. In California, the Dangerous Weapons Control Law, which places certain restrictions upon the possession of weapons, has been approved and supported by numerous state Supreme Court decisions.[15]

2.2:4   Amendment 4

The right of the people to be secure in their persons, houses, papers, and effects, against unreasonable searches and seizures, shall not be violated; and no warrants shall issue, but upon probable cause, supported by oath or affirmation, and particularly describing the place to be searched, and the persons or things to be seized.

A simple breakdown of the elements or parts of this amendment is as follows:

Search and Seizure

The right of the people to be secure in their
  (a) persons,
  (b) houses,
  (c) papers,
  (d) effects (belongings)
against unreasonable searches and seizures.

Warrants

No warrant shall issue, but upon probable cause, supported by oath (or affirmation), and particularly describing:
  (a) the place to be searched, and
  (b) the person to be searched or seized, or
  (c) the things to be seized.

This is an area of great importance and today one of great debate. Those who work in the administration of justice have to be alert to recent Supreme Court decisions in the area of search and seizure because the interpretation of this amendment seems to change so rapidly.

Protection against unreasonable search and seizure was part of English common law. The concern of the colonists was that search warrants were issued too easily and often for political reasons. The concept of protection was there; it was just a matter of its not being applied to the colonies.

Illegally Seized Evidence & Its Admissibility in Court

In most English-speaking countries, illegally seized evidence is admissible in court. For many years, American courts followed this common law doctrine, but in 1914 the United States Supreme Court, in Weeks v. United States,[16] rejected the common law rule and declared illegally obtained evidence to be inadmissible in federal courts of law. However, this did not exclude such evidence from being admissible in state courts. This is referred to as the Exclusionary Rule. It simply means that evidence obtained by an unreasonable search and seizure will not be admissible in court.

Mapp v. Ohio:[17] In 1961 the Supreme Court, in this landmark case, extended the Exclusionary Rule to every state and every court in the nation.

The problem in following the dictates of this rule is in the interpretation of the words "unreasonable search & seizure." There are many books written on this topic. Because it is well covered in the course "Legal Aspects of Evidence," it will not be covered in any detail in this book.

The term "probable cause" used as a condition for issuing warrants is also debatable, but that is a matter for the issuing judge to decide. Peace officers must develop an understanding of the term so they can substantiate probable cause when requesting search warrants.

2.2:5   Amendment 5

No person shall be held to answer for a capital, or otherwise infamous crime, unless on a presentment or indictment of a grand jury, except in cases arising in the land or naval forces, or in the militia, when in actual service in time of war or public danger; nor shall any person be subject for the same offense to be twice put in jeopardy of life and limb; nor shall be compelled in any criminal case to be a witness against himself, nor be deprived of life, liberty, or property without due process of law nor shall private property be taken for public use, without just compensation.

A simple breakdown of the elements or parts of this amendment is as follows:

(1) No person shall be held to answer for:
    (a) A capital crime (Death penalty) or
    (b) Other infamous crime (Felony)
Unless:
    (a) On a presentment or
    (b) An indictment of a Grand Jury
Except in the military forces
    (a) When in actual service
    (b) In time of war or
    (c) Public danger
(2) Nor shall any person be subject, for the same offense, to be twice put in jeopardy of life and limb. (**Double Jeopardy**—tried twice)

(3) Nor shall be compelled, in any criminal case, to be a witness against himself.
(Self-Incrimination)
(4) Nor be deprived of life, liberty, or property without due process of law.
(Proper and Fair Trial)
(5) Nor shall private property be taken for public use, without just compensation.
(Eminent Domain)

Discussion of the Amendment by Its Parts

(1) Accusatory Pleading

An accusatory pleading is a formal document that initiates criminal proceedings. The two most common accusatory pleadings are:
(1) the criminal complaint, and
(2) the indictment

Procedure in Charging Serious Crimes

This part applies only to "infamous crimes" (felonies) and "capital crimes" (ones for which the defendant could receive the death penalty). It states that, in order for a person to go on trial, the evidence supporting the accusation must be examined to see if a trial is sufficiently justified. In early times, a person could be taken directly to trial with little or no evidence just because the king or one of his subordinates felt that the person should be tried.

One of the best ways in which to ensure that there is enough evidence, is through an impartial hearing conducted by the suspect's fellow citizens. This is called a grand jury hearing. In colonial times the term "Presentment" referred to an examination of evidence by a grand jury

Through the Grand Jury: The grand jury consists of not more than twenty-three persons. It meets in secret, and in this way the government or ruler does not know who voted in what way. This allows the jury to protect a suspect from wrongful prosecution. Evidence is presented to a grand jury in support of an accusation that a crime was committed, and that the suspect(s) committed it. If twelve members of the grand jury agree that the evidence is strong enough to justify a criminal trial, they issue a "True Bill," which means they officially recommend that a trial take place. The "True Bill" then becomes the basis for the official document called an Indictment, which starts the wheels of criminal justice in motion toward the trial.

Today, apart from the grand jury, we have a system which involves the issuance of a Criminal Complaint. The District Attorney examines the evidence and decides whether a case is justified in reaching court. Since District Attorneys are evaluated on the number of cases they win, they have a tendency to be strict in the selection of cases that actually go to court. Either the police or a citizen can initiate a complaint by bringing the facts to the District Attorney or a deputy District Attorneys.

In both these systems the evidence is examined or reviewed by someone who is not personally involved in the matter. This helps eliminate prosecutions based on personal feelings. Some states do not have a grand jury system, and all charges must go through the prosecuting attorney.[18]

The amendment states that this right does not apply during times of war or great public emergency. If members of the military were granted the same legal rights as citizens in time of war, very few battles would be won; wars would be lost, and possibly, the freedom of the nation also.

(b) Double Jeopardy

The details of "Double Jeopardy" will be covered later in the chapter on Defenses to a Crime. The purpose of this right being included in the amendment is that in prior times, if the Crown "had it in" for a person, and they took him to trial and he was found innocent, they would later try him again, and would keep trying him in the hope that sooner or later some jury would convict him. It also put him to great expense in attorney fees. Today, this right mostly serves as a means of avoiding justice. It is used as a "loophole" by many guilty persons to escape criminal prosecution. Yet it is an essential right that protects people from an overbearing executive branch of government, and is therefore important.

(c) Protection Against Self-Incrimination

To fully understand the need for this right, one must be familiar with methods allowed, not only in times past, but still in some countries today. The "Rack" could legally be used to force a person to testify against himself. There were many forms of torture used to obtain confessions from suspects. Below are drawings of a thumbscrew and hand crusher that were used for this purpose.

Fig. II–1: Thumbscrew

Fig. II–2: Handcrusher

Peine Forte et Dure

Although used to frighten suspects into pleading rather than remaining silent, this was actually a form of punishment for those who remained silent in the face of accusation. The suspect was "staked out" and heavy weights were placed on his chest a little at a time until he was crushed to death. It was often a contest in bravery for the suspect. If he gave in and confessed, his estate was forfeited to the Crown and his family left without support. If he held out until he died, his family inherited. Blackstone claimed it was seldom carried out in England because most suspects would make a plea rather than suffer this punishment.[19] Compulsory self-incrimination was still practiced 400 years after the Magna Charta, and was accepted in some of the early colonies. Records of a trial in 1673 showed that Governor Winthrop of Massachusetts did not allow the privilege against self-incrimination.[20]

During the late 1800's and early 1900's in the United States, the use of the "Third Degree" by law enforcement officers was well known. Modern, professional officers have had much difficulty overcoming this reputation. Because of this, confessions were often "thrown out of court" when defendants pleaded that their statements had been made under great duress or actual beatings.

Fig. II–3:   A device of torture.

The Miranda Decision

In 1966, the United States Supreme Court under the liberal leadership of Justice Warren, set down a series of very strict rules regarding protection against self-incrimination. In Miranda v, Arizona[21] the high court not only reversed a conviction for rape against the defendant Miranda, it set down a series of rules which it felt would better ensure Fifth Amendment protection for all citizens. Many in the field of administration of justice claim that this ruling amounted to actual legislation rather than just interpretation of the Constitution. This ruling has certainly affected the administration of justice more than most others.

The court felt that the voluntary status of the confession was not the only criterion to be considered. Just as important was the suspect's awareness of his constitutional rights, and that he not be verbally persuaded into a confession once he had indicated he did not wish to discuss the matter.

The present Supreme Court, under more conservative leadership, has indicated that if the case came before them today, they would not reverse it. The court did indicate, however, that they do not plan to eliminate the rules of the decision because it has resulted in more good than harm overall. In practice though, they have been "chipping away" at Miranda by making exceptions to some rules and modifying the interpretation of others.

(d) Due Process of Law
(Pertaining to life, liberty & property)

This term can be traced to the English Petition of Right in 1628. This document used the term "law of the land" and stated that no man should in any manner be "destroyed but by the lawful judgment of his peers or by the law of the land; or put out of his land or tenements, nor taken, nor imprisoned, nor disinherited, nor put to death without being brought to answer by due process of law,"

What Is Due Process of Law?

In 1855, the United States Supreme Court answered this question by stating that in order to assure due process, a trial or other legal proceeding (it can be other than a trial) must conform to:
(1) The guarantees in the Constitution
(2) Other guarantees adopted from English law

The Constitution does not state what is meant by "Due Process." The court did state, however, that the article is a restraint on the legislative, executive, and judicial branches of government. The answer, according to the court, is to examine the Constitution to see if the process is in conflict with any of its provisions. If not, then the "settled usages" of English common law prior to the Constitution must be examined for conflicts. Basically, "Due Process" is governmental fair play.[22]

In Solesbee v. Balkcom (399 U.S. 9) (1947), Mr. Justice Frankfurter expressed his definition of "due process" in the following words:

> The "due process" clause embodies a system of rights based on moral principles so deeply embedded in the tradition and values of our people as to be deemed fundamental to a civilized society as conceived by our whole history. "Due process" is that which comports with the notion of what is fair and right and just. The more fundamental these beliefs are, the less likely they are to be explicitly stated; respect for them is the very essence of the "due process" clause.

This process ensures safeguards for the protection of individual rights as established by "settled" procedure. In 1908 the Supreme Court stated that "liberty" is not absolute when the welfare of society is involved.

(e) Protection Under Eminent Domain

The law of "eminent domain" is old. It means that the government has the right or power to take private property for public use when just compensation has been made. This was also a rule under Roman Law. The law stated that if property was taken for public use, the owner would be paid "an estimated value made by good men." The Magna Charta stated that property would not be taken from a person except through proper law or by a jury. The Code Napoleon also contained a provision for "eminent domain." It stated that compensation must be a "Just and previous indemnity."

The previous part of the Fifth Amendment also stated "shall not be deprived of life, liberty, or property without due process of law." This would indicate a trial if requested. Today, many citizens will ask for a jury trial to determine the fair amount due them for property seized under "eminent domain." The most common example of this process is land taken for the building of military bases and facilities. As a rule, the public agency taking the property will offer the owner more than the established value just to avoid the high cost of going to court on the matter. This amendment applies to the federal government only.

2.2:6   Amendment 6

In all criminal prosecutions, the accused shall enjoy the right to a speedy and public trial, by impartial jury of the state and district wherein the crime shall have been previously ascertained by law, and to be informed of the nature and cause of the accusation; to be confronted with the witnesses against him; to have compulsory process for obtaining witnesses in his favor, and to have the assistance of counsel for his defense.

A simple breakdown of the elements or parts of this amendment is as follows: In all criminal prosecutions, the accused shall enjoy:

(a) The right to a speedy trial.
(b) The right to a public trial.
(c) By an impartial jury.
(d) In the state and district where the crime was committed.

(e) To be informed of the nature and cause of the accusation.
(f) To be confronted with the witnesses against him.
(g) To have compulsory process for obtaining witnesses in his favor.
(h) To have the assistance of counsel for his defense.

Discussion of the Amendment by Its Parts

(a) The Right to a Speedy Trial

This means a trial without unreasonable delay. There are two major problems in enforcing this right. First, there is so much crime that court calendars are packed. Second, there are so many loopholes in criminal procedure that a sharp attorney can find many ways to delay the process of criminal justice. Attorneys are taught in law school that the longer time between the crime and the trial, the better off they are in trying the case. As a result of time, the memories of investigating officers and witnesses will tend to fade. There is also a greater chance that witnesses will die or leave the state and be impossible to locate. There is also the chance that evidence will be lost or misplaced.

If the attorney can keep up the delays long enough, the District Attorney's office will also be more willing to settle for a lesser charge. (Plea Bargaining). Then, as a last resort, the defense attorney can complain to the court that his client has been denied his right to a speedy trial under the Sixth Amendment.

The Federal Speedy Trial Act

In 1977 Congress passed the "Speedy Trial Act" which stated that a defendant be brought to trial within 90 days of arrest or by 1979 he be brought to trial within 60 days of arraignment.

In the same year a U.S. District Court judge ruled the law unconstitutional on the grounds that it represented an "unwarranted congressional intrusion into the internal functions of the judicial process." Citing the "Separation of Powers Doctrine" in the Constitution, the judge stated that this was a job for the courts and not Congress.

✄ (b) The Right to a Public Trial

The purpose of this right is to prevent a "Star Chamber" type of trial where it is held in secret. The only way to ensure that a trial is fair and proper is for it to be open to scrutiny. There are some exceptions to this rule. In the case of child molesting, the judge may ask that the trial not be public to protect the feelings and emotions of the victim. However, every part of the trial is recorded and will be open to review, so in a sense it is public. Before the Revolution, the colonists were often tried before courts that were strictly private, in trials in which the defendant did not have the rights normally given to English citizens.

(c) By an Impartial Jury

This is usually accomplished in two ways.

(1) Jury Selection (*Voir Dire*—to speak truth)

Today there are two main methods used for proper jury selection. They are:

(A) Challenge for Cause Both the prosecution and the defense are allowed as many challenges for the removal of a juror as can be justified. The challenge must, however, be based on an obvious bias or prejudice evidenced by the juror. For example, a jury is being selected for a vehicular manslaughter trial in which the defendant is nineteen years old. If a prospective juror is questioned regarding his feelings about teenage drivers, and he responds that they should all be hung up by their thumbs, he has shown an obvious bias or prejudice. The defense will ask the judge to remove him on Challenge for Cause. The judge has the final authority to decide. (There is no limit.)

(B) Peremptory Challenges Sometimes attorneys get a feeling or premonition about the qualifications of a prospective juror. They will not be able to "put their finger on it" because it is not obvious. To take these feelings into account, and to help select the most impartial jury possible, the law allows the attorneys for each side to eliminate up to ten prospective jurors without giving any reason. In cases where the death penalty can result, each side gets twenty peremptory challenges.

(2) Change of Venue

This means a change of location for the trial. It is used to ensure an impartial jury. If the defense attorney feels that his client cannot obtain a fair trial in the county where the crime was committed because of a particular prejudice or possible prior press coverage, he will ask the judge for a Change of Venue. It is up to the judge to decide.

Sometimes a crime is committed in a small community where everyone is related to the victim, and they are all upset about the crime. It is doubtful they can be impartial in their decision if they are selected for the jury. The obvious answer is to move the trial to another location where people are not in any way involved and do not have strong personal feelings about the crime or defendant.

(d) A Trial in the State and District Where the Crime Was Committed

One of the complaints by colonists was that the English rulers would arrest a colonist and take him to England for a trial. In this way they denied the suspect the moral support of his family and possibly of a trusted attorney. The term "district" means county. The term used when referring to the court that will handle the case is Jurisdiction. For example, municipal courts have jurisdiction over misdemeanor offenses, and superior courts have jurisdiction over felonies. Juvenile courts have jurisdiction over cases dealing with juveniles. The term used to determine the location of the court is Venue. For example, a felony committed in Santa Clara County would have to be tried in the superior court of Santa Clara County. It could not be tried in San Francisco County. An exception can be made when defendants feel they cannot get a fair trial in the county where the crime was committed and ask for a "Change of Venue."

(e) And to Be Informed of the Nature and Cause of the Accusation

The word "accusation" means the charge or offense for which the defendant has been arrested. In California, Penal Code section 841 states that the person making the arrest must inform the suspect of the cause of the arrest. This charge is again explained to the suspect when he first goes before a judge. This is called the Arraignment. This is the first appearance before the judge, and where he explains the nature and cause of the charges. He also makes sure that the defendant has an attorney who appears to be outwardly competent. He also asks the defendant how he pleads to the charges.

(f) To Be Confronted with the Witnesses Against Him

This is the right to cross-examine any witnesses who may testify against the defendant. It is important because when cross-examined under oath, a witness may admit things that would indicate his or her testimony is not reliable or valid. It is also an opportunity for the defendant or attorney to bring out the other side of the story or special circumstances. Juries also make better decisions when they can see a witness testify and not just have a deposition read in court. An exception to this rule would be a written "dying declaration."

Under English common law, this right was not allowed. The prosecution could take a deposition and then read it in court.[23] A deposition is a form of written testimony that is taken under oath. It is usually taken before the trial. The Romans also required the confrontation of accusers by the accused. In Acts XXV:16, Festus, the Roman procurator of Judea, told Paul that the high priests and elders had laid an "information" against him, to which he answered: "It is not Roman practice to hand over any accused man before he is confronted with his accusers and given an opportunity of answering the charge." (New English Bible)

(g) To Have Compulsory Process of Obtaining Witnesses in His Favor

In order for a person to have a fair trial, it is sometimes necessary to almost force a witness to come to court and to testify under oath. Some people just do not want to "get involved." This part of the amendment gives the defendant the same right as the prosecutor as far as having a judge order certain persons to appear in court to testify about a certain matter. This official order from the judge is called a Subpoena (a Greek word meaning "under penalty," pronounced "suh-pea-na.") Refusal to obey a subpoena will result in the judge issuing a Bench Warrant for "Contempt of Court."

(h) And to Have Assistance of Counsel for His Defense

Until the Miranda Decision in 1966, it was assumed that when this part of the Sixth Amendment was written, it meant during any trial resulting

from being arrested or officially charged with a crime. Five of the nine justices of the Supreme Court stated in that decision that it should start when it is obvious the suspect will end up in court, and that officers should notify suspects of their right to attorneys when they are arrested or interrogated in a formal way. The court also stated for the first time that if the suspect is indigent (poor) the county must provide an attorney. In the past, if a person appeared at the arraignment and did not have an attorney, the judge would either delay the arraignment, or appoint one from the courtroom; the county would then pay the attorney a set fee. This occurred only at the arraignment and not at the time of the arrest. Because of this Supreme Court decision, each county has a Public Defender's Office with about the same number of attorneys as the District Attorney's Office.

2.2:7 Amendment 7

In suits at common law, where the value in controversy shall exceed twenty dollars, the right of trial by jury shall be preserved, and no fact tried by a jury, shall be otherwise re-examined in any court of the United States, than according to the rules of the common law.

This amendment contains two parts. They are:
(a) Trial by federal jury shall be guaranteed in cases involving over $20.00
(b) No jury decision shall be re-examined by a federal appellate court unless under the rules of appeal at common law.
    This, basically, covers two areas:
(1) Constitutional error
    (which can be quite broad), and
(2) Error in court procedure
    (which denies the defendant a fair trial)

2.2:8 Amendment 8

Excessive bail shall not be required, nor excessive fines imposed, nor cruel and unusual punishments inflicted.

(a) Excessive Bail

The bail system is a means whereby an arrested person puts up money or property as a guarantee that, when released, he will return for the arraignment or trial. It should be high enough to ensure that he will return, yet not so high as to prevent his being released. The exact amount is difficult to establish in all cases since there are so many varying factors involved.

As far back as 1444, under Henry VI, there was an act of Parliament that required sheriffs and other officers to "let out of prison all manner of persons upon reasonable sureties (money or property) of sufficient persons." Before the Revolution, it was a common practice to set bails so high that the defendant could not possibly raise the money and would, therefore, stay in jail.

Since the right amount of bail is such a debatable subject, most attorneys will ask the judge to lower the bail on the grounds that it violates the Eighth Amendment. If the amount is considerably high, the judge will ask the prosecutor why such a high bail was set, and if he cannot justify it, or doesn't know, the judge will lower it at that time.

Sometimes officers will ask the judge to set a high bail so that the arrested person will remain in jail while they search for evidence that he might destroy if he were to bail out. Some judges will go along with this reasoning, but will grant a lowering of bail after a day or two.

The Magna Charta declared that bail should fit the crime, and that a man should not have to put up so much money that he would not be able to continue his trade or business when out of jail.[24]

(b) Excessive Fines

Excessive fines, like excessive bail, are debatable (unless they are completely unreasonable). Most states limit the fine for each offense in their statutes. If one man was given the maximum fine listed, and the two thousand defendants before him were fined half that amount, he might have grounds for claiming a violation of the Eighth Amendment, on the precedent set by the previous two thousand.

(c) Cruel and Unusual Punishment

Before the revolution, the history of England (and the world) was filled with examples of exceedingly cruel forms of punishment. These often amounted to torturing a person to death. In England it was a common punishment to have the defendant "hung and quartered." This meant that he was hung with a rope so that his neck was not snapped. Before he was strangled, he was cut down and disemboweled while still alive. His head was then cut off and his body cut into four pieces.

It was practices such as this that the writers of the Constitutional amendments wanted to prevent, but the U.S. Supreme Court has interpreted this section in many ways. In 1958 the high court stated that taking away a soldier's citizenship for an act of desertion under the Nationality Act of 1940 was cruel and unusual. (Trop v. Dulles)

The Death Penalty & the Eighth Amendment

The death penalty was not intended to come under the Eighth Amendment. The death penalty existed when the Amendments were written. If our forefathers felt the death penalty itself was cruel and unusual, they would have put it down in writing. The issue, however, is not so much the death penalty in itself, but the procedures for sentencing a person to death, and for carrying out the sentence.

Furman v. Georgia[25] In this famous case, the Supreme Court, in a five to four decision, declared that capital punishment, as it existed then, violated the Eighth Amendment. Those who agreed or disagreed did so for various reasons which almost amount to nine separate decisions. They felt the matter should be resolved by the individual states. Basically, the problem was one of discrimination. The poor and members of minority groups were more likely to be sentenced to death than others.

Since that time, several states have rewritten the laws on the death penalty The Supreme Court has stated that some of them are still in violation, but has not handed down clear guidelines. In the near future, the court will have to resolve this matter conclusively.

2.2:9 Amendment 9

The enumeration in the Constitution, of certain rights, shall not be construed to deny or disparage others retained by the people

The rights listed in the first eight amendments are specific. It was not possible at that time for the writers of the amendments to list all the possible rights which the people wanted to keep for themselves. The national government is one of delegated and enumerated powers. These powers are limited by the Constitution. The Ninth Amendment was written to back up this concept and prevent the government from later trying to take away people's rights simply because they were not listed in the Constitution or its amendments

2.2:10 Amendment 10

The powers not delegated to the United States by the Constitution, nor prohibited by it to the states, are reserved to the States respectively, or to the people.

The purpose of this Amendment is to make clear to the federal government that it has only those powers given to it by the Constitution. It divides power among three groups. First comes the people, then the states, and finally, the federal government.

This is the last amendment in the Bill of Rights. It gives the states the power to make their own laws, providing they do not violate the Constitution, or contradict an area of law preempted by the federal government. Under this amendment, the states can establish systems of police protection, education, public health, road and highway building, and other services necessary to the welfare of the people. This amendment makes the United States different from most other countries in that they do not have a national police or a national education system.

Powers that were delegated to the federal government and not allowed to the states included the power to declare war, to coin money, raise armies, make treaties, regulate commerce, and impose duties on exports and imports.

The states, in turn, can delegate powers to counties, cities and towns. This is done through a state charter, and is limited by the state constitution. As with the federal constitution, the state constitution gives to the state only those powers that the people are willing to give to it.

Grant of Power and Limitations on Power

Because the U.S. Constitution gives to the federal government only those powers that the people of the various states have specifically granted, it is often referred to as a "grant of power." Because the people, through their state constitutions, have limited the power of the states, state constitutions are often referred to as "limitations on power." The Tenth Amendment states, "The powers not delegated to the United States by the Constitution, nor prohibited by it to the States, are reserved to the States respectively, or to the people." The people, through the state constitution, limit the powers of the state legislature. The state legislature can pass laws on anything not forbidden through or limited by the state constitution. In 1823, Jefferson wrote:

I believe the States can best govern over home concerns and the General Government over foreign ones. I wish, therefore, to see maintained that wholesome distribution of powers established by the Constitution for the limitation of both, and never see all offices transferred to Washington.

In 1911, the United States Supreme Court listed some of the powers of the state:

Among the powers of the state not surrendered is the power to guard the public morals, the public safety, and the public health, as well as to promote the public convenience and the common good.[26]

2.2:11 Amendment 14 (1868)

All persons born or naturalized in the United States, and subject to the jurisdiction thereof, are citizens of the United States and of the state wherein they reside. No state shall make or enforce any law which shall abridge the privileges or immunities of citizens of the United States; nor shall any state deprive any person of life, liberty, or property, without due process of law; nor deny to any person within its' jurisdiction the equal protection of the laws.

A breakdown of the parts of this amendment for discussion is as follows:

(1) All persons who are either born in the United States or naturalized in the United States are citizens of this country and of the state where they reside.

(2) No state shall make or enforce any law which shall abridge (interfere with) the privileges or immunities of citizens of the United States.

(3) Nor shall any state deprive any person of life, liberty or property without Due Process of Law (also in Fifth Amendment).

(4) Nor shall they deny to any person within its jurisdiction equal protection of the laws.

The purpose of this amendment is to guarantee that states will ensure that:

(1) Former slaves were given the rights of citizens.

(2) They will use fair and legal methods when a person is tried for a crime.

(3) The law will be applied equally to all citizens, and not be used against some and not others, or for some and not others.

(4) Protection from state government

The Bill of Rights was ratified in 1791. The Fourteenth Amendment was not ratified until 1868, seventy-seven years later. Many changes had taken place in the United States in the intervening time. The Fourteenth Amendment was drafted primarily to protect newly freed Negro slaves from discriminatory action by individual states. However, continued interpretation of this amendment by the U.S. Supreme Court has broadened its concepts considerably. In recent years it has become one of the most important and most used amendments. This started with the so-called "shorthand doctrine" which, in effect, states that the Fourteenth Amendment is a "shorthand" version of the Bill of Rights and applies to the states rather than just the federal government.

In 1884, in Hurtado v. California[27] the high court stated that if the writers of the Fourteenth Amendment intended for the amendment to include all the detailed rights in the Fifth Amendment, they would have listed those rights in the new amendment. This case involved a man convicted of murder and sentenced to hang when the whole process was initiated by a criminal complaint rather than a "presentment" from the grand jury as listed in the Fifth Amendment.

In 1947, in Adamson v. California[28] the high court again upheld this trend of legal thought. They stated that the "due process" clause of the Fourteenth Amendment does not draw all the rights of the federal Bill of Rights under its protection.

The Fundamental Rights Theory

In making decisions, many Justices refer to the "Fundamental Rights Theory" which states that certain rights are fundamental, and that people are protected against state invasion because these are "fundamental rights," and not just because they happen to also be listed in the Bill of Rights.

Reversal Trend

Starting with the case of Griffin v. California[29] in 1965, the high court began reversing itself, feeling that the rights listed in the first eight amendments were implied in the Fourteenth. This was based on a broad interpretation of the words "due process," which the court now felt should include all the legal protections in the Bill of Rights.

From Whom Does the Fourteenth Amendment Protect Us?

The Fourteenth Amendment, by its language, speaks only to the states. It does not protect us from strictly private conduct, however wrong. Private conduct can in some circumstances be tied in with the state if that private conduct is financed by the state, or through some contract the state has a great influence on the decisions of that private entity.

An examination of the various parts of the Fourteenth Amendment is as follows:

All persons born or naturalized in the United States, and subject to the jurisdiction thereof, are citizens of the United States and of the State wherein they reside.

Under the theory of "states' rights" the citizen was not in contact with the national government. He dealt with the state, which in turn dealt with the nation. He was, therefore, a citizen who owed allegiance to his state.

The Fourteenth Amendment definitely set aside this theory. It now clearly stated that a person was a citizen of both the state and the nation, and as such, he was entitled to all the constitutional protections, not just from the national government, but from the state as well. When the Constitution was written, the major fear of colonists was an overly strong federal government. Later, it was discovered that the states could be just as oppressive as any federal government.

No state shall make or enforce any law which shall abridge the privileges or immunities of citizens of the United States.

This is not a protection from individuals or groups of individuals, but protection against the legislative, executive and judicial branches of state government.

It should be remembered that unless a power has been specifically given to the federal government, the individual states have jurisdiction over certain areas and can make special laws in those areas. For example, education and police protection are state functions. State regulations in the area of professions, manufacture of foods, jury trials and criminal prosecutions are part of state and not federal rights, providing such regulations are not a blatant violation of the Constitution.

This section uses the term "citizens," and although this protection is extended to those persons who are not actually citizens, it does not include corporations. Because of this, the state can place greater restrictions on corporations and businesses than they can upon individual citizens.

Nor shall any state deprive any person of life, liberty, or property without due process of law.

This is undoubtedly the most important section of this amendment. The term "due process" has, in recent times, been very broadly interpreted. The courts are now saying that it includes all the basic rights mentioned in the Bill of Rights.

This section now extends to the states an obligation to use due process when taking private property under "eminent domain." Today, the states are probably using this means of taking private property more than the federal government. The most common examples are taking property for state freeways and for schools.

In 1884 the United States Supreme Court held that the Fifth Amendment section requiring the administering of the death penalty be initiated through a presentment or an information from a grand jury, applies only to the federal government, and not to the states.[30]

Personal Liberty:

In 1905 the Supreme Court held that liberty is not absolute when the welfare of society is involved.[31]

Nor deny to any person within its jurisdiction the equal protection of the laws.

Although the term "Negro" was not used, this section was primarily written for the newly liberated Negro. Along with the "due process" part of this amendment, this is one of the most important sections. Today, it is one of the most widely used sections when appealing cases to the Supreme Court. It is usually a "companion" section; one that is included with other violations of amendments. For example, a case might go to the Supreme Court based on a violation of the Fifth and Fourteenth Amendments.

The general intent of this section was to prevent any person or class of persons from being singled out as a special subject for laws that are discriminatory. As early as 1879, the Supreme Court found a city ordinance to be unconstitutional because it required that the hair of prisoners be clipped. The court stated that the ordinance was directed against persons of Chinese origin, to whom "pigtails" were a very important cultural and religious tradition. They felt that it was degrading and cruel punishment.

The Separate but Equal Doctrine

The "separate but equal" doctrine was an early attempt to resolve the Fourteenth Amendment in the southern states. In Plessy v. Ferguson,[32] in 1896, the Supreme Court ruled that the Fourteenth Amendment was not violated if the races were separated in railroad cars, but given equal facilities. This was the beginning of "Jim Crow" laws that separated races in the South by supposedly providing separate but equal facilities. This lasted until 1954 when, in Brown v. Board of Education, the high court stated that separate facilities were not equal, and that the Fourteenth Amendment was, in fact, being violated.[33] This case involved segregated schools. The Brown decision along with efforts of the NAACP laid the groundwork for the Civil Rights Acts of 1957, 1960 and 1964. These acts gave further muscle to the federal government in its efforts to enforce the rights given to all citizens under the Fourteenth Amendment.

Today, the "equal protection clause" is being applied more to sex discrimination than it is to racial discrimination. The term "equal pay for equal work" was one of the "battle cries" used to rally women together for the promotion of "women's rights." We are also finding cases of "reverse discrimination" being presented to the United States Supreme Court on the basis of violation of the Fourteenth Amendment.

2.3:0   GENERAL AND SPECIFIC SOURCES OF LAW

American law can trace its origins from many sources. In this chapter eight of these sources will be covered. The eight, and the derivations of their authority, are as follows:

(1) United States Constitution
    (fountainhead of American law)
(2) State Constitutions
    (from U.S. Constitution)
(3) Federal Legislature (Congress)
    (from U.S. Constitution)
(4) State Legislatures
    (from state constitutions)
(5) Counties, Cities & Towns
    (from state charter issued by legislature)
(6) Decisions of Appellant Courts
    (from U.S. Constitution)
(7) Historical
    (Cultural Background of the People):
    (a) English Common law
    (b) Religion & Morality
    (c) Social control through customs & mores
(8) Executive Agency Rules

2.3:1 United States Constitution

The United States Constitution is the fountainhead of American law. This is the legal source and the basis for our law. It also restricts our law within certain limits based on fundamental human rights, and the will of the people who can change the Constitution when a large majority of them feel that it is essential. There is an interrelationship with the Supreme Court in that the Constitution has assigned it the duty of interpreting the meaning of its articles and amendments.

Neither the Executive, Legislative nor Judicial branch of government can change the Constitution. This power lies only with the people. At times, it seems to be a long and involved process, but the ultimate control of law is in the hands of the people. The Constitution protects this right through its guarantee of a republican form of government. The Constitution establishes the legislature (Congress) which is the lawmaking branch of government.

2.3:2 State Constitutions

State constitutions get their authority from the United States Constitution. The only restrictions placed upon this authority are that the state maintain a republican form of government, and not violate the fundamental rights enumerated in the U. S. Constitution. The state constitution establishes the state legislature, and this body of government makes state law within the limitations established by the state constitution.

2.3:3 Federal Legislature (Congress)

The federal legislature is limited in its lawmaking ability. The U. S. Constitution set definite limits to the area in which it can make law. The Constitution allows Congress to define and punish crimes within set limitations. It has no inherent power to make law like state legislatures. To maintain a balance of power within the Congress there were established two Houses, the Senate and the House of Representatives. They must both approve a bill before it can become law. Even then, the President has the power of a veto, which furthers the balance of power.

Congress may legislate when it pertains to taxes, the common defense and general welfare of the United States, establishing duties on imports, regulating commerce with foreign nations and among the states, naturalization, weights and measures, the coining and printing of money, post offices and roads and communications for mail delivery, patents, establishing lower federal courts, piracies and felonies on the high seas, declaring war, raising armies, governing the military, regulation of military bases within the states, (this is considered a federal jurisdiction rather than a state jurisdiction) and laws that are necessary to enforce the articles and amendments of the Constitution.

Over the years, Congress has found a way to expand its law-making ability by enlarging the areas in which the Constitution allows it to make law. For example, "to regulate commerce among the states" the laws on interstate commerce have grown constantly, and many of them are based on a very broad interpretation of the definition of the word "commerce." There seems to be no limit to the laws that have been passed under the heading "general welfare of the United States."

Another way to measure the increase in federal law is by measuring the increase in the number of federal executive officers required to carry out the federal law. The Federal Bureau of Investigation was a very small and powerless organization in the early 1920's since the Constitution does not provide for a federal police force. Because of the public fear of gangsterism in the twenties and thirties, the fear of Axis spies during World War II, and the fear of Communist spies afterwards, the people have allowed their state representatives in Congress to give the federal government an increasing amount of legislative power, even within the confines of the Constitution. If one were to compare the FBI of the 1920's to the present organization, and also examine other federal agencies such as the Treasury Department, it would be obvious that a great expansion of federal legislative power has taken place since that time. However, if the legislature does overstep its bounds as set down by the Constitution, the Supreme Court can declare its actions illegal or unconstitutional.

It should be remembered that the United States is not just a democracy, but a constitutional democracy. The will of the majority of the people is not the major determining factor in lawmaking. For example, the majority of Americans recently polled indicated that they favored non-denominational prayers in public schools. Congress, wishing to please a majority of voters, would gladly pass a law allowing such prayers, or even making them mandatory. The Supreme Court, however, has made itself quite clear in this matter, and has stated that this would be a violation of the First Amendment. This does not restrain all further action of the people. They can, if enough support is obtained, actually change the Constitution to allow such legislation. This rarely happens, however, because it requires the consensus of a very large percentage of the population for such a change to take place. The repeal of the Eighteenth Amendment in 1933, which changed the Constitution to allow the consumption of alcoholic beverages, is an example.

2.3:4 State Legislatures

The real power to make law lies with individual state legislatures. Unlike the federal legislature, state legislatures have the inherent power to prohibit and punish any act that is not limited by the restrictions of the federal or state constitutions. The Fourteenth Amendment is the most restrictive of all the amendments in restricting state legislatures.

Article IV, Section 1, of the California Constitution states: "The legislative power of this state is vested in the California Legislature which consists of the Senate and Assembly, but the people reserve to themselves the powers of initiative and referendum." (This is the power to propose new laws and repeal old laws by public ballot.) The source of power for the state legislatures is found in the Tenth Amendment to the United States Constitution. Later in this chapter, a brief step-by-step description of the process by which a state legislature makes new laws or repeals old ones will be given.

It is easier for state legislatures to resolve the controversy that can arise when proposing new laws because they are dealing with demands, needs and vested interests that are more similar in nature than they would be on a national level. For example, the elected representatives from the state of Maine, which has a large fishing industry, would probably not vote for a proposal that would help the meat or cattle industry of Texas. States that produce a large amount of dairy products would be against legislation helping industries producing synthetic dairy products.

2.3:5 Counties, Cities, And Towns

On the local level, there is a need for legislation that fits the needs of the community. These laws are called city or county ordinances. From a legal standpoint, it is questionable whether ordinances fit the definition of regular laws and whether violations of ordinances can be treated as crimes. This topic will be covered in a later chapter.

Local Boards of Supervisors and City and Town Councils obtain their power to enact ordinances from a charter issued by the state. Because counties, cities and towns operate on state charters, they are often referred to as public corporations.

2.3:6 Appellate Court Decisions

It was not the intent of the writers of the Constitution that the judicial branch of government be involved in the making of law. They delegated that job to the legislative branch. The appellate courts do, in fact, make law, and they claim that authority from the Constitution in an indirect way. The Constitution established a judicial branch of government which, among other duties, was to oversee the law-making activities of the legislative branch of government and make sure they follow the Constitution. They were to also review lower court decisions to see if they in any way violate the United States Constitution. Rather than just rule for or against lower court decisions, the higher court will write detailed legal explanations as to why they decided the way they did. They will also, on occasion, set down a series of rules which future lower courts must follow in order to avoid further violations of a defendant's constitutional rights.

The best recent example is the Miranda Decision. Here, the Supreme Court not only reversed the conviction, but established a "law" stating that, in order for a confession to be acceptable in court, the enforcement officers must notify the suspect of certain rights which they listed, 1, 2, 3, etc.

The justices of the high court admit that their job is not to make law. On the other hand, if, through interpreting the law, they happen to establish rules that are effectively "laws," this "legislation" is indirect and a "spin-off" of their constitutional duties of legal interpretation; and is, therefore, legal.

It is interesting that this has only been a serious problem in the last twenty years. People often think of the President and the Congress as the ones who battle each other, but today it is Congress and the Supreme Court. Congress feels the Supreme Court oversteps its bounds through law-making activities that were granted to Congress by the Constitution.

2.3:7 Historical and Cultural Background of the People

So far, the topic of the source of law has been approached from a legal standpoint. The coverage of this topic would not be complete without covering the influences that affect what type of law is passed by the legislative branches of government. Three of these sources are:

(A) English Common Law

English common law was the basis of American law because that was the law in which our founding fathers were trained. They felt that the law was good. Their complaint was not against English common law, but the fact that the colonists were denied their rights under that law.

When the colonies became independent, the transition was made easier by the fact that the same system of law under which they had lived for so long was continued after independence. The law libraries of colleges, attorneys and legislators were all common law. It would be difficult to develop a new system of law and then write numerous volumes of books on it. English common law relied heavily on precedence; new laws would have none and attorneys would feel lost in not being able to make a legal defense based on prior decisions.

The entire history of American law has been a slow and steady move away from English common law toward a more just Roman type of law. Most of the amendments are steps in this direction. Yet, our law had to have its start in some form, and the form that was best suited at the time of independence was that of English common law.

Even states like California, which joined the Union at a much later date, and which started its law on the "statutory" system, used English common law as the foundation for its "statutory" law. Until 1975, the California Penal Code had a crime called "The Infamous Crime Against Nature" in which there was no description of the offense. It was taken from English common law and when the appellate courts were asked to decide on the elements for that offense, they went to Blackstone's Commentaries on English Common Law for the description of the acts that made up the offense.

Since English common law developed over such a long period of time, its substantive part (dealing with criminal offenses) was well settled in the customs of the people and had served a long period of trial and error to reach the point where it was during colonial times.

Today, about half the states in the Union still have some form of common law as their state law. Some, like Louisiana, have a combination. They use the statutory system for their substantive (crimes) law and common law for their criminal procedure with a few changes.

(B) Religion and Morality

Starting with the first colonists, religion, in the form of the Old Testament not only influenced, but was the major source of their "Draconian" type of law. Their laws were not only taken word-for-word from the Old Testament, but at the end of each law the scriptural reference was quoted.

As with all countries strongly influenced by the Judeo-Christian religion or culture, laws concerning sexual practices are overly severe in their penalties. This influence has affected even present day laws in certain areas of the country. For example, in the New England states the "blue laws" still prevail to some extent.

In the so-called "Bible Belt," in the southern states, the influence of the Bible is ever-present in existing legislation. In the State of Utah the conservative influences of the Mormon Church play a strong part in the legislation of that state.

Changes do take place. In the State of California, a new series of "consenting adult laws" were passed in 1975. These laws permit just about any type of sex act between consenting adults. Although this is a trend away from religion-related laws, it seems to be commensurate with the change

in the religious attitudes of the people of that state. This further affirms the relationship, in a negative way, between religion and law.

(C) Social Control Through Custom &Mores

The strongest laws are those based on custom or mores (social behavior). Human beings, by their nature, are social creatures. With rare exceptions they need and want to live with other people. They also need the approval of other people. One cause of anti-social behavior among delinquents is first, their rejection by society, and then their acceptance by members of a group (i.e. a street-gang) whose customs are anti-social and criminal in nature. They need to be accepted by some group.

In places like England, a person who disobeys a social custom or a law based on custom, will be rejected by the other members of his society. They use the term "Putting him in Coventry." This term was taken from the story of Lady Godiva, around 1040 AD, and her ride through the street naked. All the townspeople, in deference to her personal sacrifice, refused to look. The one exception was a man called Tom. He was later called "Peeping Tom," and was completely ignored by the whole town. He became a "non-person" which had a very strong effect on his future behavior.

The need for social acceptance is a strong influence on the acceptance of social based law. Some customs and mores are based on superstition, and this further encouraged people to follow the dictates of custom based laws.

In large cities, where people are highly transient, and neighbors do not know each other, this type of law loses its effect. It is more suited to small towns or cities that do not have a subgroup to which a deviant can escape and be accepted.

2.3:8   Executive Agency Rules

California has more than 200 agencies actively issuing regulations on everything from automobiles to household commodities. Each year these agencies issue, delete or amend more than 5,000 regulations. Since these executive agencies seem to be on the increase, and since their regulations affect the average citizen more than criminal laws, some political scientists feel that the executive branch of government is exceeding its bounds by entering the law-making business. Although they are called regulations, they are laws.

2.4:0   POLICE POWER AND ITS LIMITS

A difficult thing for young people entering the enforcement area of administration of justice to accept is that, from a legal standpoint, the "cards are stacked" against the enforcement officer. "It doesn't seem fair," they say. What they do not understand is that it was planned that way by the founding fathers. An examination of the existing conditions at that time shows a plan of continued oppression on the part of the English who controlled the colonies. This caused the colonists to become almost paranoid about personal freedom. As a result, when they wrote the Constitution and its amendments, they purposely "stacked" things against the executive branch of government (which includes the police) and in favor of the people.

Enforcement officers who would like a "soft touch" in the area of enforcement should go to a country where a dictatorship exists. There the police are always right, and are not bothered by a restrictive Constitution. However, after a while they would undoubtedly find that their own rights, which they take for granted, are also being violated, and that the country could be a very unpleasant place in which to live.

Legally, police power originates from the Tenth Amendment and state constitutions. The state has the inherent power to prohibit and punish any act not unconstitutional. It can legislate in areas such as public heath; safety; morals; general welfare; and general prosperity. Under State Charter it can delegate police authority.

Article XI, Section 5b, of the California Constitution states:

> *It shall be competent in all city charters to provide in addition to those provisions allowable by this Constitution, and by the laws of the State for: (1) the constitution, regulation, and government of the city police force.*

Article XI, Section 7, of the California Constitution states:

> *A county or city may make and enforce within its limits all local, police, sanitary, and other ordinances and regulations not in conflict with general laws.*

Article XII, Section 8, of the California Constitution states:

> *The police power of the State shall never be so abridged or construed as to permit corporations to conduct their business in such manner as to infringe the rights of individuals or the general well-being of the State.*

2.5:0   THE MODEL PENAL CODE

The American Law Institute, whose headquarters are located in Philadelphia, has long recognized the need for a uniform penal code that is not based on ancient concepts of law, but reflects the needs of modern America. Because of the original "states' rights" concept in our early history, the penal laws of each state, although similar in many respects, have gone their own way in certain areas, and are extremely antiquated in others. It was the hope of the American Law Institute that through years of work, a model penal code could be developed that would serve as an example for those states desiring to revise their penal codes. Today, most modern books on criminal law make some reference to the Model Penal Code in order to compare its recommendations to the existing law.

2.6:0   HOW LAWS ARE MADE

It is most important that any person studying the concepts of law have some idea how the laws are made. Because of this, a short step by-step explanation will be given of this process.

2.6:1   The Legislature and Terminology

The only branch of government that can initiate and enact laws is the legislature. There is both a federal and state legislature. On the federal level, the legislature is called "Congress" and is made up of two Houses: the Senate and the House of Representatives. On the state level, our legislature is also made up of two Houses. They are called the "Senate" and the "Assembly." Each House can initiate new laws, but the laws must be approved by the other House before being sent to the executive (president or governor) for final approval. At this point they can be vetoed, but vetos can be overcome by a large vote from both Houses.

When a new law is first written and presented by a member of the legislature it is called a BILL. When the law is finally passed, it is called a STATUTE. The statute is then put into a book or series of books called CODES. In California there are twenty-nine different State Codes. They are:

- Business and Professions
- Civil
- Civil Procedure
- Commercial
- Corporations
- Education
- Elections
- Evidence
- Family
- Financial
- Fish and Game
- Food and Agricultural
- Government
- Harbors & Navigation
- Health and Safety
- Insurance
- Labor
- Military & Veterans
- Penal
- Probate
- Public Contract
- Public Resources
- Public Utilities
- Revenue and Taxation
- Streets and Highways
- Unemployment Insurance
- Vehicle
- Water
- Welfare & Institutions

Many corrections laws are found in the Penal Code, but there is also a separate code called the California Code of Regulations that contains many corrections laws.

2.6:2 Procedures Involved in the Making of a New Law

Since the procedure is similar for both the federal and state legislatures, the California state legislature will be used in the example.

There are three legal processes used in the California state legislature by which laws are made or revised:

(1) The making of new laws;
(2) The repealing of old laws;
(3) The amending of the state Constitution.

There are two legal approaches in which these processes can be accomplished. They are:

(1) Through the state legislature;
(2) Through a Referendum or an Initiative.

2.6:3 Through the State Legislature

The following are basic steps in making law through the State Legislature.

(A) Have a legislator sponsor the bill. (Proposed Law)

This can be done by either an Assemblyman or a Senator. Since he is concerned about pleasing as many voters as possible, he is more likely to support a suggested change in the law when you approach him as a member or representative of a large group or organization rather than as an individual. This doesn't mean that an individual cannot get a legislator to sponsor a bill, it just means that it would be more difficult.

For example, you belong to a service club and have obtained the backing of that club. You approach the legislator and tell him that you are a member of the county PTA, and that there are 5,000 members, and that you have been asked by that group to contact him in hopes that he will support a bill dealing with education. He will probably be very receptive to the proposal because he is thinking that when he runs for re-election, he will call you and remind you that he did his best for you and ask you to assist him in his re-election, and seeking the help or assistance of the organization. He may just want the opportunity to make a political speech before the group.

(B) The legislator introduces the bill in his own house.

The legislator will have the bill written in proper form and will present it in his own House (Senate or Assembly). The bill is given a number so that it can be identified from all the other bills that are proposed. If the legislator is a Senator, the bill will be called SB #...(the SB means Senate Bill). If he or she is an Assemblyman, the bill will be identified as AB #... (the AB means Assembly Bill). Later, if it has passed, it will be given a special code number (depending upon in which code it is to be placed).

Many legislators will submit bills which they know are not likely to pass in both houses. They feel that the simple action of proposing these bills will make their constituents feel that they are being properly represented, and thus will incur their favor in the next election.

(C) The bill is reviewed by a special committee

Legislators cannot be experts in all areas, so each House sets up committees that specialize in particular areas. In this way they can devote their efforts in one direction and increase their knowledge and expertise in that area.

These committees are very important in deciding whether a proposed bill will continue along the road to becoming official law. They have three main courses of action. They can give the bill their approval; they can make a negative recommendation, or they can "shelve" the bill for further study. If the bill will cost the public some money in one way or another, the bill will also have to be reviewed by the Finance Committee.

If the committee makes a negative recommendation, it is still possible that the House could vote for approval over the recommendation of the committee. There are times when a proposed law is a "hot potato," and they don't want to offend either side of the issue by either approving or rejecting it. The answer here is to "shelve" the bill for further study. This means the bill is being put aside until they have an opportunity to look into the matter more deeply later. In this case, "later" usually means "never," and the bill "dies in committee." Because of this, membership on such a committee gives a legislator great political power. Committee members who do approve a bill will expect that the legislator proposing the bill will, if he is on a committee, approve a later bill proposed by one of the present committee members.

(D) The committee holds hearings to allow the pros and cons to be heard

Because the state of California is a very large state in area, there are often two hearings for a bill; one held in Los Angeles, and the other in San Francisco. This makes it easier for the general public to attend the hearings and make their feelings known. Not all hearings are held in two places. If a bill is not very controversial, it is usually just held in Sacramento. The hearing allows an opportunity not only for the public to be heard, but the various lobbies as well. If the bill will affect a special interest group or business, they are sure to hire a lobbyist to attend the hearing and give good arguments why the bill should pass or fail. Today, all lobbyists must register as lobbyists, and disclose the group they represent. Some lobbyists are very skilled attorneys who have a special talent for presenting convincing arguments at hearings.

There is always the problem that powerful groups might spend considerable amounts of money to sway the committee members, but today new laws require that any such moneys be recorded for public inspection, if desired. Today, we not only have large oil companies with influential lobbies, but on the other end of the issue, we have very powerful conservation groups who support lobbies. The legislator, however, is still elected to his position, and he had better keep in mind the wishes of his constituents if he wishes to be reelected. Again, it should be remembered that our new laws on pubic disclosure of gifts make it more difficult for special interest groups to "buy" their way when these bills are being reviewed.

The hearings on a bill are not just a matter of show. The committee members cannot always think of all the possible effects that a bill will have if passed. At the hearings, new ideas can be presented and the committee members will often gain new insights regarding the overall scope of the bill if it is passed into law.

(E) The committee may then amend the bill according to the evidence that was presented in the hearings

Because of the hearings, the committee members might want to change or "amend" the bill so that it would be more applicable or suitable to groups who object to the bill in its present form. Sometimes a bill is amended to such a great extent that it has no resemblance to the original bill. Sometimes a member of a committee will tack on an amendment that will make the bill useless for the purpose for which it was proposed. This is another political tactic to avoid the approval or rejection of the bill by the committee. It is just "amended to death."

In some cases the legislator proposing the bill makes it very strong, knowing that it will raise objections, but hoping that he or she will be able to dicker with the committee members and settle for an amended version that will cover what he wanted in the first place, but might have had difficulty in getting passed. Now it appears they had to settle for part of what he wanted. It is a game of politics.

It should be remembered that a large number of legislators are also attorneys, and in their practice have been conditioned to the system of mediation and dickering. You always ask for more and settle for what you originally wanted.

(F) The bill is brought to the floor for the readings

Once the bill has been approved by the committee, it is brought to the floor of the House where the bill originated, and is given three readings. The bill is then debated on the floor and finally put to a vote by that House.

(G) If the bill passes the house where it originated, it is sent to the other house

Since a bill must be approved by both Houses, once it passes one House, it must then go to the other House of the legislature for its examination and possible approval.

(H) The other house then gives the bill the same routine as in (D) and (E)

If the second House finds the bill unacceptable, the committees of the two Houses will then get together and try to "iron out" their differences and come up with a bill that is worded in a way that is acceptable to both committees. This process might seem to be long and involved, but it is part of the system of "checks and balances" which ensures that new laws are not just passed at the snap of a finger or at somebody's whim or fancy. History has shown us that the more "going over" a bill receives, the longer it will probably last.

(I) When both houses agree, the bill goes to the Governor for signing

If the governor signs it, it becomes law on a set date. If it is a special emergency bill that is so indicated, it becomes law the minute the governor signs it. If he vetoes it, it will then take two-thirds of the votes of both Houses of the legislature to override the veto. If the Houses are close to being evenly divided between Democrats and Republicans, the chances of an override are slim. Overrides are usually voted on by political party. It is somewhat rare for the legislature to effect an override, but it does happen. In 1976, President Ford's veto of a major public works bill was over-ridden by both houses of Congress. In California, Governor Brown vetoed the death penalty bill in 1977 but both houses of the legislature overrode his veto.

If the governor fails to sign it within 12 days, it will automatically become law. This prevents the governor from "playing games" and stalling a bill he does not want to sign (in some cases, he is allowed more time). (Calif. Const. Art. 4 Sect 10)

2.6:4   Through a Referendum
The purpose of the referendum is to change or recall existing law or change the state constitution through an amendment.

(A) Changing Existing Law
Signatures must be obtained from registered voters in a number that equals 5% of those who voted in the last election for governor (gubernatorial election). If these signatures are checked and found to be valid, the proposed change will be put on the ballot of the next general election.

(B) Changing the State Constitution Through an Amendment
The same procedure is followed as for (A) above, but the number of signatures of registered voters must now be 8% of those who voted in the last election for governor. Because the constitution is more important, it requires more signatures.

2.6:5   Through an Initiative
The purpose of the initiative is to propose a new law, or to propose a new amendment to the state constitution.

(A) Proposing a New Law
Signatures must be obtained from registered voters in a number that equals 5% of those who voted in the last gubernatorial election. If these signatures are checked and found to be valid, the proposed law will be put on the ballot of the next general election.

(B) Proposing a New Amendment to the State Constitution
The same procedure is followed as that for (A) above, but the number of signatures of registered voters must now equal 8% of those who voted in the last gubernatorial election. Because it involves the Constitution, more signatures are required.

2.6:6   Discussion
If referendums or initiatives are to succeed, a large organization, formal or informal, is needed to gather such large numbers of signatures.

Formal Organization
(1) The Highway Patrol Pay Initiative
Highway Patrol Officers wanted a law passed to fix their pay scale on a ratio to the average of the five highest paid police departments in the state. Because there are such large numbers of Highway Patrol officers in the state, they and their families set up tables in shopping centers throughout the state on off-duty hours. As a result, they obtained more than the required number of signatures, and the proposal went on the ballot of the next election.
(2) Jarvis-Gann Tax Initiative
This is a classic example of the legislature being hesitant to correct a tax problem, and the people, through the Initiative, taking the matter into their own hands.

Informal Organization
(1) The Marijuana Referendum
In an effort to change existing laws prohibiting the use of marijuana, college students attempted to put a Referendum on the ballot. College students throughout the state joined together in an organization of informal campus groups. The movement was spearheaded by the more radical groups. They set up tables on campuses and solicited signatures from the students who could now vote at the age of 18. Enough signatures were obtained to put the initiative on the ballot of the next general election. The voters of California voted it down by 85%.

The Legislative Counsel
In 1913, the position of Legislative Counsel was enacted into law. The Legislative Counsel is the attorney for the Legislature. Because not all legislators are attorneys or experts in the legal wording of new laws, the Legislative Counsel provides legal assistance to legislators in drafting and amending new bills. He or she also assists them by rendering legal opinions and is likewise available to help any non-legislator who has sponsored an initiative and needs help with its' legal composition. The Legislative Counsel is elected by the Legislature at the beginning of each regular session. Under the State Civil Service Law, he or she is permitted to appoint qualified attorneys to assist in the duties of the office. This person also advises the Governor on the legality of newly passed laws.

HOW A BILL BECOMES LAW

A simplified chart showing the route a bill takes through the California Legislature

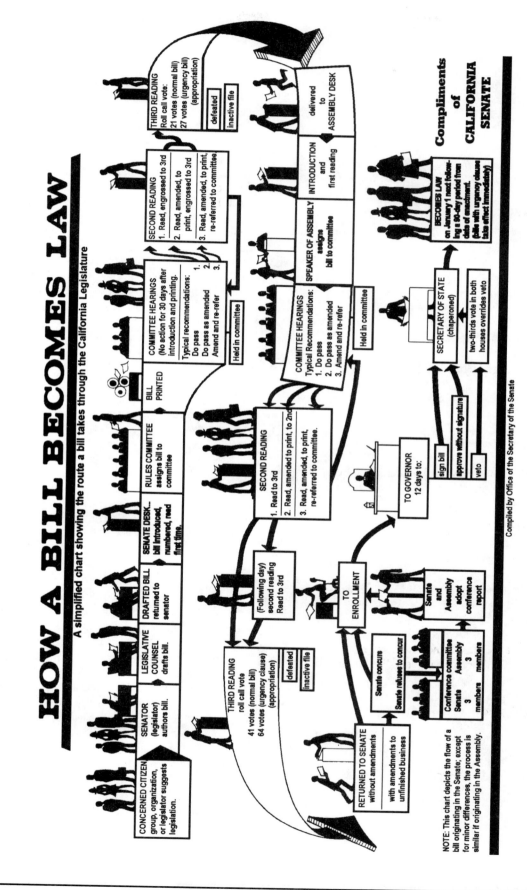

Compiled by Office of the Secretary of the Senate

REFERENCES FOR CHAPTER II

(1) Rene A. Wormser, The Story of the Law, Simon & Schuster, New York, p. 332.

(2) Federalist Papers, 788.

(3) Rene A. Wormser, The Story of the Law, Simon Schuster, New York, p. 338.

(4) Edward Conrad Smith, The Constitution of the United States, Barnes and Noble Books, New York, p. 11,

(5) Rene A. Wormser, The Story of the Law, Simon Schuster, New York, p. 343.

(6) Bruce and Esther Findlay, Your Rugged Constitution, Stanford University Press, Stanford, p. 169.

(7) Ibid., p. 185.

(8) Schenck v. U.S 249 U.S 47,52.

(9) George Seldes, The Great Quotations, Pocket Books, Simon Schuster, New York, p. 746.

(10) Thomas James Norton, The Constitution of the United States, World Publishing Company, Cleveland, p. 199.

(11) George Seldes, The Great Quotations, Pocket Books, Simon & Schuster, New York, p. 763.

(12) Cox v. Louisiana, 379 U.S. 559

(13) U. S. v. Cruikshank, 92 U. S. 542.

(14) U. S. v. Miller, 307 U. S. 174.

(15) People v. Washington, 237 C. A. 2d 59 (46 Cal Rptr 545)

(16) Weeks v. U. S., 232 U. S. 383.

(17) Mapp v. Ohio, 367 U. S. 643.

(18) Thomas James Norton, The Constitution of the United States, World Publishing Company, Cleveland, p. 199.

(19) Sir William Blackstone, Commentaries on the Laws of England, Robert Small Publishers, Philadelphia, 1825, p. 41.

(20) Thomas James Norton, The Constitution of the United States, World Publishing Company, Cleveland, p. 213.

(21) Miranda v. Arizona, 384 U. S. 436.

(22) Thomas James Norton, The Constitution of the United States, World Publishing Company, Cleveland, p. 215.

(23) Ibid., p. 219.

(24) Ibid., p. 222.

(25) Furman v. Georgia, 408 U. S. 238.

(26) Thomas James Norton, The Constitution of the United States, World Publishing Company, Cleveland, p. 226.

(27) Hurtado v. California, 110 U. S. 56.

(28) Adamson v. California, 332 U. S. 46.

(29) Griffin v. California, 380 U. S. 609.

(30) Thomas James Norton, The Constitution of the United States, World Publishing Company, Cleveland, p. 242.

(31) Ibid., p. 243.

(32) Plessy v. Ferguson, 163 U. S. 537.

(33) Brown v. Board of Education, 347 U. S. 483.

STUDY QUESTIONS

CHAPTER II

(1)   Congress gets its law-making powers directly from the Constitution.   T or F

(2)   Members of Congress are protected from arrest on the way to the Legislature during a session and on the way back home. Exceptions would be arrest for:

    (A) _✓_ Treason, felonies or breaches of the peace.   (B) ____ No exceptions.
    (C) ____ They are protected from arrest for all crimes.   (D) ____ Only federal crimes.

(3)   If the President does not sign a new bill within ten days, it automatically becomes law.   T or F

(4)   A Presidential veto can be overcome by a ___2/3___ vote of both houses.

(5)   A Writ of Habeas Corpus is one of the few rights actually mentioned in the U.S. Constitution itself (outside of the amendments).   T or F

(6)   The police are considered to come under the __executive__ branch of government.

(7)   The Constitution allows the President to grant pardons for all offenses in the United States.   T or F

(8)   When a vacancy exists in the U.S. Supreme Court, the President can nominate someone to take that position. However it must be approved by a simple majority of the __Senate__.

(9)   The Constitution of the United States clearly states that juries must consist of twelve members, and that all verdicts must be unanimous in criminal convictions.   T or F

(10) Article I of the Constitution establishes the "law making" branch of the government; it is called the __legislative branch (Congress)__. It is divided into two parts, the __Senate__ and the __House Representatives__.

(11) The English concept of punishing children for the crimes of their parents was called:

    (A) ____ Law of reciprocity   (B) _✓_ Rule of vengeance
    (C) ____ King's right   (D) _✓_ Corruption of blood

(12) Since there are many types of law-making branches of government in the United States, there could easily be a conflict between two laws. To prevent this from happening, the Constitution established the laws of __pre-emption__.

(13) The Constitution provides for a system where the Governor of one state can officially petition the Governor of another state to release a wanted felon so that he can be tried in the state requesting the transfer. This is called __rules of extradition__.

(14) The Constitution provides for a guarantee that each state has a Republican form of government. This requires that each state have a written constitution.   T or F

(15) The U.S. Constitution has a provision that allows it to be amended.   T or F

(16) The Congress has preemption in their laws over the laws of state constitutions.   T or F

(17) The Constitution can be amended by a proposal from congress and a ratification of a certain percentage of the states. __2/3__   __3/4 (states)__   T or F

(18) It is difficult to find a simple rule in dealing with first amendment rights to freedom of speech. Justice Holmes developed a doctrine he hoped would solve the problem. It was the:

    (A) _✓_ Clear and present danger doctrine   (B) ____ Divine right doctrine
    (C) ____ Absolute right doctrine   (D) ____ Balanced scale doctrine

(19) Harry Hassel is selling pornography on the street, and is arrested. he claims that his rights of expression are being denied under the __1st first__ amendment to the Constitution.

(20) Red Arrow, a member of a Southwestern Indian tribe is arrested for being under the influence of peyote (a hallucinogenic drug). He claims that it is part of a religious ceremony, and that his rights are being denied him under the __first (1st)__ amendment.

(21) TV and radio come under the protection of "freedom of the press."   **T** or F

(22) The high courts have stated that a reporter must reveal sources of information when questioned by a grand jury, and that it is not a privilege covered by the First Amendment (freedom of the press).   **T** or F

(23) In the Second Amendment, militia means __National Guard__.

(24) The "exclusionary rule" is based on the __fourth__ Amendment.

(25) A search warrant must describe the person or things to be seized.   **T** or F

(26) The famous U.S. Supreme Court decision, Mapp v. Ohio, stated that the exclusionary rule applies to the states as well as the federal government.   **T** or F

(27) The key word when applying the law on "search and seizure" in the Fourth Amendment is __reasonable__.

(28) In the "Bill Of Rights" (Fifth Amendment) the term "infamous crime" means __felony__.

(29) The term "capital crime," as used in the Fifth Amendment, means __death penalty__.

(30) An indictment is a criminal charge that originates from the __grand jury__.

(31) The term "presentment" as used in the Constitution means a criminal complaint.   **T** or F

(32) Some states do not have a grand jury system.   T or **F**

(33) In early English and European history, a person could be forced to testify against himself by putting heavy weights on the suspect's chest. It was called:

    (A) ____ Third Degree   (B) ____ Croiz De Lead
    (C) ____ Gravity Persuader   (D) __✓__ Peine Forte Et Dure

(34) The "due process" mentioned in the Bill of Rights can be traced to the English "petition of right."   **T** or F

(35) "Due process" is basically governmental fair play.   **T** or F

(36) The Constitution protects a person from being tried twice for the same crime. This is called __Double Jeopardy__. (1 of 2 terms)

(37) There was a law of "eminent domain" in ancient Rome.   **T** or F

(38) If Freddie Furd believes that the government is not offering him enough money for the land that they want to seize, he can have a jury decide the proper amount or value.   **T** or F

(39) Officer Hardrock tells Percy Persimmon that if he does not give him a confession, he will hang him out of the fifth story window by his heels until he does. This is a violation of the __Fifth__ Amendment.

(40) The right to a "speedy trial" means one without unreasonable delay.   **T** or F

(41) When selecting proper jurors, prospects can be removed when they have an obvious prejudice. This is called a challenge for __cause__.

(42) In a normal trial, each side is allowed _____TEN_____ *AS LONG AS ITS NOT BASED ON SEX OR CAUSE* "peremptory challenges."

(43) If an attorney tells the judge that the trial should be moved to another location so the defendant can receive a fairer trial, he or she will ask for a change of _____Venue_____. This right is covered under the _____FOURTEENTH_____ Amendment.

(44) The term used when referring to the particular court that has the authority to try a certain case is called _____JURISDICTION_____.

(45) When a suspect is first taken before a judge to hear the charges against him, it is called a(an) _____ARRAINGMENT_____.

(46) The Constitution states that a person accused of a crime has the right to be confronted with the witness against him. He can then ask them questions under oath. This is called _____CROSS - EXAMINATION_____

(47) The Constitution allows for a compulsory process of obtaining witnesses for a defendant if they can help him by their testimony. The court order demanding that the witness appear in court is called a(an) _____SUBPEONA_____

(48) Tilly Toadtoes is arrested for shoplifting. She says that she cannot afford an attorney. Under the Constitution she is entitled to one free. This is the _____SIXTH_____ Amendment.

(49) Mervin Muskatell is an alcoholic. He has been sentenced to two weeks in jail for theft. He objects to the sentence on the grounds that making him go two weeks without a drink is "cruel and unusual punishment." If this were true, it would be a violation of the _____EIGHT_____ Amendment.

(50) There are records of bail being allowed in England in the 15th century. **T** or F

(51) Furman v. Georgia is a Supreme Court case dealing with the death penalty. **T** or F

(52) The bail system has often been called discriminatory against the poor. **T** or F

(53) Our forefathers and writers of the Constitution felt that the death penalty was really "cruel and unusual punishment." T or **F**

(54) Under the Constitution, people have only those rights that are listed in the Constitution. T or **F**

(55) What amendment allows the states to establish their own police systems? _____TENTH_____.

(56) The Federal Constitution is called a "grant of power." The State Constitutions are called _____LIMITATIONS_____ of power.

(57) The "shorthand doctrine" states that the rights listed in the Bill of Rights are all covered in the Fourteenth Amendment and granted to the states. **T** or F

(58) What amendment requires that all persons receive "equal protection" under the law? _____FOURTEENTH_____

(59) The Fourteenth Amendment in effect, states that an American is both a citizen of the state in which he lives and also a citizen of the nation. He is entitled to protection from both. **T** or F

(60) At first the high court felt that the Fourteenth Amendment did not include all of the rights in the Bill Of Rights. **T** or F

(61) When the Fourteenth Amendment refers to the word "citizen," it also applies to non-citizens. **T** or F

(62) Originally the Fourteenth Amendment "equal protection" clause applied mostly to racial discrimination. Today it is increasingly applied to _____SEX DISCRIMINATION & orientation_____.

(63) In 1905 the U.S. Supreme Court held that a person's liberty was absolute. T or **F**

1-4-5-6-8-10-14 AMENDMENTS

(64) Even though the federal government is quite limited in the areas in which it can make law, over the years it has greatly expanded on those areas. **T** or F

(65) The "equal but separate doctrine" applied to the _FOURTEETH_ Amendment.

(66) The source of power for State Legislatures is found in the Tenth Amendment of the U.S. Constitution. **T** or F

(67) Laws that are passed by cities, towns and counties are called _ORDINANCES_.

(68) Towns, cites and counties obtain their power to make law from state charters. **T** or F

(69) Even though the Constitution limits law-making to the Legislature, the Judiciary branch of government in effect does make law by making decisions that interpret the Constitution. **T** or F

(70) Countries that are strongly influenced by Judeo-Christian religions have very strict sex laws. **T** or F

(71) The strongest of all laws are those based on custom or mores. **T** or F

(72) "Putting a person in Coventry" is an English method of:

(A) ____Punishing violators of criminal law. (B) √ Enforcing social laws or rules.
(C) ____Denying a person his inheritance rights. (D) ____Excusing a person from local law.

(73) The enforcement of "mores" or social laws is much easier in cities. _TEACHER→_ **T** or **F**

(74) In the United States, the law is purposely "stacked" against law enforcement agencies and the Executive branch of government, and in favor of the accused. **T** or F

(75) Police power originates from the Tenth amendment and state constitutions. **T** or F

(76) The Model Penal Code has been written by the _AMERICAN LAW INSTITUTE_

(77) The two houses in the California Legislature are the _SENATE_ and the _ASSEMBLY_.

(78) The two houses in the Legislature give us a system of "checks and balances." **T** or F

(79) When a law is passed by the Legislature and signed by the Governor, it is put into a set of law books and called a _ordinances & state statues_. Until it is officially a law and while it is still in the formative stages, it is called a _Bill_. It is finally put in a set of law books; these books are called _CODES_. There are 27.

(80) A new law is presented to the Legislature As "SB-140." Which house originated this law? _SENATE_

(81) A bill that is "shelved" will often "die in _COMMITTE_."

(82) If you want to change the existing law without going through the Legislature, you can gather enough signatures to have it put on the next election ballot. This is called a(an) _REFERENDUM_. If you want to propose a new law without going through the Legislature, you can also gather enough signatures to have it put on the next ballot. This is called a(an) _INITIATIVE_.

(83) A Constitutional change by referendum requires what percentage of registered voters to sign the petition in order to have it put on the ballot? _8%_.

CHAPTER III

LEGAL RESEARCH AND METHODOLOGY

3.0   RAMIFICATIONS OF LEGAL RESEARCH
3.1   JUDICIAL REVIEW
3.2   STARE DECISIS
3.3   CASE LAW AND CASE CITATIONS
3.4   THE USE OF THE LAW LIBRARY
3.5   THE LEGAL BRIEF AND ITS OUTLINE
3.6   ATTORNEY GENERAL OPINIONS

3.0:0 RAMIFICATIONS OF LEGAL RESEARCH

Legal research is important because it often determines the outcome of a criminal case. Enforcement officers who are familiar with legal research, and do their best to keep abreast of the latest case law, will be able to assist prosecutors by gathering evidence and conducting investigations so that cases will not be later thrown out of court because they might violate the latest case law. Officers who wish to keep abreast of the latest case law must have a basic understanding of simple legal research.

Legal research can be fun. The research involved in criminal law is easier than that involved in general law simply because the field is more restricted. Once students have learned the basic techniques, it is not difficult to locate the particular case or cases they are trying to find. It can, however, sometimes present a challenge, but this results in a feeling of satisfaction once the answer is located or partly solved. The greater the challenge, the greater is the feeling of accomplishment.

In the beginning, it must be made clear that doing legal research does not make one an attorney, nor should it become the basis for giving legal advice to friends and acquaintances. Locating one or more cases does not qualify a student to always properly interpret those cases from a sound legalistic approach. Granted, some of the cases are very simple, and most college students can easily understand the basic concepts involved. Giving legal advice, however, can be dangerous. If the advice is wrong, or based on a false interpretation, the person receiving this erroneous advice can suffer dire consequences. Four different types of basic legal research will be covered in this chapter. They are:

(1) Locating a particular case (or cases);
(2) Researching or locating all of the cases on a particular topic or sub-topic (This is obviously a more difficult task);
(3) Checking the case or cases to see if they have been superseded
(4) Reading a particular case and writing a legal brief on the case.

Computerized Research

The LEXIS computer system, located in New York, holds all the U.S. Supreme Court decisions since 1938, the Courts of Appeals from 1959, and the District Courts cases since 1970, along with many other federal and state materials. For example, it contains 16,000 California high court decisions. There are 900,000 cases in the system.

Lawyers who subscribe to this system have keyboard terminals in their offices with a video monitor. From the keyboard, they can ask the computer to give them all the cases on a certain topic or subject. They must narrow down their descriptions or they may receive a voluminous number of cases. If they find a case that will be important to their research, they just press a button and the computer will give them a printout of the case or cases wanted. These terminals can be attached to normal phone lines with a modem.

3.1:0 JUDICIAL REVIEW

Judicial review is the right of the Supreme Court to review laws that have been passed, and to overturn them if they violate the Constitution of the United States. One would think the legal basis for granting power to the United States Supreme Court would be found in the Constitution. Unfortunately, it is not. In number 78 of The Federalist Papers, Alexander Hamilton argued forcefully for judicial review based on his belief that the Constitution was superior to ordinary legislation. However, The Federalist Papers had no official enaction, and amounted to just the opinion of the writer.

3.1:1 The Judiciary Act of 1789
Section 25 of the Judiciary Act of 1789 states:

> Where...the validity of a statute is questioned...on the ground of being repugnant to the constitution...or the construction of any clause of the constitution...may be re-examined, and reversed or affirmed in the Supreme Court of the United States.

This seems to give a legal basis for judicial review, yet it does not set forth in clear terms whether the high court has the power to declare acts of Congress unconstitutional.

3.1:2 John Marshall and "Marbury v. Madison"

John Marshall was the fourth Chief Justice of the United States Supreme Court appointed by President John Adams just before Jefferson became President. He has been referred to as "The father of American constitutional law." He also established the precedent for judicial review.

Fig. III–1; John Marshall

Marbury v. Madison

In 1803, John Marshall declared a congressional act in conflict with the Constitution, and therefore, void. This case set the precedent for judicial review, by declaring that the Supreme Court could overrule a law passed by Congress.

Fletcher v. Peck

In 1810, the United States Supreme Court, for the first time, declared a state law to be unconstitutional and, therefore, set the precedent for judicial review over the states. Chief Justice Hughes once remarked, very clearly describing the power of the Supreme Court, "The Constitution means what the Supreme Court says it means."

3.1:3 Judicial Review of Lower Court Decisions

Article 3, Section 2, of the Constitution gives the Supreme Court appellant jurisdiction over the lower courts. Once a trial produces a verdict, and that verdict is appealed to a higher court on the ground that the trial was not run in a proper manner, or that there was a legal violation of the defendant's constitutional rights, the higher court can rule on the decision of the lower court as provided for in Article 3 of the U.S. Constitution, and Article 6, section 11, of the California Constitution.

That court not only decides if the lower court decision was right, but it lists the legal reasons for arriving at such a decision. The court majority will even set down a series of rules, on occasion, if they feel that it will clarify the problem and establish procedures which will, hopefully, protect citizens from further violations in the future. The Miranda Decision is a good example of this.

It should be remembered that it only takes a simple majority of the high court Justices to uphold or overturn a decision of the lower courts. Four Justices of the U.S. Supreme Court could absolutely disagree with the decision, but if the other five Justices agreed, the decision would stand. Since many high court decisions are "split decisions," it is wise to study the "Minority Report" of those Justices who disagree. If there is a change in the Justices in the near future, it is possible that they could overrule the first decision.

The reporting of court cases goes back to 1066 in England, after the Norman conquest. This was done in an effort to establish a common system of law. The king sent representatives to courts to listen to the decisions and then record them. They, in turn, would inform the other courts of the decisions that they had already recorded, and this, in turn, became a guide for the other courts in deciding new cases before them. In the United States, the U. S. Supreme Court decisions were first officially reported in 1790, and called the "United States Reports." The same title is used to this day.

3.2:0 PRECEDENT (*STARE DECISIS*)

The procedure mentioned in the above paragraph soon developed into a system that was called "Stare Decisis," which is a Latin term meaning "Precedent." It really means adhering to precedent, or what the previous courts have decided in cases that are of a similar nature. Precedent is a common law doctrine in which precedent is binding. That is, once a case has been decided by the high courts, all cases with the same circumstances must, in the future, be decided in the same way.

In 1761, Blackstone, the famous English jurist who helped interpret English common law, and wrote his interpretations in his famous "Commentaries," stated that Stare Decisis meant "Rigidly finding precedent." In other words, precedent MUST be followed in English common law.

In California, we still adhere to precedent, but not as strictly as under the English common law. The importance of the concept of Stare Decisis in California is that it is necessary to locate prior cases decided by the higher courts in order to present some good legal basis for the arguments used before the judge. As a rule, judges will go along with precedent because it means that the higher courts have already ruled on a very similar case, and it would be "playing it safe" on the part of the judge to follow the concepts of these prior decisions. To do otherwise would invite the appellant courts to overrule the judge's decision, and in that way make him look bad because he was not able to apply properly the basic concepts of law in making his decisions.

In California, precedent is not absolute. Occasionally, judges of the high courts will reverse the rules of their predecessors. An example would be the case of the People v. Hernandez. In 1965 the California Supreme Court changed an old and established rule pertaining to "Statutory Rape." Before this reversal, if the girl in the case was under 18 years of age, the law was violated despite any extenuating circumstances. This was backed up by all the high court decisions such as People v. Sheffield (1908) (9 C.A. 130). In the People v. Hernandez (61 Cal 2d 529) (39 Cal Rptr 361), the defendant claimed he lacked criminal intent based on the fact that to a reasonable, prudent person the victim looked well over 18 years of age. The trial judge

FEDERAL JUDICIAL SYSTEM

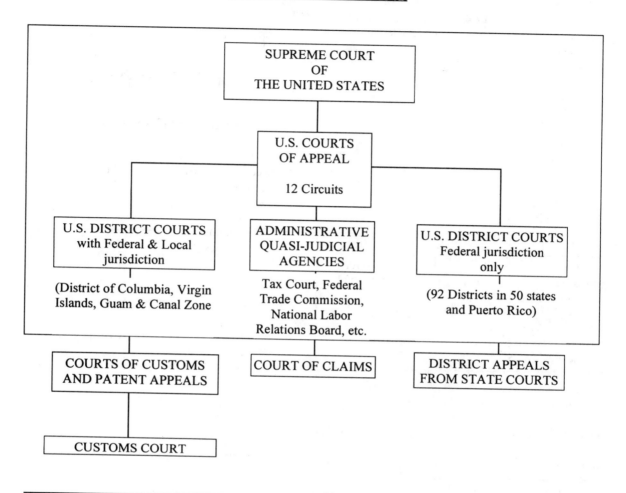

UNITED STATES COURTS OF APPEAL FOR THE TWELVE CIRCUITS

1st	2nd	3rd	4th	5th	6th	7th	8th	9th	10th	11th	12th
Maine Mass. N.Ham. R.Isl. Puerto Rico	Conn. N.Y. Vrmnt.	Del. N.Jer. Penn. Virgin Isl.	Maryld. N.Car. S.Car. Virg. W.Virg.	Ala. Fla. Ga.	Ky. Mich. Ohio Tenn.	Ill. Ind. Wisc.	Ark. Iowa Minn. Mo. Nebr. N.Dak. S.Dak	Alaska Ariz. Calif. Hawaii Idaho Mont. Nev. Org. Wash. Guam	Colo. Kans. N.Mex. Okl. Utah Wyo.	La. Miss. Texas Canal Zone	Dist. of Col.

Fig. III–2; Federal Judicial System

COURT STRUCTURE FOR THE STATE OF CALIFORNIA

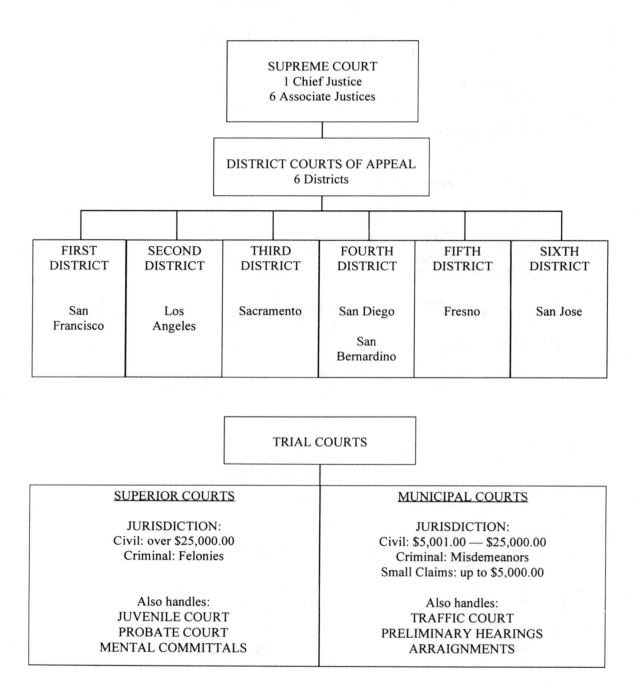

In June 1998, Proposition 220 allowed the unification of the two courts above into one Superior Court with jurisdiction over all cases. All it takes is a majority vote of the judges of both courts. So far, the majority of counties have voted to unify their trial courts. Prior to 1995, California had a "Justice Court" in judicial districts of less than 40,000 population. With Proposition 191, the Justice Courts were eliminated.

Fig. III–3; Court Structure for the State of California

refused to allow the jury to consider this aspect based on prior case law or on precedent. The California Supreme Court, however, overruled the conviction, and stated that the jury should have been allowed to view the victim to judge for themselves whether a reasonable person would think that she was over 18 years of age. If they felt that she did appear to be well over 18, they could find the defendant not guilty.

In Miranda v. Arizona, (384 U.S. 43S (1966), the United States Supreme Court ruled that juveniles were not covered by these rights. However, in 1967, the same court in In re Gault (387 U.S. 1, 13) reversed themselves and stated that juveniles are very definitely protected under these rights.

3.2:1 Basis For Appeal

Criminal cases may be appealed to higher courts if there are questions of constitutional violation or improper trial procedure, which would deny defendants a fair trial. If a defendant or attorney believes there is error in the decision of a lower court, the case may be appealed to the state high court. If the decision of the state high court is not satisfactory, they can appeal to the Federal Courts of Appeal, and finally to the U.S. Supreme Court (often referred to as the "Court of Last Resort").

3.2:2 Case Law and Its Uses

Case law also provides the courts with interpretations of words or phrases that are found in criminal statutes. For example, in the law on burglary (459 PC), the term "Building" is used. What is a building? Is a garage a building? Is a carport a building? Is a cave to be considered a building under the law on burglary? What about an old style telephone booth?

It can become very important to know, before actually going to court, what the high courts have said in previous cases about the interpretation of certain words and phrases. In the case of burglary, it could mean the difference of charging the suspect with the serious crime of burglary, or the minor crime of petty theft. There is a great difference in punishment between the two. By using case law, we can look up the definition used by a higher court in one of its decisions. This can most easily be found by looking in a set of books called Words and Phrases which give cases and high court interpretations of key words in alphabetical order.

3.2:3 Decisions Of The Higher Courts

In an Appellate Court decision, a simple majority of votes will decide the outcome of a ruling and make it law. Because of this, and in an effort to avoid tied decisions, Appellate Courts always have an odd number of Justices. The United States Supreme Court has nine Justices and the California State Supreme Court has seven. If one of the Justices is sick or absent, and the vote is a tie, the lower court decision will stand. It will be the same as upholding the conviction by the lower court.

3.3:0 CASE LAW AND CASE CITATIONS

In order to find the cases that have established precedent, there has to be a system of locating them. The easiest method is when the person conducting the search already has the citation number. A system has been developed where each case is given a case citation number. The explanation of this number is as follows:

The Case Citation Number

The case citation has five parts. They are as listed in the following example:
[A]People v. Roe, [B]21 [C]Cal.App. [D]3d [E] 114

    (A) Parties Involved
    (B) Volume
    (C) Reporter (or set of books)
    (D) Edition (or series)
    (E) Page

Explanation

(A) **Parties Involved:** The name of the first party is the one who commenced the action, In California, if the state prosecuted the case, the term "People" is used. In some states the term "State" is used. In a civil case, such as "Jones v. Smith," Jones would be the party who commenced the civil action (the Plaintiff). Juvenile cases are recorded as "In re Bobby J." "In re" means "in the case regarding." since juveniles are not charged criminally, it is not "People v. Bobby J."

(B) **Volume:** Each separate book. Each one has an individual number on the spine. They are found on the bookshelf in numerical order.

(C) **The Reporter:** The Reporter is the set of books in which the case is reported. It is originally the Appellate Court handing down the decision, but since the case may be reported in other reporters, the second part may not be listed as the court itself, but as the reporter.
Examples:

(1) Courts:
- (a) U.S. . . . . U.S. Supreme Court
- (b) USCA . . . . U.S. Court of Appeals
- (c) USCC . . . . U.S. Circuit Court
- (d) USDC . . . . U.S. District Court
- (e) C or Cal. . . . . CA Supreme Court
- (f) C.A. or Cal App
  California District Court of Appeals
- (g) AC . . . . Advance Reports of Cal. (Temporary paperback). It precedes the court designation. Later, it will be given a regular case citation.

(2) Special Reports
- (a) Ops. Atty. Gen.
  . Opinions of the Attorney General

(3) Reporters
- (a) F (&the district) . . . . . Federal Reporter
- (b) P or Pac. . . . . Pacific Reporter
- (c) Cal Rptr. . . . . California Reporter
- (d) ALR . . . . American Law Reports

The original court is always cited first, and then the reporter, or reporters. For example, 21 Cal 3d 417, 131 Cal Rptr 518.

Some law libraries only contain the reporters rather than the official court report. They often have the California Reporter which contains California Supreme Court, California District Court of Appeals and Superior Court appeals in the same volume. If you have the court reference, but not the reporter, such as Cal Rptr., there are cross-index books that will give cross indexes for different case citation sources. In California it is called the Blue and White Book (because some pages are blue, and others white).

(C) **Edition or Series:** If no series is listed, it is assumed that it is the first series. The second and third will be listed 2d & 3d

(D) **Page:** The last number is the page where the case starts.

Explanation of case People v. Clark (see p. 81)

(1) This is the original case citation. It shows that it can be found in volume 12 of the reporter for the California Appellate Court in the 4th series on page 665.

(2) This tells two things: the party originally bringing the case before the court—in this case it is the People of the State of California.; and whether the plaintiff is the party appealing the case or defending the appeal.

(3) Here the name of the defendant is listed. It also shows whether the defendant was the respondent (the one who must answer the appeal) or the appellant.

(4) The court case number or docket number.

(5) Shows the particular district of the Court of Appeals that heard the case. In this case it was the First District in San Francisco.

(6) Briefly tells what occurred and how the Court of Appeals ruled on the matter.

(7) Shows whether the high court upheld or reversed the decision of the lower court. In this case the decision was upheld (affirmed).

(8) Lists the important legal points that apply to the case.

(9) Shows the attorneys who represented the appellant. In this case, there was only one: Leo Paoli.

(10) Lists the attorneys responding to the appeal (and representing the State of California). Since appeals are handled by the Attorney General's Office, the name of the Attorney General is always listed, even though he was not in attendance during the appeal.

(11) Names the Justice who wrote the decision for the Court of Appeals. In this case, his name is Anderson, and he is the presiding Justice for the First District.

(12) The upside down "T" with the small number shows that in the original reporter (California Court of Appeals) this spot starts on page 665.

(13) Explains the reason why Clark appealed the case.

(14) Shows why the appellant's contention was not valid.

(15) Shows that the original judgment was proper and affirmed by the Court of Appeals.

(16) Lists the Justices who agree with Justice Anderson. They are Justices Poche and Reardon. The "JJ" means the plural of Justice.

3.4:0 THE USE OF THE LAW LIBRARY

(A) Searching for Particular Cases

There are many ways to search for a particular case. Five of these methods will be covered in this chapter.

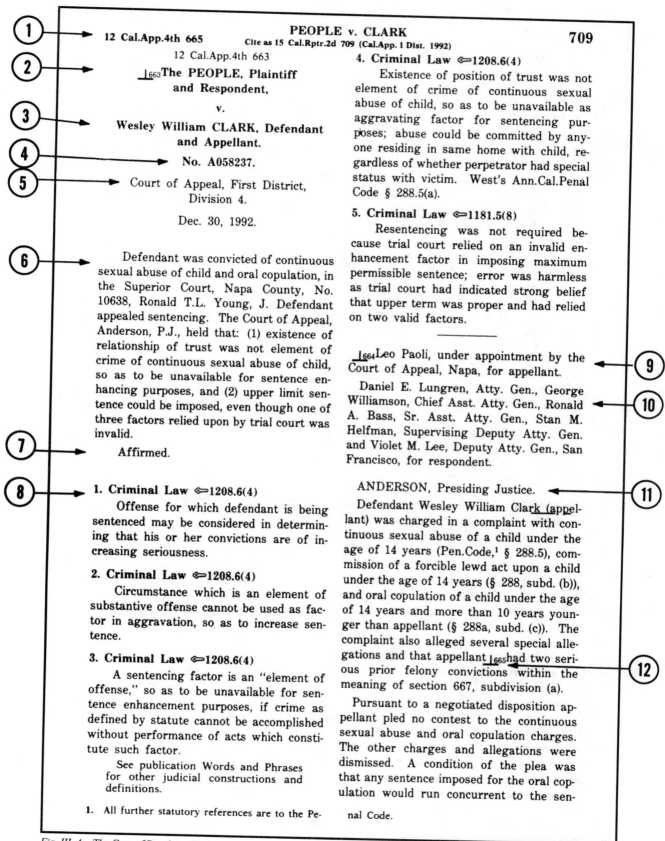

PEOPLE v. CLARK
Cite as 15 Cal.Rptr.2d 709 (Cal.App. 1 Dist. 1992)
709

① 12 Cal.App.4th 665

12 Cal.App.4th 663

② ⌐663The PEOPLE, Plaintiff and Respondent,

v.

③ Wesley William CLARK, Defendant and Appellant.

④ No. A058237.

⑤ Court of Appeal, First District, Division 4.

Dec. 30, 1992.

⑥ Defendant was convicted of continuous sexual abuse of child and oral copulation, in the Superior Court, Napa County, No. 10638, Ronald T.L. Young, J. Defendant appealed sentencing. The Court of Appeal, Anderson, P.J., held that: (1) existence of relationship of trust was not element of crime of continuous sexual abuse of child, so as to be unavailable for sentence enhancing purposes, and (2) upper limit sentence could be imposed, even though one of three factors relied upon by trial court was invalid.

⑦ Affirmed.

⑧ **1. Criminal Law ⬤1208.6(4)**

Offense for which defendant is being sentenced may be considered in determining that his or her convictions are of increasing seriousness.

2. Criminal Law ⬤1208.6(4)

Circumstance which is an element of substantive offense cannot be used as factor in aggravation, so as to increase sentence.

3. Criminal Law ⬤1208.6(4)

A sentencing factor is an "element of offense," so as to be unavailable for sentence enhancement purposes, if crime as defined by statute cannot be accomplished without performance of acts which constitute such factor.

See publication Words and Phrases for other judicial constructions and definitions.

1. All further statutory references are to the Pe-

4. Criminal Law ⬤1208.6(4)

Existence of position of trust was not element of crime of continuous sexual abuse of child, so as to be unavailable as aggravating factor for sentencing purposes; abuse could be committed by anyone residing in same home with child, regardless of whether perpetrator had special status with victim. West's Ann.Cal.Penal Code § 288.5(a).

5. Criminal Law ⬤1181.5(8)

Resentencing was not required because trial court relied on an invalid enhancement factor in imposing maximum permissible sentence; error was harmless as trial court had indicated strong belief that upper term was proper and had relied on two valid factors.

_____

⌐664Leo Paoli, under appointment by the Court of Appeal, Napa, for appellant. ⑨

Daniel E. Lungren, Atty. Gen., George Williamson, Chief Asst. Atty. Gen., Ronald A. Bass, Sr. Asst. Atty. Gen., Stan M. Helfman, Supervising Deputy Atty. Gen. and Violet M. Lee, Deputy Atty. Gen., San Francisco, for respondent. ⑩

ANDERSON, Presiding Justice. ⑪

Defendant Wesley William Clark (appellant) was charged in a complaint with continuous sexual abuse of a child under the age of 14 years (Pen.Code,[1] § 288.5), commission of a forcible lewd act upon a child under the age of 14 years (§ 288, subd. (b)), and oral copulation of a child under the age of 14 years and more than 10 years younger than appellant (§ 288a, subd. (c)). The complaint also alleged several special allegations and that appellant ⌐665had two serious prior felony convictions within the meaning of section 667, subdivision (a). ⑫

Pursuant to a negotiated disposition appellant pled no contest to the continuous sexual abuse and oral copulation charges. The other charges and allegations were dismissed. A condition of the plea was that any sentence imposed for the oral copulation would run concurrent to the sen-

nal Code.

Fig. III–4; The Case of People v. Clark

Courtesy, West Publishing Company

tence for the continuous abuse. The superior court sentenced appellant to state prison for the upper term of 16 years for the continuous abuse. A concurrent sentence was imposed for the other offense.

⑬ Appellant contends: "The trial court stated invalid reasons for imposing the upper term." This contention lacks merit.

At the sentencing hearing probation was denied because appellant was an active rather than passive participant and his performance on probation or parole was not satisfactory.

With regard to the term, the superior court commented that "it is very difficult to find any circumstances in mitigation that fit this gentleman's case." Nevertheless, defense counsel had set forth several factors which "lead the court to believe that there is some positive in [appellant's] life...." The factors were appellant's "good bond" with his wife, his activities on behalf of the Salvation Army and his early plea of no contest.

However, these factors were "greatly" outweighed by those mandating an aggravated term. Appellant "was in a position of trust or confidence, specifically trust with the youngsters involved here ages seven and nine, and that ... position of trust was indeed taken advantage of." Appellant's prior convictions were numerous and of increasing seriousness. He progressed from traffic offenses to burglary, to arson and then to the instant sex crimes.

The trial court also remarked, "the [appellant] has been convicted of ... one other crime for which a consecutive sentence might have been imposed. And I'm not saying it would have been imposed.... All I'm saying is that there is going to be a concurrent sentence in this case. [¶] Counsel, correct me if I'm wrong on that. Is there at least the possibility that this could have been a consecutive sentence? [¶] [Prosecutor]: It would have been except for the plea bargain, correct."

Appellant argues that each of the cited aggravating factors was invalid. Position of trust is an element of the crime, offenses of increasing seriousness includes the instant conviction which is improper,

and the possible |666consecutive sentence factor is barred because of the plea bargain. On the basis of *People v. Simpson* (1979) 90 Cal.App.3d 919, 924, 154 Cal.Rptr. 249, the Attorney General agrees with the latter argument.

[1] The offense for which a defendant is being sentenced may be considered in determining that his or her convictions are of increasing seriousness. (*People v. Searle* (1989) 213 Cal.App.3d 1091, 1098, 261 Cal.Rptr. 898; *People v. Marshall* (1987) 196 Cal.App.3d 1253, 1260–1261, 242 Cal.Rptr. 319.)

[2, 3] A circumstance which is an element of the substantive offense cannot be used as a factor in aggravation. (*People v. Wilks* (1978) 21 Cal.3d 460, 470, 146 Cal. Rptr. 364, 578 P.2d 1369.) A sentencing factor is an element of the offense if the crime as defined by statute cannot be accomplished without performance of the acts which constitute such factor. (*People v. Garcia* (1989) 209 Cal.App.3d 790, 793–794, 257 Cal.Rptr. 495; *People v. Marshall, supra*, 196 Cal.App.3d at pp. 1259–1260, 242 Cal.Rptr. 319; *People v. Young* (1983) 146 Cal.App.3d 729, 733–734, 194 Cal.Rptr. 338.)

[4] The offense involved herein is defined by section 288.5, subdivision (a), in pertinent part, as follows. "Any person who either resides in the same home with the minor child or has recurring access to the child, who over a period of time, not less than three months in duration, engages in three or more acts of [proscribed] sexual conduct with a child under the age of 14 years at the time of the commission of the offense ... is guilty of the offense of continuous sexual abuse of a child...."

It is undisputed that appellant was the victim's stepfather and was entrusted with caring for her and her sister. Thus, he was placed in a position of trust and confidence regarding the children. Since continuous sexual abuse can be committed by anyone residing in the same home with the children, whether or not they have special status with the victim, such sentencing factor is not an element of the crime. ⑭

Moreover, in *People v. Fernandez* (1990) 226 Cal.App.3d 669, 680, 276 Cal.Rptr.

Fig. III–4; The Case of People v. Clark, Continued.   Courtesy, West Publishing Company

Chapter Three

AVIS RENT A CAR v. SUPERIOR COURT (KOCH)

12 Cal.App.4th 222   Cite as 15 Cal.Rptr.2d 711 (Cal.App. 1 Dist. 1993)   **711**

631—a case where the charged crimes were lewd and lascivious conduct on a child under section 288, subdivisions (a) and (b), but the defendant was a "resident child molester"—the court held that abuse of the parental relationship could be utilized as an aggravating factor. This factor fell under the sentencing categories of victim's vulnerability or position of trust and confidence. It could only be credited to one and could not be counted as two aggravating circumstances. To the same effect see *People v. Garcia* (1985) 166 Cal.App.3d 1056, 1069–1070, 212 Cal.Rptr. 822.

[5] |667Since one of the three reasons given by the superior court for the upper term was improper, we must next determine if the error was prejudicial. A case will not be remanded for resentencing based on the use of an invalid factor if the superior court's remarks indicate a strong belief that the upper term was proper and other valid factors were mentioned. (*People v. Avalos* (1984) 37 Cal.3d 216, 233, 207 Cal.Rptr. 549, 689 P.2d 121.) Herein, the superior court expressed its choice of the upper term in no uncertain terms and two out of three stated reasons were proper. Accordingly, the error is harmless.

The judgment is affirmed.

POCHÉ and REARDON, JJ., concur.

12 Cal.App.4th 221
|221AVIS RENT A CAR SYSTEM, INC., Petitioner,

v.

The SUPERIOR COURT of Alameda County, Respondent;

Julia KOCH et al., Real Parties in Interest.

No. A057731.

Court of Appeal, First District, Division 3.

Jan. 11, 1993.

Car rental agency being sued by motorist who was injured when her car was rammed by stolen rental vehicle being chased from scene of shoplifting petitioned for writ of mandate to compel the Superior Court, Alameda County, No. 659744–9, James R. Lambden, J., to grant summary judgment for agency. The Court of Appeal, Chin, J., held that car rental agency could not be held liable under "special circumstances doctrine" for its failure to take adequate precautions to prevent theft of its vehicles.

Peremptory writ issued.

1. Automobiles ☞173(8)

"Special circumstances doctrine" imposes duty upon owners of heavy construction machinery to use due care to prevent the injurious use of the machinery by others; special circumstances exist when heavy vehicles are left unattended and available for use by those not accustomed to driving them.

See publication Words and Phrases for other judicial constructions and definitions.

2. Automobiles ☞173(8)

Car rental agency could not be held liable under "special circumstances doctrine," based on its failure to take adequate precautions to prevent theft of its vehicles, for injuries sustained when plaintiff's car was rammed by stolen rental vehicle being chased from scene of shoplifting; agency's conduct of parking its cars in negligently attended lot with keys in ignitions did not create duty to control the conduct of a thief, and even if duty existed, it would not extend to subject accident, which occurred in another county one week later during police chase not caused by report of vehicle theft.

|222James R. Heisey and Michael F. O'Leary, Law Offices of Michael F. O'Leary, San Francisco, for petitioner.

No appearance for respondent.

Fig. III–4; The Case of People v. Clark, Continued.

Courtesy, West Publishing Company

PARTIES INVOLVED IN A CASE

HIGH COURT	JUSTICE	**APPELLANT**: Person who appeals the case to the high court. **RESPONDENT**: Person against whom the suit is taken.
LOWER COURT	JUDGE	**PLAINTIFF**: Person bringing the case to the lower court. **DEFENDANT**: Person who is brought to court and must defend himself or herself.

(1) When the Searcher Has the Actual Case Citation

When reading books on criminal law, it will be seen that most authors will cite one particular case, or even several cases, in order to illustrate the legal basis for a particular point. Once the searcher has the case citation, the job of locating that case in the law library becomes a simple one. It is just a matter of going to the law library and pulling out that particular volume, and then turning to the page indicated.

In the case citation, 55 C.A. 3d 179 (127 Cal Rptr 454), you would go to volume 127 of the California Reporter and look on page 454 and find the case.

Below is part of a page from a common criminal law book, dealing with the topic "Gross Negligence" as used in Vehicular Manslaughter. Notice the use of several different case citations to back up the statements made in the book.

Gross Negligence

Since the amended section does not define the term "gross negligence" it must be assumed that the legislature intended that these words should be construed as having the same meaning as had been applied to them in the decisions of our appellate courts. In these cases gross negligence is defined as being such a degree of negligence or carelessness as to amount to the want of slight diligence, an entire failure to exercise care or the existence of so slight a degree of care as to justify the belief that there was an entire indifference to the safety of the property and persons of others and a conscious indifference to consequences (People v. Costa, 40 Cal. 2d 160; and cases cited). To constitute gross negligence, it is not, however, necessary that there exist and be present either willfulness or wantonness. (See Kastel v. Stieber, 215 Cal. 37, 46; Krause v. Rarity, 210 Cal. 644, 654; Cooper v. Kellogg, 2 Cal. 2d 504,510.)

(2) When the Searcher Has Only the Name of the Appellant

This type of search is made much easier if you have an approximate date of the decision. Maybe you heard the case mentioned in class as being a recent decision, or heard some officer discussing the case. If you do have an approximate date of the decision, you can go to the Reporter that covers that particular time. So many cases are being appealed today that it takes several volumes to cover one year. In the front of the Reporter you should locate a heading entitled "Cases Reported," and look alphabetically for the name of the appellant. If the case is not there, then you go to the next reporter and repeat the process. It really only takes seconds to check alphabetically for an appellant once you have the Reporter in your hands. As a result, you can go through quite a few Reporters in a very short time. In this section, the cases involving two last names are listed first (e.g., **Smith v. Jones**), then the cases involving the "People" (e.g., **People v. Harrison**).

Some law libraries do not have the volumes that contain just the California Supreme Court reports, or the District Court of Appeals reports. They are both included in a reporter called the California Reporter. Figure III–5 (page 87) is a page from the "Cases Reported" section of Volume 15, second series, of the California Reporter. If the case we were trying to locate was People v. Clark, we would look alphabetically down the list until we came to that name. Just to the right of the name we would find the page listed in volume 15. In this case, it would be page 709. If we turned to page 709 we would find the case of People v. Clark. It would not take long to read the introduction and determine if this was the case we were trying to locate, or whether it was another one with a defendant by the same name. If it was the wrong one, we would then go to the next volume and repeat the process.

(3) When the Searcher Knows Only the Type of Offense Committed

This type of search can be a little more difficult because there can be many cases involving the same offense in each Reporter.

If you know the approximate year of the decision, you can go to the reporter that covers that particular time, and look in the front of the Reporter under "Statutes Construed" and check the cases which are listed numerically by code number, (e.g., 211 under Penal Code for robbery). If you don't know the year, you start with the most recent volume and then move back. If you find a citation that could be the one you are looking for, you can quickly turn to the page listed and check it out. If we were looking for a recent case involving Child Molesting, we would look for section 288.5 PC in the "Statutes Construed" section of the California Reporter. Figure III–6 (page 88) is a page from the "Statutes Construed" section of volume 15, second series. If we look down the page numerically, we will find 288.5 PC at the 26th number from the top. If there were several, we would have to briefly check each one. In this case, there is only one 288.5 PC and it is located on page 709 of volume 15. When we turn to that page, we find that it is the People v. Clark.

(4) When the Searcher Knows the Offense and Some Special Condition or Quality About That Offense

If the case you are trying to locate has a special condition or quality, you can look in the California Digest under that topical heading. This, in turn, will list case citations for all the cases broken down under further sub-classifications.

Let us say that we were looking for a case involving "Disorderly Conduct," and that the case dealt with the sub-classification of the "Nature and Elements" of that offense. We would go to the set of books called the California Digest and find the volume that alphabetically covered "Disorderly Conduct," which would be volume 19. On page 123 we would find the topic and the sub-topic. See Figure III–7, page 89.

Cumulative Annual Pocket Parts

Since the bound California Digest is so expensive, it cannot be reprinted every year. The simple solution to keeping the volume up-to-date is to issue a yearly update that can be inserted into the pocket in the back cover of each volume. This "Cumulative Pocket Part" should always be checked to see if there have been recent court decisions that have changed or added to the particular topic. A new set of Digests is reprinted about once every ten years. The updates in the back list the additions by the year and the court that handed down the decision. See Figure III–8, page 90)

As with the California Digest, the California Codes cannot be updated more than once every ten years, so it is most important to check in the back of the book for the "Cumulative Pocket Part." This will show whether the law has changed or has been amended. It will also show whether or not the law has been repealed.

Figure III–9 and Figure III–10 (pages 91 and 92 respectively) are examples from the Military and Veterans Code. The law illustrated pertains to "Offenses in Connection with Flags."

In Figure III–11 (page 93) it can be seen that the law pertaining to "Offenses in Connection with Flags" was changed. The underlined part shows what was added, and the asterisks show what was deleted. (some books now indicate added words by putting them in italics and deleted words by putting them in "strikeout"). If this had not been checked, a serious error could have resulted in enforcing the law.

(5) Looking Under the Crime Committed, as Listed in the Annotated California Codes

Another source would be the Annotated Codes. After each statute there is listed a brief description of cases dealing with that offense and the citation for the cases.

There are considerable numbers of statutes in the twenty-nine different California Codes. Experience will teach you which type of code will be likely to contain what type of law. Common sense will also help in this regard.

In the last volume of each code, there will be a complete index for all the laws located in that code. Since the statutes are listed and cross-listed alphabetically, it does not take too long to check out the listing of statutes in one code.

General Areas of Law in Particular Codes

Narcotic laws . . . . Health & Safety Code
Juvenile laws. . . . . . Welfare & Institutions Code
General crimes. . . . . Penal Code
Alcoholic Beverage Control laws
. . . . Business & Professions Code
Laws on hunting . . . . Fish & Game Code
Rules of Evidence . . . . Evidence Code
Traffic Offenses . . . . Vehicle Code
Corrections Law. . . . . Penal Code
and . . . . California Code of Regulations

Other Information in the Codes

After the statutory wording of each law in the annotated code, there will be other important information such as:

(1) Legislative history of the law;

(2) Cross-references to other sources, e.g., other California Codes, Constitutional Law Reviews, California Jurisprudence, etc.

(3) Case citations of noted high court decisions concerning that particular statute.

These references will provide you with a well-grounded understanding of the statute and the meaning of its wording and interpretation.

Other Sources

On a broader national level, a search can be made in Words and Phrases. If the law being researched contains certain words and phrases that are important, a search of the set of books called Words and Phrases can be conducted. The words or phrases are listed in alphabetical order. If researching the crime itself, it also is found in alphabetical order.

Cross Reference for Case Citations

Because case citations are often cited in different reporters, there are times when a student will have to locate the case citation for the reporter that the library happens to have. In California, the Supreme and Appellate Court decisions are combined into one reporter, the California Reporter. Since this is the reporter that most libraries have, a case citation found in some law book and cited as 55 C.A. 3d 179 would have to be converted to a California Reporter number before it could be located in that reporter. This is simply done by looking in the California Blue and White Book. This book has the cross-references for the California Supreme and Appellate Courts with the California Reporter and the Pacific Reporter. See Figure III–12, page 94.

Using the Blue and White Book

(1) Find section of Blue & White Book that covers your reporter.

(2) Look numerically for the page with your reporter volume number.

(3) Look down the page to locate the page number of your citation.

(4) Next to it will be the cross reference citation.

Examples:
(See numbered arrows, Figure III–12, page 94)

(1) 81 Cal Rptr 146 shows it to be 276 Cal App 333.

(2) 81 Cal Rptr 161 shows it to be 1 Cal 3d 277.

Shepard's Citations

Although Shepard's Citations is essential to the research of practicing attorneys, it can also be of value to criminal justice personnel. It provides a quick and easy reference to all later cases which have mentioned or affect a particular case that the student is researching.

The process of doing this type of research is called "Shepardizing the case." It is a way to determine whether a particular case is still "good" law. Shepard's citation system consists of a set of books for the courts of each state, and for the regional Reporters such as California Reporter and Pacific Reporter. It also includes a set for the United States Supreme Court. Shepard's also has a set of books with the case citations for particular code sections such as burglary, murder or robbery, as well as one that covers the Constitution.

As with State Codes, Digests and other volumes, supplements with updated material are issued at regular intervals, so it is wise always to check the back of the book for the updated material.

At the beginning of the books will be found information that will help in using the books. Students should always go over this before starting to "Shepardize" a case.

When a case is to be "Shepardized," the student should first locate the set of books that cover the court issuing the decision. The pages go numerically by volume. When the right volume is found, then the volume is searched for the page listed in the original case citation. When the citation is located, there will also be found other citations that are related to the original one. The other citations will have a code in the form of a lower case letter before the citation. Examples of this code are as follows:

"c" —the case has been criticized

"d" —the case has been distinguished

"j" —the case was used in a dissenting opinion

"o" —the case was overruled

"q" —the case was questioned

All County law libraries have the Shepard's Citations.

CASES REPORTED

	Page
Fresno County Dept. of Social Services v. Nicki P.—Cal.App. 5 Dist.	308
Garamendi; State Farm Mut. Auto. Ins. Co. v.—Cal.App. 2 Dist.	546
General Motors Acceptance Corp.; Pearl v.—Cal.App. 4 Dist.	100
General Motors Corp. v. Superior Court (Ticich)—Cal.App. 4 Dist.	622
Griset v. Fair Political Practices Com'n (Mem.)—Cal.	893
Grothe v. Cortlandt Corp.—Cal.App. 4 Dist.	38
Guevara; Fish v.—Cal.App. 6 Dist.	329
Harmon v. St. Joseph's Catholic Church—Cal.App. 2 Dist.	1
Harris; People v. (Mem.)—Cal.	892
Hartsuiker v. W.C.A.B.—Cal.App. 1 Dist.	719
Hayes v. Commission on State Mandates (Holmes)—Cal.App. 3 Dist.	547
Hill; People v.—Cal.App. 2 Dist.	806
Hines v. San Diego County Superior Court (People) (Mem.)—Cal.	892
Hollister School Dist.; Thorning v.—Cal.App. 6 Dist.	91
Ikemoto; Arcadia Redevelopment Agency v. (Mem.)—Cal.	892
Iverson, In re Marriage of—Cal.App. 4 Dist.	70
Iverson v. Iverson—Cal.App. 4 Dist.	70
Jay Hales Development Co.; Stell v.—Cal.App. 2 Dist.	220
J., Crystal, In re—Cal.App. 4 Dist.	613
Jiminez; People v.—Cal.App. 6 Dist.	268
Juge v. County of Sacramento—Cal.App. 3 Dist.	598
Juniper Garden Town Homes, Ltd.; Tsakos Shipping & Trading, S.A. v.—Cal.App. 4 Dist.	585
Kang; EPA Real Estate Partnership v.—Cal.App. 6 Dist.	209
Khamphouy S., In re—Cal.App. 4 Dist.	882
Khamphouy S.; People v.—Cal.App. 4 Dist.	882
Kizer; Siegal v.—Cal.App. 2 Dist.	607
Klvana, In re—Cal.App. 2 Dist.	512
Klvana; People v.—Cal.App. 2 Dist.	512
Laws; People v.—Cal.App. 3 Dist.	668
Linda H.; San Diego County Dept. of Social Services v.—Cal.App. 4 Dist.	613
Lockridge; People v.—Cal.App. 4 Dist.	12
Lucky Stores v. Alcoholic Beverage Control Appeals Bd.—Cal.App. 1 Dist.	886
Macaulay v. Norlander—Cal.App. 2 Dist.	204
Mack; People v.—Cal.App. 3 Dist.	193
Martinez v. City of Poway—Cal.App. 4 Dist.	644
Martocchio; California Cas. Management Co. v.—Cal.App. 1 Dist.	277

	Page
Mercury Ins. Group v. Checkerboard Pizza—Cal.App. 4 Dist.	657
Meredith; People v.—Cal.App. 2 Dist.	285
Metzger; Berhanu v.—Cal.App. 4 Dist.	191
Miranda v. Shell Oil Co.—Cal.App. 5 Dist.	569
Moore v. Conliffe—Cal.App. 1 Dist.	791
Morehart v. County of Santa Barbara—Cal.App. 2 Dist.	212
Morfin v. State—Cal.App. 4 Dist.	861
Municipal Court of Sacramento County v. Sacramento County Superior Court (J.J. & J. Porter) (Mem.)—Cal.	679
Munoz; People v.—Cal.App. 4 Dist.	21
Nasir v. Sacramento County Office of Dist. Atty.—Cal.App. 3 Dist.	694
National Identification Systems, Inc. v. State Bd. of Control (Department of General Services)—Cal.App. 3 Dist.	257
National Union Fire Ins. Co. of Pittsburgh, Pa.; Xebec Development Partners, Ltd. v.—Cal.App. 6 Dist.	726
Neve v. Norlander—Cal.App. 2 Dist.	204
New Motor Vehicle Bd. (Carl Burger's Dodge World); Chrysler Corp. v.—Cal.App. 4 Dist.	771
New Motor Vehicle Bd. (La Mesa Dodge, Inc.); Chrysler Corp. v.—Cal.App. 4 Dist.	771
Nicki P.; Fresno County Dept. of Social Services v.—Cal.App. 5 Dist.	308
Nielsen, Inc. v. Stern—Cal.Super.	676
Noguera; People v.—Cal.	400
Norlander; Macaulay v.—Cal.App. 2 Dist.	204
Norlander; Neve v.—Cal.App. 2 Dist.	204
Oberlander v. County of Contra Costa—Cal.App. 1 Dist.	182
Paoli v. Civil Service Com'n of Mendocino County (County of Mendocino)—Cal.App. 1 Dist.	874
Pearl v. General Motors Acceptance Corp.—Cal.App. 4 Dist.	100
People v. Alcala—Cal.	432
People v. Arango—Cal.App. 2 Dist.	629
People v. Barton—Cal.App. 4 Dist.	649
People v. Bishop—Cal.App. 6 Dist.	539
People v. Bowie—Cal.App. 2 Dist.	22
People v. Burnett (Mem.)—Cal.	340
People v. Burnett—Cal.App. 2 Dist.	638
People v. Cabral—Cal.App. 5 Dist.	866
People v. Clark—Cal.App. 1 Dist.	709
People v. Darwin—Cal.App. 1 Dist.	894
People v. Dominguez—Cal.App. 4 Dist.	46
People v. Fisher—Cal.App. 1 Dist.	889
People v. Harris (Mem.)—Cal.	892
People v. Hill—Cal.App. 2 Dist.	806
People v. Jiminez—Cal.App. 6 Dist.	268
People v. Khamphouy S.—Cal.App. 4 Dist.	882

Fig. III–5; Cases Reported from *The California Reporter*

Courtesy, West Publishing Company

STATUTES

190.3—15 Cal.Rptr.2d 382
190.3—15 Cal.Rptr.2d 400
190.3(a)—15 Cal.Rptr.2d 340
190.3(a)—15 Cal.Rptr.2d 382
190.3(b)—15 Cal.Rptr.2d 382
190.3(d–f)—15 Cal.Rptr.2d 340
190.3(i)—15 Cal.Rptr.2d 382
190.3(j)—15 Cal.Rptr.2d 340
190.3(k)—15 Cal.Rptr.2d 340
190.3(k)—15 Cal.Rptr.2d 400
190.3(k)—15 Cal.Rptr.2d 432
190.4—15 Cal.Rptr.2d 340
190.4(e)—807 F.Supp. 589
190.4(e)—15 Cal.Rptr.2d 340
191.5—15 Cal.Rptr.2d 4
191.5(a)—15 Cal.Rptr.2d 4
207—15 Cal.Rptr.2d 432
209—15 Cal.Rptr.2d 305
211—15 Cal.Rptr.2d 30
211—15 Cal.Rptr.2d 46
261(a)(2)—15 Cal.Rptr.2d 333
261(a)(3)—15 Cal.Rptr.2d 193
288(a)—15 Cal.Rptr.2d 66
288a—982 F.2d 344
288a(c)—982 F.2d 344
288.5(a)—15 Cal.Rptr.2d 709
422—15 Cal.Rptr.2d 889
422 [Repealed]—15 Cal.Rptr.2d 889
459—15 Cal.Rptr.2d 340
460(a)—15 Cal.Rptr.2d 77
518—15 Cal.Rptr.2d 305
630 et seq.—15 Cal.Rptr.2d 112
636—15 Cal.Rptr.2d 112
647(f)—15 Cal.Rptr.2d 107
654—15 Cal.Rptr.2d 30
654—15 Cal.Rptr.2d 268
664—15 Cal.Rptr.2d 333
667(a)—15 Cal.Rptr.2d 22
667.6(c)—982 F.2d 344
954—15 Cal.Rptr.2d 66
995—15 Cal.Rptr.2d 112
995—15 Cal.Rptr.2d 285
1000(a)(4)—15 Cal.Rptr.2d 539
1000–1000.4—15 Cal.Rptr.2d 539
1033(a)—15 Cal.Rptr.2d 340
1093(f)—15 Cal.Rptr.2d 340
1093.5—15 Cal.Rptr.2d 340
1127—15 Cal.Rptr.2d 340
1140—15 Cal.Rptr.2d 340
1170(d)—15 Cal.Rptr.2d 12
1242—15 Cal.Rptr.2d 906
1324—15 Cal.Rptr.2d 112
1387.1—15 Cal.Rptr.2d 906
1538.5—15 Cal.Rptr.2d 17
1538.5—15 Cal.Rptr.2d 285
1606—15 Cal.Rptr.2d 896
2600—15 Cal.Rptr.2d 112
2600 et seq.—15 Cal.Rptr.2d 112
2601—15 Cal.Rptr.2d 112
4574(a)—15 Cal.Rptr.2d 382
12101(b)—15 Cal.Rptr.2d 882

Probate Code

Sec.
15300 et seq.—148 B.R. 930
15304(a)—148 B.R. 930

Public Resources Code

Sec.
30001.5—15 Cal.Rptr.2d 779
30001.5(a)—15 Cal.Rptr.2d 779
30001.5(b)—15 Cal.Rptr.2d 779
30007.5—15 Cal.Rptr.2d 779
30010—15 Cal.Rptr.2d 779
30107.5—15 Cal.Rptr.2d 779
30240(a)—15 Cal.Rptr.2d 779
30512.2(b)—15 Cal.Rptr.2d 779

Public Utilities Code

Sec.
2821(b)—981 F.2d 429

Revenue and Taxation Code

Sec.
12201—15 Cal.Rptr.2d 26
12221—15 Cal.Rptr.2d 26

Vehicle Code

Sec.
3067—15 Cal.Rptr.2d 771
5600—148 B.R. 317
5600—148 B.R. 322
17001—15 Cal.Rptr.2d 234
17004.7—15 Cal.Rptr.2d 234
20001—15 Cal.Rptr.2d 268
20001(a)—15 Cal.Rptr.2d 268
23152(a)—15 Cal.Rptr.2d 107
23152(b)—15 Cal.Rptr.2d 107
40803–40805—15 Cal.Rptr.2d 21
40808—15 Cal.Rptr.2d 21

Welfare and Institutions Code

Sec.
366.21(i)—15 Cal.Rptr.2d 613
366.26—15 Cal.Rptr.2d 308
6316.1 [Repealed]—15 Cal.Rptr.2d 896
6316.2 [Repealed]—15 Cal.Rptr.2d 896
17000—15 Cal.Rptr.2d 182
17000.5—15 Cal.Rptr.2d 182
17000.5(a)—15 Cal.Rptr.2d 182
17000.5(b)—15 Cal.Rptr.2d 182
17000.5(e)—15 Cal.Rptr.2d 182
17001.5—15 Cal.Rptr.2d 182
17001.5(a)(2)—15 Cal.Rptr.2d 182
17001.5(a)(2)(A)—15 Cal.Rptr.2d 182
17001.5(a)(2)(C)—15 Cal.Rptr.2d 182

California Rules of Court

Rule
7(b)—15 Cal.Rptr.2d 382
12(a)—15 Cal.Rptr.2d 382
23(b)—15 Cal.Rptr.2d 480
29(b)(1)—15 Cal.Rptr.2d 679
36(b)—15 Cal.Rptr.2d 382
1207—15 Cal.Rptr.2d 70

Fig. III–6;   Statutes Construed from *The California Reporter*   Courtesy, West Publishing Company

19 Cal D—123

DISORDERLY CONDUCT

Scope-Note.

INCLUDES misconduct prejudicial to safety, comfort, or welfare of others, not constituting a breach of the peace or other distinct offense; nature and extent of criminal responsibility therefor, and grounds of defense; and prosecution and punishment of such misconduct as a public offense.

Matters not in this topic, treated elsewhere, see Descriptive-Word Index.

Analysis.

1. Nature and elements of offenses.
2. Defenses.
3. Persons liable.
4. Persons entitled to prosecute.
4½. Jurisdiction and venue.
5. Preliminary proceedings in prosecution.
6. Indictment or information.
7. —— Requisites and sufficiency.
8. —— Issues, proof, and variance.
9. Evidence.
10. Trial.
11. —— Questions for jury.
12. —— Instructions.
13. —— Verdict.
14. Appeal and error.
15. Sentence and punishment.
16. Security for good behavior.

1. Nature and elements of offenses.

Library references

C.J.S. Disorderly Conduct § 1(1) et seq.

Cal. 1895. An ordinance forbidding the beating of drums on the street except on permit of the president of the board of trustees, which he may grant when, in his judgment, it will not conflict with the purposes of the ordinance,—the promotion of the safety and security of public travel,—is not void by reason of the authority given such officer to decide when permits shall be given.

In re Flaherty, 38 P. 981, 105 C. 558, 27 L.R.A. 529.

Cal. 1881. Pen.Code, § 415 (West's Ann. Pen.Code), making it an offense to use vulgar, profane, or indecent language within the hearing of children, etc., does not make the offense such only when committed in the streets of an incorporated town.

Ex parte Foley, 62 C. 508, 7 P.C.L.J. 61.

Super. 1944. The statute making it a misdemeanor for any person to maliciously and willfully disturb the peace or quiet of any neighborhood or person, by loud or unusual noise, or by tumultuous or offensive conduct, prohibits a disturbance, by the specified means, of the peace of "any neighborhood or person", and it is not necessary to establish that it is a disturbance of the "public" peace in order to authorize a conviction under the statute. West's Ann.Pen. Code, §§ 415, 416.

People v. Vaughan, 150 P.2d 964, 65 C.A.2d Supp. 844.

Law Rev. 1961. On obscene matter, California's new law.

36 S.Bar J. 625.

2—5. *See Topic Analysis for scope.*

Library references

C.J.S. Disorderly Conduct §§ 2–5.

Fig. III–7; "Disorderly Conduct" page from *California Digest.*

Courtesy, West Publishing Company

defendant's use of same facts which had been made matter of record in the other cases. West's Ann.Code Civ.Proc. §§ 473, 581a.—Id.

Cal.App. 1964. In weighing motion to vacate judgment of dismissal for lack of prosecution, trial judge should consider what prejudice or injustice defendant might suffer as result of its order. West's Ann.Code Civ.Proc. § 583.—Daley v. Butte County, 38 Cal.Rptr. 693, 227 C.A.2d 380.

Cal.App. 1963. Motion for order continuing time within which to plead accompanying notice to set aside default was not a pleading within rule that application for relief from judgment must be accompanied by copy of answer or other pleading proposed to be filed therein. West's Ann.Code Civ.Proc. §§ 420, 422, 473.—Sousa v. Capital Co., 34 Cal.Rptr. 71, 220 C.A.2d 744.

Order vacating plaintiff's default and default judgment thereon after plaintiffs failed to file third amended complaint was not improper on ground that application for relief was not supported by affidavit of merits and proposed amended complaint, where before motion was heard a verified amended complaint was filed by plaintiffs and it sufficiently showed meritorious claim. West's Ann.Code Civ.Proc. § 473.—Id.

DISORDERLY CONDUCT

Library references
  C.J.S. Disorderly Conduct § 1.

☞1. Nature and elements of offenses.
  Cal.App. 1975. Statute which proscribed, as misdemeanor, advertisement of offers to procure or obtain, or to aid in procuring or obtaining, any dissolution or annulment of marriage was constitutional on its face. West's Ann.Pen.Code, §§ 158-159a, 159a; West's Ann.Bus. & Prof. Code, §§ 6125, 6126; Rules of Professional Conduct, rules 2-101 to 2-105, 3-101, West's Ann. Bus. & Prof.Code following section 6076; U.S.C. A.Const. Amend. 1—Howard v. Superior Court for Los Angeles County, 125 Cal.Rptr. 255.

Cal.App. 1975. Mere use of vulgar, profane, indecorous, scurrilous, or opprobrious epithet cannot alone be grounds for prosecution.—Jefferson v. Superior Court, In and For Alameda County, 124 Cal.Rptr. 507.

Cal.App. 1973. Statute making person guilty of disorderly conduct who loiters or wanders upon streets or from place to place without apparent reason or business and who refuses to identify himself and to account for his presence when requested by any peace officer so to do, if surrounding circumstances are such as to indicate to reasonable man that public safety demands such identification, was within legislature's power to enact, and self-identification compelled by statute was consistent with constitutional right. West's Ann.Pen.Code, §§ 148, 647(e), 834a; West's Ann.Vehicle Code, §§ 2800, 12951(b), 40302.—People v. Solomon, 108 Cal. Rptr. 867, 33 C.A.3d 429, certiorari denied 94 S.Ct. 1476, 415 U.S. 951, 39 L.Ed.2d 567.

Insofar as disorderly conduct statute required subject to account for his presence, that requirement was operative only insofar as it was reasonably used by police officer as adjunct to requirement of identification, the latter requirement being primary and controlling. West's Ann.Pen. Code, § 647(e); U.S.C.A.Const. Amend. 5.—Id.

Cal.App. 1972. A business open to the public is a "public place" within meaning of disorderly conduct statute. West's Ann.Pen.Code, § 647(f). —People v. Blatt, 99 Cal.Rptr. 855, 23 C.A.3d 148.

Area behind service counter in men's clothing store open for business was a "public place" within meaning of disorderly conduct statute, and

arrest and subsequent search, which revealed contraband, of person who was found to be sitting behind service counter and who was intoxicated and unable to care for herself were proper. West's Ann.Pen.Code, § 647(f).—Id.

Cal.App. 1971. Omission of introductory declaration in disorderly conduct statute making such conduct a misdemeanor was inadvertent and legislative intent to punish prohibited conduct by penal sanction was manifest; thus, statute stated valid offense during interim between date statute was amended and date introductory declaration was reenacted. West's Ann.Pen. Code, § 647.—People v. Medina, 93 Cal.Rptr. 560, 15 C.A.3d 845.

Cal.App. 1971. Statute forbidding peaceable, nonobstructive picketing within interior of state capitol building was adequately narrow regulation designed to protect substantial state interest and was not in violation of First Amendment rights to freedom of speech and petition on theory that statute was too broad in scope or worked denial of equal protection. U.S.C.A.Const. Amends. 1, 14; West's Ann.Const. art. 1, §§ 9, 10; West's Ann.Pen.Code, § 171f, subds. 2, 3.—Simpson v. Municipal Court, Sacramento Municipal Court Dist., Sacramento County, 92 Cal.Rptr. 417, 14 C.A.3d 591.

Cal.App. 1968. Statute making it disorderly conduct to solicit anyone to engage in or who engages in lewd or dissolute conduct in a public place is intended to proscribe at least the engaging in lewd or dissolute conduct in a public place and the soliciting of lewd or dissolute conduct in a public place. West's Ann.Pen.Code, § 647(a)— People v. Mesa, 71 Cal.Rptr. 594, 265 C.A.2d 746.

Section of disorderly conduct statute regarding the solicitation or engaging in lewd or dissolute conduct in public place prohibits public solicitations of lewd or dissolute conduct regardless of where solicited acts are to be performed. West's Ann.Pen.Code, § 647(a).—Id.

Solicitation in a public bar of a homosexual act constituted violation of statute making it disorderly conduct to solicit or engage in lewd or dissolute conduct in any public place. West's Ann.Pen.Code, § 647(a).—Id.

Cal.App. 1968. Under statute providing that if it reasonably appears to officer of state college or university that person not a student or officer or employee is committing act likely to interfere with conduct of activities of campus or facility, such person may be directed to leave and upon failure to do so shall be guilty of misdemeanor, word "student" means student of particular institution whose campus or facility is involved. West's Ann.Pen.Code, § 602.7.—People v. Agnello, 66 Cal.Rptr. 571, 259 C.A.2d 785.

Cal.App. 1967. Under statute providing that person should be guilty of offense of disorderly conduct for being found in public place under influence of intoxicating liquor, offense is defined in terms of acts rather than status and statute penalizes act of being in public place while under influence of intoxicating liquor but does not punish person for being intoxicated and does not punish chronic alcoholic because of his alcoholism. West's Ann.Pen.Code, § 647(f).—Application of Spinks, 61 Cal.Rptr. 743, 253 C.A.2d 748.

Defendant who was a chronic alcoholic and whose presence under influence of intoxicating liquor in public place was allegedly compulsive and symptomatic of his disease violated statute punishing person because he appeared in public place while intoxicated to extent he was unable to exercise care for his own safety or safety of others. West's Ann.Pen.Code, § 647(f).—Id.

Statute providing that person should be guilty of offense of disorderly conduct for being found in public place under influence of intoxicating liquor, as applied to chronic alcoholic was not

West's ANNOTATED CALIFORNIA CODES

MILITARY AND VETERANS CODE
Sections 1 to End

Official
California Military and Veterans Code
Classification

Volume 46

ST. PAUL, MINN.
WEST PUBLISHING CO

Fig. III–9;   Cover page from *West's Annotated California Codes*, Military and Veterans Code   Courtesy, West Publishing Company

§ 614   EMBLEMS AND DECORATIONS   Div. 3

§ 614.   Offenses in connection with flags. A person is guilty of a misdemeanor who:

(a) In any manner for exhibition or display, places or causes to appear any work, figure, mark, picture, design, drawing, or any advertisement of any nature upon any flag of the United States or of this State.

(b) Exposes to public view any such flag upon which is printed, painted, or placed or to which is attached, appended, affixed, or annexed any word, figure, mark, picture, design, drawing, or any advertisement of any nature.

(c) Exposes to public view, manufactures, sells, exposes for sale, gives away, or has in possession for sale or to give away or for use for any purpose any article or substance being an article of merchandise or a receptacle of merchandise or article or thing for carrying or transporting merchandise upon which is printed, painted, attached, or placed a representation of any such flag, standard, color, or ensign to advertise, call attention to, decorate, mark or distinguish the article or substance on which so placed.

(d) Publicly mutilates, defaces, defiles, or tramples any such flag. (Stats.1935, c. 389, p. 1377, § 614.)

Derivation: Mil.C. § 94; Pen.C. § 310a, added Stats.1919, c. 105, p. 147, § 1, amended Stats.1929, c. 59, p. 135, § 2.

Cross References

Misdemeanor defined, see Penal Code § 17.

Law Review Commentaries

Adoption of Uniform Flag Act. Victor R. Henley (1951) 39 C.L.R. 68, 73.

Notes of Decisions

In general 2
Validity 1

1. Validity

The right of personal liberty guaranteed by U.S.Const. Amend. 14, is not infringed by the provision of Neb. act April 8, 1903, making it a misdemeanor to use representations of the national flag upon articles of merchandise for advertising purposes. Halter v. State of Nebraska (Neb. 1906) 27 S.Ct. 419, 205 U.S. 34, 51 L.Ed. 696, 10 Ann.Cas. 525.

Property rights are not invaded without due process of law, in violation of U.S. Const. Amend. 14, by the provision of Neb. act April 8, 1903, making it a misdemeanor to use representations of the national flag upon articles of merchandise for advertising purposes. Id.

2. In general

The protection of the national flag against illegitimate uses is not so exclusively intrusted to the Federal government as to prevent the state of Nebraska from making it a misdemeanor, by the act of April 8, 1903, to use representations of such flag upon articles of merchandise for advertising purposes. Halter v. State of Nebraska (Neb.1906) 27 S.Ct. 419, 205 U.S. 34, 51 L.Ed. 696, 10 Ann.Cas. 525.

No privilege of American citizenship is denied by the provision of Neb. act of April 8, 1903, making it a misdemeanor to use representations of the national flag upon articles of merchandise for advertising purposes. Id.

186

Fig. III–10; Page from Military and Veteran's Code, Emblems and Decorations   Courtesy, West Publishing Company

MILITARY AND VETERANS CODE § 614

DIVISION 3. EMBLEMS AND DECORATIONS

CHAPTER I. EMBLEMS

§ 611. "Flag" defined

(a) "Flag," as used in this division, means the State Flag of California and the Flag of the United States, as defined in this section.

(b) "State Flag of California" includes any flag, standard color, or ensign authorized by the laws of * * * this state, and every picture or representation thereof, of any size, made of any substance, or represented on any substance evidently purporting to be any such flag, standard color, or ensign of * * * this state, and every picture or representation which shows the design thereof.

(c) "Flag of the United States" includes any flag, standard, colors, or ensign authorized by the laws of the United States or any picture or representation of either, or of any part or parts of either, made of any substance or represented on any substance, of any size evidently purporting to be either of said flag, standard, colors, or ensign of the United States of America, or a picture or a representation of either, upon which shall be shown the colors, the stars and the stripes, in any number of either thereof, or of any part or parts of either, by which the average person seeing the same without deliberation may believe the same to represent the flag, standards, colors, or ensign of the United States of America.

(Amended by Stats.1970, c. 1364, p. 2531, § 1.)

§ 612. Colors and standards; delivery of colors to family of deceased member

The colors and standards carried by organizations of the National Guard or Naval Militia shall be such as are borne by similar organizations of the United States Army, or United States Air Force, or United States Navy, except that the regimental or battalion colors or standards may have thereon the state coat of arms, instead of the coat of arms of the United States.

The Adjutant General may, pursuant to rules and regulations adopted by him, deliver to the members of a family of a deceased member of the National Guard or of the * * * State Military Reserve one of the national colors to be used during the disposition of the remains of the deceased member according to the custom and usual practice of the United States Army, United States Air Force or United States Navy and to thereafter become the property of the members of said family. (As amended Stats.1963, c. 94, p. 726, § 16.)

§ 614. Offenses in connection with flags

(1)

A person is guilty of a misdemeanor who * * * knowingly casts contempt upon any Flag of the United States or of this state * * * by publicly mutilating, defacing, defiling, burning, or trampling upon it.

(Amended by Stats.1970, c. 1364, p. 2531, § 2.)

(2)

1970 Amendment. Substantially rewrote section.

United States Supreme Court. Mass. Phrase "treats contemptuously" in flag misuse statute was constitutionally vague, see Smith v. Goguen (1974) 94 S.Ct. 1242, 415 U.S. 566, 39 L.Ed.2d 605.

1. Validity

Subd. (d) of this section, as defined by § 611, making it a misdemeanor to publicly mutilate, deface, defile, or trample flag is unconstitutional because it is void for overbreadth. Alford v. Municipal Court for Sacramento Judicial Dist. of Sacramento County (1972) 102 Cal.Rptr. 667, 26 C.A.3d 244, certiorari denied 93 S.Ct. 912, 409 U.S. 1109, 34 L.Ed.2d 690.

This section does not apply to words but only to acts and therefore does not violate constitutional right of free speech. People v. Cowgill (1969) 78 Cal.Rptr. 853, 274 C.A.2d Supp. 923, appeal dismissed 90 S.Ct. 613, 396 U.S. 371, 24 L.Ed.2d 590.

This section does not prohibit the use of the American flag as a shoulder patch on police uniforms provided flag is not altered in any way. 53 Ops.Atty.Gen. 249, 8-18-70.

2. In general

Defendant who caused flag of United States to be cut and sewn into vest and wore vest on public streets defiled flag within this section making it misdemeanor to publicly mutilate, deface, defile or trample upon flag of United States. People v. Cowgill (1969) 78 Cal.Rptr. 853, 274 C.A.2d Supp. 923, appeal dismissed 90 S.Ct. 613, 396 U.S. 371, 24 L.Ed.2d 590.

Asterisks * * * indicate deletions by amendment

43

Fig. III–11; Cumulative Pocket Part for Military and Veteran's Code.

Courtesy, West Publishing Company

CAL. & PACIFIC REFERENCES FOR CAL. REPORTER CASES   **355**

81 CALIFORNIA REPORTER—Continued

Page	Parallel Citation	Page	Parallel Citation	Page	Parallel Citation	Page	Parallel Citation
69..276 CalApp2d 630		264....1 Cal3d 41 / 459 P2d 680		432..276 CalApp2d 795		698..2 CalApp3d 87	
73..276 CalApp2d 436		270..276 CalApp2d 744		436..1 CalApp3d 138		701..1 CalApp3d 442	
79..276 CalApp2d 601		273..276 CalApp2d 694		440...1 CalApp3d 13		705..276 CalApp2d 762	
86..276 CalApp2d 429		276..276 CalApp2d 198		444..1 CalApp3d 123		710..1 CalApp3d 467	
91..— CalApp2d —		281..276 CalApp2d 787		448...1 CalApp3d 63		713.1 Cal.App.3d 1001	
103..— CalApp2d —		287..276 CalApp2d 715		451..1 CalApp3d 105		716..1 CalApp3d 591	
107..276 CalApp2d 622		296..276 CalApp2d 729		453.1 Cal.App.3d 156		722..1 CalApp3d 320	
112..276 CalApp2d 534		301..276 CalApp2d 638		457...1 Cal3d 80 / 460 P2d 129		726..1 CalApp3d 226	
120..276 CalApp2d 156		305..276 CalApp2d 774		465....1 Cal3d 56 / 460 P2d 137		732..1 CalApp3d 355	
130..276 CalApp2d 492		310..— CalApp2d —		478...1 CalApp3d 35		738..1 CalApp3d 486	
135..276 CalApp2d 574		314..276 CalApp2d 738		481...1 CalApp3d 173		742..1 CalApp3d 602	
140..276 CalApp2d 391		318..276 CalApp2d 801		492..1 CalApp3d 217		748..1 CalApp3d 457	
146..276 CalApp2d 333		320..276 CalApp2d 610		498..1 CalApp3d 267		750..1 CalApp3d 461	
154..276 CalApp2d 249		329..— CalApp2d —		503...1 CalApp3d 94		753..1 CalApp3d 517	
161..276 CalApp2d 461		332..276 CalApp2d 770		510..1 CalApp3d 129		755..1 CalApp3d 316	
173..276 CalApp2d 649		334..276 CalApp2d 813		516..1 CalApp3d 145		757..1 CalApp3d 471	
193..276 CalApp2d 517		336..276 CalApp2d 781		519..276 CalApp2d 680		765...1 Cal3d 253 / 460 P2d 965	
195..276 CalApp2d 386		340..276 CalApp2d 816		525..276 CalApp2d 595		769...1 Cal3d 198 / 460 P2d 969	
197..276 CalApp2d 61		342..276 CalApp2d 810		529..1 CalApp3d 292		774...1 Cal3d 180 / 460 P2d 974	
201..276 CalApp2d 700		345....1 Cal3d 1 / 459 P2d 897		535..276 CalApp2d 805		780...1 Cal3d 207 / 460 P2d 980	
207..— CalApp2d —		348.....1 Cal3d 74 / 459 P2d 900		539..1 CalApp3d 248		784...1 Cal3d 168 / 460 P2d 984	
216..276 CalApp2d 264		352....1 Cal3d 8 / 459 P2d 904		544..— CalApp2d —		792...1 Cal3d 261 / 460 P2d 992	
221..— CalApp2d —		360....1 Cal3d 20 / 459 P2d 912		551..1 CalApp3d 286		795..1 CalApp3d 627	
226..— CalApp2d —		373....1 Cal3d 50 / 459 P2d 925		555..1 CalApp3d 167		800..1 CalApp3d 499	
229..276 CalApp2d 754		378..1 CalApp3d 29		558..1 CalApp3d 150		804..1 CalApp3d 578	
234..276 CalApp2d 689		381...1 CalApp3d 20		562..1 CalApp3d 339		812..1 CalApp3d 563	
237..276 CalApp2d 750		386...1 CalApp3d 78		565..1 CalApp3d 263		817..1 CalApp3d 651	
241..71 Cal2d 1200 / 459 P2d 657		391.1 Cal.App.3d 931		568..1 CalApp3d 212		833..1 CalApp3d 506	
251..71 Cal2d 1215 / 459 P2d 667		396...1 CalApp3d 115		570..1 CalApp3d 109		840..1 CalApp3d 637	
258..71 Cal2d 1226 / 459 P2d 674		401..1 CalApp3d 161		574..1 CalApp3d 178		845..1 CalApp3d 645	
		405..1 CalApp3d 1		577...1 Cal3d 122 / 460 P2d 449		849..1 Cal3d 266 / 461 P2d 33	
		414..276 CalApp2d 820		592...1 Cal3d 93 / 460 P2d 464		855...1 Cal3d 301 / 461 P2d 39	
		418...1 CalApp3d 68		609...1 Cal3d 190 / 460 P2d 481		863..1 CalApp3d 572	
		424...1 CalApp3d 50		613...1 Cal3d 144 / 460 P2d 485		866..1 CalApp3d 547	
		428...1 CalApp3d 58		623...1 Cal3d 160 / 460 P2d 495		871..1 CalApp3d 748	
				629..1 CalApp3d 274		875..1 CalApp3d 756	
				635..1 CalApp3d 361		879..1 CalApp3d 762	
				639..1 CalApp3d 256		883..1 CalApp3d 729	
				643..1 CalApp3d 493		885..1 CalApp3d 607	
				646..1 CalApp3d 326		897..1 CalApp3d 961	
				655..1 CalApp3d 344		900..1 CalApp3d 698	
				662..1 CalApp3d 449		904..1 CalApp3d 867	
				666..1 CalApp3d 555		907..1 CalApp3d 942	
				671..1 CalApp3d 308		910..1 CalApp3d 657	
				675..1 CalApp3d 367		914..2 CalApp3d 11	
				683..1 CalApp3d 184		917..1 CalApp3d 704	
						924..2 CalApp3d Supp. 1	

82 CALIFORNIA REPORTER

Page	Parallel Citation	Page	Parallel Citation	Page	Parallel Citation	Page	Parallel Citation
1.1 Cal.App.3d 384		84.1 Cal.App.3d 716		129.1 Cal.App.3d 683		175....1 Cal.3d 214 / 461 P.2d 375	
42.1 Cal.App.3d 821		92.1 Cal.App.3d 688		131.1 Cal.App.3d 769		205.1 Cal.App.3d 477	
48.1 Cal.App.3d 521		98.1 Cal.App.3d 891		138.1 Cal.App.3d 733		210.1 Cal.App.3d 968	
52.1 Cal.App.3d 976		102.1 Cal.App.3d 812		147.1 Cal.App.3d 856		215.1 Cal.App.3d 907	
55.1 Cal.App.3d 982		108.1 Cal.App.3d 841		154.1 Cal.App.3d 947		218.1 Cal.App.3d 913	
61.1 Cal.App.3d 831		117.1 Cal.App.3d 1013		157.1 Cal.App.3d 925		221.1 Cal.App.3d 919	
67.1 Cal.App.3d 790				161....1 Cal.3d 277 / 461 P.2d 361		225.3 Cal.App.3d 17	
78.1 Cal.App.3d 664		121.1 Cal.App.3d 672					

Fig. III–12; Page from *Blue & White Book*.   Courtesy, West Publishing Company

3.5:0 THE LEGAL BRIEF AND ITS OUTLINE

3.5:1 Writing a Case Brief

This is similar to the assignment in an English class where you are asked to read a book and make a summary of the book. The legal case brief would be more like reading an article in a magazine and then writing a summary of that article, for it can often be a few pages long. A case brief is a condensation of the important elements of the case.

Purpose

The purpose of the brief is to enable a person reading the case to locate the important parts of that case. It may seem difficult at first, but it becomes much easier with a little practice. Once the case has been briefed in the words of the person doing the research, it can be of help to others in quickly understanding what the case is really about.

Three Good Rules

Three good rules that should be followed in briefing a case are:

(1) Read the case completely before trying to brief it. It will give you a better overall view of the case, and you will be better able to organize the brief.

(2) Write the brief in your own words, and do not just copy from the book. You could be good at copying and not really understand the case. Instructors and professors can quickly tell when you are using words that are not your own.

(3) Be concise, and arrange things in a logical order.

The Face Page

Before covering the parts of the brief, the face page should be discussed. If the brief is to be handed in as a class assignment, there should be included certain information that will identify the student, the class, and the case. The following is an example of the information on a "face page."

All four in upper right hand corner

1. Student's name
2. Class for which the report is made
3. Instructor or professor's name
4. Date that the report was submitted

5. Name of the parties involved in the case (in center of page)
6. The case citation (just below the name of the parties)

3.5:2 Parts of the Case Brief

A case brief normally contains six parts, and can often be reduced to about two or three pages. The parts are as follows:

I. The Title:
The names of those involved in the case*
The case citation
The court that ruled on the case
The date of the decision
*The person appealing the case will be called the "Appellant."

II. The Type of Case:
What charges were brought against the defendant or appellant? Do not put the issues of the case here, only the particular charge or charges.

III. Facts of the Case:
These are the major facts of the case. Do not go into any detail as far as names and places. Briefly tell what happened, but do it in brief by just including the important facts.

IV. Issues:
The issues should not be confused with the facts of the case. What were the legal questions? On what grounds did the case reach the higher court (e.g., Violation of the Fourth Amendment). Many cases are appealed on more than one issue. If there is more than one, they should be listed numerically. Issues should be worded as questions (e.g., "Can an officer take fingernail clippings from an arrested suspect without violating his rights under the Fourth Amendment?"). These will usually be numbered in the case. The issues should contain no details of the particular case such as names and places; just the general legal questions

V. Rules of the Decision:
These are the answers to the legal questions that were listed under the ISSUES heading. This is a general statement as to what the court decided. It should have no reference to names or places, simply the legal answers given by the court in general terms, an indication of how many justices were for or against the decision, and a list of their names if they are listed after the decision. Did they affirm or reverse the decision of the lower court?

VI. Discussion or Explanation:
This can sometimes be given in two parts. Since few cases that are decided by the higher courts are unanimous, there will sometimes be a split decision, and each group will write the reasons for its decisions. These are called the Majority Report and the Minority Report. They will often have the names of the Justices at the end Many times the Minority Report will contain some important points of law that will be valuable later. This is especially true if the make-up of the high

court should change. This is even more important in cases involving a split decision where one vote decides the outcome. Although the high courts do not usually reverse themselves, they are able to do so, and in some cases they have done it.

What were the reasons given by the Justices for their decision? They will usually cite prior case law (Precedence) as a basis for their decisions. Their reasoning is very important in that it can often become the basis for cases of the future. This is why it is so important for you to list them.

3.5:3   Sample Case Briefs

Title:
The People of the State of California, Plaintiff and Appellant
v.
Gary Lee Moss and Dennis Lance Grant, Defendants and Respondents
55 Cal. App. 3d 179
California Court of Appeals, 2d District
February 10, 1976

Type of Case:
Defendants Moss and Grant were arrested for attempted Receiving of Stolen Property.

Facts:
The Ventura County Sheriff's Office received information that Moss was dealing in stolen property. An undercover officer was sent to the defendant with property that he stated was stolen, and the defendant purchased it. After the Preliminary Examination, the defendant asked that the case be dismissed because if the facts in the case were true, it would not be a legal charge of Receiving Stolen Property. The judge of the Superior Court dismissed the case and the prosecution appealed.

Issues:
(1) Does the law require that the property actually be stolen in order to convict for Receiving Stolen Property?
(2) Does the law allow the prosecution to appeal a Superior Court judge's order setting aside an information or criminal charge, following a preliminary examination?
(3) Does the law have to prove that a defendant, in a case of Receiving Stolen Property, had any connection with the thief?

Rules:
Sections 496, 664, 995 and 1238(a) of the Penal Code do not prohibit prosecution when there is a lack of connection between the thief and the receiver of stolen property, or when the items received were not, in fact, stolen. The Court of Appeal reversed the order of the Superior Court Judge, ruling that the defendants should stand trial.

Discussion:
The defense used writings from various criminal law writers from out-of-state to back up their arguments that the information should be dismissed. Justice Files, writing for the Majority Report, stated that out-of-state writings do not have precedence over state decisional law, and that the cases of People v. Rojas, People v. Meyers, People v. Parker, Young v. Superior Court, and Lupo v. Superior Court showed clearly that the evidence presented by the state was sufficient. The lower court erred in its judgment. Justices Kingsley and Jefferson also signed the decision as being in agreement with the legal reasoning of Justice Files.

Title:
The People of the State of California, Plaintiff And Respondent
v.
William Hernandez, Defendant and Appellant
61 Cal. 2d 39
Supreme Court of the State of California
July 9, 1964

Type of Case:
Defendant Hernandez was charged with 261 P.C. Statutory Rape.

Facts:
The appellant, William Hernandez, was observed by a police officer engaged in an act of sexual intercourse in the back seat of his car with a female who later turned out to be 16 years of age.

Issues:
(1) Since intent is required for a criminal act, can "Mistake of Fact" be used as a defense on the grounds that the female in this case looked well over the age of 18, and that the defendant claims to have believed her to be well over that age and legally able to consent to sexual intercourse, when he engaged in an act of sexual intercourse with her.
(2) Must there be criminal intent or criminal negligence in all cases?

Rules:

Since it is legal in California for unmarried persons over the age of 18 to engage in sexual intercourse, the jury should be allowed to view the female to determine whether or not she appears to them to be over the age of 18.

Discussion:

Section 20 of the California Penal Code states that there "Must exist a union or joint operation of act and intent, or criminal negligence."

The major issue involved a lack of criminal intent on the part of the defendant, and his right to have this issue examined during his criminal trial. Although this offense has long been called "Statutory Rape" because the age factor was considered to be a matter of statutory law and not subject to the consideration of criminal intent, the law clearly should allow for such consideration.

The very principle of "Mens Rea," or the guilty mind, is based not on conduct alone, but a mental state that either shows intent or a negligence that shows lack of care.

Since the defendant was not allowed to present proof of his reasonable belief in the age of the female, the court concluded that it was an error of the lower court to reject the offer of such proof, and reversed the judgment of the lower court.

3.6:0   ATTORNEY GENERAL OPINIONS

There are times when local prosecutors and enforcement agencies have a need for good legal opinion regarding some matter that has arisen on an emergency basis. In order to obtain an opinion from the high courts, a person would have to be arrested for a criminal offense and then appeal it to the high court. Then it might take a year or two before it is finally resolved. Obviously, this is not a practical way to resolve an immediate problem.

The way that such problems can be resolved is to appeal to the Attorney General of the state for a legal opinion. The Attorney General's staff includes a battery of legal researchers who can devote considerable time to researching a problem for local prosecutors and, indirectly, local enforcement agencies.

The Attorney General has been designated the chief law officer of the State by section 13 of the California State Constitution, and the Government Code gives him or her "direct supervision over the district attorneys of the various counties," and "over the sheriffs of the several counties of the State." (12550 and 12560 Government Code)

Section 12519 of the Government Code gives the Attorney General the duty to issue legal opinions when requested. The law states:

> The Attorney General shall give his opinion in writing to the Legislature or either house thereof, and to the Governor, the Secretary of State, Controller, Treasurer, State Lands Commission, Superintendent of Public Instruction, any State agency prohibited by law from employing legal counsel other than the Attorney General, and any district attorney when required, upon any question of law relating to their respective offices.

For example, a problem developed involving misuse of the Karate weapon known as the "Nunchaku." In this case, the Attorney General was asked for an opinion regarding whether or not such a weapon could be included under section 12020 of the Dangerous Weapons Control Law. The law lists weapons by name, but does not include the Nunchaku. The Attorney General issued an opinion stating that such a weapon by its very nature fit the legislative intent of the section, and because the training in the use of the Nunchaku involved holding both sticks together and using them as a club, that it would come under the heading of a "billy."

The opinion enabled district attorneys to prosecute violators for mere possession under section 12020. The following year, the legislature resolved the issue by including the term "Nunchaku" in section 12020, but in the meantime the problem was resolved through the issuance of an Attorney General's Opinion. The title of these opinions is Opinions of the Attorney General of California.

3.6:1   Weight and Effect of Attorney General Opinions

In 1866 (before the Penal Code was enacted in 1873), the California Supreme Court stated that, due to the nature of the duties of the Attorney General and their relation to the general government, opinions of the Attorney General are considered quasi-judicial in character, and are entitled to great respect although they are not of controlling authority. (People by McCullough v. Shearer, 30 C.645.)

Later in 1934, the California Appellate Court stated that opinions of the Attorney General are not of the same weight or authority as those of the court; yet, if the Attorney General's opinion coincides with the opinion of the court; the court can properly adopt that opinion. (Hutchins v. County Clerk of Merced County, 140 C.A. 348)

In a more recent decision, the California Appellate Court again upheld the importance of the Attorney General's opinions by stating that the interpretations of the Attorney General pertaining to laws do not have control over the courts, but nevertheless they are accorded substantial weight. (Mountain View Union High School District of Santa Clara County v. City Council of City of Sunnyvale, 168 CA 2d 89).

3.6:2 Types of Opinions

There are two types of opinions issued by the Attorney General:

(1) **Formal:** The formal opinion is issued when the topic involved is of general statewide importance. In this case, the opinions are published in the series of books called "Opinions of the Attorney General of California." The earlier example of the "Nunchaku" problem would be the type of issue that would result in a formal opinion.

(2) **Informal:** The informal opinion deals with problems that are localized to one particular city or area, and not of state-wide importance. In this case, the opinion is sent in letter form to the individual agency requesting it. Although not published in book form, these opinions are available to proper authorities who request them.

Attorney General

DEPARTMENT OF JUSTICE

STUDY QUESTIONS

CHAPTER III

(1) A student who masters the technique of legal research will be able to give legal advice to his or her friends.   T or F

(2) Judicial review means:

    (A) ____the right of the Supreme Court to overrule a law passed by Congress.
    (B) ____the right of the people to overrule new laws.
    (C) ____the obligation of Congress to review each new law.
    (D) ____the right of the President to veto new laws.

(3) The basis for general judicial review can be found in the Constitution.   T or F

(4) The "father of American Constitutional law" was:

    (A) ____Washington.   (B) ____Marshall.
    (C) ____Fletcher.   (D) ____Adams.

(5) The right of the Supreme Court to overrule lower court decisions is clearly set forth in the Constitution.   T or F

(6) The Supreme Court can overrule a decision of a lower court by a simple majority.   T or F

(7) In California, we follow strict precedent like the English do.   T or F

(8) The U.S. Supreme Court is often referred to as the "court of last resort."   T or F

(9) Prior cases reviewed by the higher courts provide us with the only legal interpretation of some of the words used in criminal statutes.   T or F

(10) The high courts always have an odd number of justices.   T or F

(11) The U.S. Supreme Court has how many members?

    (A) ____Seven.   (B) ____Nine.
    (C) ____Eleven.   (D) ____Thirteen.

(12) In a full case citation, the first name listed is the party bringing the case to court.   T or F

(13) In California, if the state takes the case to court, the term "State" would be used at the beginning of the citation. (E.g., State v. Jones)   T or F

(14) The set of books in which high court decisions are reported is called "The Reporter."   T or F

(15) What are the abbreviations for the following courts and reporters?

    (A) U.S. Supreme Court: _____
    (B) Calif. Supreme Court: _____
    (C) Pacific Reporter: _____
    (D) California Reporter: _____
    (E) California District Court Of Appeals: _____

(16) In California, the book that gives us the cross index for different case citations from different reporters is called the "Black and White" book.   T or F

(17) If a case citation refers to the first edition of that reporter, it must be listed in the citation as the first edition.   T or F

(18) In the case citation 21 C.A. 3d 114, the "21" means: _____.

(19) In the case citation 21 C.A. 3d 114, the "C.A." means: _____.

(20) In the case citation 21 C.A. 3d 114, the "3d" means: _____.

(21) In the case citation 21 C.A. 3d 114, the "114" means: _____.

(22) Match the terms used in an Appellate court case with the definitions listed to the right. Place the letter of the definition in front of the term which it most closely matches in the left hand column. (See the case on p. 79)

(1) ____plaintiff	A.	page in the original case reporter.
(2) ____appellant	B.	against.
(3) ____v.	C.	person taking case to court.
(4) ____defendant	D.	person charged in the original trial.
(5) ____respondent	E.	person appealing case to higher court.
(6) ____Anderson PJ	F.	person against whom the appeal is taken.
(7) ____jj concur	G.	name of presiding justice.
(8) ____¡181	H.	the justices who agree with the decision.
(9) ____cases reported	I.	alphabetical list of names listed in cases.
(10) ___Statutes Construed	J.	numerical list of code sections of cases.

(23) In the back of each law book there are paperback updates called:

(A) ____Cumulative Annual Pocket Parts.   (B) ____Legal Updates.

(C) ____Pocket Updates.   (D) ____Paperback Pocket Parts.

(24) The annotated codes give considerably more information about laws than just the legal wording of the law.   T or F

(25) Important case citations pertaining to each particular type of law can be found in an annotated code.   T or F

(26) If a law has been changed, it will be indicated in the paperback update insert located in the back of the code. If wording has been added to the new law, the new words will be underlined.   T or F

(27) Researchers who want to quickly determine if a law has been changed or updated should look in the:

(A) ____Blue and White Book.   (B) ____Shepard's Citations.

(C) ____Blackstone's Commentaries.   (D) ____Wilson's Guide.

(28) In writing a brief, the whole case should be first read before starting to write.   T or F

(29) The "issues" and "facts" of a case brief are really the same.   T or F

(30) If the justices of a high court are divided on how to decide a case, they will write two reports. the report that dissents from the majority viewpoint is called the:

(A) ____dissenting report.   (B) ____mini report.

(C) ____correcting report.   (D) ____writ of dissent.

(31) The Attorney General is the chief law officer of the state according to the California State Constitution.   T or F

(32) The opinions of the Attorney General provide officials with quick legal opinions without having to go through the long process involved in the appellate courts.   T or F

(33) The opinions of the Attorney General are considered quasi-judicial in character or nature.   T or F

(34) There are two types of Attorney General opinions, formal and informal. Informal opinions are sent only to the agency requesting that opinion.   T or F

CHAPTER IV

GENERAL ASPECTS OF CRIMINAL LAW

4.0   **THE ADVERSARY SYSTEM IN AMERICAN LAW**

4.1   **THE PURPOSE OF CRIMINAL LAW**

4.2   **RULES CONTROLLING THE LANGUAGE AND CONSTRUCTION OF PENAL STATUTES**

4.3   **RULES CONTROLLING THE CONVICTION OF CRIMINAL ACTS**

4.4   **LEGAL REQUIREMENTS FOR CITIZEN ACTION WHEN CRIMES OCCUR**

4.5   **THE MEANING OF TERMS USED IN PENAL CODE STATUTES**

CRIMINAL LAW

by PAYTON

4.0:0　THE ADVERSARY SYSTEM IN AMERICAN LAW

The adversary system is an Anglo-American system of law. Basically, it is a contest between two sides. The defendant or accused is on one side, supported by the expertise of an attorney, and the victim (as a person or the state) is supported by the state. The judge is in the middle as an impartial referee.

Our founding fathers were very much aware of how the whole power of the state against one citizen could be an unfair contest, so they purposely established constitutional rules to not only even things up, but to give the defendant an extra edge and weigh things more favorably toward the defense. For example, he or she is allowed:

(1) to have notice of the exact charges against him or her,
(2) to be considered innocent until proven guilty,
(3) to be convicted only on guilt proven "beyond a reasonable doubt," and not just on a preponderance of evidence as in a civil trial,
(4) to be represented by an attorney, even if he or she cannot afford one,
(5) to be released from jail on bail so as to better help prepare a defense,
(6) to be released from jail on a writ of habeas corpus if there is a lack of good evidence,
(7) a public trial, not one in secret,
(8) a fair trial with numerous rules to ensure its fairness,
(9) protection from self-incrimination,
(10) protection from unreasonable searches and seizures,
(11) prohibition of illegally seized evidence being used in court,
(12) a trial before peers,
(13) to be convicted only as a result of a unanimous verdict,
(14) to be tried only once for each offense,
(15) to examine and cross-examine witnesses (through a skilled attorney),
(16) to appeal a conviction, where the state cannot appeal an acquittal.

It is the function of the advocate to persuade the judge whose duty it is to weigh the facts and arguments and then make a decision. The advocate must present an argument in the most favorable light possible, presenting an aspect that best shows his or her client's point of view. There are at least two sides to each situation, and the same situation can appear different to different persons. For example, the optimist sees a bottle that is filled to the half-way mark and says that it is half-full; the pessimist sees the same bottle as half-empty. From one point of view, a person's behavior can be called ingenious and enterprising; from another, the same behavior can be called sneaky and aggressive.

4.0:1　The Function of the Judge in the Adversary System

One purpose of the adversary system is to keep the function of the judge and/or jury separate from that of the advocate. It allows the judge to be objective and as free from bias as is humanly possible. The early constitution of Massachusetts stated: "It is the right of every citizen to be tried by judges as free, impartial and independent as the lot of humanity will admit." This is not the role of one who should take sides.

In order to judge the full value of an argument, it must be presented without the restraints of judicial office. It must be presented by one who has devoted all efforts to investigate and prepare this presentation in the best manner possible.

Some believe that the judge should remain passive in this contest, and only be stirred into action when a point must be resolved. This is not so. The essence of the adversary system is that each side is allowed to participate effectively toward the objective which is the final decision. That participation requires presenting proofs and arguments, which, if they are to be effective or meaningful, must take place within an orderly frame. It is the duty of the judge to prevent the presentation from becoming a disorderly shouting match in which the valid and essential issues are lost from view.

He or she must also prevent an excessively aggressive attorney from "taking over the whole show." Good arguments lose their value when presented to a vacuum. If the judge does not respond, the attorney has no idea of what is going on in the mind of the judge, and cannot alter the presentation to better persuade the judge's thinking in the matter.

In the continental system of law, the state investigates the case and satisfies itself concerning the guilt of the accused before it brings him or her to trial. Because of this, when the trial actually begins, the defendant is presumed to be guilty until proven innocent.

In England, where they use the adversary system, the judge is allowed to "sum up" against the accused by telling the jury why, in his or her opinion, the defendant is guilty.

In the United States, a judge, in a jury trial, cannot comment on "questions of fact," such as the value or weight of evidence or the trustworthiness of witnesses, and may comment only on "questions of law" which deal with the legality of the issues.

The adversary system ensures due process and a fair hearing because the defendant has a "champion" whose expertise will alert him or her to any move by the prosecutor to violate these rights.

4.0:2 The Ethics of Defending Guilty Persons

Although the ethical standards of the legal profession make it proper for lawyers to defend persons they believe are guilty, they do not condone acts which go far beyond that. Examples would be the intentional fabrication of lies for the defendant and witnesses. The use of tactics that are grossly beyond the bounds of professional ethics are also forbidden. However, the reputation of the adversary system has suffered greatly from those attorneys who "pull all the stops" in order to obtain acquittals for their clients. In some cases, it is a matter of the attorney being "carried away" because of personal involvement and the desire to win. In other cases, it is premeditated and coldly calculated, with the intention of winning the case "at all costs." The answer here might be better internal control within the profession through local and state bar associations. It would amount to keeping their own house clean.

Why do attorneys take cases when they believe the defendant is guilty? One reason is that only the trial can bring out all the facts, and in some cases persons admit their guilt to protect others, or are mentally ill and want to punish themselves by being convicted for crimes they did not commit. In some cases, they honestly believe that they did commit a crime when, in truth, they did not. It is not so much these defendants who are on trial, but the whole system of justice. If a person cannot receive a fair trial and a proper defense because everyone feels that he or she is guilty, justice would not prevail. The wrong of a guilty person being acquitted could not outweigh the damage done to the justice system as a whole when even the assumed guilty are not given the same benefits as those whose guilt is uncertain.

4.0:3 Other Systems

In countries that do not have the adversary system, there is the tendency among judges to speed up cases at the expense of justice. A heavy case load will certainly promote this policy. There is also the natural tendency for judges to make up their minds early in the trial, and then view all succeeding evidence with bias. This can be done unconsciously, with no intent to thwart justice. It can be done with the intent to bring the hearing into some order and coherence, and to establish standards on which to base further testimony and evidence. This can easily result in a fixed conclusion. We are all familiar with the old saying, "Don't bother me with facts once I have made up my mind."

According to the American Bar Association, "An adversary presentation seems the only effective means for combating this natural human tendency to judge too swiftly in terms of the familiar, that which is not yet fully known."

4.0:4 The Juvenile Court System

The Juvenile Court is a branch of the County Superior Court. All Juvenile Court judges are Superior Court judges. The accusatory pleading in this court is called a "petition." The petition does not accuse the juvenile of violating a particular criminal code section. Instead, under section 602 W & I, it simply states that the suspect has violated one of the federal, state, or local laws.

If, during the hearing, the juvenile petition is "upheld," (e.g., the evidence shows that the juvenile did violate some law), instead of sentencing him to the California Youth Authority, it is said that the case has been "adjudicated." (A fancy word meaning that if he were an adult, he would have been found guilty and sentenced.)

For years in California, the juvenile court system avoided the adversary type of hearing. The Juvenile Probation officer acted as both defense and prosecutor. Recommendations were made to the judge of the juvenile court that were, hopefully, in the best interest of the juvenile.

Since the 1968 case of In re Gault[1] the high court stated that juveniles were now covered under Miranda, and that they were entitled to an attorney and Fifth Amendment protection against self-incrimination. However, the court felt that juveniles did not have the right to a trial by jury. As a result, the entire philosophy of the juvenile court system in California has been changed, having now become adversarial in nature. The District Attorney now provides a prosecutor and when the juvenile is found guilty, it appears that the punishment is greater than it would be under the old system. The juvenile seems to be the loser.

4.0:5   The Claimed Injustice of Inadequate Counsel for the Poor

It is common today to hear complaints that when poor persons are provided attorneys through the Public Defender's Office, they are getting the least capable type of attorney, and that they suffer an injustice; also, that the rich are not convicted.

There are many misunderstandings here. First, let us make the assumption that the attorneys for the rich are much better than those for the poor. It is certainly an easy assumption to make. In dealing with this question, it would be wise to examine the term "justice." What does it mean? If rich persons are acquitted through the efforts of sharp (and well-paid) attorneys when they are really guilty, is that justice or injustice? If all attorneys' names were put into a hat and you picked one by lottery, and they were all paid the same, do you honestly think that attorneys who had great capabilities would work as hard or put in as much effort as they would if paid what they are worth? Unfortunately, such attorneys can only be hired by those with a lot of money.

The injustice lies not in the fact that poor persons do not have the best attorneys, but in that rich persons can afford attorneys who are too good. All people are not equal. They all have special talents Some better than other people. The talents vary from person to person. Some are more intelligent. Some are better artists. Some are better auto mechanics. There is no way to make all people equal. The Russians tried it,

and those with talent and ability have still worked their way up to the top of the heap.

The fact that a poor person has an attorney who has passed the California Bar examination means that he or she is being represented by a person who is certainly able to see that all rights are protected during the trial.

The poor who obtain the services of a public defender are not getting the "short end of the stick." What few people realize is that under the adversary system, this attorney is competing with an attorney from the District Attorney's Office. In all fairness, both of these attorneys are from the same "cut of cloth."

It is like a football game in which the teams are evenly matched. With the rich person's attorney it is different. It can be like having a high school football player go against one of the Top Ten collegiates. Again, the result is injustice, not justice.

If the Prosecutor and the Public Defender are from the same "cut of cloth," and the laws on prosecution and conviction are purposely stacked against the state, the poor person, even with a Public Defender, is receiving better defense than one would in any other country in the world.

4.0:6   Plea Bargaining

"Plea Bargaining" is a term used in the criminal justice system to define the procedure in which the prosecutor allows the defendant to plead guilty to a lesser offense or degree in return for saving the state the cost and time of a possibly long trial.

Another often-heard complaint regarding "poor man's justice," is that Public Defenders are so busy that, rather than spending time trying the case, they try to get their clients to plead to lesser offenses. Afterwards, these clients tell everyone that they were "sold down the river" by their attorneys.

If there is an injustice to "plea bargaining" it is upon the general public and citizen in the street. It is argued that considerable money is saved the public through "plea bargaining" and that if the practice were halted, it would at least quadruple the cost of prosecution and corrections. This might be true at first, but today we are finding the same persons being arrested time and time again for felonies and then "copping a plea" to a misdemeanor, and in a short time they are back on the street again victimizing the general public. At first, the court load would be tremendous; but in a while it would be less and less because those criminals who are playing a "revolving door" game with the courts would be in prison. In the long run, the time spent on conviction, from an over-all standpoint would be less.

Career Criminal Program

In California we have a system called the "Career Criminal Program." Under this program, if a person is charged with a serious offense and has been convicted of a set number of prior serious offenses, the District Attorney can declare him to be a "Career Criminal." Each county in the state has a number of special prosecutors whose sole duty it is to try "Career Criminals," and their caseloads are lighter to enable them to devote full time to these prosecutions.

Under this program, no plea bargaining is allowed. The defendant is tried for each and every offense he committed. Critics of the effort to eliminate plea bargaining often state that if this practice were eliminated, prosecutors would only convict criminals for a small number of crimes they have committed. To refute this, Career Criminal prosecutors have a conviction rate of over 80%. This shows that convictions can be more readily had than most people believe.

The California Peace Officers' Association and other such organizations have constantly promoted the elimination of plea bargaining unless all the attorneys involved present to the court a very qualified and justified statement as to the reasons for the agreement.

It is a fact that in the State of California today only about two percent of all persons arrested for felonies ever see a state prison. Whatever the cause, something is wrong with our system, and it needs to be examined very closely.

4.1:0   THE PURPOSE OF CRIMINAL LAW

The true purpose of law has seldom been clearly defined or accepted by society. It seems that all writers in criminal law set down their own sets of purposes. In this chapter, nine purposes will be discussed.

When people live together in a society and they work and play together, there is a need for them to know what they can and cannot do in relation to their neighbors.

Because of the need of people to protect themselves from other individuals, societies throughout history have exercised their inherent right to protect both individuals and the society in general.

The ultimate source of our American law is the Constitution. In the Preamble to the United States Constitution, it states the purpose of the Constitution (and, in effect, the law). It sets the purposes as being "...to establish justice, ensure domestic tranquillity...promote the general welfare and secure the blessings of liberty..."

In Sauer v. United States, the Federal Court declared that the purpose of criminal law is to define socially intolerable conduct, and to hold that conduct within reasonable limits from an acceptable social point of view.[2]

Listed Purposes

(1)   Protection of Life and Property

There has always been the need to protect life and property from dangerous individual and collective conduct. In the Code of Hammurabi, one of the stated purposes of the law is to protect the "widow and orphan." The Mosaic code also stated this as a purpose of law. This can be done either through prevention of crime, or through imprisonment of law violators. When a violator is removed from society, society is protected from him.

(2)   Establishment of Peace and Order Through Regulation

In crowded societies there has always been a need for the establishment of peace and order through defining and regulating conduct.

When Solon established his Code, he stated the purpose of the law in the following statement:

> These things my heart prompts me to teach the Athenians, and to make them understand that lawlessness works more harm to the state than any other cause. But a law-abiding spirit creates order and harmony, and at the same time puts chains upon evil-doers; it makes rough things smooth, it checks inordinate desires, it dims the glare of wanton pride and withers the budding bloom of wild delusion; it makes crooked judgments straight and

softens arrogant behavior; it stops acts of sedition and stops the anger of bitter strife. Under the reign of law, sanity and wisdom prevail ever among men.[3]

(3) Resolving Problems in a Fair and Just Manner

Through established legal procedures, a person can resolve everyday problems in a fair and just manner by resorting to the written law which establishes rules that apply to all alike. It is not up to the judge to decide what the law is, and decide differently each time. He or she may interpret the law in difficult cases, but the general law and the way trials are conducted are established as a set rule based on constitutional protection.

(4) Prevention of Crime

The prevention of crime through the self-restraint of the individual citizen, based on fear of punishment, is a purpose of law. When persons believe that there is a good chance they will be caught if they violate the law, this will act as a form of crime prevention, and will usually stop them from violating the law. No purpose is 100% effective. When the English hung pickpockets, there were still pickpockets at work in the crowds that were gathered to witness the hangings. To measure the true degree of effectiveness of a law, we would have to look into the minds of all citizens and determine whether they had thought of committing a crime at one time, but changed their minds because they feared detection and punishment.

(5) To Establish Predictability

In a crowded society, predictability is very important in our everyday behavior. Predictability is based on expected behavior of others. It occurs when one person assumes that others will obey the law. Today, we drive through a green light at a fairly high speed based on the belief that automobiles approaching from either side of the intersection will stop for the red light. At times it is a foolish assumption. Yet, in a great majority of the time, the other persons do obey the law and stop for the red light. This enables society to function better because persons can predict the actions of their fellow citizens with a fair certainty.

This applied even in early history when rules were established for ships when they approached each other, either in crowded channels, or on the high seas. The captain of one ship would steer his ship based on the belief that the other ship would follow the regulations and a collision would be avoided.

(6) Preserving Morals and Social Behavior

Although this has been long established as a valid purpose of the law, today it is being questioned with greater frequency. The protest is based on the belief that it is not the place of the state to regulate morals. This involves the free will of the individual and moral behavior is for that person alone to decide. Others feel that individual moral decay results in the decay of the whole society. They can cite many examples throughout history. They, therefore, feel that the state must, for its own preservation, legislate morals for its people. There is no doubt that this is an area where the law often gets into trouble today. If a law exists that is not obeyed, and is not enforced, it can affect the whole area of obedience to the law.

It is noteworthy that in atheistic, totalitarian countries, morals are strictly enforced. It is not because the government is necessarily moral, but because leaders know that people who obey moral laws are more inclined to obey other laws, and this is an objective that they seek. In more democratic countries where there is more personal freedom, it is difficult to enforce moral laws.

(7) Preservation of Freedom and Liberty

In countries which have a constitution based on basic human rights and a legal system of due process, the law has a very valid purpose. It is the preservation of freedom and liberty. In the United States v. Watson, the U.S. District Court stated that the object of American criminal law is not only to protect the public from criminals, but "also to prevent the conviction of the innocent, or the conviction of a person whose guilt is not established beyond a reasonable doubt."[4]

John Locke, the philosopher whose thought greatly influenced the patriots of the American Revolution, wrote that "the end of law is not to abolish or to restrain, but to preserve and enlarge freedom: for in all the states of created beings capable of laws, where there is no law, there is not freedom."[5]

In the last twenty years there has been a criminal law revolution in the United States, and it has been based on the interpretation of amendments to the Constitution. Some have called it a civil rights revolution, but it amounts to the preservation of freedom and liberty through the law.

(8) Punishment or Vengeance

Although punishment is more the result of law rather than a purpose of law, it is mentioned in many writings as a purpose. Probably what the law does is prevent vengeance. In ancient times, both the Babylonians and the Israelites left the punishment for murder up to the families of the victims. As a result, the practice of the "vendetta" became a law unto itself. Once a vendetta starts, very little justice results. Modern law takes punishment out of the hands of the victim and lets the state administer it in a more just and fair manner.

Sir James Stephen, the famous British author on criminal law, felt that the law has the same relationship to revenge that sex has to marriage. Both control a deep impulse of human nature that, if not given legitimate expression, is bound to find disruptive outlets.[6]

(9) Prevention of Anarchy or Illegal Interference with Government

Although sometimes looked upon as a means of keeping the status quo, or protecting the existing government, without law, this could easily happen in two ways. First, without law the government could not protect itself. Second, without law, the government, in an effort to protect itself, could create a totalitarian state that would in effect mean the end of the existing democratic form of government. There are many examples in the past of our

government taking harsh measures to protect itself against the so-called "Communist threat," but the courts have interfered on the grounds that such measures were illegal and unconstitutional. Some criticize the courts on the basis that they are protecting avowed enemies of our country. The courts reply that, without law, the government could well become the enemy,

4.2:0 RULES CONTROLLING THE LANGUAGE AND CONSTRUCTION OF PENAL STATUTES

(1) All California Law Is Statutory

This means that all the laws in California have been proposed by an elected representative of the people. They have then been voted on and passed by a body of persons elected by the people, and then printed in a book of law as statutes. There is no common law in California. All law here is statutory. If it is not written in a book of law, there can be no violation of the law. Many times we are confused by what we might feel is wrong, and by what is actually listed in the statutes of the state as a criminal act. For example, moral law states that sex outside of marriage is wrong. Many states have statutes against fornication. Fornication is sexual intercourse between two unmarried persons over the age of eighteen. In California, there is no law or statute against fornication. Therefore, if a police officer were to catch two 18-year-old people engaged in an act of sexual intercourse in the back seat of a parked car, legally nothing could be done. The officer might feel that it is wrong, but California law is wholly statutory. If it is not on the books, there is no violation.

(2) The Statute Must Be in English

Section 24 of Article IV of the Constitution states that all official writings and judicial proceedings shall be conducted in the English language. Exceptions would be "terms" in another language like Latin or Spanish that are understood and accepted.

(3) No Statute Will Be Too Vague, Broad, or Uncertain

Laws that are vague or uncertain in their wording have long been illegal under statutory law. If it is difficult to determine exactly what act is meant by the law, or if a great number of actions could fit under the description, then either the whole statute or the part that is vague can be declared unconstitutional under the Due Process clause of the Fifth Amendment.

An example would be part of the old 650½ PC. It states that it is illegal to "openly outrage public decency." The California Supreme Court ruled that this section was too vague and broad and, therefore, unconstitutional. It is like saying that a person is bad. What does that mean? Does it mean that he murders people, or that he picks his nose? Some people would call both acts bad, but there is quite a difference in the two.

(4) Statutes Denouncing a Series of Acts

Many times a statute will list a number of verbs describing various actions in an effort to close possible loopholes and to further illustrate the general intent of the law. For example, the law against the illegal dumping of garbage states: "No one shall leave, drop, throw, bury, or burn any rubbish, trash, or garbage on any public or private property." If a person was observed throwing trash on public property, and then burying some trash on that same property, and then burning some garbage on that property, that person would not be guilty of three criminal offenses, but of just the one offense of illegally dumping garbage on public property. The object of listing a series of acts is for the purpose of illustration and clarification, not the listing of different offenses.

(5) Resolving Conflicts Between Statutes

There are two areas in which we find problems dealing with a conflict between statutes. The first deals with pre-emption, which is covered in Article 6 of the United States Constitution. This deals with which level of government has the highest priority in the making of law. As covered in Chapter II, the order is as follows:
(1) United States Constitution
(2) Federal Law (passed by Congress)
(3) State Constitutions
(4) State Law
    (passed by the state legislature)
(5) Local Law
    (passed by city councils, county Boards of Supervisors, and town councils)

(A) Conflict between Different Levels of Government

Pre-emption

As can be seen by the list above, the order for pre-emption is firmly established as far as the order of precedence. The real problem for local law-making bodies is to determine exactly what areas of law have been pre-empted by the higher jurisdictions.

Whenever the higher jurisdiction has passed a particular "body of law" and has given it a special name such as the "Alcoholic Beverage Control Law," it is safe to assume that a lower jurisdiction cannot pass contradictory laws in that particular area. Other examples of special acts or bodies of law are:
(1) Dangerous Weapons Control Law
(2) Invasion of Privacy Laws
(3) Uniform Controlled Substances Act
    (narcotics)
(4) Juvenile Control Act
(5) ABC Laws (Liquor Laws)

Sometimes there is a question whether a particular law really falls under one of the established special bodies of law. In the final outcome, only the high courts can resolve the problem.

Sometimes, the high courts have declared certain laws to have been pre-empted by the state when there were really no practical guidelines for local jurisdictions to use in determining pre-emption status. For example, section 647f of the Penal Code states that it is illegal to be under the influence of alcohol when in public. It is part of the Disorderly Conduct law, but does not have the earmarks of an area of pre-emption.

One town in California was having a problem with intoxicated husbands beating up their wives. To prevent this from happening, the town council passed a local ordinance making it illegal to be drunk in your own home. It was a very effective law because it allowed the police to arrest a known "wife beater" for being intoxicated before he started punching his wife. However, the California Supreme Court declared the law invalid on the grounds that the state had pre-empted the area of illegal intoxication, and a lower jurisdiction could not pass an ordinance that differed or contradicted the original law.

In another case, a large California city was having serious financial problems and decided to pass an ordinance that placed a five cent tax on each mixed drink that was sold. After a year, the California Supreme Court declared the ordinance illegal on the grounds of pre-emption. They felt that the state had pre-empted the control of alcoholic beverages and that a local jurisdiction could not pass laws in that area. They ordered the city to pay back the tax to those persons who could prove that they had paid it.

Another large city in California was having a problem with prostitution, and felt that it would be easier to obtain convictions and control the problem with an ordinance that outlawed fornication (a sex act between an adult male and female who are not married to each other). The California Supreme Court declared this ordinance to be illegal on the grounds of pre-emption. The state of California does not have a law on fornication, and it has no major set of laws with a title indicating the area of sex laws. However, the high court stated that there are so many laws dealing with sex in the Penal Code that it, in effect, gives the state pre-emption in the area of sex laws. Since California law is statutory (an act is not illegal unless it is written in a law book) and there is no law against fornication, it is legal. Any law or ordinance that makes it illegal goes against the pre-emption of the state.

If a local ordinance is just on the same general subject matter, and not in conflict with the state law, the local ordinance does not violate the rule of pre-emption. This is further backed up by In re Iverson.[7]

(B) Conflict Between Laws on the Same Level of Government

There are some cases where a new law is passed on the state level, and the new law is in conflict with an existing law. This does not happen if the legislature has properly done its "homework." When proposing a new law, legislators, as human beings, do occasionally slip up. In cases of this matter, the following rules apply:

Where two laws punish exactly the same act, they are in conflict, and the last one passed into law is the one to be accepted. If, however, there are parts of the earlier law that are not in conflict with the later law, they will remain in effect.

The way that new laws are written is important. Many will state that they repeal any older laws on the same subject. If the new law does not have a repealing clause, the two laws must be clearly inconsistent or conflicting in order for the latter to overrule the former.[8]

Because the law does not favor repeal by implication when there is no repealing clause, the two laws must be irreconcilably inconsistent in order for the latter to repeal the former.

(6) When a New Law Is Found to Be in Part Unconstitutional

There are times when the high courts will declare a part of a particular law to be unconstitutional. This does not necessarily make the whole law unconstitutional. Many laws or sections of law include a special clause. An example is 12003 PC:

> If any section, subsection, sentence, clause or phrase of this chapter is for any

reason held to be unconstitutional, such decision shall not affect the validity of the remaining portions of this chapter.

4.2:1   Rules Controlling When Laws Are Considered To Be In Effect

(A) Ex Post Facto Laws

Ex Post Facto is a Latin term that means "after the fact." It covers laws that are changed after the act is committed. Both the Federal and State constitutions prohibit Ex Post Facto Laws.[9]

Although most authors cite three examples of Ex Post Facto laws, from a technical standpoint, there are four. They can be simplified into one classification by using the words of a Federal Court of Appeal when it stated that an Ex Post Facto law was one which by legislation "alters the situation of the accused to his disadvantage."

The four classifications are:

(1) When the legislature makes an act criminal that was not criminal when the accused committed it

Arvin Ardvark has the offensive habit of picking his nose in public. His fellow citizens are so disturbed by this act that they have their legislative representative propose a new law forbidding such an act. Once the law is passed, Arvin could not be arrested for those acts committed before the law went into effect. If he continued the practice, he could be prosecuted only for those acts committed after the law was in effect.

(2) When the law has been increased in punishment

The California legislature passed a new law that increased the severity and punishment of battery when it caused more serious harm to the victim. Harry Hardrock beat up Mervin Mushmuscle with his fists, and it was severe enough to put Mervin in the hospital. He had to have a considerable number of stitches taken. Harry could be charged with a felony, and could receive considerably more punishment than he would for "simple battery." Suppose the attack took place almost a year before, and the new law was not in effect. If Harry could not be found until after the law was passed, he could only be charged with "simple battery," and given misdemeanor punishment.

(3) When the law has been increased from a misdemeanor to a felony

As will be covered in the next chapter, a felony not only results in greater punishment, but it changes the amount of force that an officer can use in making an arrest, and it also increases the amount of time before a criminal complaint has to be filed after the crime was committed, along with other considerations.

Fred Farkle commits a crime that is classed as a misdemeanor (a minor crime). After he commits the crime the legislature changes the offense to a felony (a serious crime). This means the prosecutor has three years in which to file a criminal complaint as opposed to one year for the misdemeanor.

Let us suppose that for one reason or another, probably based on the discovery of new evidence that will increase the possibility of a conviction, the District Attorney issues a criminal complaint against Fred. However, it is now thirteen months since Fred committed the crime. The complaint will have to be dismissed under the Ex Post Facto rule because the crime cannot be treated as a felony. Its felony status occurred only after the crime was committed.

(4) When a new law changes the existing rules for conviction to make it easier to convict the defendant

The United States Constitution does not state the number of persons required for a jury, nor does it state that the agreement of the members of a jury must be unanimous. This is left up to the states. Let us assume that a very conservative legislature is elected in California, and that they want to reduce the size of juries to ten persons and allow criminal convictions based on the verdict of nine out of the ten jurors.

While the legislators are processing this new legislation, Clyde Crashcup shoots his wife. While he is in jail awaiting trial, the new regulations for conviction pass the legislature and are signed into law by the Governor. Clyde cannot be tried under the new rules. He must be tried by the rules that existed when he committed the crime. Another example would be the reducing of burden of proof on the part of the state.

(B) Repeal of Existing Laws (The reverse of Ex Post Facto)

California is different on this rule than many other states. In California, the key is simply what was the law at the time the crime was committed? (Government Code 9608)

For example, Darrel Doper is arrested for possession and use of a small amount of marijuana. On the next day the law is repealed. From a legal standpoint, Darrel is still liable for prosecution. This is because the violation was illegal when it was committed, and in California that is the determining rule.

From a practical standpoint, it is doubtful that the District Attorney would prosecute a case like this. A jury might be reluctant to convict a person for an offense that is no longer illegal, despite the fact that they may legally do so.

(C) Bills of Attainder

A Bill of Attainder is passed by the legislature and pronounces a person guilty of a criminal offense without a trial and proper sentencing. This is also mentioned in the Constitution along with Ex Post Facto laws. Although such bills were used in early history, examples are quite rare now.

4.2:2 Interpretation of How the Law Is Written

(A) The Letter of the Law (WHAT the Law says)

As previously stated, all California law is statutory. In order to obtain a conviction in court, the officers must show that the defendant violated the Letter of the Law. This means the exact way in which the law was written. It is also described as WHAT the law actually says. Therefore, the exact wording in the statute itself is quite important.

Officers will find themselves in serious trouble if they arrest someone for an act which they "think" is in violation of the law, when the act that is mentioned in the statute is slightly different. Officers cannot tell the judge, "Well, it was close." They must know the exact wording of the law or the Letter of the Law. Later, this topic will be covered under the heading of Corpus Delicti.

(B) The Spirit of the Law (WHY the Law was written)

The Spirit of the Law is also called "legislative intent." This simply means WHY the law was written. This is most important when enforcing the law. Every California peace officer should be very familiar with the Spirit of the Law when dealing with the public.

Penal Code Section 4 states:

> The rule of common law that penal statutes are to be strictly construed, has no application to this code. All its provisions are to be construed according to a fair import of their terms, with a view to effect its objects and to promote justice.

The wording in this section is a little difficult. It simply means that, in California, law should be enforced according to the original intent of the law.

To illustrate, Section 12420 of the Penal Code states that it is illegal for anyone other than a peace officer, reserve, or special authorized private patrol officer to possess tear gas. Yet, Police Science Instructors in many colleges throughout the state are required to teach in-service police courses to police officers on the use of tear gas. They both purchase and possess tear gas in violation of the Letter of the Law.

The question here is, do they violate the Spirit of the Law? The answer is obviously, no. When the legislators wrote the law, they did not anticipate all the situations that would arise where someone other than a peace officer would need to possess tear gas. If a police officer were to arrest a Police Science Instructor for the possession of tear gas at a college training course, he or she would be following the Letter of the Law, but not the Spirit of the Law. The District Attorney would never issue a complaint in a case of this type. In fact, the officer would probably be "chewed out" by the sergeant for not using some common sense. The key to applying the Spirit of the Law could be the two words, "common sense."

Now, let us change the situation a little. Suppose the Police Science Instructor was drunk in a bar downtown, started an argument with the bartender and then squirted him in the face with a Mace container. Would this possession of tear gas be in violation of the Spirit of the Law? Of course. An arrest should be made for this offense.

Another example would be a case of the traffic signals at an intersection jamming with the red facing all four directions. The letter of the law states that drivers will not proceed until the light turns green (a right turn being an exception). When the cars start to back up for blocks, what do the drivers do? When it becomes obvious to everyone that the signals facing in all directions are stuck on red, the only solution is to apply the spirit of the law and treat the signal as if it were flashing red, or a four-way stop sign. The drivers would then violate the letter of the law and proceed through the red light at intervals.

(C) Corpus Delicti

Corpus delicti is a Latin term that means "body of the crime." This can be confusing if you take the term literally. It really means the "parts of the crime." A term that is used more often is the "elements of the crime."

Just as a human body has many parts, so does the legal description of a crime have many parts. Each crime is made up of at least two elements or parts. These parts are very important because each one must be proved in court in order to obtain a conviction. It is like a three-legged

milking stool—if one of the legs is missing, and you try to sit on it, you will fall on your posterior. If one of the elements of a crime is missing, the same thing will happen to you in court.

The law requires that the prosecution establish the corpus delicti of a crime being charged. Failure to prove or establish any part of the corpus delicti is a bar to further prosecution—in other words, no conviction. Some people describe corpus delicti as the facts that prove that the crime was committed.

Since the first officers responding to a call are in the best position to gather evidence, they MUST KNOW THE ELEMENTS OF THAT CRIME so that they can gather evidence or obtain statements that can later be used in court to prove the elements.

Since all law in California is statutory, all the necessary elements of a crime needed to prove that the law was violated will be in the code. A sharp police officer will always carry a Penal Code in his or her patrol car. Failure to consider one element of a crime can result in a false arrest or the case being lost in court. For example, let us consider the offense of carrying a concealed revolver on one's person. There are four elements:

(1) The weapon is designed to be used as a gun;
(2) It fires a projectile by force of an explosion;
(3) The barrel length must be less than 16 inches;
(4) The gun must be carried concealed.

If Officer Jones stops Percy Puke under suspicious circumstances and has reason to believe he might be armed and dangerous, he may "pat down" the suspect in an effort to locate weapons. If he finds that Percy is carrying a concealed (but unloaded) 38 caliber Colt revolver, and it has a special barrel that is 16½ inches long, he'd better not arrest him for Section 12025 of the Penal Code (Carrying a Concealed Weapon) because one of the elements is that the barrel length must be under sixteen inches. The third element of that crime is missing. Any arrest for that section would be a false arrest.

Breaking Down a Crime By Its Elements

The elements for each crime are found in the Penal Code. It is sometimes difficult to separate them because they are usually lumped together in a sentence or two, and some of them are subtle. There are law books available that give a breakdown of criminal elements in a 1–2–3 fashion.

In this book, most of the crimes mentioned will be broken down into their elements. Still, it is a good idea to learn how to do it yourself. The key to separating the elements in a crime is to determine which parts would have to be proved in a separate manner. The thing that will help is to look for the small, but important, words "and" and "or." Sometimes they are implied. You can tell this by reading the section. "And" means that there is a separate section following; "or" means that there is an optional section following. Read the following section from the Penal Code and try to break it down without looking at the explanation following it.

289 PC
Sexual Penetration by a Foreign Object

Every person who causes the penetration, however slight, of the genital or anal openings of another person, by any foreign object, substance, instrument, or device, when the act is accomplished against the victim's will, by means of force, violence, duress, menace, or fear of immediate and unlawful bodily injury on the victim or another person, for the purpose of sexual arousal, gratification, or abuse. "Foreign object" shall include any part of the body, except a sexual organ.

Elements of the Crime Broken Down
(1) Penetration, however slight,
(2) Of the
    (a) Genital opening of another person, or
    (b) Anal opening of another person,
(3) With any object
    (that is not the perpetrator's penis),
(4) By means of:
    (a) Force, or
    (b) Violence, or
    (c) Duress, or
    (d) Menace, or
    (e) Fear of bodily injury
(5) That is immediate
(6) And unlawful
(7) Against either
    (a) the victim, or
    (b) another person
(8) When it is against the victim's will
(9) For the purpose of either
    (a) Sexual arousal, or
    (b) Sexual gratification, or
    (c) Abuse

How Are the Elements of the Corpus Delicti Proved?

The elements can be proved by circumstantial evidence. Circumstantial evidence is evidence that tends to prove. It does not have to be proof that is absolutely conclusive. It can be proved through photographs.

It can also be proved by any one of the five senses, NOT just the sense of sight. Thieves have been convicted in court on the testimony of blind persons. In one California case, the blind person was able to positively identify the suspect by his footsteps. Several experiments were conducted in court where the suspect came into the courtroom with other persons, and each time he was in a different position with the group. Each time, the blind witness was able to pick him out of the group just by the sound of his footsteps.

Five Senses Used In Court

Proof of the corpus delicti only has to be "beyond a reasonable doubt." Many times it appears that the case was lost because the defense was able to find a good loophole. When this happens, it is the fault of the prosecution. They were not able to prove the elements of the corpus delicti.

Corpus delicti is very important to the police officer in knowing exactly what charge to use in "booking" the suspect. If he is "booked" for an offense for which the elements cannot all be proved, the officer is at fault.

For example, in a case of "purse snatch," the crime can be either robbery or grand theft. To be robbery, there must be some force or fear. The force must be more force than is needed just to carry off the goods. If the suspect approached the victim so quietly that she didn't see or hear him, and if he grabbed the purse off her arm before she had the chance to resist, hold on to the purse, or give it up voluntarily because of fear, it would be grand theft (theft from the person of another). Knowing the elements of the corpus delicti can be very important.

Confessions and Admissions

The difference between a confession and an admission is that a confession is an admission of guilt, whereas an admission is simply an admission to a particular fact. For example, if a person admitted that he murdered his ex-wife, that would be a confession. If he admitted that he was at her apartment on the night that she was killed, that would be an admission.

Confessions and admissions cannot be used by themselves to prove the elements of the corpus delicti. The elements must be proved FIRST. Once the elements of the crime are proved, then the confession or admission can be accepted,

The reason for this is that many emotionally disturbed persons come to the police department and confess to crimes they did not actually commit. Sometimes the crimes are real, sometimes they are not. It would be a miscarriage of justice to convict such persons when the only proof that a crime existed is their confession. We must be able to prove in court that a crime was actually committed.

Prima Facie proof is all that is needed to make a confession admissible. Prima facie is a Latin term meaning on "first face." It means the way that things would be judged on first appearance, or on first examination.

An officer hears a woman scream and then hears a shot. He runs up an alleyway and finds a woman lying dead. A man is standing next to her with a gun in his hand. It would be natural for the officer to assume, on prima facie evidence, that the man was the one who shot her. In reality, the man might have heard the woman scream and ran out to find her lying in the alleyway, and then picked up the gun next to her without thinking. Police officers do not have a crystal ball. Therefore, they must go on prima facie evidence until such time as other evidence changes the situation.

4.3:0   RULES CONTROLLING THE CONVICTION OF CRIMINAL ACTS

(1) Burden of Proof

In the United States, all persons are assumed innocent until proven guilty. In many countries, the opposite is true. The burden of proving guilt initially lies with the state. The prosecution must prove two major things: first, it must prove that a crime was in fact committed; then, it must prove that the defendant was the one who committed it. (1096 PC)

Insanity

If the defendant admits the act, then uses insanity as mitigation for sentencing, the defense must assume the burden of proof for it. The defense must prove that the defendant was insane. The state does not have to prove the defendant's sanity.

The state always has the burden of proof to show that each element of the crime was committed, and that the defendant committed it.

If the jury in this case was undecided whether the defendant was insane, they must assume that he or she was sane. This is because defendants have the burden of proving to the jury by a preponderance of evidence that they were insane at the time of the act.

Article 28 of the English Common law states: "Every person is presumed to be sane and responsible for his acts." Burden of proof also shifts to the defendant when the crime charged is a "presumptive" crime. The state must still prove the elements of the crime itself, but the defendant must prove the presumption.

Preponderance of Evidence

A preponderance of evidence has less weight than evidence that is beyond a reasonable doubt. A preponderance of evidence is just enough evidence to slightly tip the scale in one direction or another.

(2) Presumptions of Guilt

There are certain statutes in the Penal Code that include presumptions of guilt. In cases of this type, the burden of proof is on the defendant to counter the presumption.

For example, 12091 of the Penal Code states that if a person has in his possession a gun with the serial number removed, it is presumed that he was the one who removed it. In court he carries the burden of proof to show that he did not remove the serial number. (The presumption can be rebutted, however.)

Section 484 of the Penal Code states that employers owing wages to any employees must tell this to any new employee they hire. If they fail to do this, and then do not pay the new employee, the code presumes the employer had the intent to defraud. Because it is actually written in the law, the burden of proof is on employers to show that they had no intent to defraud. The presumption must be written in the statutory law.

(3) Reasonable Doubt (1096 PC)

The prosecution must not only convince the jury of the defendant's guilt, but must do so beyond a reasonable doubt. Reasonable doubt does not require absolute proof. It is not proof to a mathematical certainty. It is simply a reasonable and honest doubt in the mind of an unbiased, average person. After the evidence is considered and compared, the minds of the jurors are such that they cannot say they feel an abiding conviction of the truth of the charge. Conclusive proof is not required. Reasonable doubt must be based on some evidence. It is a doubt for which some reason can be given, arising from the evidence presented. Reasonable doubt does not mean a mere possible or speculative doubt.

(4) Questions of Fact and Questions of Law

In a trial there are two types of questions:
(1) Questions of fact . . . . . . Who did what?
(2) Questions of law . . . . . What is the law?

Generally speaking, a jury is concerned only with questions of fact. The judge deals with questions of law. However, there are two types of trials:

(1) **Jury trials** The jury hears the evidence and decides guilt with a judge assisting them with legal points.
(2) **Court trials** A trial before a judge only. In this type of trial, the judge decides questions of fact and questions of law.

If the jury believes that the defendant killed his wife, that is a Question of Fact. If they believe that he killed her by the use of poison, that is a Question of Fact. You might say that a Question of Fact is a question that asks: "Did a particular act really occur?"

The judge can then rule that the law is clear that all murders by poison are murders of the first degree. That is a Question of Law. Only the judge is qualified to pass on Questions of Law. Once the judge has established this Question of Law, the jury can only find the defendant guilty of first degree murder if they accept that the murder was committed by means of poison.

(5) Convictions Can Only Result From Unanimous Verdicts

All members of the jury must vote for conviction, or there can be no conviction. If one member of the jury votes for acquittal, and won't change his or her mind, it becomes a "hung jury," and the trial is ended. However, the defendant may be tried repeatedly if each trial results in a "hung jury." A "hung jury" is not an acquittal. In most cases, however, it amounts to the same thing. This is because a trial is very expensive. The District Attorney must watch that the public's money is not wasted on a trial in which a conviction cannot be obtained. If it is a very important case, the D.A. will try it several times, especially if mistakes were made in the earlier trials and there is a good chance of obtaining a conviction in the next trial.

(6) All Crimes Are Crimes Against the State

A fundamental principle in criminal law is that a criminal action is prosecuted by the People. It is not prosecuted by the injured party as would be the case in civil law.

This is a greatly misunderstood concept. Many times a victim of a crime will call the police or the District Attorney and tell them that he or she has decided not to prosecute. In most cases, the District Attorney will drop the case because there is a very heavy backlog of cases Another reason is that the victim is usually the main witness for the prosecution, and if the victim is not willing to go to court, the case will not be very strong. Because of this, many citizens have come to believe that the power of prosecution rests with the victim. This is simply not so.

Let us take the case of a woman who calls the police department every Saturday night to have her husband arrested for intoxication and battery. Monday morning she always drops the charges. After a while, the police get tired of being used as temporary bouncers and would·like the wife to take some positive action to stop these occurrences. They go to the District Attorney, report the circumstances and ask for a prosecution. The District Attorney may decide to take some action to stop the woman from playing games with the administration of justice by issuing a criminal complaint against the husband, and obtaining a subpoena (a court order to appear) for the wife. At the trial, the wife is cross-examined under oath, and the officers who responded to the calls testify under oath. What can the judge do if the evidence is obvious? He or she must find the defendant guilty. This can occur even when the victim wants the charges dropped. A wife can be asked to testify against her husband when the crime is one against her, her property, or her children.

4.4:0 LEGAL REQUIREMENTS FOR CITIZEN ACTION WHEN CRIMES OCCUR

The state encourages its citizens to take positive action to prevent criminal acts. This is obvious by the passing of Good Samaritan laws which provide citizens with monetary compensation for any injuries or loss suffered while assisting in enforcing the law. The law of Posse Comitatus and the California Labor Code also provide a citizen with Workman's Compensation for any injuries occurred while assisting a full-time peace officer. However, only full-time, sworn peace officers have the legal obligation to prevent criminal acts which they observe. There are certain occupational responsibilities that involve special jobs such as guards and watchmen, but that will be covered under negligence in a later chapter.

If a person just stands by and watches a crime take place, and makes no effort to apprehend the criminal, or even stop the crime, he is not liable unless he in some way assists the criminal.

In the People v. Weber, the Appellate Court stated that if a person has knowledge of a crime, or a belief that a crime is being committed, or even likely to be committed, and he in no way aids and abets that crime, he is not legally responsible and cannot be prosecuted for his failure to act.[10]

The fact that a person was at a crime scene, and did not take steps to prevent the crime, does not make him in any way legally responsible.

Exception (Misprision of Treason)

Section 38 PC states that it is a felony to have knowledge of treason and to conceal that knowledge. Since treason is nearly always handled on a federal level, the section is not of great practical importance.

Posse Comitatus

Posse Comitatus is a very old concept that means the power of the state to summon assistance in order to carry out the law. This term is the origin of the word "Posse" that is used so often in Western movies.

In California, Penal Code section 150 makes it a misdemeanor not to assist a peace officer when he requests such assistance in order to carry out some emergency duty. However, it applies only to able-bodied persons over the age of eighteen. This law still does not alter the rule that a citizen, on his or her own, does not have to take any action to prevent a crime being committed.

4.5:0 THE MEANING OF TERMS USED IN PENAL CODE STATUTES (7 PC)

General Terminology

(1) **Tense:** The present tense includes the future as well as the present;

(2) **Gender:** Words used in the masculine gender include the feminine and neuter genders;

(3) **Number:** The singular number includes the plural, and the plural the singular;

(4) **Person:** The word "person" includes a corporation as well as a natural person;

(5) **County:** The word "county" includes "city and county";

(6) **Writing:** The word "writing" includes printing and typewriting;

(7) **Oath:** The word "oath" includes affirmation or declaration;

(8) **Testify:** Every mode of oral statement, under oath or affirmation, is embraced by the term "testify";

(9) **Deposition:** Every written statement, under oath or affirmation, is embraced by the term "depose";

(10) **Mark:** Signature or subscription includes mark, when the person cannot write, his name being written near it, by a person who writes his own name as a witness; provided that when a signature is made by mark it must, in order that the same may be acknowledged or serve as the signature to any sworn statement, be witnessed by two persons who must subscribe their own names as witnesses thereto.

The following words have in this code the signification attached to them in this section, unless otherwise apparent from the context:

(11) **Willful:** When applied to the intent with which an act is done or omitted, implies simply a purpose or willingness to commit the act, or make the omission referred to. It does not require any intent to violate law, or to injure another, or to acquire any advantage;

(12) **Neglect:** Implies a want of such attention to the nature (Negligence) or probable consequences of the act or omission (Negligent) as a prudent man ordinarily bestows in acting (Negligently) in his own concerns;

(13) **Corruptly:** Indicates a wrongful design to acquire or cause some pecuniary or other advantage to the person guilty of the act or omission referred to, or to some other person;

(14) **Malice:** Implies a wish to vex, annoy, or injure another (Maliciously) person, or an intent to do a wrongful act, established either by proof or presumption of law;

(15) **Knowingly:** Implies only a knowledge that the facts exist which bring the act or omission within the provisions of this code. It does not require any knowledge of the unlawfulness of such act or omission;

(16) **Bribe:** Signifies anything of value or advantage, present or prospective, or any promise or undertaking to give any, asked, given, or accepted, with a corrupt intent to influence, unlawfully, the person to whom it is given, in his action, vote, or opinion, in any public or official capacity;

(17) **Vessel:** When used with reference to shipping, includes ships of all kinds, steamboats, canal boats, barges, and every structure adapted to be navigated from place to place for the transportation of merchandise or persons;

(18) **Peace Officer:** Signifies any one of the officers mentioned in Chapter 4.5 (commencing with Section 830) of Title 3 of Part 2;

(19) **Magistrate:** A judge. Signifies any one of those judicial officers mentioned in Section 808 PC;

(20) **Property:** Includes both real and personal property;

(21) **Real Property:** Is coextensive with lands, tenements, and hereditaments;

(22) **Personal Property:** Includes money goods, chattels, things in action, and evidences of debt;

(23) **Month:** Means a calendar month, unless otherwise expressed;

(24) **Daytime:** Means the period between sunrise and sunset;

(25) **Nighttime:** Means the period between sunset and sunrise;

(26) **Will:** Includes codicil (addition to a will);

(27) **Writ:** Signifies an order or precept in writing, issued in the name of the people, or of a court or judicial officer;

(28) **Process:** A writ or summons issued in the course of judicial proceedings;

(29) **State:** When applied to the different parts of the United States, includes the District of Columbia and the territories, and the words "United States" may include the district and territories;

(30) **Section:** Refers to the Penal Code, unless some other code or statute is expressly mentioned;

(31) **Book:** Signifies the recording of an arrest in official police records, and the taking by the police of fingerprints and photographs of the person arrested, or any of these acts following an arrest;

(32) Words and phrases must be interpreted according to the context and the approved usage of the language; but technical words and phrases, and such others as may have acquired a peculiar and appropriate meaning in law, must be interpreted according to those peculiar and appropriate meanings;

(33) Words giving a joint authority to three or more public officers or other persons, are construed as giving such authority to a majority of them, unless it is otherwise expressed in the act giving the authority;

(34) When the seal of a court or public officer is required by law to be affixed to any paper, the word "seal" includes an impression of that seal upon the paper alone, or upon any substance attached to the paper capable of receiving a visible impression. The seal of a private person may be made in like manner, or by the scroll of a pen, or by writing the word "seal" next to name.

Other Common Terms Used in the Penal Statutes (not listed in 7 PC)

(1) **Crimen Falsi:** A class of crime that involves falsification such as forgery, perjury, false declarations, counterfeiting, making false keys or using false weights and measures.

(2) **Feloniously:** With deliberate evil intent. Maliciously or malignantly.

(3) **Infamous Crime:** Today it means a crime that is a felony. In common law it included only certain felonies and some crimes that today would be misdemeanors and in some instances civil crimes in falsification. Anyone under common law who was convicted of an infamous crime could not be a competent witness.

(4) **Moral Turpitude:** Moral Turpitude involves an act of baseness, vileness, or depravity in the social duties which a man owes to his fellow man or to society in general, contrary to the accepted and customary rule of right and duty between man and man. (Slander & Libel, 4th Edition, Newell) "Everything done contrary to justice, honesty, modesty or good morals is said to be done with moral turpitude." (Bouvier's Law Dictionary)

(5) **Wantonly:** Describes the morally unrestrained act of one person against another. Committed without any regard to the rights of another.

REFERENCES FOR CHAPTER IV

(1)   In re Gault, 387 U.S. 1

(2)   Sauer v. U.S. (241 F 2d 640)

(3)   M. Frances McNamara, 2,000 Famous Legal Quotations, Aqueduct Books, New York, p. 361

(4)   U.S. v. Watson, 146 F Supp 258

(5)   John Locke, Second Treatise of Government, section 57.

(6)   Sir James F. Stephen, History of the Criminal Law of England, MacMillan and Company, London, 1883

(7)   In re Iverson, 199 C 582 (250 P 681)

(8)   People v. Superior Court, 199 C.A. 2d 303 (18 Cal Rptr 557)

(9)   United States Constitution, Article 1, Sections 9 and 10, and the California State Constitution, Article 1, section 16.

(10)   People v. Weber, 84 Cal. App. 2d 126 (190 P 2d 46)

(11)   Pennel v. Superior Court, 232 Cal. App. 2d 284 (42 Cal Rptr 676)

STUDY QUESTIONS

CHAPTER IV

(1) The American system of law is called the _____ system.

(2) The fathers of the Constitution wrote the law so that a trial would be weighted in favor of the defendant.   T or F

(3) In the American system, the judge can tell the jury how he or she would vote if a juror.   T or F

(4) In the American system, the judge can comment on "questions of fact."   T or F

(5) The adversary system seems to slow down a trial.   T or F

(6) Persons who are obviously guilty should not be provided with attorneys.   T or F

(7) The juvenile system has changed from one of the "hearing" approach to one that is adversarial in nature.   T or F

(8) Juveniles are entitled to attorneys just the same as adults.   T or F

(9) A poor defendant who is given a public defender is seldom given the protection of basic rights during a trial.   T or F

(10) Public defenders and criminal prosecutors from the District Attorney's office are usually of the same quality.   T or F

(11) When a suspect is allowed to plead guilty to a lesser offense than that which was actually committed in order to save time and money for the district attorney, it is called

_____.

(12) What percentage of persons arrested for a felony end up in prison? _____.

(13) The United States Constitution states that the purpose of law is "...to establish justice, ensure domestic tranquility...to promote the general welfare and secure the blessings of liberty..."   T or F

(14) "Prevention" is listed as one of the purposes of criminal law. It is 100% effective.   T or F

(15) Establishing predictability is a stated purpose of law.   T or F

(16) The government has no Constitutional right to pass laws regarding morals.   T or F

(17) Punishment is a legitimate purpose of law.   T or F

(18) All law in California is statutory.   T or F

(19) The law "Thou Shalt Not Be Bad" would be classed as unconstitutional because it is too broad and vague. It would come under the _____ clause of the Fifth Amendment.

(20) If a law stated that it was illegal to "drop, throw, bury or burn rubbish" and you were to throw, bury and drop some rubbish, you would be guilty of three different crimes.   T or F

(21) When the law predetermines which level of government has the highest priority for issuing laws, it is called _____.

(22) In California, the state has pre-empted laws dealing with public drunkenness.   T or F

(23) In California, the state has pre-empted laws dealing with sex offenses.   T or F

(24) If a new law is passed, and by accident it contradicts an old law, the old law will have been considered to be pre-empted by the new law.   T or F

(25) When a new law is declared in part unconstitutional, the whole law is considered to be invalid.   T or F

(26) When a person commits a legal act that is later declared to be illegal and the person is then arrested, a legal defense would be that the law is a(an) _____ _____ law.

(27) Give two examples of Ex Post Facto laws.

　　(A) _____.
　　(B) _____.

(28) In California, the rule regarding the repeal of laws is "we go by what the law was when the act was committed."   T or F

(29) The exact way in which the law is written is called the _____ of the law.

(30) The term "Legislative Intent" is also called the _____ of the law.

(31) The literal meaning of "Corpus Delicti" is _____.

(32) The practical meaning of "Corpus Delicti" is _____.

(33) All elements of the Corpus Delicti must be proved in court or there can be no conviction.   T or F

(34) The elements of the Corpus Delicti can be proved by any of the five senses.   T or F

(35) The elements of the Corpus Delicti can be proved by circumstantial evidence.   T or F

(36) The burden of proof regarding the elements of a crime rests with the state.   T or F

(37) If a person pleads not guilty by reason of insanity, he or she has the burden of proof for that defense.   T or F

(38) If a defendant pleads not guilty by reason of insanity, the state must still prove that he or she committed the crime.   T or F

(39) Burden of proof in a criminal case is burden of proof to show beyond a _____ _____ that the suspect is guilty.

(40) Henry Horntoad tells officers that he killed his wife. Is this an admission or a confession? _____.

(41) Confessions and admissions cannot be used to prove the elements of the Corpus Delicti without other evidence.   T or F

(42) The evidence or proof upon which an officer makes a judgment after first looking into the situation is called _____ _____ proof or evidence.

(43) The burden of proof for a "presumptive law" or crime with a listed presumption of guilt, rests with the defendant regarding that presumption.   T or F

(44) A question of fact is determined by _____.

(45) A question of law is determined by _____.

(46) In some cases a conviction can be had without a unanimous verdict.   T or F

(47) All crimes in California are crimes against the state.   T or F

(48) Unless requested by an officer, a citizen has no legal obligation to stop or prevent a crime from being committed.   T or F

(49) Laws written in the penal code in the masculine gender include both sexes.   T or F

(50) If the word "county" is used in the law, it also includes "city and county."   T or F

(51) If the word "writing" is used in a law, it refers only to "handwriting."   T or F

(52) The word _____ means every written statement under oath.

(53) An "affirmation" is legally the same as an oath.   T or F

(54) If a person cannot read or write, and is asked to sign a paper, he or she can put any mark on the paper as a signature if it is witnessed and signed by _____ persons.

(55) If the word "willfully" is used in a law, it means that the person violating that law intended to violate the law.   T or F

(56) If the word "knowingly" is used in a law, it means that the person had knowledge of the unlawfulness of that act.   T or F

(57) Property that can be easily moved or carried away, is called _____ property.

(58) If the word "month" is used in a law, it means a _____ month.

(59) If the word "will" is used in a law, it also includes the word "codicil." This word means _____.

(60) An order issued by a judge in his or her legal capacity is called either a _____ or a _____.

(61) If the word "state" is used in a law, it does not include the District of Columbia.   T or F

(62) The word used for the process of recording information on arrested persons, photographing them and taking their fingerprints is _____.

(63) If the law requires a "seal," it can be substituted by writing the word "seal" next to the person's name.   T or F

(64) The type of crime that involves falsification or forgery is called a _____ _____ crime.

(65) The term "feloniously" means with intent to commit a felony.   T or F

(66) Give an example of a crime of "moral turpitude." _____ _____.

(67) If a person commits an act that shows no regard for the rights of others, it is said that the act was committed _____.

CHAPTER V

CLASSIFICATION OF OFFENSES AND PUNISHMENT

5.0   **CLASSIFICATION OF OFFENSES BY TYPE OF LAW: CRIMINAL AND CIVIL**

5.1   **CLASSIFICATION OF OFFENSES BY SERIOUSNESS: MALA IN SE AND MALA PROHIBITA**

5.2   **CLASSIFICATION OF OFFENSES BY PURPOSE: SUBSTANTIVE AND PROCEDURAL**

5.3   **CLASSIFICATION OF OFFENSES BY PUNISHMENT: FELONIES AND MISDEMEANORS**

5.4   **PUBLIC OFFENSES: INFRACTIONS AND ORDINANCES**

5.5   **IMPORTANCE OF CLASSIFICATION BY PUNISHMENT**

5.6   **SYSTEMS OF LAW: STATUTORY AND COMMON LAW**

5.7   **PUNISHMENT: TYPES OF SENTENCING AND SPECIAL PENALTIES**

5.8   **LESSER OFFENSES AND LESSER DEGREES OF CRIME**

5.9   **CRIMES WITHOUT VICTIMS**

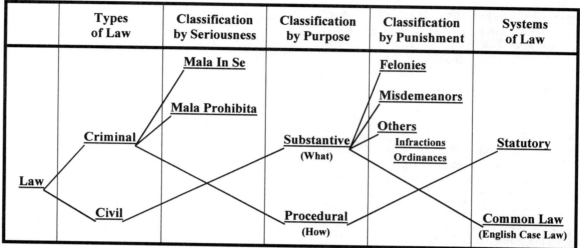

Types of Law	Classification by Seriousness	Classification by Purpose	Classification by Punishment	Systems of Law

Fig. V–1   Law Chart

5.0:0 CLASSIFICATION OF OFFENSES BY TYPE OF LAW: CRIMINAL AND CIVIL

Although the ancients did not distinguish between civil and criminal law, there is a very definite distinction between the two in American law. One of the best ways for police officers to get into trouble is trying to enforce civil law. It is often difficult to distinguish whether offenses are criminal or civil. Since the body of civil law is so extensive, the best approach for officers is to learn criminal law, and then ask themselves if the current situation falls into any criminal category. If it does not, then the officers should advise the complainant to contact a lawyer or the District Attorney.

Below is a list of some of the major differences between criminal and civil law. A civil offense is referred to as a "Tort."

5.0:1 Major Differences Between Civil and Criminal Law

Crimes
(1) There is criminal intent (or mental state)
(2) The state is the prosecutor
(3) Few complete settlements out of court
(4) Damages (fines) go to public treasury
(5) Contributory negligence not a defense
(6) Punishment is objective of judgment
(7) Punishment or fines are limited by statute

Civil Offenses (Torts)
(1) No intent
   (unless it is also part of a criminal act)
(2) The victim (plaintiff) is prosecutor
(3) Most cases settled out of court
(4) Damages go to victim

(5) Contributory negligence is a good defense or mitigating factor
(6) Objective of judgment is to restore to original condition if possible
(7) No limit on damages

5.1:0 CLASSIFICATION OF OFFENSES BY SERIOUSNESS: MALA IN SE AND MALA PROHIBITA

Classification By Seriousness of the Offense
When a crime is classified by the seriousness of the offense, its severity, or the nature of the crime, there are two classifications:

(1) **Mala In Se (bad in itself)**
(Also called "True Crimes")
These are crimes that are inherently bad and would be considered bad in all societies, such as murder, rape, and assault (also theft). Exceptions would be crimes of moral turpitude since they can vary from society to society.

(2) **Mala Prohibita (bad because it's prohibited)**
(Also called "Regulatory Crimes")
These laws are necessary to regulate a crowded society and protect individual rights such as property rights (for example, traffic laws and trespassing). There is nothing inherently wrong with going 3 miles over the speed limit or going through a stop sign if you are the only person on the road. The purpose of these laws is to regulate traffic when there are many cars on the road (or if that possibility exists). The act itself is not evil. There is also nothing wrong with walking on someone's property (unless he has just planted a new lawn). Yet if we are to have personal property rights, we must have laws regulating illegal trespassing.

5.2:0 CLASSIFICATION OF OFFENSES BY PURPOSE: SUBSTANTIVE AND PROCEDURAL.

There are two classifications of law when considering the purpose of the law. They are Substantive and Procedural.

(A) Substantive Law:

This is often referred to as the law of crimes. It deals with the obligations of each person in relation to other persons and to society as a whole. It lists exactly WHAT the law requires a person to do or not to do. Examples would be the law that lists the elements on Murder, Rape, Robbery and Riot. It includes the definition and classification of crimes.

In California, our law must be written (Statutory) in a code, and in order to convict a person in court, we must go exactly by the way it is written in that code.

(B) Procedural Law
(Also called Adjective Law):

Once a person has committed a crime (or violated a substantive law) Procedural law sets the rules for:

    (a) Making an Arrest
    (b) Gathering Evidence
    (c) Holding a Trial

Procedural law is HOW the law is carried out.
These activities must be written down in a code just like the Substantive Law. In that way one rule is not applied to one person and another to another person, and differently at different times. It is sometimes referred to as the legal machinery for enforcing the Substantive Law.

5.3:0 CLASSIFICATION OF OFFENSES BY PUNISHMENT: FELONIES AND MISDEMEANORS

In using the classification of law by punishment, most sources will use the terms "crimes and public offenses." The word "and" indicates a difference between the two words, and rightly so. They are different.

In California, there are only two classifications of crimes. They are felonies and misdemeanors. The term "infractions" comes under the heading of "public offenses."

(1) Felonies

The word felony is an Anglo-Saxon term that is derived from two words, "fee" meaning land, and "lon" which means forfeiture. In early English times the forfeiture of land was a set punishment when convicted of a felony. A person's estate was forfeited to the Crown upon conviction.

In California, Penal Code Section 17 defines a felony as: "A felony is a crime which is punishable with death or by imprisonment in the state prison."

(2) Misdemeanors

Penal Code Section 17 states;

Every other crime (other than a felony or public offense) is a misdemeanor except those offenses that are classified as infractions.

Section 19 of the Penal Code states that a misdemeanor is punishable by not more than one year in county jail for a single conviction. Fines may also be part of the punishment for both felonies and misdemeanors.

(3) "Wobblers"

There are some crimes for which the punishment is EITHER prison or county jail. This type of offense is called a "Wobbler" because it can "wobble" between the two punishments depending upon the court. Example: 273.5 of the Penal Code

Any person who willfully inflicts upon his or her spouse, or any person who willfully inflicts upon any person of the opposite sex with whom he or she is cohabiting, corporal injury resulting in a traumatic condition is guilty of either a felony or a misdemeanor.

(4) Graduated Offenses

There are some crimes in the Penal Code that are listed as misdemeanors for the first offense, and felonies for later convictions of the same offense. (E.g., 666 PC, Petty Theft with Prior.)

5.4:0   PUBLIC OFFENSES
(technically these are not crimes)

(1) Infractions

Infractions were first initiated in 1968.

Penal Code Section 19.6 states that an infraction is not punishable by imprisonment. It also states that a person charged with an infraction shall not be entitled to:

(a) A trial by jury (Only by a judge)

(b) A public defender at public expense

Penal Code Section 19.7 states that in all other respects, an infraction will be handled the same as a misdemeanor. This is for the purposes of laws of arrest and court procedures.

The only punishment for an infraction, therefore, would be a fine. However, if a person were to be cited for an infraction, and ignored the citation, he or she could be arrested, but the arrest would not be for the infraction, but for contempt of court. Many traffic offenses are now being classified as infractions. The best example would be a parking ticket.

(2) Ordinances

There is much debate as to whether municipal and county ordinances are really crimes or whether they should be classed as offenses like infractions. Infractions are statutorily classed as being separate from crimes by the Penal Code, but ordinances are not singled out for this distinction. It is the opinion of the author that they are not crimes. The definition of crime varies from book to book in a small way, but there are certain elements that are basic to the definition. The power to make laws is given to the states in the 10th Amendment. All crimes are crimes against the state, and crimes are prosecuted in the name of the state and by the state.

There is only one law-making body for the state. This avoids conflicting laws. On the other hand if the state could delegate the authority to make laws to the counties and cities, there would be a constant conflict in state law. Because of this, ordinances cannot be classed as crimes, but as offenses.

Cities are sometimes referred to as public corporations because they operate under charters from the state just as a private corporation operates under a charter. Because of this, many writers in law refer to ordinances as quasi civil offenses, and feel that any fines that result from violating an ordinance are really assessments rather than fines.

5.5:0   THE CLASSIFICATION OF CRIMES BY PUNISHMENT

What is the importance of the classification of crimes by punishment? There are two important aspects to consider when answering this question: working with suspects before sentencing and dealing with persons who have already been convicted of felonies (after sentence has been passed).

(1) Before Sentencing

Working in the Field with Suspects who Have Just Committed a Crime.

Officers must consider the maximum punishment listed in the criminal code for the offense that the arrestee is believed to have committed. What if the code lists the crime as being either a felony or a misdemeanor? It is then called a WOBBLER, and the maximum punishment will be considered. It would be classed as a felony and treated as such for the following reasons:

(a) **Laws of Arrest:**

Officers cannot arrest for misdemeanors not committed in their presence (with few exceptions), but they can arrest for felonies. Being able to treat the offense as a felony could mean the power to arrest on the spot, or not to arrest.

(b) **Amount of Force Used:**

Officers can never use deadly force when the suspect has only committed a misdemeanor. They can use maximum force in the arrest only if the crime is a felony. (Local policy also affects the amount of force that can be used.)

(2) After Sentence Has Been Passed

Dealing with Persons Who Have Already Been Convicted of a Felony

(a) **Restrictions upon certain felons:**

A felon cannot own or possess a handgun. He cannot possess any firearms if the crime for which he was convicted involved the use of a gun.

(b) **Felons on Probation or Parole:**

Felons who are on probation or parole often have many stringent restrictions pertaining to the driving of vehicles, drinking, being out on the streets after certain hours, their residence, out-of-county travel, and association with other ex-felons.

(c) **Potential Hazards:**

Although officers in the field should be cautious about handling all suspects, they should be even more careful when dealing with ex-felons. This is especially true of those who have a record of violence.

The Key to the Final Classification of a Crime

The key when dealing with a person who has already been sentenced is to learn WHERE HE WAS SENTENCED, not WHERE HE WAS SENT. There is a major difference between the two. If the person was sentenced to state prison he stands guilty of a felony. However, many times a defendant is sentenced to state prison, but never spends a day in prison. This is because of a trend among judges to avoid, if possible, sending first offenders to state prison. This is done by first sentencing the defendant to state prison, suspending the sentence in favor of five years probation, and then, as a condition of probation, sending the defendant to county jail for three months. Notice, he is not SENTENCED to county jail; he is SENT there as a condition of probation. Too often we automatically think of a person serving time in a county jail as being a misdemeanant. He was sentenced to state prison, and if he goofs up it is possible that he can then be "violated" on his probation and then sent to prison.

GO STRAIGHT TO JAIL - DO NOT STOP AT GO - DO NOT COLLECT $200⁰⁰. BY THE WAY, HOW'S MOM DOIN', POP?

5.6:0   SYSTEMS OF LAW: STATUTORY AND COMMON LAW

Classification by System

Generally speaking there are two major systems of law in the world today.

(A) Statutory Law:

In some places it is referred to as "Civil Law." It should be remembered that, for centuries, civil and criminal laws were all considered to be one law. The technical name for the Justinian Code was Corpus Juris Civilis, (Body of civil law).

To be classed as a statutory law, it must be written down in some book of statutes. To be legal it MUST be written. In most countries in Europe and the West, law is basically Roman law. It has been passed by a legislature, written and then codified in some book of law. Statutory law has sometimes been referred to as Permissive law because it allows a person the permission to do anything that the written law does not prohibit.

(B) Common Law:

A law developed through custom and usage. It is not necessarily written down at first. Later it is often written in some form. This happens when a case goes to a higher court on an appeal, and a complete record of the trial and the decision of the judges is written down.

In this system of law, a person can be convicted of some obscure criminal offense that is not found written in any law book at the time, but is an offense for which someone was convicted at some previous time in history.

In the United States we have a combination of these two categories of law. Even though we started out as English colonies under English common law, when we gained independence, we did so with a "states' rights" concept, and gave the power to the individual states to establish the type of law which suited them best. At the present time about half of the states have some type of common law. Some states have a mixture. Some use statutory law for their criminal law and common law for their civil law. The trend is to move in the direction of statutory law. As a general rule, the older states have common law, and the newer states have statutory law.

5.7:0   PUNISHMENT: TYPES OF SENTENCING AND SPECIAL PENALTIES

As will be seen later when the definition of crime is covered, there must be a listed punishment in order for a crime to be complete. There is an old Latin maxim (rule) "Nullum Crimen Sine Poena" which means, "No crime without punishment."

About 200 years ago, Noah Webster, who later wrote our first dictionary, stated: "A law without penalty is mere advice." In the California Penal Code, "all bases are covered" by a general statute that gives the punishment for all crimes listed in the code which do not have a specified punishment following that crime.

5.7:1 Sentencing

In September, 1976, Governor Brown signed into law a new system of sentencing for the state of California. The Determinate Sentence is now the type of sentencing to be used in California.

The Old Indeterminate Sentencing Law

The old system was the Indeterminate Sentence system. It was enacted in 1917, and was looked upon as being an enlightened move toward a more just system of corrections. Rather than making what could possibly be a rash and emotional decision, the judge merely sentenced the defendant to the indeterminate sentence that was listed in the Penal Code. After the crime was described in the Penal Code, the punishment was then listed in an indeterminate form. For example, "Upon conviction shall be sentenced to state prison from one to five years." When the defendant arrived at the state prison, he was given an intensive battery of tests by persons who were in no way involved with the crime or the trial. Their decision was thus an objective one. Once he had served his minimum sentence, he went before a board who then decided whether he would be released on parole, or made to serve another year. In most cases the prisoner was released after the minimum time because prisons were crowded. If the prisoner was turned down for parole, he could apply again after another year.

Prisoners did not like the indeterminate sentence. For one thing, it made them behave. The time that they served depended upon their behavior in prison. They claimed that it was too easy for someone to trip them up. In truth, most prisoners served the minimum sentence. Still, prisoners did not like correction officers, in effect, holding a club over their heads. Corrections officers liked the indeterminate sentence since it gave them some control over the prisoners. A prisoners' association was able to convince liberal legislators that this system was not fair, and they, in turn, were able to push through the new determinate sentence.

(A) Procedure in Sentencing Under the New Determinate Sentencing Law:

The punishment for each felony is listed in three choices. For example: 2 yrs.-3 yrs.-4 yrs. Judges have a choice as to which of the three sentences to give the convicted defendant. If the middle sentence is chosen, the sentence does not have to be justified. However, if the judge chooses the larger or smaller sentence, he or she must state in writing the special circumstances that justify that particular sentence. This will, in effect, cause the judges to play it safe and choose the middle sentence in most cases.

(B) Enhancements

The new law allows the court to impose additional sentences called enhancements if certain conditions exist. A general description of those conditions follows:
(1) Prior prison terms for serious felonies
(2) Prior prison terms for less serious felonies
(3) When committing a crime while armed with a firearm
(4) When committing a felony & uses a firearm
(5) When during a felony, takes, damages or destroys property over $50,000
(6) Who, while committing a felony, personally & intentionally inflicts great bodily injury

(C) Probation and Suspended Sentences

Use of firearms during certain serious felonies will result in no probation or suspended sentence.

(D) Limit on Enhancements

There is a complicated formula that limits the total amount of time a defendant can serve as a result of enhancements.

(E) Good-Time Credit in Prison

A prisoner can earn good-time credit for proper behavior while in prison. It can reduce up to one-third of his sentence.

(F) Parole

Parole is a maximum of three years (5 for "lifers") and lifetime parole for "lifers" sentenced for murder.

5.7:2 Types of Sentencing

In California there are two types of sentencing in relation to the number of crimes committed:

(1) Consecutive Sentencing

Under this type of sentencing, the defendant is sentenced to a term in prison for each separate crime for which he has been convicted.

(2) Concurrent Sentencing

Under this type of sentencing, the defendant is given just one sentence for all the crimes for which he has been convicted. They are all lumped into one sentence.

Because of practical reasons, the concurrent type of sentencing is the most common. Since it is a better deal for the defendant, he or his attorney will often dicker with the police or the District Attorney for this type of sentencing. For example, he will plead guilty to all the crimes that he has committed in exchange for just one sentence under the concurrent sentencing system.

The reason that the police go along with this type of sentencing is that it enables them to clear many crimes from their books that they might not be able to clear through normal investigations. The District Attorney (who generally has a very heavy case load) might agree to this type of sentencing in return for a guilty plea. This will save the District Attorney's Office both time and money by not having to conduct a long and expensive trial.

5.8:0   LESSER OFFENSES AND LESSER DEGREES OF CRIME

California law allows a jury or a judge (in a trial before a judge) to find the defendant guilty of a lesser offense or lesser degree than that originally charged. Only certain crimes, however, fit into this category. The key is that the lesser offense or degree must be contained within the elements of the crime originally charged.

Let us look at the elements of grand and petty theft. Generally speaking, the only difference between the two is one element. If a person is charged with grand theft, the jury may find him guilty of petty theft instead, if they believe that the item stolen did not have a value of over $400

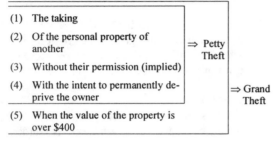

(1)   The taking
(2)   Of the personal property of another   ⇒ Petty Theft
(3)   Without their permission (implied)
(4)   With the intent to permanently deprive the owner   ⇒ Grand Theft
(5)   When the value of the property is over $400

Another example of lesser offense can be in the crimes of robbery and theft as it can often occur in a case of "Purse Snatch."

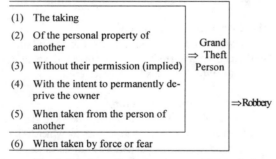

(1)   The taking
(2)   Of the personal property of another   Grand Theft Person
(3)   Without their permission (implied)   ⇒
(4)   With the intent to permanently deprive the owner
(5)   When taken from the person of another   ⇒ Robbery
(6)   When taken by force or fear

If a defendant slipped a purse off the victim's arm so fast that she did not have a chance to either resist or give up the purse out of fear, the crime would not be robbery. (Notice element #6 in Robbery.) In this case the jury could find the defendant guilty of grand theft rather than robbery. As you can see, the elements of grand theft in this case are included in those of robbery.

Lesser Degrees

The "trier of fact" can also find the defendant guilty of a lesser degree of the crime originally charged.

Example of a Lesser Degree in the Charge of Burglary

The crime of burglary has two degrees. The elements of second degree burglary are as follows:

(1)   The entry
(2)   Of a building (or specially listed place)
(3)   With the intent to commit theft or a felony
      In 1984, the fourth element that made burglary first degree was changed from "of an inhabited dwelling in the nighttime" to just "of an inhabited dwelling."
(4)   Of an inhabited dwelling.

What does "inhabited" mean? It does not mean that someone is there at the time, but that the dwelling is normally inhabited. The owner might be away at the grocery store or to Lake Tahoe for the weekend, but will return to that dwelling as his or her residence. That is the key.

How Does this Rule Apply?

Sam Snerd is a community college instructor. At the end of the spring semester, he has had all he can take of students, and goes to his summer cabin for two months. He occasionally spends the weekends and some holidays there. Because of this, the cabin is completely furnished with everything he would need if he wanted to go there on a moment's notice. Sam collects rare stamps and mentioned to a student once that he takes his rare stamps up to the cabin to relax and forget teaching. The student mentioned this to Burnie Burgle, a friend, and Burnie thought that this might be an opportunity to make a few bucks by breaking into the cabin and stealing the stamps.

Burnie goes to the cabin and breaks in, but cannot find the stamps anywhere. He decides to leave without them, and as he is climbing out the window, a deputy sheriff, who noticed a strange car parked nearby, spots him and arrests him. After looking at all the furnishings inside the cabin, the deputy assumed that it was inhabited and charged Burnie with first degree burglary.

During the trial, the defense attorney convinced the jury that the dwelling was not "inhabited" according to the strict definition of the law. As a result, they can find Burnie guilty of second degree burglary instead of the crime first charged, first degree burglary. This is because the elements of second degree burglary are included in the elements of first degree burglary.

5.9:0   CRIMES WITHOUT VICTIMS

An entire chapter could be written on the topic of "Victimless Crimes." Today it is a topic of great debate. It is one in which both sides can become quite emotional and irrational.

What are the essentials of a "Victimless Crime"? Why is it called a victimless crime? Is it really "victimless"?

Examples of "victimless" crimes are Prostitution, Narcotics, Gambling, Pornography and Abortion. Some even include public intoxication.

First, a "victimless" crime is one that is moral in nature rather than one causing direct physical harm or loss. It is called "victimless" because the victim does not report it to the police. Some say that the so called "victim" is not really a victim since he or she freely participates in the crime.

...*"VICTIMLESS CRIME" YOU CALLED IT LAST TIME! WELL, HOW COME AFTER THREE SHOTS OF PENICILLIN AND A DIVORCE I FEEL SO MUCH LIKE A DARN VICTIM?!!*

Some citizens feel that there should be no laws against the so-called "victimless" crimes. They feel that the police should be spending more time trying to apprehend and convict the serious criminals such as burglars, bank robbers and rapists.

They feel that we are legislating against human nature and that it is an impossible task. The idea is promoted that if we are to be truly a free society, that the law must allow the citizens more freedom of choice in what they do as long as it causes no harm to others.

On the other side, it is said that the "victimless" crime will cause the destruction of our society. Organized crime obtains its major source of money from these crimes. There is really no such thing as a "victimless" crime since someone, or society in general, is eventually harmed by the existence of the crime. It is not an unnecessary drain on police personnel. Los Angeles statistics show that 15% of arrests are for "victimless" crimes while only 6% of their personnel are involved in handling these cases. It might be well to quote here the thoughts expressed by Edmund Burke, a member of Parliament, in the 18th century:

> Men are qualified for civil liberty in exact proportion to their own disposition to put moral chains upon their own appetites. Society cannot exist unless a controlling power upon will and appetite be placed somewhere and the less of it there is within, the more there is without. It is ordained in the external constitution of things that men of intemperate minds cannot be free. Their passions forge their fetters.

STUDY QUESTIONS

CHAPTER V

(1) A civil wrong is called a _____.

(2) A civil wrong must have criminal intent.   T or F

(3) Name two differences between a civil and a criminal law as listed in the book.

    (a) _____

    (b) _____.
    _____.

(4) Another term used for "Mala In Se" crimes is _____ crimes.

(5) Another term used for "Mala Prohibita" crimes is _____ crimes.

(6) Give an example of a "Mala In Se" crime. _____.

(7) Give an example of a "Mala Prohibita" crime. _____.

(8) Substantive law pertains to:

    (A) ____crimes.   (B) ____search & seizure.
    (C) ____laws of arrest.   (D) ____court rules.

(9) Give an example of a "procedural law." _____.

(10) What is another name used for "procedural law?" _____.

(11) A crime punishable by imprisonment in a state prison or by death is called a _____.

(12) The word "felony" comes from the Anglo-Saxon words "fee" and "lon." what do these words mean? _____.

(13) A crime punishable by time in the county jail is called a _____.

(14) Infractions are not crimes. Name one of the three ways in which they are different.
_____.

(15) Fitzsimmon Farklequat receives a citation for an infraction. He ignores the citation and a warrant for his arrest is issued. The arrest will not be for the infraction, but for _____ of _____.

(16) Violation of a city ordinance is really a crime.   T or F

(17) All offenses classified as crimes are prosecuted in the name of the state and by the state.   T or F

(18) Violation of an ordinance has often been referred to as a _____ civil offense.

(19) Give one reason listed in the book why it is important for an officer in the field to know whether a suspected crime is a felony or a misdemeanor. _____.

(20) A crime that is listed in the Penal Code as having a punishment of either state prison or county jail is referred to as a _____.

(21) If an officer arrests for a crime that lists in the penal code both types of punishment as mentioned in the last question, what classification by punishment should be used?
_____.

(22) The key to the final classification of a crime is where the defendant is _____ not where he is _____.

---

(23) Fred Farkle is sentenced to state prison for burglary. However, the judge gives him three   T or F
years probation and sends him to county jail for three months as a condition of probation.
Since he served his time in the county jail rather than in state prison, he would be considered
a misdemeanant rather than a felon.

(24) In California we have only statutory law. In about half of the other states they have
_____ law.

(25) Statutory law must be written in a code or book of law.   T or F

(26) In some countries statutory law is called "civil law."   T or F

(27) Some states in the U.S. have a combination of statutory & common law.   T or F

(28) Who stated "a law without penalty is mere advice"?

    (A) ____Washington.   (B) ____Webster.
    (C) ____Blackstone.   (D) ____Marshall.

(29) Our system of sentencing in California is called the _____ sentence.

(30) When a defendant is sentenced to five separate prison terms for five separate burglaries, it is
called a _____ sentence.

(31) When a defendant is sentenced to just one prison term for five separate burglaries, it is called
a _____ sentence.

(32) In California, it is possible for a jury to find a defendant guilty of a lesser offense than that   T or F
originally charged.

(33) Petty theft can be a lesser offense of a charge of grand theft.   T or F

(34) Grand theft can be a lesser offense of the charge of robbery.   T or F

(35) The law on "lesser offenses" also includes "lesser degrees."   T or F

(36) The topic of "victimless crimes" is one of great debate.   T or F

(37) "Victimless crimes" are usually based on moral principles.   T or F

(38) Organized crime obtains most of its money from "victimless crimes."   T or F

(39) A "victimless crime" is called "victimless" because:

    (A) ____Dead persons have their valuables taken and they are no longer humans.
    (B) ____The victim does not normally report this type of offense.
    (C) ____The victim is usually not a U.S. citizen and subject to the law.
    (D) ____The victim is usually poor.

CHAPTER VI

COMPONENTS NEEDED FOR A CRIMINAL OFFENSE

6.0   DEFINITION OF CRIME
6.1   THE PARTS OR ELEMENTS NEEDED TO
        CONSTITUTE A CRIME
6.2   THE CRIMINAL ACT, OR CRIMINAL CONDUCT
6.3   THE MENTAL ELEMENT NEEDED FOR A
        CRIME (INTENT)
6.4   MALICE
6.5   MOTIVE
6.6   CRIMINAL NEGLIGENCE AND RECKLESSNESS
6.7   PRESUMED KNOWLEDGE AND STRICT
        LIABILITY
6.8   PRESUMPTIVE LAWS
6.9   THE JOINT RELATIONSHIP BETWEEN
        ACT AND INTENT
6.10   CAUSE AND EFFECT RELATIONSHIP AND
        DOCTRINE OF PROXIMATE CAUSE

6.0:0 DEFINITION OF CRIME

The definition of crime varies from book to book. It can be as simple as "an act in violation of the law,"[1] or it can go into great detail. Black's Law Dictionary defines crime as:

> any act done in violation of those duties which an individual owes to the community, and for the breach of which the law has provided that the offender shall make satisfaction to the public.[2]

Writers of criminal law often have their own definitions. For example, Rollin M. Perkins, Emeritus Professor of Criminal Law at the University of California at Los Angeles, and author on criminal law, defines crime as "any social harm defined and made punishable by law."

Today most criminal codes seem to follow the definition set down by Sir William Blackstone, the famous English jurist:

> A crime or misdemeanor is an act committed or omitted in violation of a public law either forbidding or commanding it.[3]

California Penal Code Definition

Penal Code section 15 states:

> A crime or public offense is an act committed OR omitted in violation of a law forbidding or commanding it, and to which is annexed, upon conviction, any of the following punishments:
>
> (1) Death;
> (2) Imprisonment;
> (3) Fine;
> (4) Removal from office;
> (5) Disqualification to hold and enjoy any office of honor, trust or profit in this state.

Section 20 of the Penal Code further defines some conditions of a crime:

> In every crime or public offense there must exist a union, or joint operation of act and intent, or criminal negligence.

These definitions are not complete definitions. That is to say they do not list all the requirements necessary in order to have a crime. The elements that they do list are certainly necessary, but they are not all inclusive. They are just basic.

6.1:0 PARTS OR ELEMENTS NEEDED TO CONSTITUTE A CRIME

One of the best ways to cover this topic is to use the Triangle of Crime as an illustration.

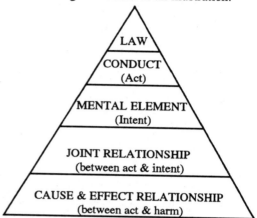

Fig. VI–1: The Triangle of Crime

Law

The first part of the Triangle of Crime is "Law." In California, all law is statutory. Therefore, an act is not a crime unless there is a law written on the books that forbids or commands it.

This is not a new concept. There is an old Latin legal maxim (rule) that states "*Nullum Crimen Sine Lege,*" or "No crime without law." As mentioned in Chapter V, and the definitions just listed, a law must have a punishment to be complete. Under English common law, the law need not be written. If a precedent could be found in some old law book where a person was at one time convicted for violating that law or act, then it would be sufficient for prosecution. Again, in California, the law must be written in a code or there is no crime.

At times it is easy to become confused by what we feel is illegal, and by what is actually listed in the statues as a criminal act.

6.2:0 CRIMINAL CONDUCT

The second part of the triangle of crime is Criminal Conduct. It is often simply called the criminal act, but "conduct" is a better term because many of the types of conduct that satisfy this legal requirement do not involve any act or action on the part of the perpetrator.

California Penal Code section 20 states: "In every crime or public offense there must exist a union, or joint operation of act and intent, or criminal negligence." Case law and legal precedent tell us that the term "act" does include all the types of conduct that will be covered here. In many law books the Latin term "*Actus Reus*" is used in place of criminal conduct. It means the same thing.

Types Of Criminal Conduct

(1) Voluntary, Physical, Positive Act

For example, Arvin Ardvark gets mad at Betty Binklehippy and shoots her. His act is voluntary. It is physical, and it is a positive act. The legal term for this act is "malfeasance."

(2) Omission Or Failure To Act.

When the law statutorily requires that a person perform a certain act, and he fails to perform it, he is guilty of a crime even though he did not do a positive act.

For example, the Vehicle Code states that you will stop at a stop sign. If you fail to stop you would violate the law. 270 of the Penal Code requires all parents to provide the basic necessities of life for their children. If a parent allowed his child to go hungry when he was able to provide food for that child, he would be guilty of a criminal act.

A term that is often used for this omission or failure to act is Nonfeasance. This is opposed to Malfeasance, which means performing an act, but performing it in an improper manner.

(3) Illegal Possession Or Transportation.

Illegal possession can violate the law and yet not involve any physical act. If a person is standing on a street corner, and is not moving a muscle, but possesses an illegal gun, he is violating the law even though he is doing nothing physical. The same applies to illegal transportation.

There are some basic requirements needed to satisfy this type of illegal conduct:

(a) The person must have knowledge of his possession. He must be aware that he is possessing the illegal item or contraband.

(b) The person must have control of what he possesses. This simply means that he has the ability to get rid of what he illegally possesses if he so desires.

(4) Constructive Acts.

The term "Constructive" means "in place of." In this type of conduct, the perpetrator himself does nothing, but some animal or some mechanical device under his control performs the act or conduct for him. For example, Mervin Mushmuscle has a trained monkey that goes into houses and steals purses. Even though the monkey does the stealing, Mervin is guilty of criminal conduct that we class as a constructive act.

This would also apply to the use of a mechanical device such as an explosive device. Mervin could be a hundred or a thousand miles away from the crime scene when the bomb explodes.

Principal – Agent Rule

Under the Principal–Agent rule, a person who is under the control of another is called an agent. The person who control that agent is called a principal. A principal is criminally responsible for the acts of an agent under that principal's control. An agent can not only be a human, but also an animal or some mechanical device such as a fishing pole or any extension of the human principal.

This type of conduct also covers the use of a mentally deficient person through fraud or misrepresentation. If Mervin were to ask Denny Dumwitty, a mentally deficient person, to take a note to the bank and get some money for him just like he gets groceries for his mother, and the note stated that Denny had a gun and a bomb under his coat and to fill the bag with money, Denny would have unknowingly robbed the bank. Although Mervin did not himself rob the bank, he would be guilty through committing a constructive act.

This would also apply to a case of using a young child to innocently participate in a crime.

(5) Passive Participation.

When a person allows an act to occur, or consents to that act, even though he does nothing himself, it is classed as passive participation, and is considered a criminal act. For example, Harvey Humpinstump is a guard for a warehouse. He looks the other way, or makes sure that he is not at the gate when his brother enters the gate to burglarize the warehouse. A person who allows another to orally copulate him is guilty of a criminal act (if a minor or in prison). Although he performs no physical act himself, he participates passively.

(6) Verbal Conduct.

Verbal conduct involves the movement of the mouth and tongue only, but is classed as a form of criminal conduct. There are many different types of verbal conduct. Some are:

(a) **Soliciting or Procuring.** This involves asking another to commit a criminal act. It could be soliciting a felony such as murder, or a misdemeanor such as prostitution. Procuring means obtaining rather than asking. An example would be the verbal procuring of prostitutes.

(b) **Use of Indecent Language.** The making of "obscene phone calls" would come under this classification.

(c) **Directive or Instructive.** When one person gives instructions to another person in such a way that harm comes to the person so directed, the person doing the directing would be guilty of criminal conduct even though he or she did nothing physical.

Examples:

Telling another what chemicals to mix, knowing that those chemicals, when mixed, will explode.

Telling your wife to stand on the edge of a cliff so you can take her photograph and while she is giving her attention to the camera, you give her directions to move back, just a little, until she steps off the cliff.

(7) **Continuing Act.** The act or conduct necessary for some crimes must be the final act in a series of acts. For the crime to be completed, several continuing acts must be performed. (Sometimes called a Progressive Act.)

For example:

Felony Drunk Driving: This offense requires three continuing separate acts in order for the offense to be complete.

(1) The person must become intoxicated.
(2) The person must drive a vehicle.
(3) Someone other than the driver must be injured.

STATUS AS AN ACT.
(Although not really an act)

Since the term "status act" is often used in criminal law, the term will be discussed here. Status, unlike the other examples, is not a type of criminal conduct, but rather a type of situation under which conduct could be criminal. Because of status, two persons could perform the same act or type of conduct; one of them would be guilty of a crime, and the other would not.

Examples of Status Acts.

(1) **Age:**

Two persons, one 22 years of age and the other 19 years of age are sitting in a bar having a cocktail. They are both performing exactly the same act, but because of the status of age, one is guilty of a crime and the other is not.

A six-year-old child sets fire to his house. His age will excuse criminal prosecution. An 18-year-old would not be excused if he committed the same act.

(2) **Blood Relationship:**

Two couples are in the same motel having sex. A & B are over 18 and are in no way related. They are not committing a crime. C & D are related by blood, and are therefore guilty of incest just by their status of blood relationship.

(3) **Marriage:**

Fred Farkle has sexual intercourse with his sixteen-year-old wife. There is no crime. Denny Dork has sex relations with his sixteen-year-old girlfriend, Fanny. Although both girls consented to the act, the fact that Denny was not married to Fanny makes him guilty of Unlawful Intercourse (old Statutory Rape).

Unconstitutionality

In some cases "status crimes" violate the Constitution. Under the 14th Amendment, "Equal protection under the law" certain types of "status crimes" are unconstitutional. For example if a particular law only applied to Blacks, and to no other race, it would violate the 14th amendment. The old "Vagrancy Laws" have been declared unconstitutional in that a person could be arrested for being on the street without "visible means of support." It might be that the person's financial problems are beyond his or her control. In most cases the person was not arrested just for being on the street without visible means of support, but due to being a transient. A local resident who happened to be on the street without any money would not be arrested.

Examples of Unconstitutional Status Acts

(1) **Vagrancy:** Covered above.
(2) **Addiction:** The Supreme Court stated that a person could become addicted through no fault of his or her own[4] (e.g., cancer patient), and just plain addiction without any other criminal act cannot be against the law.
(3) **Citizenship:** There have been many laws that required citizenship as a pre-requisite. Under section 12021 of the California Penal Code it stated that an alien could not possess or own a pistol or revolver. In 1972 the California Court of Appeals declared this section as unconstitutional based on status. Now aliens can own such weapons the same as the citizens who have not been convicted of a felony, or other special non-status requirements.

ROSES ARE RED
AND VIOLETS ARE TENDER—
I'D MUCH RATHER BE
A STATUS OFFENDER

Important Cases Regarding Status

In Powell v. Texas[5] the United States Supreme Court was asked to declare alcoholism to be a status act on the grounds that a "wino" who is arrested hundreds of times for being drunk is the same as an addict, and cannot help himself or herself; free will has been destroyed and the person cannot control his or her condition.

The conviction of Powell was upheld, but by a close vote. The majority of Justices felt that if alcoholism were to be allowed as an uncontrollable act, it would "open a can of worms," and there would be no end to the defenses that a person could use to avoid criminal prosecution.

6.3:0   THE MENTAL ELEMENT

The third step in the Triangle of Crime is the Mental Element. The mental element covers four main areas. They are:
 (1) Criminal Intent;
 (2) Criminal Negligence;
 (3) Recklessness;
 (4) Presumed knowledge
       (Constructive knowledge)

Intent
(The most common of the mental elements)

In law the Latin term "*Mens Rea*" is used for intent. It means "guilty mind." The difficulty in defining criminal intent is the fact that it is in the mind of the person doing the act, and we do not have a machine or device that will look into the mind of another and record that actual intent. We can only assume what the intent might be, or make a guess based on what the person said or did at the time the act was committed or prior to the act.

If we look far back into the early history of English common law, there seems to be a lack of writing on the subject of intent. This could lead us to believe that intent was not a necessary requirement for a crime. If we examine those offenses listed as crimes in early English times, we will see that they were all "mala in se" types of crimes. Crimes that would by their very nature contain obvious general intent. Examples would be murder, robbery, burglary and rape. With crimes of this nature, intent was probably seldom a legal issue.

Some researchers in criminal law feel that intent was not a part of English law under the rule of the Anglo-Saxons. This is based on their concept of law that stressed responsibility over all else. This type of legal philosophy does not take into account criminal intent. The perpetrator was always responsible for the results of his acts despite the presence or absence of intent. As an example of this philosophy in operation, they divided people into groups of ten, and if any one of the ten committed a crime, the other nine were also punished. The idea was to make people take some responsibility for each other's actions.

It was not until around the ninth century that the doctrine of mens rea appeared in legal writings. It came into being under the influence of the penitential books of the Catholic Church. The writings of both St. Augustine and St. Thomas Aquinas had a great effect on the need to show intent in any wrongdoing. Their doctrine of free will became the basis for the need of showing intent as a means of identifying the purpose of the person committing the crime.[6] Roman law, which considered crime to involve a moral aspect, also affected the changeover to the importance of why a crime was committed rather than what was done. A very important side-effect of this change in philosophy of law was that it opened the door for such legal defenses as insanity and infancy.

It was not until the end of the twelfth century that there developed a firm foundation in legal writings pertaining to the need for mens rea. There soon developed legal maxims such as "Actus non facit reum nisi mens sit rea"(The act does not render one guilty unless the mind is guilty). The rule before this time was, "The doer of a deed was responsible whether he acted innocently or inadvertently because he was the doer."

What Is the Definition of Intent?

When a definition of intent is attempted from a theoretical standpoint, it becomes difficult to define intent in a manner that will suit all experts in law. This is because criminal intent varies from crime to crime and intent is something that exists only in the mind of the person committing the act. Although an attempt will be made to define intent, it should be remembered that it is really a "question of fact" for the jury to decide.[7] It is probably based more on a "gut feeling" than any legal definition.

Although criminal intent is basically a mental process needed to accomplish a criminal result, it is difficult to nail down the definition into exact terms. One approach to this problem is to see what famous writers in criminal law have said about intent. For example, Justice Learned Hand defined intent as: "the awareness of the fact that a particular conduct is illegal, and is the purpose to use a certain means to achieve a certain result."

In 1889, Sir James Stephen remarked that mens rea (intent) "was impossible to define in such a way that would apply to all crimes, because of the great difference in mental attitude in different crimes." Strict liability laws, which do not require intent, will be covered later in the chapter.

6.3:1   Types of Criminal Intent

There are three types of criminal intent, classified by the need to prove guilt. They are:

(1) General Intent

This involves crimes where the finding of fault is objective. Any person who becomes aware of the facts involving the case would be able to determine that intent was involved. The manner of the crime will tend to show the intent. It is presumed from the commission of the act, based on the concept that a person is presumed to intend the natural and probable outcome of his voluntary acts.

In a case of armed robbery, the intent is obvious by the action involved, and what is said during the crime. This applies to most mala in se crimes, but not those that involve specific intent as one of the elements.

If a person of proper mental capacity commits a criminal act without legal justification or excuse, mens rea is assumed. Criminal intent can involve nothing more than the intent to commit the act regardless of whether one knows the act is wrong. Therefore, the old legal rule, "Ignorantia legis neminem excusat" (ignorance of the law excuses no one) applies here and it also does not excuse a lack of particular intent.

General intent is not only expressed in the wording of the laws that define a crime, but it is also judged by the standards that are expected of persons by the society in which they live. Since intent is a "question of fact," the jury's expectation of normal conduct helps them determine the existence of intent.

(2) Specific Intent

This type of intent shows the special reason why the act was committed.

Some statutes, by the way they are written, define the crime not as merely doing an act or series of acts, but doing an act with a set, special, or specific intent in mind. This specific intent cannot be proved just from the commission of the general act listed in the statute, but must be proved apart from the physical conditions of the criminal act.

Specific intent involves doing something for a special purpose. When the same physical act can be criminal or non-criminal depending upon the intent, specific intent will enter the picture. In most cases, the wording of this special intent is clearly spelled out, but in some cases the special intent is either implied or the wording does not include the actual word "intent." For example, the crime of theft seldom has an element written into the statute that the taking must be with the specific intent to permanently deprive the owner, yet this has always been considered a legitimate element of theft.

Specific intent is the hardest type of intent to prove because it is not always easy to infer the intent from the action performed. It is a special intent in the mind of the perpetrator, and since it is an element apart from the physical elements of the crime, an ordinary, prudent, reasonable member of the jury might find difficulty in inferring this intent from what the perpetrator did.

Although voluntary intoxication is not accepted as a legal defense to a criminal act, it can be a defense to specific intent. A state of intoxication can alter the reason for committing the act, or if the state of intoxication was very intense, it could remove what would normally be thought of as the obvious reason for committing the act. A highly intoxicated person breaks into a neighbor's house, thinking that it is his own, and that his wife had locked him out. He has committed the same physical act as would be committed by a burglar, but his state of intoxication changes the specific intent.

If a man were to hit a woman and knock her down, he could be guilty of "assault and battery." If specific intent could be proved he might also be guilty of a more serious offense, "assault with intent to commit rape." Both offenses can involve exactly the same physical act, that of hitting and knocking down a woman. If by some means the prosecution could show the jury that the defendant had the specific intent of raping the victim, they could find him guilty of the more serious crime .

Normally the defendant's past record cannot be brought into the trial because it might prejudice the jury. The fact that one has committed a burglary before does not necessarily mean that he is guilty of the one he is presently charged with. If the crime charged is one involving specific intent, then past records can be brought in as evidence to help prove that the intent was present. If the defendant has been convicted on two previous occasions of forcible rape, this could be admitted into court as helping to prove that the reason he hit and knocked down the woman in the offense he is now accused of was to rape her.

It is important not to charge a suspect with a crime involving specific intent unless there is sufficient evidence to prove that special intent. If a man takes a knife and cuts off the genital organs of another man who raped his daughter, he should not be charged with assault with intent to commit murder. His intent was to emasculate the victim not to kill him. Mayhem would be the proper charge. Even if the charge was attempted murder, the prosecution would not have to prove that the defendant attacked the victim with the specific intent to murder him. This crime has no specific intent. Say the victim was attacked with a knife. Under the doctrine of Proximate Cause, it would be a natural and probable outcome that the victim could die from a loss of blood. In this case there need be no proof that the defendant actually intended that the victim die in order to be charged with homicide. If he could be charged with homicide if the victim died, then he could also be charged with attempted murder if the victim did not die.

(3) Transferred Intent
(Also called Constructive Intent)

In transferred intent a person has a criminal intent toward some particular person, place or object, and by accident or misfortune, some other person, place or object becomes the recipient of this criminal intent. When this occurs, it is said that the original criminal intent is carried over or transferred to the act actually committed.

For example, Huey Hardhat is going with Kitty Krump. He hears that she has been secretly seeing Homer Hashbrown. He becomes insanely jealous and buys a gun with which to shoot Homer. He goes to Kitty's apartment and finds both Kitty and Homer there. He aims the gun at Homer and fires. He misses Homer and by accident kills Kitty. Here we have a criminal act but no intent as far as killing Kitty. In criminal law this would be called a case of transferred or constructive intent. Huey would be just as guilty of murder as if he had originally intended to kill Kitty.

This concept applies even if the crime that results is different from the one originally intended. However, the final result must be within the probable limits of the original act. It must be a result that would be a natural and probable outcome of whatever was originally intended. For example, Sam Snerd and Willard Whomp go into a liquor store with intent to rob the store. They had no intent to cause any harm to the clerk. They are armed with revolvers. When they tell the clerk to give them the money, he quickly reaches for what appears to be a gun. Sam shoots and kills the clerk.

There was no original intent to kill the clerk. However, when two men go into a store armed with loaded revolvers in an attempt to rob the store, it is a natural and probable outcome of that act that someone might be killed.

Let us examine a case where transferred intent would not apply. Humphrey Hucklestump tells Larry Letcher to stay away from his daughter Lulubelle. When he finds out that Larry has still been seeing her, he gets his revolver and goes over to Larry's farm looking for him. He sees Larry next to a haystack and fires at him. He misses Larry, but the bullet hits some rocks near the haystack. This causes sparks which ignite the haystack. The haystack catches fire and the flames spread to the barn next to the haystack. Can Humphrey be charged with arson? The answer is no. The reason is that the setting of the barn on fire was not a probable and natural outcome of an attempted murder. Under the doctrine of proximate cause, the final result would be too unusual for a normal, reasonable person to anticipate or expect it.

In the State v. Whitfield[8] the defendant was held responsible for murder when he accidentally killed a woman while raping her. The killing was done without malice and was not intentional. Still the courts felt that the felonious intent of the original act was such that it carried over to the killing as a probable outcome. In California there are statutory provisions making any death resulting from the commission of a felony at least second degree murder.

Constructive or transferred intent cannot be applied to crimes that involve a requirement of specific intent. It applies only to crimes in the general intent area. To have specific intent means that the intent is a special intent pertaining only to the original planned crime.

For example, Fred Farkle plans to burglarize the Consolidated Laundry. He makes the plans and learns the location of the safe from a brother who works there. Because Fred is nervous, he starts drinking before going out on the job. He then drives up the back alley and breaks into what he thinks is the back door of the Consolidated Laundry. He goofs. He breaks into the L & M warehouse instead. He also sets off the silent alarm and is arrested. Fred can be guilty of malicious mischief or vandalism for breaking into the building, and trespassing, but not burglary. The crime of burglary requires a specific intent, and Fred's specific intent was toward the Consolidated Laundry not the L & M Warehouse. Specific intent cannot be transferred.

Transferred Intent Over a Period of Time

Apart from original intent being transferred from the original act to the unintended results of that act, it can also be transferred to later acts that are part of a particular criminal objective.

Transferred intent also applies when dealing with an act or series of acts covering a period of time. Sometimes the series of acts are all leading to one objective. In cases of this sort the law can treat the original intent as being "continuing," and covering the whole span of time needed to achieve the set objective of the criminal action. This can be important, because some of the acts might be more crucial than others, and some of the acts might lack the criminal intent that is associated with others.

For example, in the case of Jackson v. Commonwealth (100 KY 239) which occurred in 1898, and is therefore a case of fairly long precedent, two men gave a woman a large dose of drugs with the intent to kill her. However, she did not die, but went into a comatose state that gave the appearance of death. Because they believed that she was dead, the next day they decided that they should dispose of the body and disfigure the face so that no one would be able to recognize the victim. Their first step was to behead her. Since she was really not dead, the act of beheading her did kill her. However, there was present no criminal intent to kill because they believed her to be already dead. Since the law requires both act and intent in order for a crime to be complete, it appeared on the surface that they were not guilty of murder. However, the high court, in reviewing the case, held that the conduct involved a continuous act which brought the original intent over to the act that caused the death. It would be easier to say that the intent was continuous rather than the act, but it amounts to the same thing.

Another example that involves a fine point in law is the case involving an assault that later becomes a murder. Arvin Ardvark shoots Mervin Mushmellow in attempt to murder him. Mervin doesn't die and Arvin is tried for attempted murder. He is convicted and sentenced to state prison. Three months later Mervin dies from the gunshot wound. By this time Arvin no longer had bad feelings about Mervin, and when Mervin actually died, Arvin had no intent for him to die. His dying however, was an element of murder that was not an element of the attempted murder. Now we have another act resulting in a new crime, but there was no intent accompanying the act. Since this is sort of a technical exception to double jeopardy, Arvin is brought back from prison and now tried for the new crime of murder.

From a legal standpoint, the original criminal intent is said to have transferred or continued to the final act three months later. This legal concept also comes under the doctrine of proximate cause in that the shooting was the proximate cause of the death, which is a natural and probable outcome of a shooting. Since intent and responsibility are closely related, this doctrine would be valid.

Criminal Intent Cannot Transfer Backwards

Criminal intent can only be transferred to later acts or results of an initial act. It cannot be transferred back to an original act for which there was no criminal intent. It may, however, be used as circumstantial evidence to show that if there was criminal intent in a later act, that it would be probable that it was also present in a previous act.

"Trespass ab Initio"
(Does Not Apply to Criminal Law)

"Trespass ab Initio" is a legal term that means if wrongful intent is proven in a recent act, it can be assumed that previous acts were also wrongful. This legal concept does not apply to criminal law. It applies only to civil law. Sometimes there are borderline cases. For example, the Internal Revenue Service finds that a waiter has not been declaring the full amount of his tips for a period of one month. Under the doctrine of "trespass ab initio," they can assume that he has been guilty of the same error for the previous months of the year, and can assess him accordingly. Although this can be a criminal act, the assessment of tax is a civil matter.

6.4:0   MALICE

Under common law, malice had the same meaning as general intent. Today there is still a close relationship. Black's Law Dictionary defines malice as:

> The intentional doing of a wrongful act without just cause or excuse, with an intent to inflict an injury or under circumstances that the law will imply an evil intent.—A conscious violation of the law. —A condition of the mind showing a heart regardless of social duty and fatally bent on mischief.

It defines "general malice" as:

> A wickedness, a disposition to do wrong, a diabolical heart, regardless of social duty and fatally bent on mischief.

Ballantine's Law Dictionary, in its definition of malice, states:

> In its legal sense, malice means a wrongful act, done intentionally, or with evil intent, without just cause or excuse, or as the result of ill will. It does not necessarily imply spite against any individual, but rather in many instances, merely a wanton disposition grossly negligent of the rights of others.

As can be seen from these law dictionary definitions, there is not too much difference between general intent and malice. In one higher court decision, the court stated the difference between malice and general intent was that malice contained a condition of the mind that was more intent on wrongdoing or injuring another than would be the case of general intent.[9] In Bias v. United States, the court stated that malice was "of such character as to show an abandoned and malignant disposition." This would indicate that the difference is a matter of degree rather than a real difference.

Malice in Murder

The term malice is very important in the crime of murder because the type of malice is often used to distinguish the difference between Murder of the First Degree and Murder of the Second Degree.

According to Section 188 PC, the definitions of malice in murder are:

Express Malice: When there is manifested a deliberate intention unlawfully to take away the life of a fellow creature.

Implied Malice: When no considerable provocation appears, or when the circumstances attending the killing show an abandoned and malignant heart.

6.5:0   MOTIVE

People often get motive and intent confused. It is easy to do. Motive is WHY the person committed the crime. It is the reason for intent, and the reason for the crime. It has been sometimes called the moral quality of intent while intent is the mental quality of a crime. It gives birth to a purpose which then grows into the intent.

Motive does not have to be shown or proved in order to obtain a conviction. It can, however, be used as an approach to prove intent. A lack of motive may be used by the defense to help show a lack of criminal intent or even to counter circumstantial evidence relating to identity.[10] The absence of motive can also be used to support the presumption of innocence.[11] In other words, motive is not relevant to the substantive or written statutes, but it does have importance in the procedural or trial aspects of law. It certainly affects the type and degree of punishment after conviction.

A bad motive cannot make an act illegal if no law is violated. Similarly, a good motive cannot reduce the criminal liability of a bad act. If a person tries to cheat another, but by chance does not cheat him, he has a bad motive, but there is no criminal act. There have been many people who have committed murder with the best of motives. Mercy killing is an example. Still, it cannot be used as a legal defense. Persons belonging to religions that advocate the practice of polygamy are still guilty of bigamy if they engage in this practice; religion is not a legal defense in such a circumstance.

When we consider that intent relates to the means of committing the crime and motive relates to the result of the crime, the line between motive and "specific intent" becomes a thin one.

An exception in which motive may be considered a defense is when the motive involves "necessity" as a defense. In order for necessity to be used as a defense, it must be shown that the defendant was avoiding an immediate harm that is greater than the harm for which the law involved seeks to prevent. For example, if a jail catches fire and an inmate breaks out of jail to avoid burning to death, he has violated the letter of the law as far as "Jail Breaking" is concerned, but the motive was "necessity" rather than an attempt at permanent escape. The inmate was avoiding an immediate harm (burning to death) greater than the harm which the law involved seeks to prevent (allowing persons convicted of crimes to roam loose in society). Since juries are human beings, and want to know WHY the defendant committed the act, the prosecutor will undoubtedly present motive as part of the prosecution's case. Still, from a legal standpoint, a conviction can be had without motive ever being proved or even presented. For example, Professor Thadwick Humpastump is lecturing to his class of 70 students, and all of a sudden he turns to Flossie Furd in the front row and states, "I have thought about this for a week, and it's the only way." He then pulls out a gun and shoots her. His statement would show some premeditation, and there would be 69 witnesses to the shooting. (Flossie can't talk.) If Professor Humpastump refuses to tell anyone why he shot Flossie, he could go to the gas chamber without anyone ever knowing the motive for the shooting. He could be convicted in court without motive ever being shown. From the standpoint of the prosecution, it is much easier to obtain a conviction if some motive can be shown. Because of this the investigating officer should make every effort to gather evidence that will show motive. Once motive is established, it can present clues that will lead to other forms of evidence that can be accepted in court.

6.6:0 CRIMINAL NEGLIGENCE AND RECKLESSNESS

Criminal Negligence

Criminal negligence may be substituted for criminal intent in order to make a certain conduct criminal in nature. The most common application of criminal negligence involves traffic offenses, and especially cases of vehicular manslaughter.

There Are Five Elements Normally Involved In Negligence

(1) **An Obligation** or responsibility on the part of the defendant toward proper conduct.

(2) **A Standard Of Proper Conduct.** The conduct that would be expected of an ordinary, reasonable, prudent person under the same conditions.

(3) **A Breach Or Violation Of That Standard.** There must be some conduct that violated the standard.

(4) **A Chain Of Causation.** There must be some connection shown between the negligent conduct and the result or final criminal outcome.

(5) **Some Harm Or Injury.** Results from the negligence.

There are two difficult elements to prove in court, First, what would be expected conduct under the conditions at that time and place? Second, what did the defendant do that violated the standard of conduct?

6.6:1 Discussion Of Elements Normally Involved In Negligence

(1) **An Obligation**

There are three general types of obligations:

(a) **Statutory** (Some written law pertaining to the obligation) E.g., Providing necessities for children (270 PC).

(b) **Unwritten Obligation Involving Safety & Welfare of Others** (Including their property). A man obtains a hunting license and goes deer hunting He is performing a legal act. However, suppose he sees a movement in the bushes, yet cannot see exactly what it is. He fires his rifle into the bushes and kills another hunter. His action would be negligent based on the fact that it is an unwritten, yet valid, obligation that a hunter will not fire his rifle at something he cannot see clearly. It is a responsibility expected of a reasonable person. This is sometimes called a common sense obligation.

An unwritten obligation does not involve dangerous risks to the person obligated.

(c) **Occupational Responsibilities**

Railroad switch-persons have an unwritten, yet legal, responsibility to properly perform their jobs in a way that ensures the safety of others. That is what this job is all about. If the switch-person is drunk, or falls asleep, and fails to throw the switch for an oncoming train, and that train runs into another, causing great damage and/or personal injury, the switch-person would be guilty of negligence and could be charged with manslaughter if someone was killed.[12] Police officers and security guards also come under this type of occupational responsibility, as do lifeguards (who, for example, might waste time talking to members of the opposite sex while someone is in need of help). The key to this category is the purpose or objective of each particular occupation.

If a person suffers some harm or damage because of the action or failure to act, of another person, the first step to consider in determining whether there was negligence is to establish whether there was an obligation or duty required of the person responsible.

In some cases the courts have held that the defendant must have been aware of such duty and had the required knowledge to perform the duty, or the negligence becomes questionable.[13]

Moral Obligations

Moral obligations are not legal obligations. Once they are undertaken, however, proper care must be used in carrying them out. (E.g., If a person stops at the scene of an accident, and as a moral obligation tries to give first aid to one of the victims, he or she takes on the legal responsibility to act in a normal, prudent, and reasonable manner.)

If one person observes another drowning, that person has a moral obligation to try to save the drowning victim if he or she is able. However, from a legal standpoint the observer does not have an obligation to do anything, and could, in fact, be so depraved as to take photographs of the person drowning to sell to a newspaper.

6.6:2   A Proper Standard of Conduct

This can be difficult to prove. What does it mean? It is a deviation from that standard of care and conduct that exceeds the accepted norm. (This still leaves much room for difference of opinion.) It is difficult to define. Most laws use words like:

(a) Prudent

(b) Reasonable

(c) With due caution

These presume the behavior of an ordinary person acting under the same circumstances, including time and place. (can be an act or failure to act)

It is difficult to define expected conduct for all occasions, under all circumstances. The so-called "ordinary, reasonable, prudent person" is a myth who simply does not exist. Yet members of the jury are asked to examine the circumstances in a case and arrive at a decision regarding that conduct in relation to the conduct that would normally be expected of a prudent and reasonable person under the same set of circumstances. If the standard does involve some occupation or skill, expert witnesses are usually brought to court to testify as to what they consider to be a proper standard of conduct.

The legal definition of words found in statutory laws provides the members of juries with little real guidance in determining what should be a standard of proper conduct. They must often react to a "gut feeling" that is influenced by the persuasive ability of the attorneys for both sides.

6.6:3   A Breach or Violation of that Standard of Conduct

Once a proper standard of conduct is established, the jury must then decide whether the defendant violated that standard by his act or his failure to act. In order for negligence to take the place of criminal intent, the act or failure to act must involve a negligence that is reckless or indifferent to consequences.[14]

Witnesses or physical evidence can be invaluable in establishing evidence of a breach of a standard of care, but there is often a lack of evidence or witnesses to properly establish exactly what happened. The jury has to decide on the testimony or deposition (a sworn written statement) of the defendant. The degree of the breach is often the determining factor as to whether the case is classed as criminal or civil.

Abilities of the Defendant

It must be shown that the defendant had the ability to perform the required duty, otherwise he or she would not be liable for not performing that standard of conduct (State v. Miller (Mo App) 33 SW 2d 1063). If a man had no knowledge of medicine, he would not be guilty of failing to help his wife who was ill or sick when the required conduct involved some medical ability. On the other hand, if he refused to seek help from neighbors or others when it was available, (or from those who had the skills or knowledge) he would be liable. (Stehr v. State 92 Neb 755) If the victim is a relative, this affects responsibility,

6.6:4   A Chain of Causation Exists Between the Original Act and the Final Result

The topic of causation and the Doctrine of Proximate Cause will be covered later under the "Relationship of Conduct and a Criminal State of Mind." In the case of negligence, more consideration is given to unpredictable or unforeseen interfering circumstances that add to or affect the final outcome. In cases of outright criminal intent, this is given little weight. The "but for" rule of the Doctrine of Proximate Cause is applied to negligence, but ONLY to the Proximate Cause, and not the actual or physical cause. In the case of an accidental shooting, the <u>proximate cause</u> would be the <u>pulling of the trigger</u> (or firing of the gun). The <u>physical cause</u> would be the <u>bullet entering the victim's body</u>.

ORIGINAL ACT
(Proximate Cause)

END OR FINAL
RESULT

CONNECTION

Fig. VI–2: The Chain of Causation

Connection

In order to show that a chain of causation exists between the original act and the final result, each link in the chain must be shown to connect. If there is a break in the chain, the defendant cannot be held responsible for the end or final result.

6.6:5 Some Harm or Injury Results from the Negligence

Even if the injury or damage is very slight, there is still liability, In the case of traffic offenses, such as ignoring a stop sign without intent, the harm or injury is to society since this act has caused a potential danger to the safety of others.

It is important that investigating officers give attention to the exact details of injury or damage when first observed, and use some logic in determining whether the injury or damage is a likely or probable result of the suspect's initial act.

Although the same rules apply both to civil and criminal negligence, criminal negligence is of a greater degree than ordinary negligence. Even in the area of criminal negligence, the statutes of California divide it in two classifications:

(1) Ordinary negligence
(2) Gross negligence

This is done to establish the degree of punishment. For example, in California, Vehicular Manslaughter can be either a felony or a misdemeanor depending upon whether the negligence involved is Gross or Ordinary.

There are simply no fixed rules in distinguishing the two classes. Only facts and circumstances can be used in the final determination, aided by descriptions of what the higher courts have declared to be examples of gross and ordinary negligence. The conduct of the defendant is the determining factor, not the extent of the injuries suffered by the victim.

Some Rules on Negligence

(1) Negligence cannot be attributed to crimes that involve specific intent; this is willful intent, and can in no way be classed as negligence.
(2) Criminal negligence can be present in an otherwise lawful act. For example, the driving of a vehicle when the driver is licensed and when driving under the speed limit, is a lawful act.

If, however, the driver fails to use due caution, and is not alert to traffic and pedestrians, then this lawful act becomes an act that involves negligence. If the driver were to hit another car or a pedestrian in a cross walk, the negligence would make the act criminal.

(3) Negligence can also involve the failure to perform a legal act.
(4) If a person's acts indicate gross and wanton negligence or even recklessness in regard to exposing others to danger, that person is presumed to have intended the natural and probable consequences of those negligent acts.[15]

6.6:6 Example of Negligence By Applying Five Elements

(1) **Obligation:** Arvin Ardvark works as a switchman for the Coast Railroad Company. His job and obligation is to switch the tracks when a particular train is passing by so that it continues on its way and doesn't go into the passenger loading area.

(2) **Standard of Proper Care:** The Railroad regulations state that the tracks will be switched when the train is at least one quarter of a mile away from the switch. This is to ensure safety in case the switch is broken. In this case the switchman can use a red flag or lamp to stop the train.

(3) **A Breach or Violation of That Standard of Care:** One night Arvin falls "asleep at the switch," and doesn't realize the train is approaching until it is almost there. He runs for the switch but pulls it too late and the train continues along the wrong track hitting a passenger train that is loading at the platform.

(4) **A Chain of Causation:** Because of Arvin's negligence, the track was not switched. Because the track was not switched, the train continued along the wrong track. Because the train continued along the wrong track, it hit another train stopped on that track. Because it hit the other train, ten people were killed and fifty people were injured. All the links in the Chain of Causation can be joined to show that the deaths and injuries would not have occurred if Arvin had not been negligent in his occupational duties.

(5) **Harm or Injury Results:** This can be shown by death certificates, photographs of the scene and victims, doctor's depositions, and witnesses.

6.6:7   Recklessness

Recklessness is somewhere between negligence and criminal intent. Some of the major differences are:

(1) In negligence the defendant need not be aware of the consequences of his conduct. His actions are just not those of a normal, reasonable, prudent man.

(2) In recklessness, the defendant is aware of (or should be aware of) the possible risk that his or her actions involve, and is therefore, from a mental standpoint, more guilty or liable for the result of his or her acts. The key is awareness of increased risks. (Foreseeability)

6.6:8   Degrees of Care or Responsibility Between Classification of Criminal Offenses

To better understand the relationship between the degrees of care that are required for different types of criminal conduct, or the lack of criminal conduct, the illustration on the next page shows how the change of conduct can change from a lawful act to an unlawful act. This, of course, is a simplification of this relationship, but it will help to illustrate a point.

6.7:0   PRESUMED KNOWLEDGE OFFENSES

A key to these offenses is that the persons responsible have some control over their actions.

6.7:1   Strict Liability Crimes

Strict liability crimes involve statutory obligations, unlike negligence which simply involves lack of due caution.

One of the apparent paradoxes in criminal law is the statutory law in many states that require both act and intent in order for there to be a crime. Yet there is a classification of crimes that does not require the mental state we call criminal intent, or even criminal negligence. These are the "Strict Liability" (sometimes called "Absolute Liability") crimes. There are not many of these types of crimes on the books.

Legality of Strict Liability Crimes

(1) There is nothing in the U.S. Constitution that requires both act and intent to be present in order for there to be a crime.

(2) Historically, there has always existed a small but special class of offenses which required no criminal intent. As we go farther back, we find greater numbers of strict liability crimes.

(3) These crimes affect the general welfare, health or convenience of society, outweighing individual needs in the interest of the community.

(4) State Supreme Courts have recognized the power of the state legislature to enact strict liability laws in the public interest, and within their Police Powers (10th Amendment).[16]

(5) Chief Justice Cooley in the People v. Robey[17] stated that the need for intent in a crime was not a universal rule. He felt the purpose of statutes in the nature of Police Regulations was to "require a degree of diligence for the protection of the public."

(6) Justice Cardozo,[18] in referring to the legality of Strict Liability crimes, stated: "Prosecution for minor penalties have always constituted in our law, a class by themselves. That is true though the prosecution is criminal in form." He seems to be saying that these offenses are not really crimes although they are prosecuted as such. Many other writers in criminal law feel they are more civil in nature.

6.7:2   Justification for Strict or Absolute Liability Crimes

The justification for these offenses is based more on practical aspects than on strict legal theory. Some of the reasons most often given are:

(1) The penalties are usually very light. (Fines)

(2) A great amount of time and expense is saved for both sides if intent need not be proved in cases where the punishment is so light.

(3) Most people are aware of these offenses and know their liability in the matter. Many pertain to special occupations.

(4) There is little chance of inflicting great injustice upon the people as a whole, from the existence of such laws.

(5) Far more good than bad results from the existence of such laws.

(6) These are crimes against the general public and not against an individual.

(7) The needs of the community far outweigh the needs and rights of the individual.

Strict liability crimes do not cover "*Mala in se*" offenses, but only "*Mala Prohibita*" offenses.

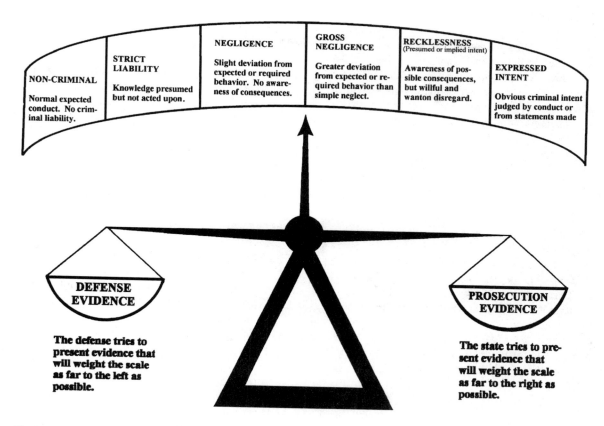

NON-CRIMINAL	STRICT LIABILITY	NEGLIGENCE	GROSS NEGLIGENCE	RECKLESSNESS (Presumed or implied intent)	EXPRESSED INTENT
Normal expected conduct. No criminal liability.	Knowledge presumed but not acted upon.	Slight deviation from expected or required behavior. No awareness of consequences.	Greater deviation from expected or required behavior than simple neglect.	Awareness of possible consequences, but willful and wanton disregard.	Obvious criminal intent judged by conduct or from statements made

DEFENSE EVIDENCE

The defense tries to present evidence that will weight the scale as far to the left as possible.

PROSECUTION EVIDENCE

The state tries to present evidence that will weight the scale as far to the right as possible.

Fig. VI–3: The Scale of Criminal Liability

Examples:

(1) Parking tickets in which the registered owner of the car is responsible even he or she was not driving the car.

(2) The selling of tainted or bad foods in which the owner of the production company is responsible. (Serious as a threat to public health.)

(3) Public sanitation laws where the owners of buildings are responsible even if they were not personally negligent. It makes them more conscious of the duty to ensure proper sanitation.

(4) The mechanical condition of a car is the responsibility of the registered owner of the car.

(5) Under Alcoholic Beverage Control Laws, the owners of liquor stores are liable when their employees sell liquor to minors.

6.7:3 Responsibility Under Strict Liability Offenses

The fact that the defendant had good faith or that it was an innocent mistake is no defense regarding strict liability crimes. That is why the term "strict liability" is used.

Constructive Knowledge

The theory here is that criminal intent is not required because of a principle called "Constructive Knowledge." (sometimes called "Presumed Knowledge") It is assumed that if the defendant had such knowledge, he or she then failed to act upon that knowledge. It goes back to the old legal maxim about ignorance of the law being no excuse. The legal thinking is that if the defendant did not know the law, he or she should have.

The term "constructive" has been used before in this book. The meaning is "in place of." It has been used in the term "Constructive Entry" where a burglar would be guilty of entry even if he did not himself make entry into a building, using instead a trained monkey to make the entry and steal valuables. It was referred to as a "Constructive Act." The term "Constructive Intent" was also used.

In constructive intent, the defendant intended to kill one person, but by mistake killed another. In this case, the original intent was used "in place of" the intent needed for the final killing.

The U.S. Supreme Court has held that as long as strict liability statutes are not vague or indefinite in their wording, they are constitutional.[19]

Resolving the Conflict of Strict Liability and the Intent Requirement for Crimes

Many states are attempting to solve the problem of contradiction with state penal codes that list a requirement for both act and intent in order for there to be a crime. The solution used in most states is to create a special classification of offense that is not regarded as a crime. This type of offense is called an "Infraction."

6.7:4 Strict Liability and Responsibility Under the Principal-Agent Rule

The principal is the person who controls another; the agent is a person who is controlled by another. The most common example of the Principal-Agent concept are employers and employees.

Under the Strict Liability laws, an employer (Principal) is responsible for the acts of his or her employees (Agents) if they pertain to the Strict Liability class. Examples would be employees selling alcohol to minors, selling tainted (bad) food, or dumping litter or garbage into a stream or waterway next to the place of employment.[20]

The theory behind this responsibility is that employers have some control over their employees if they are working at the place where they are employed. There is supervision over their actions, and there is always the threat of losing their jobs if they do violate one of the Strict Liability laws. Otherwise, employers could tell their employees to forget about cleanliness and turn out the food faster so they can make more money, but that they will not back them up if they get caught.

Control Over Employees for Non-Strict Liability Offenses

There is an assumption here that employers do in fact have some control over their employees. Exceptions to this rule would be when they are out-of-town on business, or home sick. Under Strict Liability, employers have no excuse if their employees violate these laws. When it pertains to other types of violations, it must be shown that the employer does, or should, have some control.

Offenses Committed by Either the Principal or Agent, but Unknown to the Other

There are sometimes conditions where either the employer or the employee violate the law, but it is unknown to the other party. For example: A youth is hired as a delivery person, and as part of the job, packages are delivered to certain addresses. Unknown to the employee, the packages contain illegal substances. Since this does not cover a

Strict Liability law, and there is no intent, the employee is not criminally responsible. In the same circumstances, the employee is hired to perform a legitimate task of delivering packages. Unknown to the employer, the employee is delivering narcotics to his customers apart from his regular delivery duties. Under these conditions the employer would not be criminally responsible.

Criminal Acts Coerced by Employer (Principal)

If an employer tells an employee to commit an act that violates the law or lose his or her job, the employee can have no legal defense by using this as an excuse for these criminal acts.

6.8:0 PRESUMPTIVE LAWS (There is a presumption of specific intent)

There are certain crimes that involve a statutory presumption of certain facts. This can pertain to the presumption that the defendant had a certain or particular:

(a) Intent, or
(b) Knowledge or
(c) performed a certain act

The major difference between a Presumptive Law and a Strict Liability Crime is that the Presumptive Law can be rebutted but the Strict Liability Crime cannot. Under Strict Liability, if you commit the act, you are guilty. Rebutted means that the defendant can present evidence in court to prove the presumption is false. However, the burden of proof is on the defendant to show evidence that contradicts the presumption.

Conditions for Presumptive Laws

(1) It is an offense that affects the general community and not just one person.
(2) No intent is required (as in Strict Liability).
(3) This presumption must actually be written into the law. (Otherwise, the District Attorney could call any law a presumptive law and put the burden of proof on the defendant.)

The state still has the burden of proof to show that all the other elements of the offense did occur.

There are not many Presumptive Laws on the books. They are usually reserved for offenses that affect public order and the general welfare of the community, and are cases in which it would be difficult for the state to prove the presumption.

Since the burden of proof is on the defendant, if the jury cannot make up their minds as to the presumption, they must assume that the presumption is in fact true.

Examples of Presumptive Laws:

(1) In California, the Dangerous Weapons Control Law states that if a person possesses a firearm with the serial number removed, it is presumed the possessor was the one who removed the serial number. The state must prove that he did in fact possess the firearm, and that the serial number was in fact removed when he was found in possession of the weapon.

Because Presumptive Laws are refutable, the defendant can show evidence that would prove to the jury that he was not the one who removed the serial number.

(2) The California law on theft states that if a person hires a new employee, and does not tell him that he owes other employees back wages, and then fails to pay the new employee, it is presumed that the employer intended to defraud the new employee.

Because these laws reverse the burden of proof, they are occasionally challenged, but they have always been declared to be constitutional by the California Supreme Court.[21]

6.9:0 THE JOINT RELATIONSHIP BETWEEN THE ACT (CONDUCT) AND INTENT (MENTAL PART)

The law is very clear that there must not only be an act and intent, (or conduct and the mental element) but there must be a joint relationship between the two. There are times when there is both act and intent, but there is no relationship between the two.

For example, a woman hates her husband so much that she decides to kill him. We now have the mental element. Her husband is out of town, and she plots different ways to "do him in." Her husband is not expected back for three days. Because he finishes his business, he returns three days early. He arrives at two o'clock in the morning, and finds that he has misplaced his key. He does not want to wake his wife, so he tries to sneak in the house by climbing through a window. His wife hears a noise and thinks that it is a prowler or burglar. She gets her husband's hunting rifle and goes to the room where she heard the noise. She sees a dark figure coming through the window, and fires the rifle at the figure. She kills her husband. She has now completed the act. However, when she killed her husband, she did not know it was him. Even though we have both the intent and the act, there is not a proper joint relationship between the two, and there is no crime.

Let us consider another example where the mental element comes after the act. Henry Hemroid is chopping down trees on his property. He has signs all around his property prohibiting trespassing. Mortimer Snort trespasses on the property to take a "short cut" home. Mortimer is hard of hearing, and doesn't hear Henry yell, "Timber." A tree falls on Mortimer and kills him. Here we have the act of a killing, but without criminal intent. When Henry discovers that the tree fell on Mortimer, he tells his helper that he is very happy about it because he has hated Mortimer for years. We now have the mental element, but it occurs after the act, so there is no joint relationship between the act and the intent, and therefore, no crime.

6.10:0 THE CAUSE-AND-EFFECT RELATIONSHIP AND THE DOCTRINE OF PROXIMATE CAUSE

The fifth element in the Triangle of Crime is the Cause-and-Effect Relationship. This simply means that a person cannot be convicted of a crime without the prosecution showing that the act the defendant committed was responsible for the final harm. This concept often comes under the general heading of CAUSATION.

6.10:1 Causation (It is really responsibility)

Causation simply means that a cause and effect relationship must be shown between the original act or conduct of the defendant, and the resulting harm. If we know who caused the harm, we know who is responsible. Causation shows criminal responsibility.

The doctrine of causation is found in both criminal and civil law. The use of this doctrine in determining responsibility for a certain harm is basically the same. One of the differences would be contributory negligence. In criminal law there is no contributory negligence. For example, a rape victim who wore revealing clothes, and even enticed the rapist may have contributed to the rape, but it would not affect the responsibility of the rapist. In civil law, however, the negligence of the victim can greatly affect the amount of the monetary judgment awarded. If the jury feels the victim in some way contributed to the resulting injury or harm, they can reduce the award accordingly.

Another difference is that in criminal law there must be intent or criminal negligence in order for there to be criminal liability or responsibility. In civil law it is just a matter of proving that the final harm or damage has a causal relationship to the original act. For example, Arvin Ardvark throws a rock through a window. By using "causation," it can be shown that Arvin is responsible for the resulting harm of the broken window. Under civil law, he is responsible for the damage. Would he also be responsible for criminal liabilities? If it could be shown that Arvin actually intended to break the window, or that his act was so negligent that a reasonable person would expect the throwing of the rock to break the window, then it is possible that Arvin could be charged criminally as well.

Criminal Negligence and Ordinary Negligence

There is a difference between criminal and ordinary negligence. In criminal negligence there is a legal obligation to perform a certain act or to maintain proper caution when performing certain acts such as driving a vehicle. In plain or ordinary negligence, there is just a simple failure to perform an act in a reasonable manner or to show a proper caution in the performance of the act.

6.10:2   Types Of Causation

(A) Direct Causation

In direct causation, it is easy for a reasonable person to conclude that the original act or conduct was responsible for the resulting harm. This is because it is so direct. Situations that involve direct causation are often those that also involve some type of intent. Crimes involving criminal intent are usually crimes with a direct causation.

For example: Melvin Milktoast tells his wife Melba that he has put up with her nagging for over 20 years, and he has had enough. He takes a shotgun and blows her head off. In this case there is a very simple and direct "chain of causation" from the shooting of the gun to the wife's death. Link one: Melvin points the gun at his wife. Link two: he pulls the trigger. Link three: the gun fires a load of pellets. Link four: the pellets blow off the victim's head. Link five: the victim dies. Because it is easy to connect the original act with the resulting harm in a case involving direct causation, few problems arise. There is another type of causation, however, which can present many problems when trying to determine responsibility.

(B) Indirect Causation

When the resulting harm was not intended by the person committing the original act, he can still be held responsible, This occurs when there are intervening circumstances or unknown conditions and is called indirect causation. It can become very complicated when the Chain of Causation involves a long series of acts or "links." These cases usually involve negligence or acts of recklessness

6.10:3   Elements Needed for Criminal Causation

To show criminal causation, three things must be proved:
(1) The conduct was the "Cause in Fact" of the final harm.
(2) The final harm was "Proximate" (proximate cause). This means that the result was either:
   (a) Actually intended, or
   (b) That it should have been expected as a reasonable outcome of the original act.
(3) There was present the necessary mental element to make the situation criminal. (E.g., intent, negligence, recklessness)

(1) Cause In Fact

Two rules are used to show Cause in Fact:
(a) The "But For" Rule

The most common way to show Cause in Fact is through the "But For" Rule. We simply ask: "but for the original illegal act of the defendant, would the final harm have resulted?" If the answer is no, then we have proved the first element. In civil law, this is all that is required to assign responsibility. The act need not be criminal as well. In civil law, this rule is held very strictly. If the Chain of Causation leads from the harm back to the original act, the responsibility is clear. In criminal law, where proving responsibility can result in taking a defendant's personal liberty or freedom for a long time, the rule has reasonable limits. The "But For" Rule tends to show the relationship between the cause (original act) and the effect (harmful result)

Examples:
(a) But for the fact that the defendant negligently used gasoline to clean the hot engine of his running motorcycle, would the fire have started in the garage that eventually spread to the entire apartment complex and resulted in the death of an elderly invalid tenant?
(b) But for the fact that the defendant knocked the victim unconscious and left him lying in the snow, would the victim have developed pneumonia and died?

(b) The Substantial Factor Rule

This becomes a problem when more than one person contributes to the final harm. It becomes difficult to assign responsibility.

Example:

Fred Farkle and Mervin Mushmuscle attack Teddy Toadtoes. Fred shoots Teddy in the heart, and Mervin shoots him in the head. Both shots are fired at the same time and both shots are fatal.

Who is responsible for Teddy's death? Can we apply the "But For" rule? But for the fact that Fred shot at Teddy, would Teddy have died? Yes, he would have died as a result of Mervin's shot. Under this rule, Fred could escape responsibility. Not only that, the rule could be applied to Mervin as well and excuse him from responsibility. Now we see the reason for the substantial factor rule.

Application of the Rule:

We ask this simple question. "Was the defendant's conduct a substantial factor in bringing about the criminal result?" In this case, the answer would be yes for both defendants. Under this rule, they would not escape responsibility.

(2) Proximate Cause
(The Doctrine of Proximate Cause)

The Doctrine of Proximate Cause states that "a person is responsible for the natural and probable outcome of his actions." This doctrine is based very heavily on what is called "foreseeability." Would a normal, prudent person be able to foresee what was going to happen when he did a certain thing?

Example:

Sammy Snerd is working for a construction company and his boss tells him to carry some leftover lumber down from the tenth floor of a building under construction. Because he is lazy, Sammy just throws the lumber off the tenth floor. He does this without even looking to see if someone might be walking around the ground area. As a result, one of the boards hits and kills a worker on the ground. Should Sammy, as a normal, prudent person, have foreseen the potential danger of such an act? Is it the natural and probable outcome?

Proximate Cause as a Question of Fact

The application of the Doctrine of Proximate Cause is a question of fact. The judge will explain the law to the jury (questions of law) but it is up to the jury to decide whether those rules actually apply to the case being tried. It is the "Trier of Fact" who determines Proximate Cause.

6.10:4   Contributing Factors In Causation

Contributing Causes and Sole Causes

In applying the Doctrine of Proximate Cause there are two types of causes to consider: contributing causes and sole causes. To be proximate, an act need only be a contributing cause and not the sole cause. Because these are difficult concepts to nail down, it is best to rely on the "Chain of Causation" concept in all cases and show that there are no breaks in the chain.

Attempting to apply the Doctrine of Proximate Cause is often a matter of trying to balance a concern for the defendant's liability as a reasonable person under a particular set of circumstances, and a desire to assign responsibility for the harm that has been suffered. Unfortunately, when we have a case of negligence and unintended consequences, the tendency, at times, is to lean in the direction of assigning responsibility to some one person.

Rules Under Indirect Causation

(A) Cases Where Contributing Factors Are Accepted In Proving Liability

(1) Unknown Circumstances Must Be Accepted

Sometimes this rule is expressed as "Taking the Victim as You Find Him." It means that the defendant cannot avoid responsibility for causation based on the defense that he did not know that certain conditions existed. For example Arvin Ardvark hits Larry Lump with a stick and Larry has a heart attack and dies. Arvin cannot avoid responsibility for Larry's death by claiming that he did not know that Larry had a bad heart.

Arvin hit Larry in the nose with his fist. It started a nose bleed, and Larry, being a hemophiliac bled to death. Arvin could not use the excuse that he did not know that Larry was a hemophiliac. Arvin must take Larry "as he finds him."

(2) Different Acts of Common Design or Purpose

The defendant's act need not be the sole cause of the resulting harm or damage. It can be a contributing or proximate cause which is accompanied by another act committed at the same time by another who is trying to achieve a common objective with the defendant.[22] If a person, by his or her actions, shortens the life of one already mortally wounded by an accomplice, that person is guilty of homicide. This is so even when the act is only a contributing factor. It is also true if two persons shoot the victim when acting together[23] or independently of each other[24] and it applies even if only one of the wounds is actually fatal. If each wound alone could not have caused death, and only the combination of wounds could have been fatal, both persons committing the acts are guilty of homicide,

(3) Effect of Contributing Acts by the Victim Are No Defense

If the cause of death is a matter of negligence or failure by the victim to properly take care of a wound, the person who caused the wound is still liable for the death.[25] If the death is brought about by suicide because the victim of the unlawful injury was in unbearable pain, the person causing the original injury is responsible for the death.[26] Even if the victim refused an operation that could have saved his or her life, the responsibility for the death lies with the person causing the original injury.[27]

The above situation also applies if the victim, because of the injury, cannot take proper preventive action and dies from bleeding, even if proper first aid would have saved his or her life.[28] If the victim, in a state of fever and delirium, tears open the wound or stitches and then dies, the rule of proximate cause applies.[29] If the victim has a bad heart and the trauma of the attack causes a heart attack,[30] or if the excitement of the attack causes a brain hemorrhage,[31] the person who created the original trauma or disturbance is responsible for the victim's death.

(4) Post Actus (After the original act) Circumstances By Victim Are No Defense

Many things that occur after the original act or injury that would make the result more serious. These intervening circumstances do not interfere with the rules of causation. This can happen if an original wound is not fatal in itself, but causes an infection, disease, or illness that later causes death (e.g., blood poisoning, pneumonia, etc.)[32] Poor or negligent medical attention in treating the original injury can also cause a death for which the person committing the original act is responsible.[33]

(B) Cases Where Contributing Factors Are Not Accepted In Proving Responsibility

(1) Intervening Acts That Are Independent of Original Design

The defendant commits an original act with a set purpose in mind. Later, another person, in no way connected with the first, commits another act that increases the severity of the original act. In cases of this nature, the high courts have felt that the "chain of causation" was broken. It often depends upon whether the second act is entirely responsible for the result, or is just a contributing factor. This is a "gray" area in the law on causation, and is difficult to nail down with simple rules.

(2) Accidental Acts

If the original act is accidental and involves no violation of law or criminal intent, and there is no negligence present, it does not matter whether it was the proximate cause of the final result. If a reasonable, prudent person could not have prevented the original act, then it is a civil matter.

6.10:5 Considerations In Applying the Doctrine of Proximate Cause

The following considerations in applying the Doctrine of Proximate Cause are referred to as "Types of Proximate Cause" in some texts.

(A) Sufficiency of Original Act

Was the original act in itself sufficient to produce the results?

Example:

Sam Slush is arrested for Felony Drunk Driving because he allegedly hit the back of another car and injured the driver. A blood test shows that he was driving under the influence of alcohol. The question is whether his act of running into the back of the other car was sufficient to cause the supposed injuries to the driver of that car. The investigating officers' report shows no visible damage to either car, and states that they just took the word of the driver of the first car that he was in fact injured. Later, Sam finds two witnesses who saw the accident and they state that the two bumpers just barely touched as both cars slowly approached a red light. It would now be a "question of fact" for the jury to decide whether Sam was guilty of just Drunk Driving, or whether his act of bumping into the other car was "in itself sufficient" to cause the supposed injuries to the other driver and therefore increase the offense to Felony Drunk Driving.

(B) Chain of Events Reaction (Also called the "Domino Reaction")

Did the original criminal act start in motion a chain of events that finally and indirectly resulted in damage or harm? (foreseeability should not be too remote)

Example:

Hector Hashbrown loses his temper with his wife while carving the turkey, and swings at her with the knife and cuts her. The wound is not a serious or fatal one. In her fear, Hector's wife runs into the bathroom and locks herself in. In her emotional state she does not try to stop the bleeding, and then faints. She then bleeds to death even though proper first aid would have stopped the bleeding and saved her life. Here the cause started a chain of events that indirectly resulted in her death.

(C) Increased Risk

Did the original criminal act place someone in a position of substantially increased likelihood that they would suffer personal injury or harm to their property?

Example:

Clyde Crashcup sees Fanny Friggit lying asleep on the beach near the water. He notices that her purse is right next to her. In an effort to steal the purse and make a successful escape, he sneaks up on her and hits her over the head with a piece of driftwood. This results in a concussion and leaves her unconscious. He runs off with the purse leaving her unconscious on the beach. In a short time the incoming tide covers Fanny and she drowns. Her head concussion was not fatal and she would have recovered had the tide not moved in and drowned her. Here the act of knocking her unconscious placed her in a position of increased likelihood that she would suffer personal harm.

Example:

Harvey Hinkle holds up a liquor store. As he starts to leave with the money, he notices a police car parked outside the liquor store and two police officers getting out with their guns drawn. Just then Lilly Laglump walks into the store to buy her nightly pint of gin. Harvey grabs her and uses her as a shield and hostage. A gunfight ensues, and Lilly is shot.

Under the "Increased Risk" classification of Proximate Cause, Harvey would be responsible for the shooting of Lilly even though he did not do the shooting himself.[34] But for the fact that he held up the liquor store, there would have been no gun battle. But for the fact that he grabbed Lilly as a shield, she would probably not have been shot. This example is not difficult to understand. However, there are borderline cases involving Proximate Cause that are more difficult to apply.

If the defendant acted criminally and intentionally, few intervening circumstances are considered unforeseeable. If the defendant's conduct amounts to criminal negligence only, he or she will be given a greater benefit of the doubt regarding any unforeseen intervening circumstances.

6.10:6 The Difference Between the Physical Cause and the Proximate Cause

(1) **Physical Cause:** The physical or mechanical cause of injury such as a gun or bullet.

(2) **Proximate Cause:** The person controlling the physical cause

In applying the rules of causation, the key is establishing a relationship between cause and effect. A simple physical cause and effect relationship is not enough. It must be shown that the defendant's original criminal act was the proximate cause of the harm or injury that resulted.

Example:

Millie Mugwit gets mad at Lester Lump while she is peeling potatoes and stabs him with the knife in her hand. The knife is the physical cause of the injury. You could say that if the knife company had not manufactured the knife, the stabbing would not have occurred. However, that is a little far-fetched. So the physical cause does not make one responsible under causation. The proximate cause is the important consideration. The proximate cause in this case would be Millie stabbing Lester with the knife. That is what caused the injury.

6.10:7 Improbability of Outcome as it Affects Rules of Causation

There are limitations dealing with improbability. If the final act is different in some way or more serious in degree than the illegal act originally intended, such difference of original intent and the result is immaterial. However, it becomes a problem when the result is entirely different from that originally intended. Now the determination of liability or responsibility becomes more difficult because "foreseeability" is greatly restricted.

If the result of an act is so accidental that it does not have a justifiable relationship between the original act and the seriousness of the result, or responsibility is so unreasonable that a normal, prudent, average person could not have possibly anticipated the end result, it is unlikely that the person causing the original act would be held responsible for the final result. If the "Chain of Causation" has so many links that the original act is too far removed from the end result, criminal responsibility is very doubtful.

Example:

An example could be of the "Rube Goldberg" variety. Elmer Dudd throws a banana peel on the sidewalk (a minor violation of the law). A lady with an armful of groceries is walking behind him; she slips on the banana peel and drops her bag of groceries on a sleeping dog who runs down the sidewalk barking. A little boy who is afraid of dogs runs into the street to get away from the frightened dog. He runs in front of an automobile. The driver sees him and turns the car sharply to avoid hitting him. As he swerves the car, he runs head-on into an 80-year-old lady driving a Volkswagen, and she is killed from a concussion when her head hit the windshield of her car.

A causal relationship can be traced from the original act to the final result, but it is so out-of-the-ordinary that even though Elmer would be civilly liable for the death of the 80-year-old lady, it is extremely unlikely that he would be held criminally liable.

Example:

Nimrod Noodledorf is walking down the sidewalk. He is smoking a cigarette. He has a cold and the cigarette tastes funny to him, so he throws it in the gutter next to the curb. This would be a minor violation of the litter laws. Unknown to him, there has been an automobile accident about a block up the street. The gas tank of one of the cars has ruptured and gasoline is leaking out and flowing down the gutter. Nimrod's cigarette ignites the gasoline and the flames race up the street to the automobiles and cause them to explode. In this case, the cause of the explosion could be traced to the act of Nimrod throwing the cigarette in the gutter. Yet the average, normal, prudent person could not expect to reasonably foresee such an outcome from his act.

With the burden of proof on the prosecution, juries are more inclined to give the defendant the benefit of the doubt when circumstances are questionable. It is also true, however, that when juries are examining the circumstances they are able to look at them with a hindsight viewpoint, knowing what actually did happen or resulted from the act. This makes it difficult to really put themselves in the defendant's exact state of mind at the time he or she committed the initial act. This state of mind has a direct bearing on what the defendant should reasonably expect to happen as a result of the act.

The famous American Jurist, Justice Holmes, once urged caution in stretching the doctrine of proximate cause too far. He stated:

> all choice...depends on what is known at the moment of choosing... A fear of punishment for causing harm cannot work as a motive, unless the possibility of harm may be foreseen. Hence the only conditions that are significant for the purpose of the judgment are those that were known or ought to have been known to the actor.

He went on to say that, when considering the possible outcome of an act, it should be based on what knowledge the person has or ought to have had at the time of the act.

REFERENCES FOR CHAPTER VI

(1) Alan Butler, The Law Enforcement Process, Alfred Publishing Co., New York,

(2) Rollin M. Perkins, Criminal Law and Procedure, Foundation Press, New York, p. 1.

(3) Ibid, p. 1.

(4) Robinson v. California, 370 U.S. 660.

(5) Powell v. Texas, 392 U.S. 514.

(6) 39 Agustini Episcopi, tome Q 72, Aquinas 2 Summa Q 7.

(7) Wechter v. People, 53 Colo. 89.

(8) State v. Whitfield, 129 Wash.134.

(9) Alt v. State, 88 Neb. 259.

(10) State v. Wilkins, 158 N.C. 603.

(11) People v. Tom Woo, 181 Cal. 315.

(12) State v. O'Brien, 32 N.J. LAW 169.

(13) Westrip v. Commonwealth, 123 Ky. 95.

(14) U.S. v. Thompson, D.C. 12F. 245.

(15) People v. Vasquex, 85 Cal. App. 575.

(16) State v. Dombroski, 145 Minn. 278.

(17) People v. Robey, 52 Mich. 577.

(18) Tenement House Department v. McDivitt, 215 N.Y. 160 (1915)

(19) Lambert v. California, 355 U-S- 225-

(20) In re Marley, 29 Cal- 2d 525.

(21) People v. Scott, 24 Cal. 2d 774.

(22) People v. Roberts, 211 Mich. 187.

(23) People v. Rudecki, 309 Ill. 125.

(24) Wilson v. State, Tex. Cr. 74 SW 409.

(25) State v. Lane, 158 Ma 572.

(26) People v. Lewis, 124 Cal. 55.

(27) Franklin v. State 41 Tex. Cr. R 21.

(28) Mason v. State, 94 Tex. Cr. R 532.

(29) State v. Angelina, 73 W.Va. 146.

(30) State v. Scates, 50 N.C. 420.

(31) People v. Studern, 59 Cal. App. 547.

(32) Bishop v. State, 73 Ark. 568

(33) People v. Freundenberg, 121 C.A. 2d 564.

(34) Taylor v. State, 41 Tex. Cr. 564.

STUDY QUESTIONS

CHAPTER VI

(1) According to Penal Code Section 20, in every crime there must exist both act and
_____.

(2) The Latin term for criminal conduct is _____ _____.

(3) The legal term for the omission or failure to act is _____.

(4) "Possession" can be classed as a type of conduct even though there is no movement on the   T or F
part of the suspect.

(5) Illegal possession requires all but one of the following:

    (A) ____The item possessed is illegal.
    (B) ____The person possessing has knowledge of his possession.
    (C) ____The item possessed belongs to the person possessing it.
    (D) ____The person possessing has control of what he possesses.

(6) If a man uses a trained monkey to steal things for him, the man is still guilty of criminal conduct. It is called a _____ act.

(7) A "status" act is a type of criminal conduct.   T or F

(8) Vagrancy is an unconstitutional status act.   T or F

(9) The Latin term for criminal intent is _____ _____.

(10) Sir James Stephen stated that intent was impossible to properly define.   T or F

(11) There are three types of criminal intent.   T or F

(12) "General intent" is found mostly in what type of crimes?

    (A) ____Mala Prohibita crimes.   (C) ____traffic offenses.
    (B) ____trespassing violations.   (D) ____Mala In Se crimes.

(13) "General intent" is often shown by the actions involved in the crime.   T or F

(14) Specific intent is found in most crimes.   T or F

(15) A defendant's past record can be used in a trial to show specific intent.   T or F

(16) Specific intent is the hardest type of intent to prove.   T or F

(17) Transferred intent is also called _____ intent.

(18) When Arvin tries to shoot Clyde, but by mistake shoots Betty, he is still guilty. This is called
_____ intent.

(19) Criminal intent can transfer backwards in time.   T or F

(20) "Trespass Ab Initio" means:

    (A) ____present intent can be applied to past acts.   (B) ____the intent found in trespassing.
    (C) ____the original intent in continuous crimes.   (D) ____trespassing at night.

(21) Under Common Law, malice was the same as general intent.   T or F

(22) Motive must be proven in order to obtain a conviction in court.   T or F

(23) A good motive excuses criminal liability.   T or F

(24) Moral obligations are also legal obligations.   T or F

(25) "Unwritten obligations" can be legal obligations.   T or F

(26) A police officer has legal occupational obligations.   T or F

(27) In laws that cover "proper standards of conduct," the words most often used are:

    (A) ____severe, intense, magnified.   (B) ____proper, regular, normal.
    (C) ____prudent, reasonable, with due caution.   (D) ____none of these.

(28) A "deposition" is:

    (A) ____a sworn written statement.   (B) ____a court order.
    (C) ____a warrant.   (D) ____a confession.

(29) In criminal negligence, the harm must be an actual physical harm.   T or F

(30) Criminal negligence cannot be attributed to a crime that involves specific intent.   T or F

(31) Criminal negligence applies only to unlawful acts.   T or F

(32) When a person is grossly negligent, intent is presumed for the natural & probable outcomes of such acts.   T or F

(33) The major difference between negligence and recklessness is that in recklessness:

    (A) ____the offense is more serious.   (B) ____the punishment is greater.
    (C) ____one is aware of the increased risk of one's acts.   (D) ____there is no intent.

(34) The key to "presumed knowledge" is that the person responsible for the act has some control over the action.   T or F

(35) Another name for "strict liability" is:

    (A) ____absolute liability.   (B) ____set liability.
    (C) ____concrete liability.   (D) ____established liability.

(36) Strict liability laws, as a class of laws, are unconstitutional.   T or F

(37) There have always been strict liability laws.   T or F

(38) State Legislatures are allowed to pass strict liability laws under "police powers" given to the states by the _____ Amendment of the Constitution.

(39) The purpose of strict liability laws is to require a degree of diligence on the part of members of society.   T or F

(40) Strict liability laws are very numerous.   T or F

(41) Strict liability laws do not cover "Mala In Se" crimes.   T or F

(42) Give an example of a strict liability offense. _____.

(43) Strict liability laws substitute "constructive knowledge" for criminal intent.   T or F

(44) The most common example of a principal-agent relationship is _____ and _____.

(45) If an employee is threatened by his boss with being fired if he does not violate a minor law, the employee may be excused from criminal liability since he was acting under instruction of his boss.   T or F

(46) The major difference between a strict liability law and a presumptive law is that a presumptive law can be _____.

(47) Presumptive laws must have the presumption actually written into the elements of the offense. T or F

(48) The defendant has the burden of proof regarding legal presumptions. T or F

(49) In presumptive laws, the state must prove all of the elements except the presumption. T or F

(50) Presumptive laws usually affect what type of offenses?

    (A) ____public order and general welfare of the community.   (B) ____Mala In Se crimes.

    (C) ____sexual offenses.   (D) ____criminal assaults.

(51) Presumptive laws cover elements that would be extremely difficult to prove in court without the presumption. T or F

(52) "Causation" is the term used for:

    (A) ____the cause and effect relationship.   (B) ____criminal intent.

    (C) ____criminal negligence.   (D) ____criminal conduct..

(53) "Taking the victim as you find him" is a rule of causation. T or F

(54) The legal term used to describe the ability of a person to know what the outcome of his or her acts might be is:

    (A) ____predictability.   (C) ____accountability.

    (B) ____foreseeability.   (D) ____determinism.

(55) To be found responsible for a resulting harm under the rule of causation, the defendant's act must have been the sole cause of the resulting harm. T or F

(56) Arvin Ardvark stabs Betsey Bloominheimer. It is not a fatal wound. Because Betsey does not take proper care of the wound, it becomes infected and she dies. Arvin is responsible for Betsey's death. T or F

(57) Clyde Crashcup punches Kenney Krumdopple in the chest. Kenney has a bad heart. Kenney dies from a heart attack. Clyde is therefore responsible for Kenney's death. T or F

(58) Denny Dork shoots Mervin Mushmuscle; Mervin dies. Under the rule of "causation," the gun in this shooting would be the:

    (A) ____physical cause.   (C) ____proximate cause.

    (B) ____real cause.   (D) ____legal cause.

(59) The doctrine of _____ _____ states that a person is responsible for the natural and probable outcome of his actions.

(60) To show "cause in fact" we use the _____ _____ rule.

(61) If a person did not intend the final outcome of his or her acts, this lack of intent will remove responsibility. T or F

(62) The "chain of events reaction" is also called the _____ reaction.

(63) Whether or not the doctrine of proximate cause applies in a case being tried is a question of fact for the jury to decide. T or F

(64) Chief Justice Holmes urged caution in stretching the doctrine of proximate cause too far. T or F

(65) To be the proximate cause, an original act must be the sole cause of the resulting harm. T or F

CHAPTER VII

PARTIES TO CRIMINAL ACTS

7.0   **PARTIES TO A CRIME IN CALIFORNIA**
7.1   **WHO IS A PRINCIPAL IN CALIFORNIA**
7.2   **WHO IS AN ACCESSORY IN CALIFORNIA**
7.3   **COMPOUNDING A CRIME**
7.4   **WHO IS AN ACCOMPLICE IN CALIFORNIA**
7.5   **CORROBORATION AND THE ACCOMPLICE**
7.6   **PARTIES TO A CRIME UNDER COMMON LAW**

7.0:0   PARTIES TO A CRIME IN CALIFORNIA

Upon achieving statehood, California adopted a new classification system for "parties to a crime" in place of common law. In 1850, the Crimes and Punishment Act listed parties to a crime as Accessories, Principals, and Accessories After the Fact. Accessories, however, were treated as Principals:

> An accessory is he who stands by and aids, abets, or assists; or who not being present aiding, abetting, or assisting, hath advised and encourages the perpetration of the crime. He who thus aids, abets or assists, advises or encourages shall be deemed and considered as principal and punished accordingly.

In 1872, the State of California adopted a Penal Code. The law on "parties to a crime" was changed — the term "Accessory" was dropped because, in the 1850 law, it meant the same as "Principal." Section 31 of the new Penal Code stated:

> All persons concerned in the commission of a crime, whether it be felony or misdemeanor, and whether they directly commit the act constituting the offense, or aid and abet in its commission, or, not being present, have advised and encouraged its commission, and all persons counseling, advising, or encouraging children under the age of 14 years, lunatics or idiots, to commit any crime, or who by fraud, contrivance, or force, occasion the drunkenness of another for the purpose of causing him to commit any crime, or who, by threats, menaces, command, or coercion, compel another to commit any crime, are Principals in any crime so committed.

7.1:0   Acts Committed Outside State

Penal Code Section 27 adds to this by including certain acts committed outside California. The following persons are liable to punishment:

(1) All persons who commit, in whole or in part, any crime within this state;

(2) All who commit any offense without this state which, if committed within this state, would be larceny, robbery or embezzlement under the laws of this state, and bring the property stolen or embezzled, or any part of it, or are found with it, or any part of it, within this state;

(3) All who, being without this state, cause or aid, advise or encourage, another person to commit a crime within this state, and are afterwards found therein.

7.1:1   WHO IS A PRINCIPAL IN CALIFORNIA

Principals

The problem of parties to a crime is simplified in California by using only one classification — Principal. **All principals are equally guilty.** There are six acts mentioned in section 31. The one pertaining to tricking or forcing a person to become drunk in order to get him to commit a crime could be covered under "Forcing" another to commit a crime, or "encouraging" a crime. Because of this, there are actually only five conditions that make a person a principal. They are:

(1) Committing the crime;

(2) Aiding and abetting another to commit the crime;

(3) Not being present, advise and encourage the crime;

(4) All persons who counsel children under 14, lunatics or idiots to commit a crime;

(5) Forcing another to commit a crime.

California case law deals mostly with those who "aid and abet" or "encourage" the commission of a crime. Case law is lacking in the area of #4. Case law has broadened the definition of the word "abet." (See "Definitions" on page 168.)

7.1:2   Advantages of the California System of Parties to a Crime

Under the California system, one who assists in a crime that can only be committed by a certain type of person is guilty even though he does not come under that classification. For example, a private person is not an executive officer, and he cannot be guilty of the crime of "Soliciting a Bribe by an Executive Officer." However, if he assists an Executive Officer in the soliciting of a bribe, he would be guilty as a principal under the California system.[1]

Other examples of advantages of the California system of parties to a crime are:

(1) A man is attacked by two men and is stabbed. Witnesses cannot determine which of the suspects was carrying the knife. In California it does not matter. Both assailants are equally guilty as principals.[2]

(2) Several men force themselves into a woman's car and then take it to a secluded spot where more than one of the suspects rape her. She cannot identify which of the men raped her. Under California law it does not matter because they are all principals and equally guilty.[3]

(3) A group of demonstrators is arrested after some of them threw bricks at responding officers, injuring one of them. Because of the conditions of the situation, identification cannot be made of the exact demonstrators who threw the bricks. Since they were acting in concert, they are all guilty of Assaulting a Peace Officer.[4]

(4) In a fight were several persons with knives; the victim cannot identify which of them actually stabbed him. Under California law they are all principals.

(1) Those Who Actually Commit the Crime

Those who actually commit the crime are classed as principals. There are two ways in which a person can come under this classification.

(A) **Actual Presence:** The accused is physically at the scene, and actually commits the act.

(B) **Constructive Presence:** Constructive presence means "in place of" actual presence.

Through an Agent

Examples:

(1) **A trained animal could be an agent.** A person who trained a monkey to enter a building and steal valuable items would be at the scene constructively.

(2) **A mail-carrier could be an innocent agent** when he or she delivers a bomb that another person mailed from a distant city.

(3) **Small children could be innocent agents** if they unknowingly commit a crime at the instruction of an adult. The person who instructed the child would be constructively present at the scene through the child, even if he or she was some distance away at the time.

If the agent becomes aware of what he or she is doing, and continues the act, the agent then becomes a principal. There can be more than one principal. In fact there is no limit on the number of principals in a crime.

(4) **A mechanical device can be an agent.** Someone who placed a bomb at a certain location and then left for some far distant place so that he would not be present when the bomb exploded, would still be present constructively.

(5) **Ammunition can be an agent.** Shooting someone with a high powered rifle from some distance away would still make that person present at the crime scene constructively through the bullet which would be his agent.

(6) **A telephone can be an agent.** Using the telephone to commit a crime, while telephoning from some distance away, would still make the perpetrator present at the scene constructively. He is there through his agent the telephone (e.g., phoning victim to distract him while partner commits crime).

(2) Those Who Aid and Abet the Commission of a Crime

Those who aid and abet the commission of a crime can do so before the crime is committed, or during the commission of the crime. They may also aid and abet the crime while it is being committed, and yet not be present at the scene physically. It can be constructive presence. For example, a thief can have a friend call the only clerk in a store on the telephone while the thief is in the store so the clerk will be distracted while the thief steals something from the store. The person who phones the clerk is quite a distance from the scene, but is still aiding and abetting the crime.

Definitions:

(1) **Aid:** Aid means to assist, and it can be done innocently without any implication of guilt knowledge or felonious intent.[5]

(2) **Abet:** Assistance accompanied by knowledge of the wrongful purpose of the person committing the crime.[6] There is a consciousness of guilt in instigating, encouraging, promoting or aiding the crime.[7] The high courts have also stated that "abet" means "to warn or encourage by gestures[8] to counsel[9] to advise the commission of a crime[10] direct the criminal with knowledge of his wrongful purpose[11] or be present at the scene in case he is needed."[12]

(A) One Who Aids and Abets Must Have Specific Intent

Just because a person is present at the crime scene does not make that person guilty of aiding and abetting. In fact he or she can be at the crime scene and actually aid the criminal without being aware of it. This is why the law requires that the aiding have specific intent.

Example #1:

Henry Honebone is walking down the street. Bernie Bergle stops him and asks for help. Bernie asks Henry to hold a ladder for him because he has locked himself out of his house and is trying to climb in the upstairs window. Henry, being a good neighbor, gives Bernie a hand. What Henry doesn't know is that Bernie doesn't live there and is a burglar. Henry has aided a crime, but without specific intent.

Example #2:

Henry parks his car in a shopping center parking lot. As he gets out of his car, he is approached by Sam Slick. Sam states that he has locked himself out of his car, and wants to borrow a coat hanger so that he can get into his car with it. Henry happens to have a coat hanger in his car and lends it to Sam. The car really didn't belong to Sam. He was trying to steal it. Even though Henry aided Sam in stealing the car, he did so without specific intent.

(B) Sympathy Alone is Not Sufficient to Make One Guilty of Abetting

A person can be sympathetic towards the actions of the criminal, yet not be guilty of aiding and abetting. On the other hand, if a person gave **verbal** encouragement to the criminal, he would be guilty of aiding and abetting, and would be classed as a principal.[13] Examples illustrating this point are:

(a) Freddie Froghair and his wife Fanny do not get along. One day, Freddie comes home and finds Larry Letcher in the kitchen having a drink with Fanny. Freddie tells Larry to get out of his house. Larry then takes a chair and hits Freddie over the head. When this happens, Fanny smiles and is obviously happy at seeing her husband hit over the head.
Question: Is Fanny a principal by aiding and abetting? WHY or WHY NOT?

(b) Under exactly the same circumstances, let us suppose that Fanny told Larry to hit Freddie one more time for good measure.
Question: Is Fanny a principal by aiding and abetting? WHY or WHY NOT?

(C) Responsibility When Several Persons Pursue a Common Design

When several persons pursue a common criminal design or objective, they all become aiders and abettors for each other.[14] For example, Fred, Howard and Clyde plan to pick pockets at the county fair. They get together and practice on each other. During the first day of the fair, Fred picks three pockets, Howard picks five pockets, and Clyde picks four pockets. Although each person committed the act by himself, they were all aiders and abettors and therefore guilty as principals of all twelve crimes.

(D) Examples of Acts That Make a Person Guilty of Aiding and Abetting

(a) Acting as a lookout for another who is committing a crime.[15]

(b) Driving a get-away car.[16]

(c) Restraining the victim while another hits him or her.[17]

(d) Entering a store where a friend works as a sales clerk and taking extra change after making a small purchase.[18]

(e) Lending a car to another, knowing it will be used in a crime.[19]

(f) Acting as a lookout while another injects heroin into his or her arm. If the person dies from an overdose, the lookout is guilty of aiding and abetting manslaughter.[20]

(g) Aiding and abetting a crime makes the person responsible for the natural, reasonable and probable outcome of any acts that he or she aids and abets. For example, a person who lends a gun to another who intends to use it in a holdup would be responsible for any death that occurs from the holdup. The natural, reasonable and probable outcome of an armed robbery is that someone might be killed.[21]

(h) Arranging for a minor to have sexual intercourse with another makes the person guilty of aiding and abetting statutory rape.[22]

(i) Preventing another from assisting the victim makes the person a principal because he or she aids and abets the act.[23]

(j) Giving false statements of injuries, in one's capacity as a physician so that the patient can sue for damages makes one a principal for aiding and abetting the crime of fraud.[24]

(k) Selling equipment and ingredients to be used for the illegal making of beer makes the seller guilty of aiding and abetting a violation of the Alcoholic Beverage Control Act.[25]

(E) Proving a Person Did in Fact Aid and Abet

Whether or not a person aided and abetted a criminal act is a question of fact for the jury to decide.[26] This fact can be determined from circumstantial evidence.[27] Since abetting a crime involves knowledge of the criminal purpose, the test of aiding and abetting is whether or not the accused directly or indirectly aided the perpetrator, and the extent of his knowledge is also a question of fact for the jury to decide.[28]

(3) Those Who Advise and Encourage the Commission of a Crime

Although section 31 of the Penal Code states one who "not being present have advised and encouraged," the high court interpretation of the word "abet" includes "advise" and "encourage," and therefore allows such action to occur either at the scene or away from it.[29]

Definition: The word "encourages" also means procures, solicits and counsels.

(A) Extent of Liability for One Who Advises and Encourages a Crime

One who advises and encourages the commission of a crime is responsible for the natural and probable outcomes of such a crime. Transferred intent can also apply.

Example:

Billy Burp knows that Harry Hitman is looking for Clyde Crashcup so that he can kill him. Billy gives Harry information as to where Clyde is hiding. By mistake Harry shoots and kills Fred Farkle. Billy is a principal in the crime of murder because of transferred intent. He advised the killer regarding Clyde Crashcup, and is therefore responsible for any killing by mistake.

Example:

A person gives a friend information about what time a store will have the most money so the friend can rob the store at that particular time. The person knows that his friend plans to use a gun in the robbery. If someone is killed in the robbery, the person who advised the robber will be a principal to murder. This is because a killing is the probable and natural outcome of an armed robbery.

WELL, WELL, HARRY - GUESS WHO MADE A BOO-BOO!

(B) Examples of Acts That Make One a Principal Through Advising and Encouraging.

(1) A woman uses information that she has to procure others to commit a robbery in exchange for a share of the loot. She is a principal through advising and encouraging.[30]

(2) A man who was not at the crime scene was found to be a principal because he "connived and encouraged" the commission of robbery.[31]

(3) The parents of a four-year-old child were found to be principals in the violation of a city ordinance prohibiting the riding of tricycles on the sidewalk. This was based on the fact, proven in court, that they encouraged the child to ride on the sidewalk.[32]

(4) A man was convicted as a principal for his "verbal" encouragement, and incitement to commit a crime.[33]

(5) A passenger in a car who urged the driver to leave after hitting another car was a principal in "Hit and Run."[34]

(C) Example of When Person Who Advises and Encourages Is Not Liable for Outcome of Criminal Act.

Sam Slurp tells Burnie Burgle when a safe will have a large amount of money in return for ten percent of the take. Burnie breaks into the safe and obtains two thousand dollars. He is mad at the small "take," so he sets the building on fire. Since the arson is not the natural and probable outcome of a burglary, Sam is only a principal to the burglary and not the arson. On the other hand, if Sam knew that Burnie was a pyromaniac, and set fire to most of the buildings that he burglarized, he should expect that Burnie would also set fire to the place where he advised the burglary. In this case, arson would be the natural and probable outcome of any burglary committed by Burnie Burgle:

(4) Those Who, Through Force or Coercion, Compel Another to Commit a Crime

The difficult part of this condition is proving that persons who claim to have been forced to commit crimes were truly forced. If they were threatened, was the threat such that a normal, prudent person would feel that he or she was in immediate physical danger, or in danger of a threat that could be carried out. The threat does not have to be physical. It could be the threat of losing one's job.

Examples:

(1) A mother forcing her 16-year-old daughter to have sex relations.[35]

(2) A woman who forces a man to rape another woman is a principal in that crime.[36]

(3) A boss who threatens to fire employees unless they falsify public records. When they do the act, both the boss and the employees are principals.[37]

(5) Persons Can Be Principals To Crimes They Could Not Themselves Legally Commit Examples:

(1) A woman who encourages a man to rape another woman could not, herself, commit rape on that woman, but as a principal, she can be legally guilty of that offense.

(2) A person who is not a peace officer could not be guilty of acting improperly under color of authority, but if he encouraged an officer to do so, he would legally be a principal to this offense.

7.2:0 WHO IS AN ACCESSORY IN CALIFORNIA

In California, there are no Accessories Before the Fact, only Accessories After the Fact. Because of this, the term "Accessory" is often used when referring to an Accessory After the Fact, since this is the only type of accessory.

7.2:1 Accessory After the Fact (After the Crime)

All states have the classification of "Accessory After the Fact." There is little difference in the wording of the law; but there are differences in exceptions to this classification.

An Accessory After the Fact Has Nothing to do With the Crime Itself. His or her acts occur after the crime has been committed. Penal Code, section 32, states:

> Every person who, after a felony has been committed, harbors, conceals or aids a principal in such felony, with the intent that said principal may avoid or escape arrest, trial, conviction or punishment, having knowledge that said principal has committed such felony or has been charged with such felony or convicted thereof, is an accessory to such felony.

The basic elements of this offense are:

(1) After a felony has been committed. (Only a felony)
(2) A person harbors, conceals or aids the felon.
(3) With the intent that the felon escape justice. (Specific intent)
(4) When he knows that the person he helped has:
   (a) Committed the felony, or
   (b) Been charged with the felony, or
   (c) Been convicted of the felony

(The term "escape justice" fits the acts mentioned)

Because there is no major difference between the elements for Accessory after the Fact in common law and California law, we are able to use the case law from many states to answer questions regarding this classification. Some of the words that have been used in court decisions to further explain acts under this offense are:

(1) Helps prevent capture
(2) Comforts
(3) Assists
(4) Rescues
(5) Relieves

(A) Definitions of Words and Phrases Used
(1) After a felony has been committed:

It is necessary that a felony was in fact committed in order for a person to be charged with being an accessory.[38] Under the rule of "Res Gestae," which means the entire events that made up the crime, a crime is not over until the escape has been completed. Therefore, driving a person away from the crime scene makes the driver a principal to that crime rather than an accessory after the fact because the crime is not yet completed. Once the principal has escaped from the scene, and someone helps further the escape, that person may be classed as an accessory, because the word "after" is now in effect.[39] (This does not apply to misdemeanors.)

(2) Aids: (This aid requires specific intent)

Simply aiding a person is not enough to make one an accessory. Acts of charity to one who is trying to escape justice do not make one an accessory as long as the acts are intended to relieve pain or discomfort and do not interfere with the felon's apprehension.[40] For example, a person who found another lying on the sidewalk, bleeding and semi-conscious, and bound the wound and gave the other a drink of water, would not be committing acts that would make him or her an accessory.

If the help is such that it aids the principal to escape justice in some way, the kind of help is unimportant.[41] If aid is given, it can be in person or through some agent. The accessory could recruit another person and provide him or her with the means necessary to assist the felon. In this case, they would both be accessories.[42]

(3) Having Knowledge:

This is the same as the word "knowingly." It means that the person doing the act either knows or should reasonably know that the person being assisted is wanted for a felony. The legal term for this knowledge is "*Scienter*," a Latin term meaning "having guilty knowledge." "Knowingly" means the act is voluntary and not committed under any duress. Because of this required knowledge, the offense of being an Accessory After the Fact <u>requires specific intent.</u>[43]

... AND JUST HOW WAS I TO KNOW MY RODNEY WAS WANTED FOR A FELONY ?!

If the person has knowledge alone, but provides no assistance, he or she is not guilty. For example, knowing that one's brother is an escaped felon, but not notifying the police of his whereabouts, does not make one an accessory because such an offense requires that some aid or assistance be given; knowledge of the person being wanted does not complete all the elements of the offense.[44]

Circumstantial evidence can be used to prove knowledge. For example, if there was wide publicity about the crime and the suspect, and it can be shown that the defendant did read the papers and watch television, this could be circumstantial evidence to prove his or her knowledge.

Common sense is also a good rule to apply. If the felon just held up a bank, and was shot in the attempt, then showed up at a friend's house with the gunshot wound, a gun, and a briefcase with $10,000 — the amount taken in the bank robbery—the accessory would have a difficult time convincing the jury that he or she did not suspect this friend to be the person responsible for the bank robbery.

In the investigation of such an offense, the details are important. Did the accessory do any particular act or acts that could be used as circumstantial evidence to prove awareness of the person's felonious involvement? Was the felon wounded? Were there newspapers in the house with headlines of the crime or the escape? Did the accessory take precautions to prevent anyone's knowing that the felon was in his or her home (such as keeping the blinds closed, or not accepting visitors)? Did he or she arrange for the felon to leave town and use fictitious names on reservations?

The most difficult element to prove in this offense is the fact that the accessory knew the person whom he or she assisted had either committed a felony or was wanted for a felony.

A mother who assists her son would technically be classed as an accessory, yet the District Attorney would be hesitant to prosecute her for that charge because a jury, or some members of that jury, would be reluctant to find her guilty. After all, she is doing what all mothers should do.

(4) Has Been Charged:

The high courts are not completely clear on the definition of this phrase. They state that it includes a formal complaint, information, or indictment filed against a criminal, and then state "possibly an arrest without warrant might be sufficient."[45] This term, "charged," has given enforcement personnel a problem in relation to the crime of escape, and the high courts have interpreted that the word, when applying to escape, means "booked or formally charged."[46] Yet the legislative intent of the two offenses is different. The legislative intent of the law on being an Accessory After the Fact is to prevent persons from assisting felons to escape justice. When this is considered, it would seem reasonable that the word, "charged" would include an arrest without a warrant, as the California Supreme Court suggested, but did not clearly state.

(B) Court Rules:

If the court or jury finds the Principal not guilty, they cannot find the Accessory After the Fact guilty.[47] This is common sense. Unlike the rule under common law, however, the Accessory After the Fact can be tried even if the Principal is not. In the case of death or absence of the Principal, a person can be charged as being both a Principal and an Accessory After the Fact if evidence shows the person aided and abetted the crime, or later assisted the co-principal to escape justice.[48]

Although there is a rule that a co-principal cannot testify against another co-principal without some corroboration (supporting evidence), the rule does not apply to an Accessory After the Fact because he or she is technically not a co-principal. An Accessory-After-the-Fact's statements can be accepted without corroboration.[49]

(C) Examples of Being an Accessory
(1) Providing the Principal with a false alibi.[50]
(2) Providing the Principal with an automobile.
(3) Providing the Principal with a hiding place.
(4) Providing the Principal with money.
(5) Going to the crime scene to destroy evidence.
(6) Offering bribes to police officers or prosecutors.
(7) Providing the Principal with a forged passport.
(8) Providing the Principal with train, bus or plane tickets.

(D) No Exceptions to Accessory Law in California

California has no exceptions to the law on Accessories. Under common law, a wife cannot be charged as an Accessory After the Fact if she helped her husband. This was supposed to be part of her marital duties. In some southern states immediate members of the family are exempt as Accessories After the Fact (based on the strong "kinfolk" obligations in southern culture.)

7.3:0   COMPOUNDING A CRIME (153 PC)

(1) Any person having knowledge of a crime
(2) Receives something of value, or agrees to receive it
(3) In return for
    (a) concealing that crime or
    (b) refraining from prosecution or
    (c) withholding evidence
(4) Except in cases provided for by law

As with Soliciting, all that is needed for the overt act is an agreement to compound or conceal the crime. The simplest definition of the word "compounding" would be "concealing."

Civil Damages: Reimbursement Permissible

As long as the victim does not make an agreement to compound the crime, he may accept compensation from the perpetrator for any injuries or damage received during the commission of the crime. This is a legal right and could be obtained through a civil lawsuit if the perpetrator were not to pay for the injury or damages.

The Compromising of Misdemeanors

The fourth element of Compounding a Crime states, "Except in the cases provided for by law." Penal Code Sections 1377, 1378 and 1379 list the conditions under which a crime may be legally compounded or compromised. The conditions are as follows:

(1) The crime is a misdemeanor;
(2) The victim is entitled to civil reimbursement;
(3) The court agrees to the compromise;
(4) The perpetrator pays the court costs;
(5) The action is officially recorded in the minutes.

Example:

The victim of an assault suffers a broken nose; the doctor bill costs him $100. Later, when his temper cools down, he realizes that he started the argument and probably deserved the punch in the nose. He makes an agreement with the perpetrator to forget the whole thing if he pays for the doctor bill.

This would probably be the end of the matter, but, if the victim was to later get angry at the perpetrator again, he could initiate criminal proceedings. The only protection that the perpetrator would have would be to follow through on the last three elements listed under "The Compromising of Misdemeanors." Once recorded officially in the minutes, further prosecution is barred, and the victim cannot later reopen the case.

Exceptions to a Compromise (1377 PC)

(1) The victim is a peace officer performing his or her duties;
(2) The criminal act was done riotously;
(3) The act was done with the intent to commit a felony.

If any of these conditions exist, the crime may not be legally compromised.

Examples of Compounding a Crime:

(1) Harry Hashbrown works with Hector Honk. One day he sees Hector put a valuable tool under his shirt then put it in the trunk of his car. The next day he tells Hector that he saw him and is going to tell the boss. Hector promises to give him $5 to forget the incident. Harry agrees. He is guilty of compounding a crime.

(2) Lester Lump sees Millie Maggot shoplift a sweater. He contacts her and tells her that if she does not have sex with him, he will tell the police and she will go to jail. Millie agrees to have sex with Lester. Is he guilty of compounding a crime? Has he actually received anything? Is what he wants something of value? Yes, he is guilty of compounding a crime. The elements of the crime include a promise as well as actually receiving anything. The state Supreme Court has ruled that a woman's sexual favors are something of value.

7.4:0 WHO IS AN ACCOMPLICE IN CALIFORNIA

Accomplices

The California Penal Code covers accomplices under Section 1111 PC which states:

A conviction cannot be had upon the testimony of an accomplice unless it be corroborated by such other evidence as shall tend to connect the defendant with the commission of the offense; and the corroboration is not sufficient if it merely shows the commission of the offense or the circumstances thereof.

An accomplice is hereby defined as one who is liable to prosecution for the identical offense charged against the defendant on trial in the cause in which the testimony of the accomplice is given.

The term "accomplice" has different meanings in different states. In California it applies to a person who is a principal, who is liable for the same punishment as the co-principals for the same offense, and who turns "state's evidence" in return for full or partial immunity. The Model Penal Code, published by the American Law Institute, gives the term Accomplice a simple definition in that it denotes "criminal complicity." Otherwise, it has no special meaning.

Under common law, the testimony of an accomplice need not be corroborated. Under California law, it is a legal necessity. The corroboration of the testimony of an accomplice applies only to trials and not to preliminary examinations, or to the issuance of indictments.[51]

Who Is an Accomplice?

Despite Section 1111 PC, which was written in 1915, we must look to the appellate courts for an up-to-date interpretation of the legal elements defining the term accomplice.[52] Common usage of the term "accomplice" means one who has participated in criminal action along with one or more other persons. He or she is one who has assisted in the crime. In California law, the term is slightly different in that it includes more than just being a principal. The elements of the definition of the term "accomplice" are as follows:

An Accomplice:

(1) is a co-principal in the offense for which the defendant is charged;

(2) is liable to prosecution for that identical offense;

(3) testifies against the co-principal in the trial in which the co-principal is being tried.

Who Is Not an Accomplice?

(1) Minors

Because an accomplice must be a principal in the crime, and since a person under the age of 14 cannot be charged with a criminal offense in absence of proof of knowledge of the wrongfulness of the act, a 13-year-old will not be considered an accomplice unless this knowledge can be proven.

Unless the Juvenile Court has declined to handle the case of a minor under the age of 18, and has certified him or her to the adult court for trial, that minor cannot be classed as an accomplice.[53]

(2) Feigned Accomplices

The law has always encouraged its citizens to assist in achieving the proper ends of criminal justice. It has allowed its citizens to feign complicity in a criminal action in order to obtain information that will later assist a criminal prosecution.

In the People v. Plascile[54] the Appellate Court defined a feigned accomplice as one who, under the direction of an officer of the law, or on his or her own initiative, and without criminal intent, feigns complicity in a crime merely to detect the perpetrator with a view to prosecution.

It must be understood that this would be a good defense when a defendant can think of no other excuse. The problem here, even if the defense is truly a valid one, is getting the jury to believe that the purpose of the involvement was just to get evidence for the prosecution. This is particularly true in the case of the feigned accomplice who does not notify the police, although the law does allow such an act. Obviously the best procedure in cases of this nature would be to notify the police or authorities of the feigned complicity.

If, however, it can be shown that the defendant had actually participated in formulating the plans for the crime from the very beginning he or she could not escape being a principal and then possibly an accomplice.[55]

7.5:0 CORROBORATION AND THE ACCOMPLICE

The corroboration needed to make the testimony of an accomplice acceptable in court need not be direct evidence or proof positive. Circumstantial evidence may be used as proof.[56]

Examples:

(1) Attempting to rig a false alibi and flight are sufficient corroboration.[56] (Ibid)

(2) Silence of the accused in the face of the confession of an accomplice which implicates both of them in the crime is sufficient corroboration.[57]

(3) "False and contradictory statements of a defendant in relation to the charge are themselves corroborative evidence.[58]

(4) The defendant's confession is enough to corroborate the testimony of an accomplice.[59]

(5) Physical evidence left at the scene that is the same as that owned by the defendant.[60]

The following is an example of a situation where a series of circumstances, that in themselves do not prove guilt, could be used to corroborate the testimony of an accomplice:

Bernie Bergle and Herbert Honebone break into a warehouse to steal some new radios that an informant told them have just arrived. He told them that the invoice with the serial numbers had been lost somewhere and that they could not be identified by their serial numbers.

Bernie took an armful of radios out to his car and put them in the trunk. Just as he was about to return to the warehouse for more radios, he noticed a patrol car approaching the warehouse. The informant forgot to tell them about the silent alarm that was inside the warehouse. Bernie hid from sight, and when the police car drove around and behind the warehouse, Bernie took off for home.

The police found the forced entry and called for more help. They later caught Herbert inside the building. He had the jimmy tool used to gain entry in his pocket. Herbert, realizing that he was caught in the act, confessed and implicated Bernie. He told them that it was really Bernie's idea and that they drove there in Bernie's car.

The next morning, investigators found Bernie at his home. They asked him where he was the night before. He told them that he was in San Francisco overnight. While talking to him in his apartment, they noticed six radios that were stacked in the corner. They asked him where he got the radios. He replied that he had just obtained a job as a salesman selling radios, and those were the ones he had not sold yet.

The investigators then went back to the neighborhood of the crime scene. At a corner gas station, they talked to Cecil Coffinstopper, who told them that he had seen Bernie Bergle standing near the warehouse just before 11:00 P.M. He had on a white scarf. The next time he saw Bernie was about fifteen minutes later. He noticed that, this time, Bernie did not have his white scarf. On checking the warehouse again, the investigators found a white scarf. The foreman at the warehouse stated that none of his workmen had a white scarf and that he had never seen the scarf before.

Let us look at the circumstantial evidence in this case. Each fact in itself does not prove that Bernie was involved in the burglary as Herbert said. Which items would be considered good enough to corroborate Herbert's testimony?

(1) Bernie lied about his whereabouts on the night of the crime.

(2) Bernie had six radios in his apartment that were the same color and make as those taken from the warehouse.

(3) A witness saw Bernie standing near the warehouse just before the time that the silent alarm went off.

(4) A witness saw Bernie wearing a white scarf. Later he saw him without the scarf. A white scarf was found in the warehouse.

(5) Investigation revealed that Bernie did not have a job as a radio salesman.

The answer to "Which facts can be used as corroboration?" is any of the five. The corroboration needed for an accomplice's testimony need be only very slight.

Why Is Corroboration Needed?

Without corroboration, criminals who have been caught in the act could implicate all their enemies and have them sent to prison. Since accomplices are principals (or criminals), their word alone would not be given full weight.

7.6:0   PARTIES TO A CRIME UNDER COMMON LAW

Under common law, there are four categories of parties to a crime. They are:

Principal in the First Degree

One who actually performs the criminal act, in person or by a constructive act such as a non-human agent, an instrument, an innocent human agent or a trained animal.

Principal in the Second Degree

One who aids and abets a Principal of the First Degree, and was actually at the scene in person, or was there in a constructive manner such as by use of the telephone.

Accessory Before the Fact

One who orders, encourages, counsels, or aids and abets the Principal in the First Degree to commit the crime—not present at the crime scene.

Accessory After the Fact

One who is not involved in the crime itself, but who, with knowledge that a person has committed a felony, conceals, or gives assistance to prevent his or her detection, arrest, trial, or punishment.

Under early English common law, an accessory or a Principal of the Second Degree could not be tried until the Principal of the First Degree was tried and convicted first. This was based on the theory that if the Principal of the First Degree was not guilty, how could the accessories be guilty of that same crime? This was basically a good rule, but it was carried to the extreme. If the Principal of the First Degree was killed during the crime, or escaped to another country, none of those who assisted him could be tried for their part in the crime. Under present English law, this rule has been changed.

Comparison of Parties to a Crime in California and Under Common Law			
Common Law Classifications			**California Classifications**
Classification	**Participation**	**Conditions**	**Classification**
<u>ACCESSORY BEFORE THE FACT</u>	Aids and abets, Advises, Encourages, Commands, Coerces, Solicits, the Principal to commit a crime.	Not present at the crime scene. Occurs before the crime. Requires specific intent.	There is only one classification of parties to a crime in California. It is the classification of PRINCIPAL.
<u>PRINCIPAL OF THE FIRST DEGREE</u>	Actually commits the crime.	Present at the crime scene, constructively or in person	**Conditions**
<u>PRINCIPAL OF THE SECOND DEGREE</u>	Aids and abets the Principal of the First Degree.	Present at the crime scene, constructively or in person. Specific intent is required.	If the person is in any way associated with or involved with the crime, before or during, that person is a PRINCIPAL. There are no degrees, and ALL PRINCIPALS ARE EQUALLY GUILTY. The principal can be present at the scene constructively or in person.
Classification Not Involving the Actual Crime			
<u>ACCESSORY AFTER THE FACT</u>	Knowingly assists a wanted <u>felon</u> escape justice by assistance, concealment of crime, hiding felon, etc. <u>after</u> the crime has been committed.	Not at the crime scene. If at the scene, is also a principal of the second degree. In some jurisdictions there are exceptions such as close family members.	<u>ACCESSORY AFTER THE FACT</u> Same as under common law, but there are no exceptions.

REFERENCES FOR CHAPTER VII

(1) People v. Anderson, 75 C.A. 365 (242 P 906).
(2) DeLa Roi in re, 28 C. 2d 264 (169 P 2d 363).
(3) People v. Enright, 140 C.A. (649 35 P 2d 1033).
(4) People v. Buice, 230 C.A. 2d 374 (40 Cal Rptr 877).
(5) People v. Dole, 122 C 486 (55 P 581).
(6) People v. Blake, 214 C.A. 2d 705 (29 Cal Rptr 772).
(7) People v. Best, 43 C.A. 2d 100 (110 P 2d 504).
(8) People v. Ortiz, 208 C.A. 2d 572 (25 Cal Rptr 327).
(9) People v. Etie, 119 C.A. 2d 23 (258 P 2d 1069).
(10) People v. Allen, 208 C.A. 2d 537 (25 Cal Rptr 351).
(11) People v. Tambini, 275 C.A. 2d 757 (80 Cal Rptr 179).
(12) Pinizzotto v. Superior Ct., 257 C.A. 2d 582 (65 Cal Rptr 74).
(13) Pinell v. Superior Ct., 232 C.A. 2d 284 (42 Cal Rptr 676).
(14) People v. Lockett, 25 C.A.3d 433 (102 Cal Rptr 41).
(15) People v. Navarro, 212 C.A. 2d 299 (27 Cal Rptr 716).
(16) People v. Ellhamer, 199 C.A. 2d 777 (18 Cal Rptr 905).
(17) People v. Whalen, 124 C.A. 2d 713 (269 P 2d 181).
(18) People v. Sparks, 44 C.A. 2d 748 (112 P 2d 974).
(19) People v. Martin, 128 C.A. 2d 361 (275 P 2d 635)
(20) People v. Hopkins, 101 C.A. 2d 704 (226 P 2d 74).
(21) People v. Cain, 216 C.A. 2d 748 (21 Cal Rptr 190).
(22) People v. Lewis, 9 C.A. 279 (98 P 1078).
(23) People v. Macchiaroli, 54 C.A. 665 (202 P 474).
(24) People v. Wallace, 78 C.A. 2d 726 (178 P 2d 771).
(25) 42 Ops Atty Gen 80
(26) People v. Fleming, 191 C.A. 2d 163 (12 Cal Rptr 530).
(27) People v. Ransom, 221 C.A. 2d 57 (34 Cal Rptr 302).
(28) People Y. Long, 7 C.A. 3d 586 (86 Cal Rptr 590).
(29) People v. Goldstein, 146 C.A. 2d 268 (306 P 2d 575).
(30) People v. Nolan, 144 C 75, (77 P 774).
(31) People v. Oldham, 111 C 648 (44 P 312).
(32) Muller v. Standard Oil Co., 180 C 260 (108 P 605).
(33) People v. Bohmer, 46 C.A. 3d 185.
(34) People v. Steele, 100 C.A. 639 (280 P 999).
(35) People v. Bartol, 24 C.A. 659 (142 P 510).
(36) . People v. Hernandez, 18 C.A. 3d 651 (96 Cal Rptr 71).
(37) People v. Shaw, 17 C 2d 778 (112 P2d 241).
(38) People v. Hardin, 207 C.A. 2d 336 (24 Cal Rptr 563).
(39) People v. Bryson, 257 C.A. 2d 201 (64 Cal Rptr 706).
(40) People v. Dunn, 6 N.Y.S. 805
(41) People v. Duty, 269 C.A. 2d 97 (74 Cal Rptr 606).
(42) Rex v. Jarvis 2 Moo. & R 40
(43) People v. Duty, Ibid.
(44) People v. Lauria, 251 C.A. 2d 471 (59 Cal Rptr 628).
(45) People v. Garnett, 129 C 364 (61 P 1114).
(46) People v. Redmond, 246 C.A. 2d 852 (55 Cal Rptr 195).
(47) People v. Allsip, 268 C.A. 2d 830 (74 Cal Rptr 550).
(48) People v. Shepardson, 48 C 189
(49) People v. Collum, 122 C 186 (54 P 589).
(50) People v. Duty, Ibid (41).
(51) Stern v. Superior Ct., 78 C.A. 2d 9 (177 P 2d 308).
(52) People v. Williams, 7 C.A. 2d 600 (46 P 2d 796).
(53) People v. Johnson, 115 C.A. 704 (2 P 2d 216).
(54) People v. Plascile, 159 C.A. 2d 622 (323 P 2d 1032).
(56) People v. Santo, 43 C 2d 319 (273 P 2d 249).
(55) People v. McCormick, 76 C.A. 688 (245 P 781).
(57) People v. Hambright, 113 C.A. 2d 140 (248 P 2d 45).
(58) People v. Simpson, 43 C 2d 553 (275 P 2d 31).
(59) People v. Baker, 25 C.A. 2d 1 (76 P 2d 111).
(60) People v. Trujillo, 32 C 2d 105 (194 P 2d 681).

STUDY QUESTIONS

CHAPTER VII

(1) A person who commits theft in Nevada and brings the stolen property into California can be charged with theft in California just as if the property had been stolen here.   T or F

(2) Ronella Rufflestomper, who lives in Oregon, writes a letter to Frank Fudd in California, encouraging him to commit a crime in California. When Ronella comes to California, she can be arrested for encouraging Frank to commit a crime.   T or F

(3) Under California law, a person can be a principal to a crime that he or she could not personally legally commit.   T or F

(4) In California, a person can be a principal without actually being at the crime scene.   T or F

(5) As used in California law, the word "aid" does not mean the person who assists another knowing that the act is criminal.   T or F

(6) Prunella Porkpickle lends Freddie Furd her car knowing that it is to be used in a holdup. Prunella is classed as a(an) _____ in California.

(7) One who aids and abets must have specific intent to be criminally liable.   T or F

(8) There is no limit to the number of principals to a crime under California law.   T or F

(9) The high courts have stated that "abet" means to "encourage."   T or F

(10) Verbal encouragement makes the person encouraging another to commit a crime liable for that crime under California law.   T or F

(11) Arvin, Burkford and Clyde plan to pick pockets at the state fair. Each of them successfully picks three pockets. Arvin is guilty of how many charges of picking pockets? _____.

(12) In California, the driver of a "getaway" car is classed as a(an) _____.

(13) In California, a lookout for a burglary is classed as a(an) _____.

(14) Arnold lends a gun to Freddie to be used in a holdup. Freddie holds up a store and kills the clerk. Arvin is only responsible for the robbery and not the killing.   T or F

(15) Clyde lends a car to Mervin to be used in a burglary. Mervin commits the burglary and just for the fun of it he sets fire to the building. Under California law, Clyde is guilty of burglary and arson as well.   T or F

(16) Rumpford Rox is driving a car when he hits another parked car. His passenger, Clyde Crashcup tells him to leave the scene quickly before anyone sees him. Clyde is now a principal to hit and run.   T or F

(17) Simply advising another person to commit a crime makes one guilty and a principal in California.   T or F

(18) Arvin Ardvark sees Harry Hardrock fighting with Mervin Mushmuscle. Arvin does not like Mervin, so he tells Harry "hit him again buddy." When Harry hits Mervin again, Arvin is a principal to battery.   T or F

(19) All states have the classification of accessory after the fact.   T or F

(20) An accessory after the fact applies to both felonies & misdemeanors.   T or F

(21) To be guilty of being an accessory after the fact, the person helping must be aware of any of the following but one:

(A) ____The person being helped has committed a felony.
(B) ____The person being helped has been charged with a felony.
(C) ____The person being helped has been convicted of a felony.
(D) ____The person being helped has committed a serious crime against property.

(22) Lenny Lump drives Larry Liverwort away from the bank that Larry has just robbed. Lenny then hides Larry in a spare room until things "cool down." Lenny is now classed as a(an) _____ and a(an) _____.

(23) Flossie Furd finds Clyde Crashcup lying in the street bleeding from a gunshot wound. Clyde had just held up a liquor store and was shot by the clerk. Flossie rips up her slip and binds Clyde's wound. Flossie is now an accessory after the fact.   T or F

(24) In California a person can only be an accessory before the fact if the crime is a felony.   T or F

(25) The legal term "scienter" means:

(A) ____hiding another.   (B) ____having guilty knowledge.
(C) ____doing something for money.   (D) ____assisting another.

(26) The most difficult part to prove in a charge of being an accessory (AF) is:

(A) ____a felony has been committed.
(B) ____that the suspect actually was assisted.
(C) ____that the person knew the suspect was escaping justice.
(D) ____that something of value was received for the aid.

(27) The legal (Latin) term used to describe the overall events that make up a crime, or its scope, is:

(A) ____Corpus Delicti.   (B) ____Mens Rea.
(C) ____Res Gestae.   (D) ____Maximus Enclosius.

(28) Corroboration means:

(A) ____to reject.   (B) ____to support or back up.
(C) ____to gather evidence.   (D) ____to disprove.

(29) An accessory after the fact cannot testify against a principal in a crime without corroboration.   T or F

(30) A person who commits a felony and the person who helps him or her escape are both co-principals in the crime.   T or F

(31) If a person conceals a crime in return for something of value, that person is guilty of the offense called a _____ crime.

(32) Compounding a crime applies only to felonies.   T or F

(33) In compounding a crime, the suspect must actually receive something of value in return for concealment of that crime.   T or F

(34) The easiest definition for the word "compounding" would be the word _____.

(35) To "compromise" a crime, the crime can only be a misdemeanor.   T or F

(36) A person who legally "compromises" a crime must pay the court costs.   T or F

(37) Fred Farkle rips Officer Ardvark's shirt while Ardvark is trying to settle a family argument. This misdemeanor can be compromised.   T or F

(38) In California, to be an "accomplice," that person must testify against his or her co-principal (or turn "state's evidence").　　　T or F

(39) In California a juvenile can be an accomplice.　　　T or F

(40) In California an accomplice who is working for the police and just pretending to be involved in the crime to gather evidence is called a(an) _____ accomplice.

(41) In order for the testimony of an accomplice to be accepted in court, it must:

　　(A) ____ be truthful.　　　　　　　　(B) ____ be corroborated.
　　(C) ____ be consummated.　　　　　　(D) ____ be direct evidence.

(42) The corroboration needed to back up an accomplice's testimony can be very slight.　　　T or F

(43) In Common Law, a person who actually committed the crime is classed as a(an)

_____.

(44) In Common Law, a person who acts as a lookout during a crime is classed as a(an)

_____.

(45) In Common Law, a person who lends a robber a gun to be used in a holdup but does not actually show up at the scene is classed as a(an) _____

_____.

(46) Under English Common Law, what person could not be charged as being an accessory after the fact? _____.

(47) In early English Common Law, a principal of the first degree could not be convicted until the principal of the second degree was convicted.　　　T or F

CHAPTER VIII

THE INCHOATE OFFENSES

8.0   **INTRODUCTION TO INCHOATE OFFENSES**
8.1   **SOLICITING**
8.2   **CONSPIRACY**
8.3   **ATTEMPTS TO COMMIT A CRIME**

8.0:0 INTRODUCTION TO INCHOATE OFFENSES

The term "Inchoate" means imperfect or not completely formed. The types of offenses that come under this classification are begun, but fall short of actual completion. The purpose of making such offenses illegal is to protect the welfare of the community by preventing or deterring persons from attempting such offenses. The three main objectives of the laws on inchoate offenses are:

(1) To prevent crimes from being completed;
(2) To apprehend those who are criminally minded and deal with them before they have a chance to complete their crime;
(3) To prevent the criminally minded from escaping justice when it is only a matter of chance or circumstance that they were not able to complete their criminal objectives.

The three classifications of inchoate offenses in California are Solicitation, Conspiracy, and Attempts.

The Model Penal Code developed by the American Law Institute sets forth strict guidelines for dealing with inchoate offenses. In it, suggestions are made that (it is hoped) will solve the problem of making such laws effective and just. They are:

(1) Eliminate the defenses of factual and legal impossibility and make criminal intent plus any overt act beyond the preparatory stages sufficient for prosecution.
(2) Make criminal solicitation a general offense like Attempt.
(3) Emphasize the element of individual agreement in Conspiracy.
(4) Remove vague words from the law on Conspiracy.
(5) Limit the defense of "change of heart" or "renunciation" in the laws on Attempt, Solicitation and Conspiracy.
(6) Align punishments with the crimes these offenses lead to rather than setting a punishment for each inchoate offense. (Example: punishment for conspiracy to commit murder should be more severe than that for petty theft.)

In this chapter, a different approach will be used than that found in most books. Usually, the order of coverage is Attempts, then Conspiracy and then Soliciting. It is more logical to start with the lesser offenses and build on those to arrive at more serious or more involved offenses. By adding elements to lesser offenses, we arrive at more serious offenses.

For example, if Arvin Ardvark asks Freddie Furd to commit robbery, Arvin is guilty of Soliciting. If Freddie agrees to the solicitation, and borrows a gun, Arvin and Freddie are now guilty of Conspiracy. If Freddie and Arvin enter the liquor store with the intent of committing robbery, they are now guilty of Attempt. Because this "building-block" approach seems more logical, it will be the approach used in this chapter.

8.1:0 SOLICITATION

As with other inchoate offenses, the purpose of the laws on soliciting is an effort to prevent the crime from being committed.

Records indicate that indictments for solicitation in England go only as far back as the 17th century. In 1679, there was a case involving the soliciting of forgery of evidence (or perjury of witnesses in court).[1] There was also a case in 1769 involving the soliciting of a public official to take a bribe.[2] These were considered the only crimes that were illegal to solicit until 1801 when, in Rex v. Higgins, the English high court clearly stated that solicitation itself was an offense even though the crime was not acted upon.[3]

California has no general solicitation law. The laws dealing with solicitations are covered in specific criminal code sections. The major law is Penal Code section 653f: Every person who, with intent that the crime be completed, solicits another to:

(1) offer a bribe
(2) accept a bribe
(3) join in the offer of a bribe
(4) join in the acceptance of a bribe
(5) join in the commission of:
   (a) Carjacking
   (b) Murder
   (c) Robbery
   (d) Burglary
   (e) Grand Theft
   (f) Receiving Stolen Property
   (g) Extortion
   (h) Rape by force or violence
   (i) Perjury
   (j) Subornation of Perjury
   (k) Forgery
   (l) Kidnapping
   (m) Assault with a deadly weapon
   (n) Arson
   (o) Sodomy by force or violence.
   (p) Oral copulation by force or violence.
   (q) Rape with foreign object.
   (r) Child molesting.

(s) Use of force or threat of force to prevent a witness from testifying.

(t) Narcotics violations (H & S Code)

(u) 14014 W & I Code

Such offenses must be proved by the testimony of two witnesses or of one witness and corroborating circumstances.

8. 1:1 Elements of Soliciting

There are four elements to the crime of solicitation. They are:

(1) The soliciting of another,

(2) To commit one of the special crimes listed,

(3) With the intent that such crime will be committed,

(4) When there are two witnesses, or one witness and corroboration.

(1) The Soliciting of Another

The term "soliciting" is a general term used to cover many acts. Examples of words that come under the heading of "soliciting" are:

(a) Ordering

(b) Counseling

(c) Inducing

(d) Instructing

(e) Advising

(f) Tempting

(g) Asking

(h) Requesting

(i) Entreating

(j) Persuading

(k) Urging

(l) Inciting

(m) Procuring

(n) Enticing

(o) Imploring

(p) Beseeching

(q) Begging

The soliciting can be done

(1) Verbally or

(2) By written request or demand

There is concern among many that the crime of soliciting is a threat to the First Amendment of the United States Constitution. This is why there are so few general solicitation laws. In California, we do not have a general solicitation law. Our only laws pertaining to soliciting are specifically directed to special crimes listed in the individual codes. (For example, those listed in 653f.)

The crime is complete when the soliciting has taken place, and the crime solicited need not be completed or even attempted.[4] Unlike conspiracy, the crime of solicitation does not require any overt act.[5] It is not important where the acts solicited are to be performed. They can be within the state or outside the state.[6] The solicitation may be proved by circumstantial evidence, and may also be corroborated by the statements of others who had also been solicited by the defendant for the same act.[7] If the soliciting has taken place, it does not matter if the person solicited refuses to go along with the solicitation, the crime is complete.[8]

(2) To Commit One of the Specific Crimes Listed

Because California does not have a general soliciting law, there must be a specific code section listing the elements of the offense and listing the particular law or laws to which it applies. Examples of special soliciting laws are:

(a) 127(c) PC Procuring another to commit perjury;

(b) 266(h) PC Soliciting, receiving support from prostitution;

(c) 647(a) PC Soliciting lewd acts in public;

(d) 647(b) PC Soliciting prostitution;

The high courts have upheld the constitutionality of soliciting laws just as long as the wording of the law is not too broad or vague.[9]

(3) With the Intent That Such Crime Will Be Committed

The purpose of this element is to give First Amendment protection to citizens, and avoid a situation where one person makes kidding or joking remarks to another, having no real intent that a crime be committed. It also prevents possible misunderstandings or misinterpretations of what was said by the person accused of the soliciting.

Example:

Harry Hotsocks visits his friend, Mervin Mushbowl, and from his upstairs window observes the girl next door sun-bathing in a string bikini. She is very good-looking and well-endowed. Harry tells Mervin that any girl who sun-bathes in an outfit like that is just asking to be raped. He then kiddingly tells Mervin that he should be the one to do it. Harry does not really mean what he says; he is just making "macho" talk. Without this element, Harry has just verbally committed an act of solicitation that violates 653f of the Penal Code.

Many states have this intent written into the law. In California, the element is not written into the law, but the high courts have confirmed that it is an essential element. In some states, the intent is just a general intent, but in California the Appellate Court, in People v. Werner, stated that "soliciting involves a specific intent."[10]

If the crime solicited, unknown to the solicitor, is impossible of being committed because of some unforeseen circumstance, the crime of soliciting is still complete as long as the solicitor believes that it is possible when he or she does the soliciting.[11]

Example:

Mortimer Snort tells Arvin Ardvark to hold up a supermarket, and lends him a gun to do it. Unknown to Mortimer, the supermarket is closed on Labor day. When Arvin goes to the store he finds that it is closed and returns to Mortimer's house. It is impossible to rob a store when none of the employees are there. Still, Mortimer is guilty of soliciting (653f PC). If you examine the elements of soliciting, they are all present in this case. There is nothing in the elements that state the crime has to be committed. It just states that the solicitor has the intent for the crime to be committed. In this case, Mortimer had that intent.

8.1:2 The Dangers of Soliciting

There is some argument as to the real danger of the crime of soliciting. Below are some of the pros and cons to this argument:

(A) Against Soliciting as a Crime
(1) Solicitors are afraid to commit the crime, and that might discourage others from doing it.
(2) Persons being solicited have free will and may not go along with the suggestion.
(3) Of all the inchoate offenses, it has the least chance of completion.

(B) For Soliciting as a Crime
(1) Solicitors can be very cunning and sly, and solicit others to do their dirty work for them.
(2) Solicitors hide in the shadows and become the masterminds, making it difficult to successfully prosecute them for their part in the crime.

8.1:3 Merging and Soliciting

The crime of soliciting does not merge with the crime solicited. This means that the person who solicits a crime that is eventually committed is guilty of both soliciting and the crime. The two offenses do not merge together into one offense.

If the crime solicited is actually committed, the solicitor then becomes a principal to that crime because he or she has encouraged its commission.

8.1:4 Soliciting as Entrapment

Entrapment occurs when the police plan a crime and, through some agent, recruit other persons to commit it so they can arrest them. This is illegal. Although the law does have some technical exceptions such as when it can be shown that the person arrested was in the business of doing what he or she was arrested for, the police have to be especially careful about charges of entrapment.

Example:

Numerous complaints regarding male homosexuals stopping men on the street and soliciting lewd acts are received. The police put an undercover detail on the street in the hope that they will be solicited. If the undercover officers do any soliciting themselves, they will be guilty of entrapment. They must be careful not even to make suggestive movements that could be interpreted as inciting a male homosexual to approach them. The rule also applies to non-police officers working under the direction of the police. They are their agents and are acting in their behalf.

8.1:5 Corroboration for Soliciting

California law requires two witnesses or one witness and corroboration to obtain a conviction for soliciting. In Kelly v. the United States, the Federal court reversed a conviction for soliciting lewd acts because the undercover officer who arrested the suspect included no corroborative statement in his report. In the transcript of the trial, the officer testified only to the fact that the defendant solicited him for a lewd act, but in no way corroborated the solicitation.[12]

Corroborating solicitation is difficult when there is only the suspect and the arresting officer, yet the corroboration need only be very slight. It should identify the suspect with the crime, remove any doubt as to intent, and show clearly that the meaning of the statement was not mistaken.[13] One way to corroborate solicitation is to "wire" the undercover officer with a transmitter so the statement can be taped on a receiver in a police vehicle.

The Federal Criminal Code suggests one way of overcoming the problem of misunderstanding is to require a fourth element — some overt act beyond solicitation, not necessarily the crime itself, but any act toward the objective.

Model Penal Code (Proposed Official Draft)
Section 5. 02 Criminal Solicitation

(1) Definition of Solicitation. A person is guilty of solicitation to commit a crime if with the purpose of promoting or facilitating its commission he commands, encourages or requests another person to engage in specific conduct which would constitute such crime or an attempt to commit such crime or which would establish his complicity in its commission or attempted commission.

(2) **Uncommunicated Solicitation.** It is immaterial under Subsection (1) of this Section that the actor fails to communicate with the person he solicits to commit a crime if his conduct was designed to effect such communication.

(3) **Renunciation of Criminal Purpose.** It is an affirmative defense that the actor, after soliciting another person to commit a crime persuaded him not to do so or otherwise pre- vented the commission of the crime, under circumstances manifesting a complete and voluntary renunciation of his criminal purpose.

Proposed Federal Criminal Code (study draft)

1003 Criminal Solicitation
(1) **Offense.** A person is guilty of criminal solicitation if he commands, induces, entreats, or otherwise attempts to persuade another person to commit a particular crime which is, in fact, a felony, whether as principal or accomplice, with intent to promote or facilitate the commission of that crime, and under circumstances strongly corroborative of that intent.

(2) **Defense.** It is a defense to a prosecution under this section that, if the criminal object were achieved, the defendant would be a victim of the offense or the offense is so defined that his conduct would be inevitably incident to its commission or he otherwise would not be guilty under the statute defining the offense or as an accomplice.

(3) **Defense Precluded.** It is no defense to a prosecution under this section that the person solicited could not be guilty of the offense because of lack of responsibility or culpability, or other incapacity or defense.

(4) **Renunciation and Withdrawal.** It is an affirmative defense to a prosecution under this section that the defendant, after soliciting another person to commit a felony, persuaded him not to do so or otherwise prevented the commission of the felony, under circumstances manifesting a complete and voluntary renunciation of the defendant's criminal intent. A renunciation is not "voluntary and complete" if it is motivated in whole or in part by

(a) a belief that a circumstance exists which increases the probability of detection or apprehension of the defendant or another or which makes more difficult the consummation of the crime, or

(b) a decision to postpone the crime until another time or to substitute another victim or another but similar objective.

8.2:0 CONSPIRACY

Conspiracy was unknown as a criminal act in early common law. It was first mentioned in 1292 (20 Edw. 1) and 1300 (28 Edw. 1), but it was not defined very well until 1304 (33 Edw. 1):

> Conspirators be they who do confeder or bind themselves by oath, covenant, or other alliance, that every of them shall aid and bear the other falsely and maliciously to indict or cause to indict, or falsely to move or maintain pleas; and also such as cause children within age to appeal men of felony whereby they are imprisoned and sore grieved; and such as retain men in the country with liveries or fees to maintain their malicious enterprises; and this extendeth as well to takers as to the givers; and stewards and bailiffs of great lords which by their seignory office or power undertake to bear and maintain quarrels, pleas, or debates that concern other parties than such as touch the estates of their lords or themselves.

Even then it was not usually applied in criminal matters.

Sir James Stephen, the famous English writer on criminal law, suggests that the first attempt to apply conspiracy to criminal acts was in the Court of Star Chamber. Before this time it was applied mostly to offenses involving civil injuries.[14] After the Restoration in the 1600's, it found its way into the Court of King's Bench, and was then widely accepted as applying to criminal matters.

8.2:1 Dangers of Conspiracy

The dangerous aspects of conspiracy lie in the fact that two or more persons must be involved. This causes an increased likelihood that the conspiracy will not be abandoned because one member becomes ill or decides not to follow through with the objective of the conspiracy. If one person were to die, the others would take over. If one person failed, the others would try to succeed in his or her place and the chance of completion would be much greater.

Because of this, in California all conspiracies are felonies, even conspiracy to commit a misdemeanor. In some cases, the punishment is optional (a Wobbler) and can be either a felony or a misdemeanor, but until judication it is classed as a felony.

The purpose of the law on Conspiracy is to prevent crimes from being committed just as are the other inchoate offenses.

8.2:2 Definition and Elements of Conspiracy

Under English common law, the definition that finally developed is listed under Article 48. The definition is as follows: "When two or more persons agree to commit any crime, they are guilty of the misdemeanor called conspiracy whether the crime is committed or not."[15]

The definition under California law has changed from the original, and is listed as follows from section 182 of the Penal Code:

If two or more persons conspire:

(1) To commit any crime.

(2) Falsely and maliciously to indict another for any crime, or to procure another to be charged or arrested for any crime.

(3) Falsely to move or maintain any suit, action or proceeding.

(4) To cheat and defraud any person of any property, by any means which are in themselves criminal, or to obtain money or property by false pretenses or by false promises with fraudulent intent not to perform such promises.

(5) To commit any act injurious to the public health, to public morals, or to pervert or obstruct justice, or the due administration of the laws.

(6) To commit any crime against the person of the President or Vice President of the United States, the governor of any state or territory, any United States Justice or judge, or the secretary of any of the executive departments of the United States.

Where, in English law, conspiracy was a misdemeanor, the punishment in California is a "wobbler." Sections 2, 3, 4 and 5 are also "Wobblers." If the crime conspired is a felony, or that listed under section 6, it is a straight felony.

Elements Broken Down

On the basis of both statutory and case law, the elements of conspiracy are:

(1) An agreement or understanding (toward common objective)

(2) Between two or more persons

(3) With specific intent to accomplish

(4) Either

   (a) An unlawful purpose (crime) or

   (b) A lawful purpose by unlawful means or

   (c) An injury to public health, morals or justice.

(5) When accompanied by some overt act beyond the mere agreement. (184 PC)

(1) An Agreement of Understanding

The agreement in conspiracy may consist of tacit, mutual understanding to commit a crime. The agreement can be implied rather than formal, and need not be written.[16] Those involved need not clearly state the terms of the common understanding.[17] It need not even be expressed in words.[18] Agreement may be shown if there is concert of action, all parties working together, understandingly with single design for accomplishment of a common purpose.[19] Conspiracy may result from actions of defendants in carrying out a common purpose to achieve an unlawful end.[20] The agreement can be inferred through conduct. The parties need not actually meet together and agree to the joint undertaking of a criminal action.[21]

The agreement of each conspirator need not be to personally participate in the crime. They can aid in just the planning stage.[22] Those agreeing need not even meet the other conspirators or know who they are.[23] It is not even necessary that those agreeing to the conspiracy know all the plans to the conspiracy just as long as they seek the common objective of the conspiracy.

The members of a conspiracy do not have to approve each part of the plan. For example: The objective is to rob the Bank of America, and all conspirators agree to this objective. Later, in working out the final details, most of the conspirators want to use a helicopter rather than a car to make their escape. Two conspirators, however, insist upon using a car because it is safer. If they do not legally withdraw from the conspiracy, they are still members of that conspiracy and are responsible for all the natural and probable outcomes of that conspiracy, such as the shooting of a teller in the bank.

(2) Between Two or More Persons

Remember, it takes "two to tango" and it takes two or more to commit a conspiracy. Without two persons or more, there can be no conspiracy.

At one time, the Church had a great influence on the law. Because of this, the religious concept that a married couple were spiritually one was carried over into common law with the rule that a husband and wife, being one person, could not be tried for conspiracy for an agreement between just the two of them. This rule remained with us until very recent times.

In 1960, the United States Supreme Court rejected the common law rule regarding a married couple being exempt from the law on conspiracy.[24] The court stated that it was fiction to assume that the two persons were really one and could not conspire to commit a crime. However, this was a 5-to-4 decision, and the four justices who disagreed with the decision felt that the husband-and-wife relationship was of such an intimate nature, if one of them was involved in the planning of some criminal act, the other would certainly be aware of it, and might be unjustly implicated on the basis of the close relationship alone. They expressed a fear that this decision could "endanger the confidentiality of the marriage relationship."

It was not until four years later that the California Supreme Court also rejected the concept that a married couple should be immune to conspiracy prosecution. In 1964, the California Supreme Court held that this rule was invalid.[25]

When Can One Person be Tried for Conspiracy?

The key to prosecution for conspiracy is "were there two or more persons involved when the agreement took place and the overt act was committed?" If there were two or more at this time, an individual person can later be singly tried for the crime. For example: If Larry Lunk and Sam Slurp conspire to commit a crime and commit some overt act toward its completion beyond the mere agreement, and then Larry dies or leaves the country, Sam can be tried for the conspiracy by himself.

If two persons commit the act of conspiracy, and one of them is granted immunity, the other can be tried alone.[26] On the other hand, if three persons are charged with conspiracy and during the trial two of them are found not guilty, and the third defendant is found guilty, there can be no conviction. The decision that the two defendants were not guilty means that they never committed the crime. That being the case, there were never two or more persons involved, and the third person cannot be charged with conspiracy.[27]

There is no limit to the number of people who can be involved in a conspiracy, as long as it is at least two. It is not essential to the conviction of a co-conspirator that any or all other co-conspirators be tried and convicted.[28]

(3) With Specific Intent to Accomplish

The purpose of the element of specific intent is to offer First Amendment protection. If it were not for this element, people could be charged with conspiracy when they were just joking and did not really intend to carry out the conspiracy.

Example:

Fred Farkle and Fanny Fridgit are walking down the street together. Fanny mentions that she is really broke. Fred states that he is also very broke, points to the First National Bank across the street, and suggests that they have plenty of money. Fanny then kiddingly states, "We ought to pull a holdup there." Fred jokingly agrees. From a technical standpoint, if either of them were to make the slightest overt act (even in fun) toward such an objective, and someone overheard and saw their overt act, they could be charged with conspiracy. The element that protects them is that requiring "specific intent." Specific intent cannot be presumed from the mere commission of an unlawful act. It must be proved by the prosecution.[29] Conspiracy requires specific intent even if the crime that is the object of the conspiracy does not require that special type of intent.[30]

Personal motives are immaterial to conviction. The purpose or specific intent in conspiracy is more important than in any other crime. This is because it shows the conspirator's state of mind. This removes the possibility of making a mistaken inference from the statements of the conspirators which is easy to do. The California Appellate Court has declared conspiracy to be a "specific intent" crime, and not one requiring just "intent."[31] Statements of the accused conspirators are often better means of proving specific intent than their actions. However, both are used to prove specific intent.

In the crime of conspiracy, the specific intent is really two intents. First is the intent to agree or conspire, and the second is the intent to commit the crime which is the object of the conspiracy.[32]

Specific Intent and Resulting Objectives That Are Different

The specific intent of the conspiracy is one that is set and established before the crime or objective is completed. Since the completion of the objective is not necessary in order for the conspiracy to be complete, the original objective is the one that determines the seriousness of the conspiracy.

For example, conspiracy to commit a felony is a straight felony; to commit a misdemeanor is a "Wobbler," and a person could be sentenced for a misdemeanor on such a conspiracy charge. Let us look at an example where the conspiracy was to commit a felony, but when the crime was completed, it turned out to be a misdemeanor.

Example:

Freddie Flake and Lilly Liverlip conspire to steal five hundred dollars that Lilly's aunt keeps in her purse. The plan is for them to take her to the beach. Lilly will distract her and Freddie will take the money from her purse. Lilly is sure that there is five hundred dollars in the purse because she has seen it several times. Her aunt is rich and keeps it there in case of an emergency when the banks are closed. Unknown to Lilly, an emergency had arisen and her aunt spent four hundred of the five hundred dollars. As a result, Freddie only got one hundred dollars.

Point of Law:

In California, theft of over $400 is a felony; theft of $400 or less is a misdemeanor (petty theft).

Freddie and Lilly are guilty of conspiracy to commit a felony. They are also guilty of petty theft. Even though they only obtained one hundred dollars, the original intent of the conspiracy was to steal five hundred dollars, that intent, and not how much they finally obtained, determines the severity of the conspiracy.

Defenses That Remove Specific Intent

Since conspiracy is a specific intent crime, there are situations where that intent is missing, for example: where the accused acted in ignorance without criminal intent. A person associates with the members of a conspiracy, unaware of their purpose or association. Mere association with honest intent is not proof of a conspiracy.[33] Since some mental capacity is required, and intoxication can affect specific intent because it alters the state of mind, proof of intoxication could be a defense.[34]

(4) Either An Unlawful Purpose Or A Lawful Purpose By Unlawful Means

This element is not listed in 182 of the Penal Code, but the high courts have, since the crime became common, declared this to be an element. It probably had its origin in a statement of Lord Denman that conspiracy means "either to do an unlawful act, or a lawful act by unlawful means."[35] The U.S. Supreme Court in 1895 further upheld this element by stating that conspiracy involved "a criminal or unlawful purpose, or some purpose not in itself unlawful or criminal, by criminal or unlawful means"[36] It is further affirmed by the California Appellate Court in People v. Moran.[37]

(A) Criminal Acts

The term "any crime" as used in 182 of the Penal Code means just that. The word "crime" includes felonies and misdemeanors.[38] It also includes city ordinances,[39] and is limited to only those crimes planned in this state.[40]

Some substantive crimes are really conspiracies even though they are not called conspiracies. For example, the Sherman Act of 1890 (Anti-Trust Act) punishes conspiracy to restrict free enterprise.

(B) Lawful Acts Accomplished by Unlawful Means

The best examples of this condition of conspiracy involve business concerns and labor unions. Businesses seek to make a profit, which is lawful. However, they sometimes use unlawful means to make that profit and to restrict the trade of others. A legal association of individuals engaged in a lawful enterprise may become a criminal conspiracy. Labor unions seek to prevent businesses from taking advantage of their employees, and see that the employees get a "fair shake." This is a legal endeavor. However, they sometimes use criminal means to obtain those goals. While on strike, they rough up non-strikers (assault and battery), and cause damage to the property of the employer and non-striker (vandalism).

Example #1:

Most of the garlic in the United States is grown in the area of Gilroy. The garlic growers get together at a meeting and decide that they control most of the garlic in the United States. They feel that there are many people of Mediterranean origin in the United States who would just not be able to cook without garlic. They therefore decide to double the price of garlic. This is a conspiracy. The making of profit is legal, but to use price fixing as a means of obtaining this profit is illegal.

Example #2:

After the meeting, ninety percent of the growers double their price. Ten percent of the growers decide not to go along with the price rise. Then, representatives of the ninety percent go to the wholesale outlet and tell them that if they buy garlic from the ten percent who did not go along with their scheme, that they would not sell any garlic to them. Without ninety percent of their source of garlic, the garlic wholesalers would be out of business. They therefore refuse to buy garlic from the ten percent of growers who rebelled against the price increase. Again, the making of a profit is legal, but making it by restricting the trade of other businesses is illegal, so they are attaining lawful objectives by unlawful means. This violates the Anti-Trust Act.

(C) Through Lawful Acts That Are Injurious to the Public Health, to Public Morals or to Pervert or Obstruct Justice

The acts covered under subsection 5 of Penal Code Section 182 are very broad in their interpretation. There is not much California case law in this special area, but there is precedent in both English law and the case law from other states.

There is a very early case in English law where a gentleman of good reputation and a nearby family became involved in a personal dispute. A short time later, the daughter in the family became pregnant. The family conspired with the daughter to falsely tell everyone in the village that the gentleman, whom the family disliked, was responsible for her pregnancy. The specific intent here was to ruin the good reputation of the gentleman they disliked. The members of the family were tried and convicted for conspiracy.[41]

In Pennsylvania, there was a case of persons having a relative declared insane in order to obtain the relative's money and to have the relative out of the way.[42]

There is a case of conspiracy from New Jersey that is of interest to those in the field of Criminal Justice. In this case, a group formed a conspiracy to force the police department to fire certain officers whom they disliked. They attempted this through harassment of the department administrators and city officials, The conviction was for conspiracy to deprive the officers of their livelihood.[43]

This subsection is very broad, but as long as a complaint or indictment is clearly worded and detailed as to the acts committed, it is doubtful that it will be declared unconstitutionally broad or vague.

(5) When Accompanied by Some Overt Act Beyond Mere Agreement

Under common law, conspiracy does not have to have an overt act. The verbal act is enough. In California and on the federal level, conspiracy must have an overt act that is beyond mere agreement. The purpose of the act is to show that the conspiracy has begun an active existence.[44] It is not necessary that the act be criminal or unlawful in nature.[45] It is not necessary that each member of the conspiracy commit the act, or for that matter, any act. Only one member need commit the act that starts the conspiracy.[46]

The overt act tends to nail down the true criminal intent of conspiracy. The overt act necessary to start the conspiracy in motion need only be very slight. An example would be buying a postage stamp to be used to mail poison in a conspiracy to commit murder.[47] The act can be preliminary or preparatory in nature, such as drawing the plans for the crime. The act can be done by an innocent agent such as a delivery person or mail carrier.[48]

Examples of Acts That Can Begin a Conspiracy

(a) Raising funds to bribe a public officer
(b) Buying rope to be used in a kidnapping.
(c) Borrowing a car to be used in a holdup.
(d) Buying a gun to murder another.
(e) Buying pantyhose to be used as a mask in a robbery.
(f) Obtaining chloroform to be used in a rape.
(g) Stealing a key to be used later in a burglary.
(h) Buying special ink and paper to be used in a conspiracy to counterfeit money.

8.2:3　Criticism of Conspiracy Laws

Because a person can too easily be accused of conspiracy based on inference and association, there has been some criticism of these laws. U.S. Supreme Court Justice Jackson referred to conspiracy as "so vague that it almost defies definition."[49]

In 1925, Justice Taft became concerned about abuse of conspiracy statutes. He sent out "Recommendations to the District Judges," asking them to contact prosecuting attorneys regarding these abuses. He noted a prevalent use of conspiracy indictments to make felonies out of misdemeanors. It was suggested that the use of such tactics by prosecutors was arbitrary and harsh. He also noted that the rules of evidence for conspiracies made cases difficult for the defendant and felt that it could create undue prejudice against the innocent. In the same year, the famous U. S. Supreme Court Justice, Learned Hand called conspiracy the "darling of the modern prosecutor's nursery."[50]

Apart from the misuse of conspiracy indictments by prosecutors, there is also the concern about its use to infringe upon the free speech rights guaranteed under the First Amendment, especially in those states where an overt act is not required.

8.2:4　Conspiracy and the Federal Government

Conspiracy laws are used most often by the federal government. There are several reasons for this. On the local level, the authorities do not normally become aware of a conspiracy until the objective is actually completed. In that case, they charge the perpetrators with the completed offense rather than the conspiracy. This is true even though in many cases it is easier to prove the conspiracy than the completed criminal substantive act.

Federal government agencies often have large numbers of undercover agents and informants infiltrating organizations which present a potential danger to the United States. This is especially true of organizations whose philosophies involve the violent overthrow of the U.S. government. Some of the conspiratorial objectives of these organizations are so dangerous, detrimental or irreparable, the government cannot allow them to be completed. When they learn of such plans, they move immediately to stop their completion. For example, if they learn of a plan to blow up the Statue of Liberty, their undercover agents or informants contact them as soon as an overt act is completed toward the final objective. They will then move in and arrest all those involved in the conspiracy.

The federal government also has obligations to citizens that are easier to enforce through the use of conspiracy laws. For example: there is a tendency for certain "confidence" men to attempt to defraud large numbers of citizens through the use of the mails, or through certain types of schemes in which ordinary, prudent, citizens would not be able to properly protect themselves. The average citizen does not have the resources or capability to check out every plan in which he would like to invest his money; for example: retirement plans and insurance policies that are fraudulent and do not have the capability of paying off when citizens find themselves in a position to collect. It is here that the federal government can offer some protection to its citizens by arresting and prosecuting such illegal schemes under the conspiracy laws.

Under the "general welfare of the public" clause, the federal government has the responsibility to protect its citizens from fraudulent schemes. The federal government has many laws by which it can prosecute those who defraud the public, but it is much better to detect and arrest those persons before they actually commit the crimes. When persons try to violate the law on "Using the Mails for Fraudulent Purposes," or "Obstructing the Administration of Election Laws," or "Overthrowing the Existing Government," they can be arrested and convicted on conspiracy to violate those laws.

8.2:5 The Partnership Aspects of Conspiracy and Liability

Because in early common law, conspiracy had a civil application, the law on conspiracy today follows many of the legal rules regarding a business partnership. United States Supreme Court Justice Oliver Wendell Holmes once referred to conspiracy as a "partnership in criminal purpose."[51] Professor Perkins, author of "Criminal Law and Procedure," has stated "an agreement for a lawful purpose is a contract; an agreement for an unlawful purpose is a conspiracy."

In discussing criminal liability for participation in a conspiracy, it is important to understand the "partnership" concept. Some claim that the

liability in conspiracies is too great and sometimes unjust. Whether or not this is true, it must be understood that the offense has its origin in civil partnership. In a civil partnership, each partner is completely responsible for the business acts and debts incurred by other partners. Many persons have been ruined in business because of their partners. The legal responsibility is great in a partnership. The same is true of conspiracies.

A Conspiracy Does Not Merge With the Completed Crime

Conspiracy has a double liability in that, unlike in early common law, the act of conspiracy does not "merge" or join with the completed crime. If the crime is completed, the conspirators are responsible for both the conspiracy and the completed crime.[52]

Proximate Cause and Conspiracy

Under the Doctrine of Proximate Cause, a conspirator is liable for all acts of co-conspirators if they are done in furtherance of the common objective of the conspiracy. The rule of causation states that a conspirator is responsible for the acts of co-conspirators if the acts are the natural and probable outcome of that particular conspiracy. The key is whether the acts fit the common objective. If the conspiracy is to steal lumber, and on the way back from the theft one of the conspirators holds up a liquor store, the other conspirators are not responsible for the robbery because it was not part of the common objective of the conspiracy.

A conspirator need not be present when an act is committed in order to be responsible for that offense.[53] This applies even if he or she did not know that the act was to be committed, as long as it contributed to the objective of the conspiracy.[54]

If, as a result of a conspiracy, someone is killed, all the conspirators are responsible for the killing. This even applies to those who specifically state that they want nothing to do with a killing and even forbid the others to commit such an act.[55]

In a conspiracy to beat up a person, it is a natural and probable outcome that the victim could die from the beating. Therefore, all who conspired to beat up the victim are responsible for his or her death even if they were against killing anyone.[56]

When persons join a conspiracy that has already formed, they adopt the previous acts and declarations of their fellow conspirators[57] but they may not be convicted of a substantive offense committed by any of the other conspirators prior to their joining the conspiracy.[58] The prior acts and declarations would be used to prove that the conspiracy was in motion.

All crimes are crimes against the state. If a person who is guilty of conspiracy to defraud a mail order company makes a private deal with them to refund the money in exchange for dropping the charges, such agreement is illegal and only the state can determine whether or not to prosecute.[59]

A conspiracy to commit murder can only be murder of the first degree, because the plain fact that a conspiracy occurred shows premeditation.[60]

8.2:6   Withdrawal from a Conspiracy

Simply refraining from further activity in a conspiracy does not allow a legal claim of withdrawal. There must be an affirmative and bona fide rejection or repudiation of the conspiracy, and it must be communicated to the co-conspirators.[61] Since conspirators wishing to withdraw from a conspiracy must notify co-conspirators of their intention, and since they may not know all members of the conspiracy, it is logical that they give notice only to those persons whom they know are members. In judging whether the defendant did in fact withdraw from the conspiracy, the jury must apply the "reasonable person" rule to determine whether he or she acted reasonably in attempting to withdraw from the conspiracy.[62] Once conspirators withdraw from a conspiracy, they are no longer responsible for further acts committed as a result of that conspiracy. They are, however, still liable for acts committed before their withdrawal.[63]

The Model Penal Code recognizes withdrawal as a defense to prosecution for earlier acts. The conspirator, however, must have attempted to "thwart the success of the conspiracy." (Model Penal Code 5. 03(06)). One way would be to notify the police of the conspiracy. This however, is a proposal of the American Law Institute, not a law.

A conspirator who withdraws after the agreement, but before the overt act has been completed, is not liable for the acts of the conspiracy.[64] If the act that started the conspiracy was performed by an innocent agent under the direction of a conspirator, the conspiracy is in effect and all are responsible or liable who have not withdrawn before that act.[65]

8.2:7   Proof of the Conspiracy

Although it is difficult to show common design by direct evidence, direct and circumstantial evidence can be used to prove a conspiracy.[66] Usually a conspiracy is proved by circumstantial evidence alone. The evidence need only show an inference that the conspiracy did exist.[67]

Since a conspiracy involves specific intent, it is more difficult to prove than if only general intent was involved. The existence of a conspiracy may also be proved by the declaration of one or more conspirators if the declaration relates to the objective of the conspiracy, and is not a confession.[68]

Just because a co-conspirator is not being tried with the other conspirators, does not mean that his or her acts and declarations cannot be used in the trial of the other conspirators.[69]

Whether an act committed by an accused conspirator fits that conspiracy, or is an independent act that has nothing to do with the conspiracy is a question of fact for the jury to decide.[70] Whether the act was committed before or after the conspiracy was in effect is also a question of fact.[71]

The fact that the defendant in a conspiracy trial used different names to apply for unemployment benefits was accepted as sufficient evidence of a common design to commit conspiracy to defraud, not a case of committing a single crime. The fact that the co-conspirator registered phony businesses, enabling the fraud to be accomplished, was also accepted as proof that the offense consisted of conspiracy, not unrelated substantive crimes.[72]

The fact of conspiracy need not be proved by a preponderance of evidence or beyond a reasonable doubt. It can be proved by prima facie evidence alone.[73] A conspiracy can be proved by the testimony of a conspirator who withdrew from the conspiracy, or by co-conspirators who have accepted partial or full immunity in return for testifying. The dying declaration of a homicide victim, whose death was the object of a conspiracy, can be used to establish that conspiracy.[74]

8.3:8   The Scope of the Conspiracy

Many confuse the scope of the conspiracy with the scope of the crime that is its object. There is a distinct difference. The scope of a conspiracy is dependent upon its objective. The conspiracy does not end until its ultimate objective has been accomplished. Therefore, a conspirator's liability goes beyond the completion of the criminal act.[75] For example, the ultimate objective of a robbery is not the robbery, but the obtaining of the money and its division among the conspirators. Therefore, the conspiracy to rob or to steal is not over until the spoils have been divided.[76] In a conspiracy to kidnap for ransom, the ultimate objective is not the seizing of the victim, but the obtaining of the ransom money and its division among those involved in the conspiracy.[77] It is understood that conspiracy includes evading and resisting arrest, and any act to achieve that end. If the conspirator kills another in an attempt to escape, the other conspirators are equally guilty of murder.[78] It can also extend beyond the crime if the act committed is for the purpose of concealing the crime.[79]

8.2:9 Model Penal Code
Section 5. 03. Criminal Conspiracy

(1) **Definition of Conspiracy.** A person is guilty of conspiracy with another person or persons to commit a crime if with the purpose of promoting or facilitating its commission he:

(a) agrees with such other person or persons that they or one or more of them will engage in conduct which constitutes such crime or an attempt or solicitation to commit such crime; or

(b) agrees to aid such other person or persons in the planning or commission of such crime or of an attempt of solicitation to commit such crime.

(2) **Scope of Conspiratorial Relationship.** If a person guilty of conspiracy, as defined by Subsection 1 of this Section, knows that a person with whom he conspires to commit a crime has conspired with another person or persons to commit the same crime, he is guilty of conspiring with such other person or persons, whether or not he knows their identity, to commit such crime.

(3) **Conspiracy With Multiple Criminal Objectives.** If a person conspires to commit a number of crimes, he is guilty of only one conspiracy so long as such multiple crimes are the object of the same agreement or continuous conspiratorial relationship.

(4) **Joinder & Venue in Conspiracy Prosecutions**

(a) Subject to the provisions of paragraph b. of this Subsection, two or more persons charged with criminal conspiracy may be prosecuted jointly if:

(i) they are charged with conspiring with one another; or

(ii) the conspiracies alleged, whether they have the same or different parties, are so related that they constitute different aspects of a scheme or organized criminal conduct.

(b) In any joint prosecution under paragraph a. of the Subsection;

(i) no defendant shall be charged with a conspiracy in any county (parish or district) other than one in which he entered into such conspiracy or in which an overt act pursuant to such conspiracy was done by him or by a person with whom he conspired;

(ii) neither the liability of any defendant nor the admissibility against him of evidence of acts or declarations of another shall be enlarged by such joinder; and

(iii) the Court shall order a severance or take a special verdict as to any defendant who so requests, if it deems it necessary or appropriate to promote the fair determination of his guilt or innocence, and shall take any other proper measures to protect the fairness of the trial.

(5) **Overt Act.** No person may be convicted of conspiracy to commit a crime, other than a felony of the first or second degree, unless an overt act in pursuance of such conspiracy is alleged and proved to have been done by him or by a person with whom he conspired.

The Relationship Between Scope of the Crime and Scope of a Conspiracy

CONSPIRACY

Attempt — Crime

Overt act beyond mere agreement — Overt act beyond mere preparation — Start of crime — Escape from scene — Objective of conspiracy attained

Example in Kidnapping

CONSPIRACY TO KIDNAP

Attempted Kidnapping — Actual Kidnapping

Buying tape to bind hands of victim — Entry of victim's home — Movement of victim — Taking victim to hideout — Collection and division of ransom

(6) **Renunciation of Criminal Purpose.** It is an affirmative defense that the actor, after conspiring to commit a crime, thwarted the success of the conspiracy, under circumstances manifesting a complete and voluntary renunciation of his criminal purpose.

(7) **Duration of Conspiracy.** For purposes of Section 1. 06(4):

(a) conspiracy is a continuing course of conduct which terminates when the crime or crimes which are its object are committed or the agreement that they be committed is abandoned by the defendant and by those with whom he conspired; and

(b) such abandonment is presumed if neither the defendant nor anyone with whom he conspired does any overt act in pursuance of the conspiracy during the applicable period of limitation; and

(c) if an individual abandons the agreement, the conspiracy is terminated as to him only if and when he advises those with whom he conspired of his abandonment or he informs the law enforcement authorities of the existence of the conspiracy and of his participation therein.

8.2:10 Proposed Federal Criminal Code
1004. Criminal Conspiracy

(1) **Offense.** A person is guilty of conspiracy if he agrees with one or more persons to engage in or cause the performance of conduct which, in fact, constitutes a crime or crimes, and any one or more of such persons does an act to effect the objective of the conspiracy. The agreement need not be explicit but may be implicit in the fact of collaboration or existence of other circumstances.

(2) **Parties to Conspiracy.** If a person knows that one, with whom he agrees, has agreed or will agree with another to effect the same objective, he shall be deemed to have agreed with the other, whether or not he knows the other's identity.

(3) **Duration of Conspiracy.** A conspiracy shall be deemed to continue until its objectives are accomplished, frustrated or abandoned. "Objectives" include escape from the scene of the crime, distribution of booty, and measures, other than silence, for concealing the crime or obstructing justice in relation to it. A conspiracy shall be deemed to have been abandoned if no overt act to effect its objectives has been committed by any conspirator during the applicable period of limitations.

(4) **Defense Precluded.** It is no defense to a prosecution under this section that the person with whom such person is alleged to have conspired has been acquitted, has not been prosecuted or convicted, has been convicted of a different offense, is immune from prosecution, or is otherwise not subject to justice.

8.3:0   ATTEMPTS TO COMMIT A CRIME

In an effort to deter crime, the law tries to discourage a criminal from even attempting a crime by making such an attempt unlawful and punishable. Attempts to commit a crime are illegal throughout the United States, yet this crime differs from state to state. The major point of difference is an important one. That point is, exactly when does the attempt start?

It is difficult to know exactly at what time in history attempts were classed as crimes. Harvard Law Professor Sayre believes that it occurred in 1789 when an English high court stated: "The completion of an act criminal in itself is not necessary to constitute criminality." (Rex v. Scofield Cald. 397)[80]

Sir James Stephen, the writer on criminal law, believed it started with the infamous Court of Star Chamber. He based his belief on circumstantial evidence found in the earlier writings in Hudson's book "Treatise on the Court of Star Chamber" in which Hudson described a purpose of the court as being that it: "Punisheth errors creeping into the commonwealth, which might otherwise prove dangerous— yea, although no positive law or continued custom of common law giveth warrant to it."[81] This would place the first use of criminal attempts in the 1330's. Sir James Stephen also found recorded evidence of convictions for attempts in 1563 and in 1602 A. D.

An attempt is a separate offense, yet when the crime has been completed, there can no longer be a separate charge of attempt. The attempt and the crime merge into one offense.

8.3:1   The Law on Attempts in California

Sections 663 and 664 of the Penal Code make an attempt to commit a crime an offense. Unlike soliciting, which can only apply to specially listed crimes, an attempt to commit a crime can be illegal when attempting to commit any crime. Under 664 PC the code states: "Every person who attempts to commit any crime, but fails, or is prevented or intercepted in the perpetration, is punishable." The codes also contain specific statutory offenses that involve an attempt to commit a crime; for example: Attempted Arson, 451 PC. The law on attempts applies only to Mala In Se crimes, and not regulatory offenses.

... HOW D'YA FIGURE THIS IS 'MALA IN SE"? ...

... IT'S MY MOTHER-IN-LAW'S PLACE !!

8.3:2 The Elements of an Attempt

There are five elements for a general attempt. If the attempt also amounts to an assault, there is an added element.

(1) An overt act.
(2) Beyond mere preparation.
(3) Towards committing a crime legally capable of commission.
(4) When there is specific intent to commit the crime.
(5) Which, if not interrupted, would have resulted in the crime.

Although assaults are listed separately in the codes, they are technically attempts. The definition of an assault is as follows:

An unlawful attempt, coupled with the present ability, to commit a violent injury upon the person of another. (240 PC)

Because of this definition, any attempt that is also an assault requires a sixth element:

(6) The crime or method involved is capable of completion.

8.3:3 Two Classes of Attempt

Understanding the law on attempts can be difficult unless you first understand that there are two types of attempts. The first type is a general attempt to commit a crime; for example: attempted burglary or attempted theft. There are five elements for this type of attempt. If, however, the attempt also amounts to an assault, then there is another element that must be proved. Under this type of attempt it must be shown that the crime was actually capable of being completed.

For example, if Fred Farkle tries to shoot Kitty Krump, but the ammunition is old and does not fire, Fred is guilty of attempted murder. This is because it is possible that the ammunition could fire on the second try. In another example, unknown to Fred, his wife removed the bullets from the gun. He aims the gun at Kitty and pulls the trigger. He is not guilty of attempted murder because the crime is impossible. This crime is a type of assault and requires that the crime be actually capable of completion. Without bullets, a person attempting to fire the gun is incapable of killing anyone.

8.3:4 Discussion of the Elements

(A) An Overt Act in an Attempt

The act must reflect the specific intent of the person doing the act. It must be an act that logically fits into the "Chain of Causation" or one that could logically lead to completion of the crime.

To constitute the crime of attempt, the acts of the defendant must go so far that they would result in the completion of the crime if it were not prevented by other factors of which the defendant is not aware.[82] The acts needed for an attempt must be such that they would have resulted in the crime if it were not for intervening circumstances that were unknown to the person committing the act.[83]

The overt act needed for a criminal attempt need not be the "Last Proximate Act" prior to the commission of the crime itself.[84] The terms "Last Proximate Act" and "Point of No Return" are used in some states to indicate an act that is so close to the actual crime that the crime would be quickly committed if things were to continue as they are. The overt act needed for a criminal attempt need not to be the ultimate act in the crime, but can be a first or subsequent step moving directly toward the crime after the preparations have been made.[85]

Examples of Overt Acts

(a) Defendant took a gun to wife's house. He listened at the door to see if he could hear anyone else in the house. He then had a friend go to the door so that his wife would open the door. (Attempted Murder)[86]

(b) Defendant took woman to the house of a physician to determine whether she had a venereal disease before putting her to work in a house of prostitution. (Attempted Pandering)[87]

(c) Defendant used a false pretense to obtain money from the victim. It did not matter that the intended victim did not believe the story told; it was still attempted fraud.[88]

(d) Defendant was seen at night in front of a bedroom window with his hands raised up towards the window, and ran away when discovered. There were valuables that were visible on the bed in the room. Conviction for attempted burglary upheld.[89]

(e) Defendant was discovered standing inside door, wearing gloves; when officer approached, he dropped paper bag and then gloves. Convicted of attempted burglary.[90]

(f) Defendant was standing near a store where the door had been pried. Tools on suspect matched tool marks on door. Convicted of attempted burglary.[91]

(g) Defendant was observed at 2 o'clock in the morning leaning against door of store with hand through hole in door glass. Attempted burglary.[92]

(h) Defendant represented himself as vice officer, and threatened victim with arrest as a prostitute if she did not give him money. Convicted of attempted extortion.[93]

(i) Defendant approached victim's vehicle, showed a gun and asked for money. As victim tried to start car, defendant smashed window with gun. Convicted of attempted robbery.[94]

(j) In an attempt to obtain confidential advance telephone directory supplements, defendant formulated plan on how to photograph supplements then have them returned so they would not be missed; he then paid a large sum to have the supplements delivered to him. Convicted of attempted receiving stolen property.[95]

(k) Defendant grabbed taxi driver by the neck stating, "Give me your money." Convicted of attempted robbery.[96]

(l) Officer heard pounding on the wall of a store. He saw two men run away when he checked out the noise. When apprehended, plaster from the wall was found in cuff of one suspect. They were convicted of attempted burglary.[97]

(m) A person can be a principal in an attempt. Defendant acted as a lookout for a friend who attempted to commit a burglary. Defendant was convicted as a principal in the crime of attempted burglary.[98]

(n) Defendant rented an office above a bank. He brought in tools and started drilling a hole in the floor. Convicted of attempted burglary.[99]

(o) Defendant pulled trigger on gun aimed at victim. Convicted of Assault With Intent to Commit Murder[100]

(p) Defendant pointed a gun at a clerk without saying anything. Convicted of attempted robbery.[101]

(q) Defendant was placing time bomb under wife's bedroom when arrested. Convicted of attempted murder.[102]

(r) Defendant cut screen on a window. Convicted of attempted burglary.[103]

(s) Defendant cut lock with a bolt cutter. Convicted of attempted burglary.[104]

(t) Defendant, an operator of a furnace repair company, falsely told a housewife that her furnace was in bad shape and dangerous. He then agreed upon a price for a new furnace. Three days later, his workmen (agents) came to the house and began dismantling the old furnace. This was an overt act that made the defendant guilty of attempted grand theft.[105]

(B) Beyond Mere Preparation.

This is the "fly in the ointment." How far beyond mere preparation does an act have to go to qualify as an attempt? Even California case law seems to contradict itself in this matter. Some cases state that the act "must reach far enough towards accomplishment of the desired result to amount to commencement of consummation."[106] Others state that the overt act need not be the ultimate step, but may be the first or a subsequent step toward the commission of the crime.[107] By sheer number of cases, the last approach is the one recommended.

Examples of Preparation

Examples of preparation could be the drawing up of plans of the building to be burglarized, buying a gun to be used in a holdup, borrowing a car to carry away the loot from a burglary, buying adhesive tape to be used in a kidnapping, siphoning gasoline from a car to be used in an arson. None of these acts have really gone beyond mere preparation. How far away from mere preparation the important act must be in order to have an attempt Justice Holmes felt should depend upon the type of crime. He felt that in a serious crime such as murder, the act should be closer to the preparation simply because the perpetrator should be arrested before he committed the act. In the case of a minor crime such as petty theft, he felt that the act could be right next to the commission of the crime itself because if the crime was actually committed, the harm would not be that great.

When considering how far the act should be beyond mere preparation, it should be remembered that the purpose of laws on criminal attempts is to prevent crimes from being committed, not to see how far things can go before they are stopped.

In using the stricter concept of attempts, the required act is so close to the final crime that once the act occurs, the chain of causation if it were a train, would be moving down a clear track toward its destination, the completed crime. If something does not interfere to "derail" it, it will reach its destination in the form of the completed crime.

(C) Towards the Commission of a Crime Legally Capable of Completion

A crime can only be committed under certain conditions. There is a rule in law that the crime attempted must be legally capable of being completed. We have already learned that, in order to obtain a conviction, we must be able to prove all the elements of the corpus delicti. There is also a rule of law that if a crime cannot legally be completed, no charge of attempting to commit it can be made. If one element of the crime is missing or cannot be proved, there can be no attempt. This is called "Inability in Law to commit a crime."

Inability in Law to Commit a Crime

The law is clear that if the crime attempted cannot, by law, be committed, there is no attempt. For example, the elements of incest (285 PC) are:

(1) An act of
  (a) Marriage or
  (b) Sexual intercourse
(2) With another person who is related within the degrees of consanguinity (not cousins).

Civil Code 59 States that the law covers parents and children, ancestors and descendants of every degree, and between brothers and sisters of the half as well as the whole blood, and between uncles and nieces or aunts and nephews.

Situation:

Arvin Ardvark comes into the police station to report what he feels is a shocking situation. He states that he was on his roof installing a new TV antenna. While there, he was able to see through the bedroom window of his next-door neighbor, Larry Letcher. Both Larry and his daughter Lucie were drinking wine and giggling. Then Arvin saw Larry undress his daughter, and get on the bed with her. They were kissing and fondling each other. Just as Larry was about to make sexual penetration of his daughter he happened to look out the window and observe Arvin watching him. He quickly jumped off the bed and ran out of the room.

Mr. Ardvark is referred to a detective in the Sex Detail. Upon further questioning, Mr. Ardvark states that Lucie Letcher is a first-year college student and is eighteen years old. The detective goes to the Letcher residence and finds Lucie home alone. She is still slightly intoxicated. She is notified of her constitutional rights, and agrees to talk to the detective. She admits that her father tried to have sexual intercourse with her, but tells the detective it is "none of his damn business." The detective leaves the residence and goes to the District Attorney to obtain a criminal complaint for attempted incest. The Deputy DA who handles sex offenses tells the detective that before he will issue a criminal complaint, he wants a copy of the daughter's birth certificate. From school records the detective learns her date of birth and the name of the hospital. He then goes to the County Recorder's Office and learns that Lucie was adopted. He takes the certificate to the Deputy DA.

Question: Will the DA issue a complaint for attempted incest? Why or why not?

(D) When There Is Specific Intent

In order to have an attempt the act must involve specific intent. It must be a specific intent to commit a particular crime.[108] Since negligence is conduct performed without criminal intent, negligence cannot be substituted for the specific intent necessary for a criminal attempt. General intent will not apply to attempts. The specific intent required for an attempt applies to a particular type of crime rather than an individual victim. Transferred intent does not apply to crimes involving specific intent. Exceptions would be crimes of attempt because the specific intent is toward a type of crime. If a person attempts to murder someone, but shoots at another by mistake and misses him, he can be charged with attempted murder even though the person at whom he shot was not the person he originally attempted to shoot.

The intent to commit a crime without some overt act cannot be classed as an attempt. If there is intent and the person does something that would normally result in a crime, he is guilty of an attempt even if, unknown to him, some facts exist that would make the crime impossible to complete.[109] If the person believes he can accomplish the crime he intends to commit, his inability to commit it does not remove his liability for an attempt.[110] (Exceptions would be crimes incapable in law of being committed, or crimes classed as assault.) The intent required in the crime of attempt can be inferred from circumstantial evidence.[111] This inference is a question of fact for a jury to decide.[112]

(1) Examples of Where the Lack or Presence of Specific Intent Results in No Violation
(a) Specific Intent Is Wrongly Inferred

Harry Hardhat gets mad at Flossie Furd for telling his wife about one of his affairs. He loses his temper when he sees her walking home through the park after work, hits her and knocks her down. She calls the police and tells them she is sure Harry knocked her down with the intent to rape her; the only reason he stopped and ran off was because she screamed. Remember, an attempt requires specific intent, not just general intent. Will Harry be charged with "Assault With Intent to Commit Rape?" It appears, from the available evidence, that there is nothing to show that Harry had specific intent to commit the crime of which he is accused.

(b) There Was Specific Intent, But That Intended Was Not a Crime.

Sometimes there is a fact that is unknown to the person attempting the crime that would make the act not criminal.

Example: Freddie Flake is a sneak thief. He will steal anything that is not tied down. As he walks down the street, he notices a crowd in front of the library. He believes it is one of the annual sales of old books held by the library. Because there is such a large crowd, Freddie is sure he can sneak off with some books. He slips into the crowd and reaches for two books to hide under his coat. Just then he sees a police officer looking at him. He lets go of the books and runs off. Because the crowd is so thick, Freddie does not see the sign stating that the books are damaged and any person can have two of them free. In his mind, however, he had the intent to steal, and he committed an overt act toward what he thought would be theft.

Example: Darrel Doper arranges to buy narcotics from an undercover narcotics officer. When the undercover officer shows up for the buy, he takes Darrel's money and gives him a bag of talcum powder instead of heroin. This amounts to an attempt because the crime could have been committed if the undercover officer had not substituted talcum powder for the heroin.

Example: Larry Lump is mad at Fred Frisbie. He gets a gun and goes looking for Fred. When he finds him, he takes out the gun, aims it and pulls the trigger. Unknown to Larry, the ammunition is so old that it cannot fire. Larry is guilty of Attempted Murder. In this case the crime could have been committed were it not for chance. In these two examples, human intervention and chance prevented the act from being completed. This intervention or interruption, as opposed to the inability in law in the first example, makes the act an attempt.

Example: Ferdinand Frump, who is not a doctor, attempts an abortion on Ronella Rump. Ronella is doing undercover work for the police and is not pregnant. Ferdinand is guilty of the attempt even though she is not pregnant.[113]

(E) Due to Some Interruption or Intervention, the Crime is not Completed

If a crime is completed, there is no attempt; the attempt merges with the completed crime. An exception is, if the attempt is a statutory offense such as "assault," and is successful, the defendant can be charged with both "assault" (240 PC) and "battery" (242 PC). These are separate and distinct offenses in the Penal Code, each with its own section number. From a practical standpoint, a person is seldom charged with both assault and battery because the judge knows that a charge of battery presupposes an attempt, or the crime of "assault." In general attempts, however, the attempt does merge with the completed crime, and the offense charged is only the completed crime.

Interruption or intervention can take many forms. Common examples are:

(1) **Human Intervention:** The perpetrator is discovered and arrested just as he cut the lock with a pair of bolt cutters.

(2) **An Act of God:** Lightning, rain, flood, snow, storm, electrical blackouts are examples of "Acts of God" that can prevent a crime from being committed.

Examples: Rain washes out a bridge on the way to a building a burglar intends to break into and he has to turn around. Lightning causes a failure in electrical power; either the lights go out so the perpetrator cannot see what he is doing, or, in the case of a safe burglar who plans to drill a safe, the drill will not operate.

(3) **Mechanical Failure:** A gun won't fire because of a faulty mechanism. The car to be used in a crime won't start. The bomb timing mechanism doesn't work properly and the bomb does not explode.

(4) **Chance, Accident or Fate:** The perpetrator gave the victim a glass of milk containing poison. The victim drank only a small portion of it and became sick. It is attempted murder. The perpetrator gave the victim a glass of orange juice containing poison. The victim accidentally knocked it over and as a result did not drink it. It is still attempted murder.

(5) **Human Error:** A person placed a bomb under the wrong car. It is attempted murder. A person who, with intent to kill, mixed the wrong chemicals for a poison drink is guilty of attempted murder. A person who intended to rob a liquor store ran out of gas as he approached it and abandoned the attempt because he needed the car to escape in. The abandonment was not a true voluntary abandonment; he had committed acts beyond mere preparation, and was therefore guilty of attempted robbery.

(F) A Method is Involved That Appears Reasonably Capable of Completing the Crime

This element applies only when the attempt is also an assault. It is important to consider whether the attempt is absolutely impossible to complete, or whether the completion is based on chance alone. In the prior example of the gun with the faulty ammunition, it was by chance that the ammunition did not fire. The example of the gun without ammunition illustrates the situation where it is absolutely impossible for the crime to be completed. Another example of chance would be in a case of attempted murder. In this case, Arvin Ardvark intends to kill Clyde Crashcup. At night he goes to Clyde's bedroom window, which is open. He points a shotgun towards the bed and fires. Unknown to Arvin, Clyde was sleeping in another room on this night. Arvin is guilty of attempted murder because the fact that Clyde was not in the bed where he normally sleeps was a chance happening. It was not an absolute impossibility. Attempted murder is a type of assault when a gun is used, and therefore it must be a type of assault that is capable of completion.

The determination of whether or not the accused had the ability to commit the crime is the actual ability and not what the perpetrator thought. Or for that matter what the victim thought.[114]

8.3:5 Abandonment of the Attempt

The abandonment of an attempt to commit a crime is a defense. However, the abandonment of the attempt must occur before the overt act is completed.[115] If the abandonment is motivated by the sudden appearance of police, it is not free and voluntary and constitutes a criminal attempt.[116]

Relationship Between Solicitation, Conspiracy and Attempts			
Condition	**Solicitation**	**Conspiracy**	**Attempts**
INTENT	Specific Intent.	Specific Intent.	Specific Intent.
ACT	Verbal (or written) act.	Verbal act (some states also require an overt act).	Overt act toward completion of the crime.
PREPARATION	None needed.	Just mere agreement. The Federal government and California require a preparatory act.	Act must be beyond mere preparation. Must be legally capable of completion.
MERGING	Does not merge with crime.	Does not merge with crime.	Merges with crime if completed.
DANGER OF COMPLETION	Least danger of completion. Solicitor afraid to commit crime and solicitee might refuse.	Greater chance of completion because more than one person is involved.	A still greater chance of completion because it has progressed so far toward crime.
OBJECTIVE	Crime need not be capable of actually being completed. Solicitor must believe it capable of completion. It must be a statutory crime.	Act need not be a crime, but some act that is harmful to others. It can be a lawful act by unlawful means.	Act normally capable of completion. Varies in different states. Must be a crime.
RESPONSIBILITY	Responsible for natural and probable consequences of the act.	Responsible for all acts committed toward the common objective.	Responsible only for own acts or those of co-principal.
NUMBER OF PERSONS	At least one. Person solicited need not receive solicitation.	Two or more. No limit.	One or more persons.
ELEMENTS	(1)Soliciting of another (2)To commit a crime (3)With the intent that it be committed.	(1)An agreement toward a common objective (2)By two or more persons (3)With specific intent to: (a)Do an unlawful purpose, or (b)Do a lawful purpose by unlawful means *Special element in some jurisdictions* (4)When there is an overt act beyond mere agreement.	(1)An overt act (2)Beyond mere preparation (3)With specific intent (4)To commit a crime legally capable of commission. (5)The crime is prevented by some type of intervention. (6)When method appears reasonably capable of completion
APPLIES TO WHAT TYPE OF CRIME	Applies only to statutory offenses in California. E.g., 653f, 647(a) & (b), PC and 7210 7210.5 B & P	Applies to any crime and even civil wrongs.	Applies only to Mala In Se crimes.

REFERENCES FOR CHAPTER VIII

(1)   Rex v. Johnson 89 Engl Rep 753
(2)   Rex v Vaughan 98 Engl Rep 308
(3)   Rex v. Higgins 102 Engl Rep 269
(4)   People v. Shapiro 17 C.A. 2d 468
      (62 P 2d 436)
(5)   People v. Burt 45 C 2d 311 (288 P 2d 503)
(6)   People v. Burt Ibid.
(7)   People v. Baskins 72 C.A. 2d 728
      (165 P 2d 510)
(8)   People v. Haley 102 C.A. 2d 159
      (227 P 2d 48)
(9)   Turner v. LaVelle 251 F Supp 443
(10) People v. Werner 29 C.A. 2d 126
      (84 P 2d 168)
(11) Benson v. Superior Ct. 57 C 2d 240
      (18 Cal Rptr 516)
(12) Kelly v. U. S. 194 F 2d 150
(13) People v. Rissman 154 C.A. 2d 265
      (316 P 2d 60)
(14) Stephen, Sir James F., A History of The
      Criminal Law of England, Vol. II, Mac-
      millan and Co., London, 1883, p. 229
(15) Stephen, Sir James F., A Digest of the
      Criminal Law, F. H. Thomas and Co., St.
      Louis, 1878, p. 33.
(16) People v. Woodard 145 C.A. 2d 529
      (302 P 2d 834)
(17) People v. Kitchens 164 C.A. 2d 529
      (331 P 2d 127)
(18) People v. Anderson 90 C.A. 2d 326
      (202 P 2d 1044)
(19) Marino v. U. S. 91 F 2d 691
(20) People v. Cornell 188 C.A. 2d 668
      (10 Cal Rptr 717)
(21) People v. Brown 259 C.A. 2d 663
      (66 Cal Rptr 623)
(22) People v. Malotte 46 C. 2d 59
      (292 P 2d 517)
(23) People v. Aday 226 C.A. 2d 520
      (38 Cal Rptr 199)
(24) U. S. v. Dege 364 U. S. 51,
(25) People v. Pierce 61 C 2d 879
      (40 Cal Rptr 395)
      People v. Lockett 25 C.A. 3d 433
      (102 Cal Rptr 41)
(26) Sherman v. State 113 Neb 173
(27) People v. Gilbert 26 C.Ai 2d 1 (78 P 2d 770)
(28) People v. Calhoun 50 C 2d 137
      (323 P 2d 427)
(29) People v. Olf 195 C.A. 2d 97
      (15 Cal Rptr 390)

(30) People v. Bernhardt 222 C.A. 2d 567
      (35 Cal Rptr 401)
(31) People v. Aday 226 C.A. 2d 520
      (38 Cal Rptr 199)
(32) People v. Horn 12 C 3d 290
      (115 Cal Rptr 516)
(33) People v. Smith 63 C 2d 779
      (48 Cal Rptr 382)
(34) People v. Aubrey 253 C.A. 2d 912
      (61 Cal Rptr 772)
(35) Jones' Case 4B & Ad 345
(36) U. S. v. Cassidy 67 F 698 (1895)
(37) People v. Moran 166 C.A. 2d 410
      (333 P 2d 243)
(38) Doble v. Superior Ct. 197 C 556 (241 P 852)
(39) People v. Malotte 46 C 2d 59 (292 P 2d 517)
(40) People v. Burt 45 C 2d 311 (288 P 2d 503)
(41) Rex v. Armstrong 86 Engl Rep 196
(42) Com v. Spink 137 Pa 255
(43) State v. McFeely 25 N. J. Msc 303
      (52 A 2d 823)
(44) People v. Ragone 84 C.A. 2d 476
      (191 P 2d 126)
(45) People v George 257 C.A. 2d 805
      (65 Cal Rptr 368)
(46) People v. Aday 226 C.A. 2d 520
      (38 Cal Rptr 199)
      People v. Buffum 40 C 2d 709
      (256 P 2d 934)
(47) People v. Corica 55 C.A. 2d 130
      (130 P 2d 164)
(48) Hyde v. U. S. 218 U. S. 681
(49) Krulewitch v. U. S. 336 U. S. 440
(50) Harrison v. U. S. 7 F 2d 259
(51) Marino v. U. S. 91 F 2d 691
(52) Pinkerton v. U. S. 328 U. S. 640
(53) People v. Cook 10 C.A. 2d 54 (51 P 2d 169)
      Vannata v. U. S. 289 F 424
(54) Williams v. U. S. 295 F 302
(55) People v. Lawrence 143 C 148 (76 P 893)
(56) People v. McMannis 122 C.A. 2d 891
      (266 P 2d 134)
(57) People v. Jones 25 C.A. 2d 517
      (77 P 2d 897)
(58) People v. Feddman 171 C.A. 2d 15
      (339 P 2d 888)
(59) People v. Harris 272 C.A. 2d 506
      (77 Cal Rptr 406)
(60) People v. Snyder 50 C 2d 190 (324 P 2d 1)
(61) People v. Crosby 58 C 2d 713
      (25 Cal Rptr 847)

(62) State v. Allen 47 Com 121

(63) Orear v. U. S. 261 F 257 (5th Cir)

(64) U. S. v. Britton 108 U. S. 199 (1883)

(65) Hyde v. U. S. 218 U. S. 681

(66) People v. Catzman 258 Cal App 2d 777
(66 Cal Rptr 319)

(67) People v. Matthew 194 C 273 (226 P 424)

(68) People v. Rodley 131 C 240 (63 P 351)

(69) People v. Arnold 199 C 471 (250 P 168)

(70) People v. King 30 C.A. 2d 185
(85 P 2d 928)

(71) People v. Snyder 50 C2d 190 (324 P 2d 1)

(72) People v. Koch 4 C.A. 3d 270
(84 Cal Rptr 629)

(73) People v. Cattin 169 C.A. 2d 247
(337 P 2d 113)

(74) People v. Amaya 134 C 531 (66 P 794)

(75) People v. Tinnin 136 C.A. 301 (28 P 2d 951)

(76) People v. Lewis 222 C.A. 2d 136
(35 Cal Rptr 1)

(77) People v. Wagner 133 C.A. 775
(24 P 2d 927)

(78) People v. Kauffman 152 C 334

(79) People v. Suter 43 C.A. 2d 444 (111 P 2d 23)

(80) Sayre, "CriminalAttempts," Harvard Law
Review, 41 Harv L Rev 821 V929

(81) Stephen, Sir James F., A History of the
Criminal Law of England Vol II, McMillan and Co., London 1883, p. 223. '

(82) People v. Camodoca 52 C 2d 142
(388 P 2d 903)

(83) People v. Adami 36 C.A. 3d 452
(111 Cal Rptr 544)

(84) People v. Parrish 87 C.A. 2d 853
(197 P 2d 804)

(85) People v. Robinson 180 C.A. 2d 745
(4 Cal Rptr 679)

(86) People v. Parrish 87 C.A. 2d 853
(197 P 2d 804)

(87) People v. Benenato 77 C.A. 2d 350
(175 P 2d 296)

(88) People v. Wallace 78 C.A. 2d 726
(178 P 2d 771)

(89) People v. Davis 24 C.A. 2d 408 (75 P 2d 80)

(90) People v. Lyles 156 C.A. 2d 482
(319 P 2d 745)

(91) People v. Wilson 25 C.A. 2d 332
(77 P 2d 238)

(92) People v. Martone 38 C.A. 2d 392
(101 P 2d 537)

(93) People v. Franquelin 109 C.A. 2d 777
(241 P 2d 651)

(94) People v. Martell 197 C.A. 2d 195
(16 Cal Rptr 918)

(95) People v. Parker 217 C.A. 2d 422
(31 Cal Rptr 716)

(96) People v. Logan 257 C.A. 2 267
(64 Cal Rptr 667)

(97) People v. Burton 184 C.A. 2d 299
(8 Cal Rptr 153)

(98) People v. Hall 272 C.A. 2d 287
(272 C.A. 2d 278)

(99) People V. Staples 6 C.A. 3d 61

(100) People v. Meriweather 263 C.A. 2d 559
(69 Cal Rptr)

(101) People v. Guilbert 214 C.A. 2d 566
(29 Cal Rptr 640)

(102) People v. Lanzit 70 C.A. 498 (233 P. 816)

(103) People v. Cagle 141 C.A. 2d 612
(297 P 2d 44)

(104) People v. Calker 31 Cal 2d 290
(188 P 2d 12)

(105) People v. Keefer 35 C.A. 3d 156
(110 Cal Rptr 597)

(106) People v. Lyles 156 C.A. 2d 482
(319 P 2d 745)

(107) People v. Seach 215 C.A. 2d 779
(30 Cal Rptr 499) (1963)

(108) People v. Flemming 94 C 308 (29 P 647)

(109) People v. Siu 126 C.A. 2d 41
(271 P 2d 575)

(110) People v. Fratianno 132 C.A. 2d 610
(282 P 2d 1002)

(111) People v. Logan 257 C.A. 2d 267
(64 Cal Rptr 667)

(112) People v. Davis 24 C.A. 2d 408
(75 P 2d 80)

(113) People v. Cummings 141 C.A. 2d 193
(296 P 2d 610)

(114) People v. Mosqueda 5 C.A. 3d 540
(85 Cal Rptr 346)

(115) People v. Von Hecht 133 C.A. 2d 25
(283 P 2d 746)

(116) People v. Walker 33 C 2d 250 (201 P 2d 6)

STUDY QUESTIONS

CHAPTER VIII

(1)   The word "inchoate" means _____.

(2)   The "Model Penal Code" was developed by the:

      (A) ____American Bar Association.   (B) ____Lawyer's Guild.
      (C) ____American Law Institute.   (D) ____District Attorney's Association.

(3)   The purpose of laws on inchoate offenses is to:

      (A) ____make criminal prosecution easier.   (B) ____give longer prison terms.
      (C) ____prevent crimes from being committed.   (D) ____allow for probation.

(4)   California has no general solicitation law.   T or F

(5)   In California, solicitation must be proved by the testimony of _____ witness(es) or of _____ witness(es) and corroboration.

(6)   Solicitation can be accomplished by means other than verbal. Another way would be

      _____.

(7)   A solicitation is not criminal until the crime solicited has been completed.   T or F

(8)   A solicitation does not become illegal until some overt act has been completed.   T or F

(9)   If a person who has been solicited refuses to go along with the solicitation, there is no crime violated.   T or F

(10)   The purpose of the intent element in solicitation is to offer _____ Amendment protection.

(11)   In California, the intent in solicitation is a specific intent.   T or F

(12)   Solicitation has the least chance of completion of any inchoate offense.   T or F

(13)   The crime of soliciting does not merge with the completed crime.   T or F

(14)   If a person solicits a crime and the crime is committed, that person is guilty of soliciting and he is also guilty as a(an) _____ to the crime.

(15)   The Federal Criminal Code suggests that a fourth element be added to solicitation. It would require an _____ act toward the objective of the solicitation.

(16)   Millie Mashpott sends a letter to Mortimer Mugilicuty asking him to burn down her insured cabin. Mortimer never receives the letter. There is no crime of soliciting.   T or F

(17)   Conspiracy requires the agreement of _____ or more persons.

(18)   In California all conspiracies are punishable as _____.

(19)   To be conspiracy, the agreement must be a verbal, formal agreement.   T or F

(20)   The key to the agreement for conspiracy is that it is toward:

      (A) ____illegal goals.
      (B) ____a common purpose or understanding.
      (C) ____goals that are possible of completion.
      (D) ____the objective of the leader of the conspiracy.

(21)   In order to be a conspiracy, all conspirators must know each other.   T or F

(22) Before 1964 a certain classification of two people could not be guilty of conspiracy. That classification was _____.

(23) Under no circumstances can one person be tried for conspiracy.   T or F

(24) There is no limit to the number of persons who can be involved in a conspiracy.   T or F

(25) Conspiracy is a specific intent crime.   T or F

(26) In conspiracy, the element of intent is really _____ intents.

(27) Specific intent is only required in conspiracy when the crime conspired is a specific intent crime.   T or F

(28) The specific intent in conspiracy is the intent to commit the crime originally intended and not the crime that actually results.   T or F

(29) Intoxication can affect the specific intent in conspiracy.   T or F

(30) Conspiracy can involve a lawful act by unlawful means.   T or F

(31) Both unions and management have been guilty of conspiracy in dealing with strikes.   T or F

(32) The acts needed for a conspiracy are limited only to those acts committed within this state. T or F

(33) Price fixing is an example of an act that can be a conspiracy.   T or F

(34) Violations of "Anti-Trust" laws can amount to a conspiracy.   T or F

(35) In California, conspiracy requires an overt act beyond the agreement.   T or F

(36) Overt acts in conspiracy must be criminal in nature.   T or F

(37) Only one member of a conspiracy is needed to commit the act that is necessary for a conspiracy to begin.   T or F

(38) If an overt act in a conspiracy is committed by an innocent agent, such as a postman, the conspiracy is not in effect.   T or F

(39) In 1925, the Supreme Court sent a warning to Judges and District Attorneys, warning them about making felonies out of misdemeanors in conspiracy complaints.   T or F

(40) There is a fear of many persons that without a required overt act, conspiracy laws could infringe upon the _____ Amendment.

(41) Conspiracy is prosecuted more on the local level than it is on the federal level.   T or F

(42) The federal government has many special statutory conspiracy laws. this is an obligation founded on the Constitution's:

  (A) ____ "General Welfare Of The Public" clause.   (B) ____ "Public Safety" clause.
  (C) ____ First Amendment.   (D) ____ Tenth Amendment.

(43) The law on conspiracy has many similarities with the civil law on partnerships.   T or F

(44) A conspiracy does not merge with the completed crime.   T or F

(45) A conspiracy to commit murder can only be murder in the first degree.   T or F

(46) A conspiracy can be proved by circumstantial evidence.   T or F

(47) The scope of a conspiracy to commit kidnapping ends when the victim is kidnapped.   T or F

(48) The difficulty in the law on attempts is in knowing just at what point the attempt starts.   T or F

(49) Generally speaking, an attempt merges with the completed crime.   T or F

(50) The law on attempts applies only to:

    (A) ____Mala In Se crimes.   (B) ____crimes against the person.
    (C) ____crimes against property.   (D) ____Mala Prohibita crimes.

(51) An "attempt" is a specific intent crime.   T or F

(52) Which of the following terms applies to attempts?

    (A) ____last proximate act.   (B) ____degree of return.
    (C) ____irreversible act.   (D) ____the "set mould."

(53) In order for a person to be guilty of attempted fraud, the victim must have believed the suspect's story.   T or F

(54) Chief Justice Holmes felt that the point at which an act amounted to an attempted crime should depend upon the seriousness of the crime.   T or F

(55) The term "perpetrator" means:

    (A) ____the person reporting the crime.   (B) ____the victim.
    (C) ____the person committing the crime.   (D) ____none of these.

(56) Larry Letcher tries to have sexual intercourse with his adopted daughter, but is interrupted when his wife comes into the bedroom. Larry is guilty of attempted incest.   T or F

(57) Criminal attempts involve specific intent.   T or F

(58) An attempt to commit a crime can involve negligence.   T or F

(59) Transferred intent can apply to crimes of attempt.   T or F

(60) Fred Frisbee tries to shoot Lester Lump, but the gun does not fire due to mechanical failure. This is therefore not a case of attempted murder.   T or F

(61) A person charged with both the attempt and the completed offense can be convicted if they are separate sections listed in the penal code.   T or F

(62) A burglar prepares to drill a safe. Just as he is about to use the drill, a storm causes the electricity to go off. This intervention is called:

    (A) ____chance.   (B) ____mechanical failure.
    (C) ____an act of God.   (D) ____fate.

(63) A person cannot be guilty of attempting to commit an attempt.   T or F

(64) There can be no attempt to commit perjury.   T or F

(65) The abandonment of an attempt to commit a crime is a defense.   T or F

CHAPTER IX

DEFENSES AGAINST CRIMINAL PROSECUTION

9.0   INTRODUCTION

9.1   COMMON LAW DEFENSES

9.2   CALIFORNIA DEFENSES LISTED UNDER SECTION 26 OF THE PENAL CODE

9.3   DEFENSES INVOLVING MENTAL IMPAIRMENT OR DIMINISHED CAPACITY

9.4   DEFENSES BASED ON CONSTITUTIONAL PROTECTION, STATUTORY, OR LEGAL PROVISIONS

9.5   DEFENSES BASED ON LACK OF INTENT OR CRIMINAL NEGLIGENCE

9.6   OTHER DEFENSES

9.7   ILLEGAL OR UNTENABLE DEFENSES

9.0:0　INTRODUCTION

Since the most common defense is based on lack of intent, the establishment of a system of legal defenses came late in the history of law. It is generally accepted that the doctrine of defenses to criminal liability based on "*Mens Rea*" or criminal intent was not fully accepted by legal writers and Jurists until around the Ninth century. Christian theologians such as St. Augustine (Fifth century) and St. Thomas Aquinas (Thirteenth century) developed doctrines based on free will and the need to consider why an act was committed in order to assess responsibility.

Throughout the history of England, there was a slow development of rights for the common people. These became the basis for legal defenses. Many of these rights were later written into the U.S. Constitution and the Amendments in the form of legal protections, and therefore legal defenses. State Codes further added to the list of legal defenses. These were based both on intent and the need for civil protection.

There are many situations in California criminal law where persons who commit crimes avoid criminal liability for their actions. It is important that police officers investigating a crime be alert to the possible defenses for that particular crime. Not only will it save much embarrassment in court, but it will better serve the interests of justice.

It is a police officer's job to gather evidence to help prove a legal defense as well as to gather evidence for the prosecution. Persons having a legal defense should not have to suffer the burden of a criminal trial. The District Attorney is very alert to the possibility of legal excuses for criminal acts, and will wish to avoid the waste of time and expense of going to court if the suspect does in fact have a legal defense. The problem is that District Attorneys do not investigate crimes. They do not gather the facts or talk to the witnesses. They usually have just the officer's report to use in making a decision on whether to prosecute.

Police officers who know the various legal defenses for criminal actions can do a better job of investigation and report writing. They can also be of great assistance to the District Attorney's office.

9.1:0　COMMON LAW DEFENSES

By the Eighteenth century, English common law had become well codified. Sections twenty-five through thirty-four of their criminal law covered the basic defenses. These later became the basic defenses for American law. The English common law defenses are as follows:

Defenses to Crimes Under English Common Law

Article 25—Children under 7
(This rule was absolute)

Article 26—Children between 7 & 14
(In absence of proof that they knew the wrongfulness of their acts)

Article 27—Insanity
(Also included birth defects and idiocy)

Article 28
Every person is assumed to be sane and responsible for his acts

Article 29—Voluntary Intoxication
(Only when it affects specific intent)

Article 30—Married Women
(For crimes of theft and receiving stolen property, but only when in the presence of their husbands)

Article 31—Compulsion
(Being forced by threat of immediate and instant death)

Article 32—Necessity
(Where the potential harm outweighs the crime)

Article 33—Ignorance of the Law
(Only in very rare cases & only Mala Prohibita offenses)

Article 34—Ignorance of Fact
(Acting under good faith based on a belief which if true, would not make the act criminal)

Peculiarities in Common Law

In early English common law, persons who could read and write were able to claim "Benefit of Clergy" and be tried by an ecclesiastic court, which was much more lenient than the criminal courts. The word "clergy" means to be able to read and write, which a clergyman had to do in order to read the Bible. It was a legal "loophole" that was used to compensate for the severity of the criminal courts.

...BLIMEY, ME LORD! YAS REALLY PUT A SCARE IN TA ME BLOODY HEAD FER A MINUTE. WHEN YAS SAID "BENEFIT O' CLERGY," I THOUGHT YA WAS GONNA MAKE ME GET MARRIED!

9.2:0 CALIFORNIA DEFENSES LISTED UNDER SECTION 26 OF THE PENAL CODE

In 1872 when the California Penal Code was first written, it borrowed from and modified the English defenses to a crime. The defenses were listed in Section 26:

Section 26 PC

(Persons capable of committing crimes.)

All persons are capable of committing crimes except those belonging to the following classes:

(1) Children under the age of fourteen, in the absence of clear proof that at the time of committing the act charged against them, they knew its wrongfulness.

(2) Idiots.

(3) Persons who committed the act or made the omission charged in ignorance or mistake of fact, which disproves any criminal intent.

(4) Persons who committed the act charged without being conscious thereof.

(5) Persons who committed the act or made the omission charged through misfortune or by accident, when it appears that there was no evil design, intention, or culpable negligence.

(6) Persons who committed the act or made the omission charged under threat or menace sufficient to show that they had reasonable cause to and did believe their lives would be endangered if they refused. (Except capital crimes.)

These topics will be further discussed later in the chapter.

9.3:0 DEFENSES INVOLVING MENTAL IMPAIRMENT OR DIMINISHED CAPACITY

The title, which is self-explanatory, covers offenses committed by infants, idiots, mentally ill persons, persons unconscious of the act, and those who commit a crime while in a state of involuntary intoxication.

9.3:1 Infancy

It has long been recognized that children, because of their immaturity, are not as responsible as adults. The early Babylonians had special courts and judges for juveniles. The Romans also allowed ignorance of the law as an excuse for children. They felt that they are often ignorant of what the law requires, and what the probable outcome of their acts might be.

Our own Anglo-American legal history shows that we were slow to recognize infancy as a state that precludes full criminal responsibility. We also failed to recognize that the law should proceed in a different manner. Although we accepted the common law rules on infancy, it was not until 1899 that the State of Illinois enacted the first Juvenile Act in which a new and enlightened approach was used in dealing with juvenile offenders. It established a system of rehabilitation rather than punishment.

Under "Juvenile Control Acts," juveniles were not considered criminals and the court proceedings were not considered criminal courts;[1] juveniles could not be imprisoned with adults.

However, most state laws, including California, allow a juvenile judge to "remand"(send to another court) sixteen- or seventeen-year-old juveniles to an adult court when the juvenile authorities have not been able to handle or control them. This can also work the other way and allow an adult court judge to "remand" nineteen-year-olds to the juvenile court when it is felt that they are too mentally or emotionally immature to be properly handled by the adult court.

Many state codes have laws that recognize the lack of responsibility of young persons. Examples would be limiting the drinking of alcohol to those persons over a certain age (Business and Professions Code), or preventing junk dealers from buying metal and junk from minors.

In 1932, the federal government provided that juveniles accused of federal offenses could be tried in local state juvenile courts where their status as juveniles would be given further consideration.

Under English common law, it was recognized that children are not as mature as adults, and should therefore be excused from certain legal responsibilities. There were two classes of children who could be excused from criminal acts:

(1) **Children under seven.** This rule was absolute. No child under seven could be criminally prosecuted. It was based on the teachings of the Catholic Church that age seven is the "age of reason." It was believed that at age seven, all normal children could tell right from wrong and were therefore responsible for their sinful acts.

(2) Children between the ages of seven and fourteen. This rule applied only in the absence of proof that they knew the wrongfulness of the act.

MY LITTLE CUTHBERT IS ONLY THIRTEEN, YOUR HONOR—WHY DO YOU ASK?

This rule was strictly applied in early English times. If there was any evidence that the child over seven and under fourteen knew that what he did was wrong, he was held responsible. In one early case, an eight-year-old boy was hanged for arson.[2] In another case, a ten-year-old boy killed a girl and hid her body. The hiding of her body was considered evidence that he knew the wrongfulness of the act, and he was held criminally responsible.[3] Even in this country a strict rule was held in early times. In New Jersey, a twelve-year-old boy was hanged for murder.[4]

California

In California, we have eliminated the first part and have simply stated that any person under the age of fourteen is not liable for a crime unless he or she knew the wrongfulness of the act. This is a presumptive law which is refutable. It is a question of fact for the jury to decide.[5] The age of fourteen is also found in other laws. For example, under the old laws on rape, when the suspect was under the age of 14, the state had to prove that he had the ability to make penetration.

Although a child under the age of 14 is presumed to be incapable of committing a crime, an adult who aids and abets or advises that child is Still guilty as a principal.[6]

A four-year-old child has been declared to come under section 1 in regard to knowing that it is unlawful to ride a tricycle on the sidewalk in violation of a city ordinance.[7]

Because the juvenile court heard no expert testimony on the issue, and because the court made no effort to directly question a 9-year-old boy accused of breaking into an automobile to determine whether he had some insight or understanding about the wrongfulness of his conduct, the California Court of Appeals declared that the child was improperly made a ward of the court under section 602 W&I Code.[8]

When age becomes an issue in criminal defense, the physical age of the person, not the mental or moral age, is the legal consideration.[9] However, when a juvenile is being charged with a criminal act under section 602 W&I, the court must consider the child's age, experience and understanding in determining whether that child was mentally capable of committing the conduct described. In a 1970 case, the California Supreme Court declared that a twelve-year-old girl with a social and mental age of seven was protected from the harsh strictures of Welfare and Institutions Code section 602.[10] (This section states that a juvenile who violates a federal, state or local law can be made a ward of the court.)

In order to find a child under the age of fourteen legally responsible for a criminal act, it must be shown that he or she possessed a knowledge of good and evil and had sufficient mental capacity to understand the nature of the act. Requirements are knowledge that the act was forbidden, and that committing it would result in punishment. It must also be shown that the child was conscious at the time he or she was committing the wrongful act.[11]

Section 1111 of the California Penal Code requires that the testimony of an accomplice must be corroborated. When a juvenile commits a criminal offense with another juvenile, neither can be prosecuted in an adult court, so they cannot be classed as accomplices. Because of this, one juvenile may testify against the other, and the testimony can be accepted in court without the corroboration required in section 1111 of the Penal Code.[12]

9.3:2 Idiocy

The technical definition of an idiot from a legal standpoint is a person who is "virtually without mentality."[13] There is also a definition used by psychologists and psychometrists that is based on IQ. An idiot is one with an IQ of from 0 to 25.

Although there was evidence indicating the defendant in a rape case was mentally deficient, it was not so severe that he could not distinguish right from wrong. Threats to the victim and her family along with statements after the arrest showed that he was able to distinguish right from wrong.[14]

Very few idiots are seen in public. Most of them are either hospitalized or institutionalized. It is doubtful that any of them would be capable of committing a crime.

What most people think is an idiot is really an imbecile. Imbeciles have an IQ of between 26 and 50. They are trainable and are responsible for their acts. They are often seen on the street with relatives and are seldom involved in any criminal activity.

Although imbeciles are technically responsible for their acts, the District Attorney would be very reluctant to take them to court. It is difficult to get juries to convict imbeciles. This is because juries feel sorry for them and do not understand that they are trainable and responsible for their acts. These cases are usually settled out of court.

9.3:3   The Insanity Defense In California

Since its early history, California has allowed the defense of insanity. The rule used to determine whether a person was insane was the M'Naghten Rule.[15] In 1967, the California Supreme Court stated that only the state legislature could change this rule. (People v. Nicolaus).[16] However, in the case of People v. Drew (22 Cal 3d 333), the California Supreme Court, under Chief Justice Rose Bird, decided on its own to replace the M'Naghten Rule with the Substantial Capacity Test (constitutionally, enacting law is the job of the Legislature.) The California legislature, upset at having its authority usurped in this matter, took corrective action in 1983 by placing great limitations on the use of insanity as a defense. The following Penal Code sections reflect the changes:

26 PC—Persons Capable of Committing Crimes

The section on insanity as a defense has been completely removed.

21 PC—Diminished Capacity
(the inability to control one's conduct)

Criminal intent is now shown by the circumstances connected with the offense. Evidence that the accused lacked the capacity or ability to control his conduct for any reason shall not be admissible as to the issue of whether the accused actually had any mental state with respect to the commission of any crime (also 21b PC)

25a PC—Diminished Capacity in Criminal or Juvenile Actions

The defense of "Diminished Capacity" has been abolished in any criminal or juvenile action. This includes any evidence of a person's training, mental illness, disease or defect, to negate the ability to form a responsible mental state.

25b PC—Evidence of Diminished Capacity

Evidence of diminished capacity or a mental disorder may be considered by the court only at the time of sentencing or other disposition or commitment.

25c PC—"Not Guilty by Reason of Insanity"

A plea of "not guilty by reason of insanity" shall be accepted only when the defense can prove, by a Preponderance of Evidence, that he or she was incapable of knowing or understanding the nature and quality of the act, and was unable to distinguish right from wrong at the time the act was committed. (This is basically the M'Naghten Rule)

28a PC—Evidence of Mental Disease

Evidence of mental disease, defect or disorder shall not be admitted to show lack of ability to form any mental state. This evidence is admissible solely on the issue of whether or not the accused actually formed a required mental state, when a specific intent crime is charged, and only to show

    (1) Specific Intent,
    (2) Premeditation,
    (3) Deliberation, or
    (4) Malice Aforethought.

As a matter of public policy, there shall be no defense of Diminished Capacity, Diminished Responsibility, or Irresistible Impulse.

The above does not apply to insanity hearings listed in 1026 PC, 1027 PC and 1429.5 PC.

1026 PC:

Defendants are presumed sane and responsible for their acts. If they enter pleas beside insanity, they are tried as if they are sane. If found guilty, the court then determines insanity. (Felonies only)

1027 PC:

When a defendant pleads "not guilty by reason of insanity," the court may select two or three psychiatrists or psychologists to examine the defendant. They cannot make a judgment as to the sanity of the defendant at the time of the crime. They can give a psychological history and opinions of the defendant's present mental state. They can take the stand as expert witnesses and be subject to direct and cross examination.

1429.5 PC

The same as 1026 but for misdemeanors.

The M'Naghten Rule

This test for insanity was developed in 1843 as a result of the murder of Sir Robert Peel's male secretary by Daniel M'Naghten. The ruling is as follows: "he was laboring under such defect of reason, from disease of mind, as to not know the nature and quality of his act, or, if he did know, that he did not know that he was doing what was wrong."

Important terms in this rule.

(1) Did not know the nature and quality of the act. This means that if the accused shot someone, he or she didn't know that the object in his or her hand was a gun, or didn't understand that if it was pointed at someone and the trigger was pulled that it would kill.

(2) Did not know that it was wrong. The questions that are asked of the suspect soon after the act are very important in establishing this second condition. If the suspect thought that the person who was shot was an alien from outer space invading the world, he or she might think that this action was good rather than bad.

Other Insanity Rules

There are three other major tests for insanity used in the United States. They are:

(1) The Durham Test

(Also called the New Hampshire Test-1871)

In this test, the jury hears all the expert testimony, and then makes up their own mind as to the insanity of the defendant. Here, there can be a tendency to disregard scientific evidence and just go by a "gut feeling."

In 1954, the U.S. Court of Appeals for the District of Columbia decided in favor of this test as opposed to the M'Naghten Rule.

(2) The Irresistible Impulse Test

This test, first used in Pennsylvania in 1846, states that a defendant is insane if he knew right from wrong, but because of some mental condition, he could not prevent himself from doing it. This test is criticized due to the wide discretion that it involves. It would excuse too many people.

(3) The Substantial Capacity Test

About 1955, the American Law Institute developed a model insanity defense for their Model Penal Code. It was called the Substantial Capacity Test. The test is as follows:

A person is not responsible for criminal conduct if at the time of such conduct as a result of mental disease or defect he lacks substantial capacity either to appreciate the criminality (wrongfulness) of his conduct or to conform his conduct to the requirements of the law.[17]

Evidence or Proof of Insanity

Defendants can only use the defense of insanity when they were insane at the time that the offense was committed.[18] A defendant who was sane during a fatal attack that did not kill his father then became insane and again attacked his father also killing his mother and other members of the family. The testimony of pathologists indicated that the original attack on his father would have resulted in his death. As a result, the defendant was found guilty of murder of his father, but not of the rest of the family because he was insane during those attacks.[19]

Partial insanity is not a sufficient defense to excuse the commission of a homicide.[20] Even though the defendant has a schizoid personality, the fact that he was not legally insane, and that lay witnesses' testimony showed his mental capacity, was enough evidence for the jury to accept his criminal responsibility.[21]

As proof of mental condition, the "tryer of fact" may take into consideration any conduct or declaration made by the defendant within a reasonable time prior to commission of the alleged act.[22]

Although five psychiatrists differed as to the defendant's sanity, evidence was accepted as supporting his sanity when it showed that he prepared in advance for the act by obtaining special instruments, and then lied about their presence. After his arrest, he also stated to the police that his acts were planned and he knew that they were wrong.[23] The testimony of a psychiatrist is not binding on the jury and is only evidence to be weighed against other evidence presented in the case.[24]

Evidence That Is Not Acceptable

A doctor is not an expert on the definition of legal insanity.[22 Ibid] The fact that the family of the defendant had always treated him as insane or an imbecile is inadmissible as evidence of his mental incapacity to commit a crime.[25]

The testimony of psychiatrists who answered hypothetical questions in the courtroom, but who had never examined the defendant, nor provided reasons for their conclusions, was not "substantial" evidence to support the jury's implied finding of their conclusions.[26]

Addiction to narcotics is not a form of insanity. The fact that the defendant was addicted to morphine at the time he killed the victim is not conclusive evidence that he was insane at the time of the killing.[27]

9.3:4   Persons Unconscious of the Act

There are sometimes situations where a person commits an act that is classified as a crime, yet because of some physical or mental state the person is really not conscious of what he or she is doing. This defense does not include cases of mental illness, but only persons of sound mind such as somnambulists, or persons suffering with delirium from fever or medication. Unconsciousness is a complete defense, not just a partial defense. Unconsciousness not only includes a state of coma or immobility, but also a condition in which a person acts without being aware of those acts.[28] Although a defendant used unconsciousness as a defense, the court held that his admission to remembering 95 percent of what had occurred, could not logically support a defense of unconsciousness.

Examples:

(A) Sleepwalking (somnambulism)

Some people are subject to a condition called somnambulism in which they move about and perform normal-appearing acts, yet are asleep. It is possible that persons in this state could perform acts that would amount to crimes. If they did, they would have a legal defense in that they were really unconscious of the act that they were performing.[29] A book entitled, "The Sleepwalk Killers," written by Leslie Watkins, cites cases throughout history where sleepwalkers have killed others.

(B) Involuntary intoxication

There are times when a person can become involuntarily intoxicated by ingesting something without realizing that it contains alcohol or drugs. If, while in this state of involuntary intoxication, the person were to throw a brick through a window, he or she would have a legal defense for the crime of vandalism, but would still be responsible for the tort or civil responsibility, and would have to pay for the window.

Whenever defendants use a legal defense, the burden of proof is on them to show that the circumstances were as described. In this case, the burden of proof would be on the defendant to show that the state of intoxication was in fact involuntary.

(C) Voluntary Intoxication (22 PC)

Voluntary intoxication was used as a partial defense under the Alvarez decision (4 CA 3d) when specific intent was involved. Section (22(a) PC) states that acts committed while in a state of voluntary intoxication are not less criminal because of this condition. Such evidence shall not be admitted to negate the capacity to form any mental state for the crime charged, such as purpose, intent, knowledge, premeditation, deliberation, or malice aforethought, **when** a specific intent crime is charged; or, when charged with murder, to determine premeditation, deliberation, or the harboring of express malice aforethought. Voluntary intoxication includes the taking of drugs or similar substances. If voluntary intoxication, over a period of time, causes insanity, and the insanity is permanent as a result of a diseased brain, it is a complete defense.[30]

(D) Delirium from fever or medication

When a person is ill and has a fever, the body temperature can rise to the point where it affects the blood pressure and the person goes into a state of delirium where he can be subject to hallucinations. This is a very frightening condition, and a person so affected might, out of fear, commit some act that would amount to a crime.[31]

(E) Injuries to the head

If persons receive blows to the head that result in mental conditions causing them to perform acts over which they have no voluntary control, this is a legal defense against criminal prosecution.[32]

(F) Exceptions to This Defense (25.5 PC)

In any criminal proceeding in which the plea of not guilty by reason of insanity is entered, this defense shall not be found by the trier of fact (the jury in a jury trial or a judge in a court trial) solely on the basis of:

(1) a personality disorder.
(2) an adjustment disorder.
(3) a seizure disorder.
(4) an addiction to intoxicating substances.
(5) an abuse of intoxicating substances.

OH, COME, COME NOW, YER HONOR! THE FACT THAT MY CLIENT'S ACT RESULTED IN THE DESTRUCTION OF NEW YORK DOESN'T MATTER — HE WAS DRUNK AT THE TIME!

9.4:0 DEFENSES BASED ON CON-STITUTIONAL PROTECTION, STATUTORY PROVISION OR LEGAL RULES

Under this topic are Double Jeopardy, Entrapment, Statute of Limitations, Immunity, Consent, Status Offenses, Self-Defense, Defense of Habitation, and Legislative Intent.

9.4:1 Former Jeopardy

Former Jeopardy, sometimes called double jeopardy, simply means that once a person has been tried for a criminal offense, that person cannot be tried again for that same offense .

The purpose of this ruling is to protect citizens from legal persecution. It is unfortunate, but sometimes it does not serve the interest of justice. For example, there have been cases where the defendant has been found not guilty by a jury, and then the defendant walked up to the jury and gave them the "finger," telling them that he did commit the crime and that they were "a bunch of suckers." There are times when, after the trial and a "not guilty" verdict by the jury, new evidence is unearthed that would have definitely proved the defendant's guilt, but there is nothing that the police can do. These cases are very rare, however, and since our system of law is designed to give the defendant the benefit of the doubt, the concept of former jeopardy is valid.

The basis for this concept is found in the Constitution of the United States which says: "no person shall be...subject, for the same offense, to be twice put in jeopardy..." The California Constitution also states in Article 1, Section 13: "no person shall be twice put in jeopardy for the same offense." The California Penal Code states in Section 687: "no person can be subjected to a second prosecution for a public offense for which he has once been prosecuted and convicted or acquitted."

The law of former jeopardy applies to all crimes, both misdemeanors and felonies.

What Is a Prior Offense?

There is sometimes a problem in establishing exactly what constitutes a prior offense. Sections 656, 793 and 794 of the California Penal Code state that a conviction in another county, state, or foreign country stands as a prior conviction and would be a bar to further prosecution.

Statutes Listing Various Acts

There are many statutes that list a series of acts which could constitute a violation of that law. An example is Section 261 of the Penal Code. It lists many ways in which the crime of rape may be committed. If a man were charged with rape by force (261.2 PC) and found not guilty, the prosecution could not re-try him on a different subsection of the same law. For example, 261.1, where the victim, because of unsound mind, was incapable of giving consent. The law on former jeopardy would be a defense in a case of this nature.

At What Point in the Trial Does Former Jeopardy Become a Legal Defense?

(1) **In a trial before a jury.** Jeopardy attaches once a competent jury is duly empanelled, sworn and charged with the case. If the jury is discharged at a later time in the trial without the consent of the defendant, or for a cause the court can control, and before a verdict, it is the same as an acquittal. If this occurs, the defendant cannot be tried again on that same charge.[33] If alternate jurors are ordered, they must also be sworn to try the case, or jeopardy does not attach.[34]

(2) **In a trial before a judge.** Jeopardy attaches when a trial has commenced and the first prosecution witness has been sworn in.[35]

Examples of When Jeopardy Does Attach

A person charged with an offense and legally tried before a competent court cannot be charged later with a lesser offense of that original charge. For example, a man tried for grand theft cannot later be charged with petty theft for the same act. Similarly, a new trial cannot be undertaken simply by changing the charge for the same offense. For example, a man charged with assault and battery, and tried on that offense, cannot later be tried on assault with a deadly weapon, when it covers the same action that brought about the first trial.[33 Ibid]

Examples of When Jeopardy Does Not Attach

When there is a "hung jury," jeopardy does not attach (1140 PC). When the jury is prevented from giving a verdict by reason of accident, jeopardy does not attach (1141 PC).

If the court grants a motion for a mistrial at the request of the defendant, jeopardy does not attach, and a new trial may be initiated.[36]

If a defendant is charged with several counts of a crime, and during the trial one of the counts is dismissed, jeopardy will apply to that particular count, but not the others.[37]

If two or more defendants are on trial and one turns "state's witness," (resulting in the charges against him being dropped in return for his testimony) he may not later be tried on those same charges. However, his co-defendants are not included in this application of jeopardy. (1099 and 1100 PC)

When a person is convicted of an offense, the act of which later becomes a more serious offense, jeopardy does not attach. For example, Harvey Hinkle shoots Mervin Mushmuscle. Mervin is hospitalized. He is still hospitalized when Harvey is tried for assault with intent to commit murder. Harvey is convicted. Six months later, while Harvey is in prison, Mervin dies from the original shooting. Harvey can now be tried for murder (187 PC), but cannot use former jeopardy as a defense. It is the result of the same act, but there is a new element — the death of a human being.

Juvenile Cases

In the past, based on People v. Silverstein (121 CA 2d 140), a juvenile court hearing was not considered to be the same as an adult trial. Because of this, a juvenile could be tried in a juvenile court, and later tried in an adult court if he or she was declared to be not suited to the juvenile corrections system. Recently, however, a California Supreme Court decision has reversed this concept; it has now been declared to be double jeopardy.[38]

9.4:3   Entrapment as a Defense

Entrapment is defined as the act of police officers inducing persons to commit crimes they are not contemplating for the purpose of prosecuting them. Based on the idea that the purpose of law is to prevent crime, not to encourage it, entrapment is a legal defense in the state of California.

Prior to 1979 the key to entrapment was "in whose mind did the crime originate." It did not matter if the police officer approached the suspect and solicited him as long as the crime was one that he had originally intended to commit.

In 1979, the California Supreme Court, in People v. Barranza (23 Cal. 3d 675) changed the focus for determining whether entrapment occurred. The new determination is, "Was the conduct of the law enforcement agent likely to induce a normally law-abiding person to commit the offense?" This is directed away from the suspect and toward the law enforcement officer. It is not whether the suspect intended to commit the crime, but whether the officer's conduct was such that it would induce a person to commit a crime. In a companion decision (People v. Macintire 23 Cal.

3d 742) the high court held that third parties used by the police were agents even if they were unaware of the police objectives in using them.

The new decision may present some problems in the control of vice. The most common means of vice control is to send undercover officers or agents to an area where complaints have been received in the hope that they will be solicited. Most prostitutes will now state in court that they were solicited by the officer and cite the Barranza decision. How do you prove this? The courts have held that if the defendant has a "reputation in his community" for the type of offense he or she was arrested for, then entrapment is not a defense. In People v. Pierre,[39] it was stated that the law does not frown upon the entrapment of criminals, but the seduction of innocent people into the performing of criminal acts. If the officers use no more persuasion than is needed to make the sale, and the suspect is willing to sell the narcotics, there is no entrapment.[39 Ibid]

Decoys and Traps

If the police learn of a planned crime they would be remiss in their duties if they did not attempt to trap the suspects. In cases of on-going criminal activity, such as stopping people on the street for the purpose of soliciting lewd acts, the most efficient method of control or prevention is to use police decoys. In the People v. Hanselman, 76 Cal. 460, the high court held that it was not entrapment for officers to disguise themselves in an effort to decoy criminal suspects.

One of the problems in using decoys is that officers can get carried away in their efforts to do a good job. In one city, a problem developed of men in cars stopping women on the street and propositioning them. When police decoys were used on the streets, many arrests were made and the problem seemed resolved. However, the police decoys felt they were not doing their job when things slowed down, so they began to wave at passing cars and to make eyes at passing motorists. The court threw out all such arrests on the grounds that they were clear-cut cases of entrapment. The same applies to undercover decoys in homosexual hangouts. They must be careful not to make suggestions or gestures that could be suggestive. Otherwise, it could be entrapment.

9.4:4   Statute of Limitations

Generally speaking, the statute of limitations places a legal limit on the amount of time between the commission of a crime and the start of prosecution proceedings. Its purpose is to prevent the threat of criminal prosecution from being "held over the head" of a person for years. It also prevents a form of "behavior blackmail" where a person is forever threatened with prosecution if he "doesn't watch his step." In People v. Chapman,[40] the Appellate Court stated that there must come an end to threat of prosecution for offenses. It was also felt that it was unfair for defendants to defend their cases with or against evidence that has faded in the passage years. The statute of limitations is determined by two factors—whether the crime is a felony or a misdemeanor, and the type of crime.

Offenses for Which There are No Statutes of Limitations (799 PC)

The following offenses have NO statute of limitations:
(1) Offenses punishable by death.
(2) Offenses punishable by life imprisonment (possible parole).
(3) Offenses punishable by life imprisonment (no poss. parole).
(4) Embezzlement of public money.

Serious Felonies (800 PC)

If the punishment can involve eight or more years in prison, the prosecution shall commence within six years of the commission of the crime.

Felony Offenses in General (801 PC)

When the crime is a felony, prosecution shall commence within three years of its commission.

Exceptions: (801.5 PC)

Prosecutions regarding any offense in 803 PC shall commence within four years of discovery or the completion of the offense, whichever is later.

Misdemeanor Offenses (802(a) PC)

When the crime is a misdemeanor, prosecution shall commence within one year of its commission.

Exceptions: (802(b) & (c) PC)

If the crime is either:
(a) 647.6 PC: Annoying or Molesting Children, or
(b) 729 B & P; and the child is under 14, the prosecution must commence within two years after the commission of the crime.

Tolling the Time (803 PC)

(A) The statute of limitation does not continue once a prosecution has commenced in a court of law.
(B) If the offense is:
   (1) Felony fraud, or
   (2) A breach of fiduciary obligation, or
   (3) Misconduct in public office, or
   (4) One of the many examples in the code. (They are just examples and not mandatory.) the time does not commence until the discovery of the crime.
(C) If the suspect is out-of-state, the prosecution has up to three extra years before initiating proceedings.
(D) If the victim is under 18 years of age, and the crime is either: 261, 286, 288, 288a, 288.5, or 289 PC, the statute of limitation is one year after the victim reports the offense to
   (1) a responsible adult, or
   (2) a public agency WHEN:
      (a) the regular statute of limitations has expired. AND
      (b) at least one of the offenses listed above has occured during the period of the statute of limitation.
(E) If the victim is of any age, and is reporting one of the above sexual offenses that occurred when he or she was under 18, the statute of limitation starts when the victim reports the offense to a law enforcement agency WHEN:
   (1) The regular statute of limitations has expired. AND
   (2) The crime involves "Substantial Sexual Conduct" as listed in 1203.066 PC. AND
   (3) There is some independent corroboration that is admissible in court (not to include opinions of mental health professionals).

Commencement of Prosecution (804 PC)

Prosecution will be considered to have commenced when:
(1) An indictment or information has been filed.
(2) A complaint is filed in an inferior court.
(3) A case has been certified to the superior court.
(4) An arrest or bench warrant has been issued.

Determining Length of Sentence (805 PC)

(1) Enhancements shall not be included in the time used to compile the time of sentence for purposes of this chapter.
(2) When determining whether the statute of limitations is based on the original offense charged or a lesser included offense, the crime for which the defendant is found guilty is the one used for determining statute of limitations.

Discovery of the Offense

The burden of proof as to the fact that the offense was committed within the period established by the statute of limitations, or that the exception applies to the case being tried, falls on the prosecution.[41] Whether the prosecution has complied with the requirements is a question of fact for the jury to decide.[42]

The word "discovery" indicates a state of awareness, and mere loss of property without discovering that it was actually stolen does not mean that the victim has discovered the crime. Discovery is set in motion when either the victim or the law enforcement agency discovers the crime.[42 Ibid]

When the Statute of Limitations Ceases (799 PC)

If, after the commission of a crime, the defendant is out of the state, that time out of the state will not be counted as any of the time towards the statute of limitations. (802 PC)

Ex Post Facto Application

Ex Post Facto laws require that rules be based on the law that existed at the time the crime was committed.[43]

The Effect of Lesser Offenses on the Statute of Limitations

Finding a defendant guilty of a lesser offense can have a definite effect on the statute of limitations. If the original charge is grand theft (a felony), and the jury finds the defendant guilty of a lesser offense, petty theft (a misdemeanor), the conviction may be overruled if the limitations have run out for a misdemeanor.

For example, Herbert Hickup takes his color TV out to the back yard and puts it in his pickup so that he can take it to the repair shop. He goes back into the house to get a drink of water. While in the kitchen, he sees Lester Lump take the TV from the back of the pickup, put it in his car, and drive off.

Herbert calls the police and gives them the details. When the officers arrive to take the report, Herbert tells them that the value of the TV is $450. Because of the reported value, the officers write up a felony grand theft report.

Lester Lump hears the police are looking for him and leaves town. Two years later he is in Los Angeles and is stopped for a traffic ticket. The officer runs a file check on him, and the computer comes back with information that there is a felony warrant for Lester Lump, charging grand theft.

Lester is arrested and put on trial. During the trial, the evidence is very conclusive concerning Lester taking the TV. The jury accepts the fact that he did take the TV. However, Lester's attorney brings in some TV experts who testify that the set was broken and worth at most $250. The judge tells the jury if they feel the TV was worth less than $400, they can find Lester guilty of petty theft if they feel that he did in fact take the TV. After a short deliberation, the jury agrees that Lester took the TV, but feels that its value was much less than $400. They find him guilty of petty theft. Lester's attorney then asks the judge to set aside the conviction on the grounds that the statute of limitations has run out, since the limitation for a misdemeanor is one year, and over two years have expired since the offense. This would be a valid defense.

9.4:5   Immunity as a Defense

There are two types of immunity. They are:
(1) Statutory immunity and
(2) Contract immunity.
(also called common law immunity)
There are many situations in law where persons suspected of crimes will be given legal immunity for their acts when it serves a good purpose.

(A) Statutory Immunity (Protection Under the Fifth Amendment)

If a person were forced to testify in court and it in any way could implicate him or her in a criminal action, that person's rights under the Fifth Amendment would be violated. Yet, the California Constitution (Art. IV, Sec. 35), the California Corporation Code (25354), the California Government Code (9410), and the California Penal Code (Section 1324) all state that in certain circumstances, a person can be required to give testimony. They all agree, however, that when such testimony is given, the person testifying will receive immunity from criminal prosecution.

Statutory Immunity Involving Narcotics Investigation

Section 11367 of the Controlled Substances Act of the Health and Safety Code states that all duly authorized peace officers and persons working under their direction are immune from prosecution for narcotic offenses while conducting investigations of narcotic violations.

If it were not for this immunity, it would be difficult for peace officers or their agents to do undercover investigative work in this field.

Statutory Immunity of the Feigned Accomplice

The law, in an effort to encourage its citizens to assist in promoting the ends of criminal justice, allows a person to participate in a criminal action for the purpose of gathering information for the prosecution. This can be done either under the direction of the police or authorities, or strictly on the citizen's own initiative.[44] In such a case, if the jury believes the story, the feigned accomplice can escape criminal prosecution.

California's state legislature, in enacting laws that provide immunity, did not intend such laws to be a broad and sweeping grant of immunity against the commission of any crime, but to protect persons who are forced to testify, and to make the prosecutor's job less cumbersome.[45] California's statutes that grant immunity are not unconstitutional and, unless there is a law enforcement policy obviously being practiced by the police in an unequal and unfair manner, the statutes are valid.[46]

Diplomatic Immunity

Diplomatic immunity seldom becomes a defense in a criminal trial because the matter is resolved without going to trial. The problem is first determining whether the person does work for the foreign embassy, and second whether he is one of the persons of that embassy who is entitled to diplomatic immunity. Once this is determined, the suspect is released without any attempt made to start a criminal prosecution. A rare exception would involve a person who no longer works for a foreign embassy, and is being charged with a crime which he claims was committed when he was working for the embassy and was at that time covered by diplomatic immunity. It becomes a question of fact for the jury to decide.

(B) Contract Immunity Through the District Attorney (Turning "State's Evidence")

A person who is a co-principal in a criminal action may make a written agreement with the District Attorney to testify voluntarily. If the court approves the agreement, that person will be granted full or partial immunity. He or she may, however, be prosecuted for perjury. (1324.1 PC)

Under no circumstances should the immunity be based on the conviction of a co-principal. To do so would be a miscarriage of justice. Under that condition, the person testifying has an incentive to lie in order to retain the immunity.

The whole theory behind allowing a co-principal to testify in return for immunity, is that it is better to have a "bird in the hand than two in the bush." If this theory is valid, then immunity should only be granted in cases where the evidence is so weak that without the testimony of one of the co-principals, the case would be lost.

9.4:7 Consent as a Defense

There are certain crimes where consent is a legal defense. Most of these crimes have an element stating that it is without the consent of the owner or victim. However, this is not true in all cases.

Examples of crimes where consent is a defense are rape (where the victim is over 18), theft, and robbery. Many times it is a legitimate defense. The victim becomes angered at the defendant and accuses him or her of committing the act without consent, when at the time, the victim's full consent was given. Investigators should always consider the emotional state of the victim at the time of the report. They should also consider revenge motives.

9.4:8 Status as a Defense

Status as an act has already been discussed in Chapter VI. Once the high courts have declared a certain act to be a status act and in violation of the Constitution, the state legislature will change the law. However, someone has to challenge the constitutionality of a law, and if convicted of violating that law, would use the defense of status.

9.4:9 Self-Defense

Self-defense can only be used as a defense for a charge of unlawful homicide, assault and battery or assault with a deadly weapon. It could conceivably be used as a defense for the crime of Exhibiting a Firearm or other Deadly Weapon in a Threatening Manner (417 PC) The key to self-defense is justification based on a real and immediate threat to one's person. The more severe the threat, the more severe can be the measures taken to defend oneself. Section 197 of the Penal Code allows one person to legally kill another if there are reasonable grounds to believe that the other person is about to commit great bodily harm or injury on the defending person. Section 198 of the Penal Code states that "Bare Fear" alone is not sufficient to justify self-defense. It must be accompanied by some act that would cause a reasonable person to believe that he or she was in immediate danger.[47]

9.4:10   Legislative Intent (Spirit of the Law)

Legislative intent is a legal defense. Based on Penal Code Section 4, legislative intent is to be considered when enforcing the law. Officers and prosecutors who make an arrest or take a case to court, based solely on the "Letter of the Law" will find that it is a very valid defense. This seldom occurs because the prosecutor's office will "weed out" such cases. It will be used as a defense when the prosecutor believes that the act committed violated both the "Letter" and the "Spirit" of the law, and the defendant believes that it violated only the "Letter of the Law." Many cases end up in court based on a difference of interpretation.

9.5:0   DEFENSES BASED ON LACK OF INTENT OR CRIMINAL NEGLIGENCE

Mistake of Fact, Accident and Misfortune, Innocent Agents, and Acting under Force, Threat or Duress fall under this heading.

9.5:1   Mistake of Fact

Commiting an act or making an omission under ignorance or mistake of fact disproves criminal intent. Mistake of Fact occurs when persons commit acts they believe to be legal, based on some mistaken fact which, if it were true, would result in the act not being illegal. The fact on which this belief is based must be one that would be accepted by a reasonable, prudent, ordinary person.

Example:

Percy Persimmon goes to a restaurant and hangs up his coat. When he finishes his meal, he walks over, picks up his coat and leaves the restaurant. As he leaves, Arvin Ardvark runs after him yelling, "Stop, thief!" Arvin accuses Percy of stealing his coat. When Percy looks in the pockets, he finds articles that do not belong to him. He goes back to the restaurant and finds that his coat is still hanging on the wall. It looks exactly like Arvin's coat. Percy took Arvin's coat, yet there was no criminal intent because of the Mistake of Fact.

There have been many instances where a person's automobile has been taken by mistake. It was the same make and model, and the same key fit both cars. This seems to be more common in General Motors' products than with other car makes.

A person who believes, in good faith, that certain facts are true, and then acts based on those beliefs in a manner that would be lawful if the facts were as believed, is not guilty of a crime. A person who, based on a mistaken belief that a doctor had phoned in a prescription, told the pharmacist that it had been phoned in, and the pharmacist accepted this fact and gave the defendant narcotics, could use the excuse of Mistake of Fact.[48]

Mistake of Law

There is another term that is similar to Mistake of Fact — Mistake of Law. This is the same as "Ignorance of the Law," and is not a legal excuse.[49]

An example of Mistake of Law would be fishing out-of-season. The person is violating the law, but is not aware of the fact that it is against the law. Another example would be the person who is driving 45 miles per hour in a zone that he or she thought was a 45 MPH zone, when in fact it was a 35 MPH zone. If "Ignorance of the Law" were allowed as an excuse, it would be difficult to enforce the law and maintain order. People would be able to avoid prosecution for regulatory crimes just by saying they didn't know it was illegal.

9.5:2   Accident and Misfortune

Persons who commit an act or make an omission through misfortune or by accident, when it appears that there was no evil design, intention, or culpable negligence. There are times when a person violates no law and is not guilty of criminal negligence, yet causes injury to someone or something. This used to be called an "act of God," because no human intervention could control the results or prevent the incident from happening.

An example would be a person who is driving 30 MPH in a 35 MPH zone. No law is being violated. The person's eyes are on the road ahead and he or she is alert. A young child, chasing a ball, jumps out from between two parked cars. It is too sudden for the driver to take any evasive maneuvers, and he or she hits and kills the child.

This is an example of accident and misfortune, where the person causing the injury was not criminally at fault. The major defense involves showing that the defendant did not violate the law in some way, or was not in some way negligent. It is a question of fact for the jury to decide.

9.5:3   Innocent Agents

Usually cases of this type are weeded out through the use of the lie detector, or a thorough investigation of the suspect and his or her reputation for telling the truth. However, persons whose backgrounds or records are such that a reasonable person would not believe them to be innocent agents in the crime will probably be disbelieved by the District Attorney, and prosecution will be started. Unfortunately, if the defendant is truly innocent, it would be difficult for a jury to believe.

In most cases, the fact that the suspect was an innocent agent of another can be easily or satisfactorily proved before the case gets to the trial stage. If nothing else, such a person will be given immunity in return for providing testimony against the person who used him or her as an innocent agent, and the interest of justice will be served.

9.5:4   Acts Under Force, Threat or Duress

Persons who committed the act or made the omission charged under threat or menace sufficient to show they had reasonable cause to and did be- lieve their lives would be endangered if they refused, have a legal defense (except capital crimes).

In a defense of this type, it must be shown that the threat was an immediate one and not a threat of a future injury. In some states the law allows a defense where the fear is based on great bodily harm rather than just a fear of danger to one's life. In California, the law is clear that the fear must be a reasonable one, and that it must be a fear that is based on a danger to one's life.

A woman who is forced to orally copulate a man under threats to her life would not be liable under Section 288a of the Penal Code if it could be shown that she had reasonable cause to believe that her life would be endangered if she refused.[50]

Where it can be shown that the defendant had the opportunity to withdraw and leave the co-defendant safely, shows that participation did not involve duress.[50 Ibid] (Also the Patricia Hearst case).

As with self-defense, the threat of imminent danger to the defendant must be one that is reasonable. In a charge of escape from a state prison, the courts held that a threat to commit sodomy on the defendant if he did not escape with them, despite the fact that it might be abhorrent, fell short of great bodily harm.[51] The threats must be immediate and not threats of future danger.[52]

The court accepted the statements of a 16-year-old boy that he committed several sex acts under duress when the defendant threatened to inject him with a poisonous substance, beat him, and have him committed to a mental institution. The defendant also told the boy he was a deputy sheriff and had "private eyes" watching him.[53]

As being a principal to the crime, a woman was convicted of rape, where she made threats of great bodily harm to a man (when accompanied by

the power of immediate execution) if he did not rape another woman. The courts accepted his defense of duress, and charged the woman with the crime which resulted in her conviction.[54]

A member of the Hell's Angels claimed that he was ordered by the president of the club to kill one of the victims. The defendant claims that the president had a gun, but admits that he did not see it. The defendant stated that his patch was a status symbol, and that he would do whatever the president ordered him to do in order to maintain his membership in the club. These statements were accepted as valid evidence that the defendant did not act based on duress or compulsion.[55]

9.6:0   OTHER DEFENSES

Under this heading will be covered the defenses of Necessity, Physical Impossibility and Corporations.

9.6:1   Necessity as a Defense

In the defense of necessity, the wrongfulness of the act performed is far outweighed by the severity of what would happen otherwise. For example, a person is lost in the north woods in the winter. His car broke down and he tried to walk for help and became lost. After a few days, he was about to freeze to death and was starving. He finally came upon a cabin. There was no one there, and the door was locked. He breaks into the cabin (vandalism) and builds a fire and takes some food from a cupboard (theft). The alternatives to committing these crimes, however, were quite severe. (Death). If the owner of the cabin was a little weird and hardhearted, and wanted him prosecuted, the defense would be necessity. From a civil standpoint, the person breaking in and using the wood and food would be civilly liable to replace what he took and repair what he damaged.

To justify this exception to criminal responsibility, the courts require that there be an actual, absolute necessity. Stephen, in his *History of Criminal Law*, commented on the lack of precedence in this area. He stated:

> Compulsion by necessity is one of the curiosities of law, and so far as I am aware is a subject on which the law of England is so vague that, if cases raising the question should ever occur the judges would practically be able to lay down any rule which they considered expedient.

Necessity must have always been a defense. For example, the law about not doing work on Sunday is thousands of years old. Yet one can be sure that police officers, or their ancient equivalent, were not excused from working on Sunday. It was necessary for them to work. You can be sure that soldiers fighting a battle did not stop on Sunday.

In the United States, the Northeastern states have long had "Blue Laws" which forbid just about all work on Sunday. You can be sure that these did not apply to firemen when a house was on fire. If the law forbade working on Sunday, why were not police officers and firemen arrested? The answer is the law of necessity. The same rule would apply to nurses and doctors.

Another example of necessity as a defense would be a girl who is hitchhiking and is picked up by a man who drives her into the woods and, at knife-point, rapes her. He takes all her clothes so she will not be able to report him before he has a chance to escape. He then drives off leaving her alone and naked. She walks around looking for something with which to cover herself. In a short while, she comes to a farmhouse and notices some clothes on a clothesline. She is embarrassed to go to the door naked, so she steals a dress. She has committed the crime of theft because of necessity.

Defense of Necessity & the Execution of Jesus

Despite the prior statement of Stephen, the defense of "necessity" goes back some time in history. Records in the Vatican Library show that Jesus of Nazareth was executed in Jerusalem in violation of both Roman and Hebrew law. Because the Roman Empire thought so highly of its law, the Roman emperor, Tiberius Caesar, demanded an accounting of those involved. Herod's letter to the emperor blamed Pontius Pilate because he gave the order of execution. The charge in this case was blasphemy and, under Roman law, this was not punishable by death. Other points of Roman law were also violated during the trial and execution.

The High Priest, Caiaphas, (who was probably the instigator in this case) did not follow proper Hebrew law in his actions. At that time, Jewish law stated that any judge passing a sentence of death was required to fast one whole day before the execution. The Sanhedrin was required to review the case. One person on foot and one person on horseback were required to tour the city, loudly announcing the name of the condemned and the charge. They were to seek anyone who would testify in behalf of the condemned man. The prisoner, on his way to execution, had the right to turn back three times to make an appeal. In this case, none of these rights were afforded the condemned. Because of this, Caiaphas was called before the Sanhedrin to defend his actions.

Both Pilate and Caiaphas used the defense of "necessity." Copies of their letters of defense are in the Vatican Library.[56]

In Pilot's letter to Caesar, he claimed that he was running a short-staffed garrison, and that the people in Jerusalem were so emotionally involved in the situation, they were on the verge of rebellion. He stated that if he had not gone along with the demand for the execution, an uprising would surely have occurred, which would have cost many lives and resulted in much property damage. This, he claimed, would bring shame to the Roman Empire.

Caiaphas went before the Sanhedrin in person, but also put his defense in writing. He covered all bases by first blaming it on mob action, then stating that Jesus had challenged the religious structure of Jerusalem, and that he had many followers who were planning to overthrow the existing religious hierarchy. He further told the Sanhedrin that their very existence was being endangered and he had to take immediate action to resolve the problem.

In each case, the defense of necessity was accepted. Neither man was punished for his failure to properly carry out his legal responsibilities.

9.6:2   Physical Impossibility

Physical impossibility is used mostly with obligations or duties imposed by law. Because of physical impossibility, the law is violated.

For example, a man is driving his automobile down the street. He has not been drinking. His car is in proper working order. As he approaches the intersection, he notices a stop sign. As he is about to put on the brakes, he has a heart attack or a stroke and is unable to move his foot. As a result, he goes through the stop sign and violates the law.

A man is driving down the street, and he sees a large box that has dropped off a truck. It stops in front of his car. He stops his car which in turn blocks traffic. It is against the law to stop traffic. In this case, however, the violation is based on physical impossibility.[57]

Section 150 of the Penal Code states that all persons over 18 must come to the assistance of a peace officer when so requested. If Sammy Sadsocks has a bad heart, and is called by a police officer to assist him in making an arrest, he would have a defense against 150 PC, in that it was a physical impossibility for him to assist the officer.

9.6:3 Corporations and Partnerships
Partnerships

The federal courts have declared that partnerships, not being legal entities, cannot, as partnerships, be prosecuted for crimes. The guilty members of the partnership can, however, be held criminally responsible.[58] In the case of "Strict Liability" laws, each partner would be liable. If one partner violated the Agricultural Code and sold eggs that were not edible, his partner, who was not aware of the sale, would be liable.[59]

Corporations

As with partnerships, corporations are not capable of committing crimes unless the crime is punishable by fine. Under those circumstances, a corporation can be guilty and fined accordingly. The officer or agent of the corporation, who carries out the illegal designs or interests of the corporation, is liable for criminal prosecution as an individual.[60] This is based on the criminal law concept of moral, personal responsibility which is emphasized in our law.

9.7:0 ILLEGAL OR UNTENABLE DEFENSES

Defenses such as custom, religion, matters of honor, alibi, irresistible impulse, contributory negligence, emotional insanity, moral insanity, and sexual deviation are not accepted as defenses in law. These topics will be briefly covered.

9.7:1 Custom & Matters Of Honor as Defenses

Unless it has actually been written into law, custom cannot be used as a defense. For example, in the South, it is the custom to be "obliging to kinfolk," and not to assist another member of the family would be a gross violation of custom. As a result, the legislatures in that area have statutorily exempted relatives from being charged as Accessories After the Fact when they help a relative who is escaping the law.

This defense becomes a problem when a person comes to California from another area where the custom is different, and is either a legal excuse, or one in which prosecutors look the other way. For example, many foreign countries allow custom as a defense. In Sicily, the members of a family in which a women has been sexually violated have the legal right to go after the perpetrator and either emasculate or kill him. Some look upon this as a matter of honor. They are duty-bound to seek revenge. To do nothing would amount to cowardliness. Often, in the countries of their origin, the police might not be as effective in enforcing the law, or truly feel that it is a matter for the victim and his family to resolve.

In the Old Testament, the law allowed the family members of a murdered victim to take the law into their own hands. This was a custom in the entire Middle-East.

9.7:2 Religion as a Defense

This topic has already been covered in Chapter II under the First Amendment. The law basically states that a person cannot use religion as a defense to break the law.

If a person could use the right of religious freedom to violate positive criminal law (since the definition of religion is so broad) there would be no end to the different religions people would join or form in order to seek their own selfish personal desires. The rights of one individual do not allow him or her to deny the rights of another.

9.7:3 Alibi as a Defense

There is much misunderstanding about the use of alibi as a defense. In fact, there is argument as to whether it is or is not a defense. Many authors claim that alibi is merely a rebuttal of the state's evidence. One law dictionary defines the word "alibi" as follows:

> The literal significance of the word is "elsewhere" (Latin), and as used in the criminal law it indicates that line of proof by which a defendant undertakes to show that he did not commit, and could not have committed the crime charged, because he was not at the scene of the crime at the time of its commission. Although alibi is frequently characterized as a defense, it is not such within any accurate meaning of that word, but is merely a fact in rebuttal of the state's evidence.[61]

It would be best to approach alibi as evidence rather than as a legal defense. If there is any obvious validity to the alibi, the police investigators will thoroughly check it out, and the District Attorney will probably give it the benefit of the doubt.

As a result, a valid and legitimate alibi will be presented before the trial starts, and therefore prevent the case from ever going to court. The alibi that is brought up at the last minute, just by sheer chance, is highly suspect.

9.7:4 Irresistible Impulse (Uncontrollable impulse)

In California, irresistible impulse is not a defense. If it were, it would open the door to endless defenses. Because we have only the word of the defendant as to the fact that the impulse was impossible to resist, it would be too subjective to be fairly or justly used in court. As long as the defendant knew the nature and quality of the act, and knew that the act was wrong, he or she is responsible.[62] Judge Charles Fricke, author of criminal law, has supported California's stand based on two grounds:

(1) **Difficulty of Proof.** We do not know if the impulse was irresistible, but only that it was not resisted.

(2) **Value of Fear of Punishment.** When the will-power is weakened, although the mentality is not all or only slightly impaired, the fear of punishment must be of some value as a restraint, and the class of people referred to need that restraining influence.[63]

Sometimes, the word "compulsion" is used to indicate irresistible impulse, but the word is too easily confused with the defense of duress and force, so it is best to stick to irresistible impulse.

9.7:5 Moral Insanity and Emotional Insanity

Both of these terms are also used interchangeably with "Irresistible Impulse." They indicate an acute lack of will-power. They both lack the element of mental disease, and usually refer to perverted sexual drives, or crimes involving the lack of moral sense.[64] Neither of these defenses is allowed in California for the same reasons as irresistible impulse is not allowed as a defense.[65]

9.7:6 Homosexuality or Sexual Deviance

It is not, nor can it be, illegal to be homosexual. The reason is that it would be a status crime over which the person had no control. We do not know what causes persons to be homosexual. Because of this, we cannot lay guilt or blame at their feet for a situation over which they have little or no control. It would be like having a law against being Black or Brown. Those persons would have no control over their status.

On the other hand, those who have homosexual or deviate tendencies cannot use their particular sexual drives as a defense for actual physical acts in which they voluntarily participated. It is illegal to solicit others on the street for sexual acts whether they be heterosexual or homosexual. It is illegal to engage in sexual acts with minors, and these acts cannot be defended by a claim of a particular sexual status.[66]

Although the Consenting Adult Law was passed in 1975, it did not allow soliciting for lewd acts to be removed from the statutes.

9.7:7 Contributory Negligence

Contributory negligence means that the victim in some way contributed to the crime. Although contributory negligence is a factor to consider in civil law, it has no place in criminal law. There is a tendency (remaining from our youth, when we needed to blame others) to still put part of the blame on someone else when we have been caught doing something wrong. We seem to feel that guilt shared is guilt reduced. In California criminal law, this is no basis for a defense.

You cannot say that the woman you raped contributed to the crime by wearing a short, tight skirt. You cannot say that the victim you stole from contributed to the crime by leaving his property lying around without watching it.

REFERENCES FOR CHAPTER IX

(1)   Hill v. Pierce 113 Or 386

(2)   Emlyn, note to 1 Hale P.C. 25

(3)   York's case, Fost. 70

(4)   State v. Guild 10 N.J. Law 163

(5)   People v. Kanngiesser 44 C.A. 345
      (186 P 388)

(6)   People v. Roberts 26 C.A. 3d 385
      (103 Cal Rptr 25)

(7)   Muller v. Standard Oil Co. 180 C 260
      (180 P 605)

(8)   Michael B., In re 44 C.A. 3d 443
      (118 Cal Rptr 685)

(9)   People v. Day 199 C 78 (248 P 250)

(10) Gladys R. In re IC 3d855 (83 Cal Rptr 671)

(11) People v. Williams 12 C.A. 2d 207
      (55 P 2d 223)

(12) People v. Stanley 67 C 2d 812
      (63 Cal Rptr 825)

(13) People v. Keyes 178 C 694 (175 P 6)

(14) People v. Fisher 49 C.A. 3d 174
      (122 Cal Rptr 366)

(15) M'Naghten's Case 8 Eng Rep 718 (1843)

(16) People v. Nicolaus 65 C 2d 866
      (56 Cal Rptr 635) (1967)

(17) Model Penal Code, American Law Insti-
      tute, Philadelphia,

(18) People v. Kirby 15 C.A. 264 (114 P 794)

(19) People v. Goedecke 65 C 2d 850
      (56 Cal Rptr 625)

(20) People v. Valentine 28 C 2d 121
      (169 P 2d 1)

(21) People v. Risenhoover 70 C 2d 39
      (73 Cal Rptr 533)

(22) People v. Huddleston 275 C.A. 2d 859
      (80 Cal Rptr 496)

(23) People v. Custer 260 C.A. 2d 234
      (67 Cal Rptr 39)

(24) People v. Gentry 257 C.A. 2d 607
      (65 Cal Rptr 235)

(25) People v. Pico 62 C 50

(26) People v. Moore 257 C.A. 2d 740
      (65 Cal Rptr 450)

(27) People v. Reid 193 C 491 (225 P 859)

(28) People v. Gorshen 51 C 2d 716
      (336 P 2d 492)

(29) People v. Sedeno 10 C 3d 703
      (336 P 2d 492)

(30) People v. Heffington 32 C.A. 3d 1
      (107 Cal Rptr 859)
      People v. Goodrum 31 C.A 430 (160 P 690)

(31) People v. Goshen 51 C 2d 716
      (336 P 2d 492)

(32) People v. Cox 67 C.A. 2d 166 (153 P 2d 362)
      People v. Ray 14 C 3d 20
      (120 Cal Reptr 377)

(33) In re Harron 191 C 457 (217 P 728)

(34) People v. Hess 107 C.A. 2d 407
      (237 P 2d 568)

(35) People v. Burns 84 C.A. 2d 18
      (189 P 2d 868)

(36) People v. McDaniels 137 C 192 (69 P 1006)

(37) People v. Mills 148 C.A. 2d 392
      (306 P 2d 1005)

(38) People v. Silverstein 121 C.A. 2d 140
      (262 P 2d 656)

(39) People v. Pierre 176 C.A. 2d 198
      (1 Cal Rptr 223)

(40) People v. Chapman 47 C.A. 3d 597
      (121 Cal Rptr 315)

(41) In re Demillo 14 C 3d 598
      (121 Cal Rptr 725)

(42) People v. Swinney 46 C.A. 3d 332
      (120 Cal Rptr 148)

(43) Sobiek v. Superior Ct. of San Mateo County
      28 C.A. 3d 846 (106 Cal Rptr 516)

(44) People v. Piascik 159 C.A. 2d 622
      (323 P 2d 1032)

(45) People v. Stewart 1 C.A. 3d 339
      (81 Cal Rptr 562)

(46) People v. Williams 11 C.A. 3d 1156
      (90 Cal Rptr 409)

(47) People v. Hoover 107 C.A. 635 (290 P 493)

(48) People v. Katz 207 C.A. 2d 739
      (24 Cal Rptr 644)

(48) People v. McLaughlin 111 C.A. 2d 781
      (245 P 2d 1076)

(50) People v. Coleman 53 C.A. 2d 18
      (127 P 2d 309)

(51) People v. Richards 269 C.A. 2d
      (75 Cal Rptr 597)

(52) People v. Quinlan 8 C.A. 3d 1063
      (88 Cal Rptr 125)

(53) People v. Anderson 264 C.A. 2d 271
      (70 Cal Rptr 231)

(54) People v. Hernandez 18 C.A. 3d 651
      (96 Cal Rptr 71)

(55) People v. Moran 39 C.A. 3d 398
      (114 Cal Rptr 413)

(56) Archko Volume. Archko Press, Grand
      Rapids, MI, 1887, p. 128.

(57) Com v. Brooks 99 Mass 434

(58) U.S. v. Brookman Co. 229 F Supp 862

(59) In re Casperson 69 C.A. 2d 441
(159 P 2d 88)

(60) People v. Jevne Co. 179 C 621 (178 P 517)

(61) James A. Ballantine, Self Pronouncing Law
Dictionary, Lawyer's Cooperative Publishing Co., Rochester, N.Y. 1948, p. 43.

(62) People v. Nash 52 C 2d 36 (338 P 2d 416)

(63) Charles Fricke, California Criminal Law,
Legal Book Co., Los Angeles, 1976.

(64) People v. French 12 C 2d 720 (87 P 2d 1014)

(65) People v. Johnson 115 C.A. 704 (2 P 2d 216)

(66) People v. McDonough 198 C.A. 2d 84
(17 Cal Rptr 643)

STUDY QUESTIONS

CHAPTER IX

(1) Most legal defenses are based on a protection of basic human rights or a lack of criminal _____.

(2) Evidence for a possible defense should be investigated by the District Attorney's office rather than by the investigating police officers.　　T or F

(3) Under English Common Law, absolutely all persons under the age of _____ were incapable of committing crimes.

(4) Under English Common Law, every person was presumed sane and responsible for his acts.　　T or F

(5) In the United States, apart from the common law defense of "infancy," we did not have a special law for the treatment of juveniles until 1899. This occurred in the state of _____.

(6) If a juvenile judge "remands" a juvenile, he or she:

    (A) ____sentences him.
    (C) ____"chews him out."
    (B) ____releases him from custody.
    (D) ____transfers him to another court.

(7) In early English law an eight-year-old could be hanged.　　T or F

(8) In California, the laws state that a person under _____ years is incapable of committing a crime unless he knows the wrongfulness of the act.

(9) This knowledge is a question of fact for the jury to decide. (Re: question 8)　　T or F

(10) When age is a defense it is the physical age that applies (generally).　　T or F

(11) Sometimes mental age is considered in determining criminal liability.　　T or F

(12) An idiot has an "IQ" of from 0 to _____ .

(13) An imbecile is responsible for his criminal acts.　　T or F

(14) After the California Supreme Court decision in the case, "People v. Drew," the new test for determining insanity was the _____ _____ test.

(15) The California Legislature could not change the "Drew" decision.　　T or F

(16) When a defendant uses insanity as a defense, the burden of proof is on him to prove that he was insane during the crime.　　T or F

(17) In a defense for insanity, the burden of proof is:

    (A) ____beyond a moral certainty.
    (C) ____beyond a reasonable doubt.
    (B) ____a preponderance of evidence.
    (D) ____absolute proof.

(18) One of the most common insanity tests in the U.S. is the New Hampshire Test (1871) it is more commonly called the _____ test.

(19) Around 1955 the American Law Institute developed a model insanity test. it is called the _____ _____ test.

(20) In insanity cases, the testimony of a psychiatrist is binding upon the jury.　　T or F

(21) Addiction to narcotics is legally a form of insanity.　　T or F

(22)   Somnambulism is a legal defense. It means:

    (A) ____insanity.   (B) ____sleepwalking.
    (C) ____high fever.   (D) ____a drugged state.

(23)   Involuntary intoxication can be a legal defense.   T or F

(24)   Acts committed during an epileptic seizure are not criminal.   T or F

(25)   Double jeopardy does not apply if the prior conviction occurred outside the state.   T or F

(26)   Double jeopardy applies only to felonies.   T or F

(27)   In a trial before a jury, double jeopardy begins once:

    (A) ____the jury is empaneled, sworn & charged with the case.
    (B) ____the first witness for the defense is sworn in.
    (C) ____The first witness for the prosecution is sworn in.
    (D) ____the jury hears the first witness testify.

(28)   In a trial before a judge only, double jeopardy begins once:

    (A) ____the first witness for the defense is sworn in.
    (B) ____the first witness testifies.
    (C) ____the first witness for the prosecution is sworn in.
    (D) ____the judge calls the court to order.

(29)   Double jeopardy does not apply to lesser offenses.   T or F

(30)   Double jeopardy does not attach when there is a _____jury.

(31)   Double jeopardy does not attach when a mistrial is granted at the request of the defendant.   T or F

(32)   Juveniles are not affected by double jeopardy if tried in juvenile court.   T or F

(33)   The latest key to entrapment is "In whose mind did the crime originate."   T or F

(34)   The statute of limitations for general felonies is _____ years.

(35)   The statute of limitations for murder is seven years.   T or F

(36)   The statute of limitations for a misdemeanor is _____ years.

(37)   The statute of limitations ceases when the defendant is _____ _____ _____.

(38)   The burden of proof for the time requirement for the statute of limitations rests with the state.   T or F

(39)   Jack Hass can't find his gun. He thinks he misplaced it somewhere in the house. Later the police   T or F
        find the gun at the scene of a burglary. When they notify Jack, they examine his house and find
        jimmy marks on a window. They now know the gun was taken in a burglary of Jack's house.
        Jack can establish "discovery" of the burglary as the time when he first could not find the gun.

(40)   Mervin Mushmuscle is tried for a felony that he committed two years ago. The jury finds him
        guilty of a lesser offense that happened to be a misdemeanor. What is his punishment?
        _____.

(41)   Common law immunity is sometimes called _____ immunity.

(42)   The District Attorney decides to allow a co-principal in a criminal case to turn "state's evi-
        dence" and testify against his co-principals in return for immunity. This type of immunity is
        called _____ immunity.

(43) Tom Turkey coerces his wife to steal a bottle of wine for him (this is misdemeanor petty theft). She is caught in the act. Which of the following is true?

    (A) ____Both of them can be prosecuted.   (C) ____Only the wife can be prosecuted.
    (B) ____Only the husband can be prosecuted.   (D) ____Neither of them can be prosecuted.

(44) Consent is never a defense in a criminal trial.   T or F

(45) When a person commits a criminal act because of mistaken belief, which if true, would make the act legal, it is called _____ of _____.

(46) The legal term for "ignorance of the law" is _____ of _____.

(47) Fanny Flagel is driving 25 mph in a 30 mph zone. She is alert and driving in a careful manner. A young child jumps out from between two parked cars and Fanny hits the child. Fanny has a legal defense; it is called accident and _____.

(48) A person who committed a crime under threats or duress will be excused from criminal liability unless that crime is a(an) _____ offense.

(49) Freddie Flake is lost in the north woods. He is starving. He finds a locked cabin. He breaks in and lights a fire to stop freezing, and takes some food to keep from starving. His defense is called _____.

(50) A partnership cannot be prosecuted for a crime.   T or F

(51) Corporations cannot be prosecuted for a crime unless by fine.   T or F

(52) Custom and matters of honor are untenable defenses.   T or F

(53) The Old Testament allowed the family of a murdered victim to take legal revenge.   T or F

(54) "Alibi" is not legally a defense.   T or F

(55) "Irresistible impulse" is a legal defense.   T or F

(56) Moral and emotional insanity are interchangeable terms with "irresistible impulse."   T or F

(57) It is illegal to be a homosexual in California.   T or F

(58) Contributory negligence is a partial defense in California criminal law.   T or F

CHAPTER X

COMMON CRIMES AND THEIR ELEMENTS

10.0	HOMICIDE IN GENERAL
10.1	UNLAWFUL HOMICIDE
10.2	LAWFUL HOMICIDE
10.3	KIDNAPPING
10.4	ASSAULT
10.5	BATTERY
10.6	ASSAULT WITH A DEADLY WEAPON
10.7	RAPE
10.8	ROBBERY
10.9	EXTORTION
10.10	DISTURBING THE PEACE
10.11	BURGLARY
10.12	THEFT
10.13	VANDALISM

The breakdown of crimes in this chapter is borrowed from *The Peace Officer's Guide to Criminal Law*, Payton & Guffey.

10.0:0 HOMICIDE IN GENERAL

10.0:1 Elements of Homicide

Homicide has four elements. They are:
(1) The killing
(2) of a human being, or a fetus
(3) by a human act or agency
(4) when death occurs within 3 years and 1 day

Any of the elements can be proved by circumstantial evidence, and no body need be produced in order for a conviction to be obtained. There need be no direct evidence of death produced, nor is a confession essential to a conviction.[1]

(1) The Killing

There need not be an intent to kill. The death, however, must be the proximate result of some human act, not necessarily the direct result. It can also be caused by a person committing an act required by law.

Definition of Death

According to 7180 of the Health and Safety Code, a person shall be considered dead if he has suffered "Total and Irreversible cessation of brain function." Determination will require the opinion of two independent physicians.

Transplanting Body Parts (7181 H & S)

When a part of the deceased is used for direct transplantation, neither the physician making the determination of death nor the physician making the confirmation shall participate in the procedures for transplanting a part from the deceased's body.

Officers Right to Search Bodies of Accident Victims (27491.3 Gov. Code)

This law allows officers to search the bodies of deceased accident victims for a card that indicates a wish to donate vital organs.

(2) A Human Being, or a Fetus

A fetus becomes a "human being" when it has been born and has established its own independent circulation, not relying on the circulation of the mother. The umbilical cord need not be severed.

The definition of the term "fetus" has changed considerably over the years. In 1976, the California Appellate Court,[2] declared that a fetus must be viable (it moves) and must be capable of living if it were separated from the mother's womb.

(3) By a Human Act or Agency

The death cannot be brought about by an "act of God," such as a lightning bolt or a flood. It must be the result of some human act. Understanding of this element will be enhanced by understanding the Doctrine of Proximate Cause.

Proximate Cause

Proximate cause means that, if a death results from the natural and probable consequences of a particular act, that act is the proximate cause of the death. The key question is: If the original act had not occurred, would the victim have died?

If a row of dominoes were stacked on end, spaced about an inch apart, and someone knocked one over, it would in turn knock the next one over and so on until the last one. The proximate cause of the last domino being knocked over was the fact that someone knocked over the first one.

Examples of deaths that occurred through proximate cause:

(a) A non-fatal wound is opened by movement of the victim and he bleeds to death; the perpetrator is guilty of unlawful homicide.[3]

(b) The victim is ill. He suffers a wound that in itself is not fatal, but accelerates his death; the perpetrator is guilty of unlawful homicide.[4]

(c) The victim receives a non-fatal wound from a bullet, but then dies on the operating table due to the shock of the operation; the assailant is guilty of unlawful homicide.[5]

(d) The perpetrator hits the victim over the head and leaves him lying in a dark road at night. A short time later an automobile runs over the victim and kills him. The original assailant is guilty of unlawful homicide. If he had not left the victim unconscious in the road, he would not have been run over by the automobile.[6]

(e) The perpetrator shoots the victim in the abdomen. The pain is so severe that the victim commits suicide. The person who shot him is guilty of unlawful homicide.[7]

(f) Two men grab the victim and demand his money. In an effort to get away from them, he breaks loose and falls into the path of an oncoming cable car, causing his death. The two men are guilty of unlawful homicide.

(g) A man cuts his wife with a knife. In fear she runs to the bathroom and locks herself in. The wound, if treated, would not have been fatal, but the woman loses consciousness from loss of blood and then bleeds to death. The husband is guilty of unlawful homicide.

(h) In People v. Studern the District Court of Appeals stated that if a person creates a breach of the peace and, through the excitement thus induced, causes the death of a bystander by a brain hemorrhage, the death is that natural and probable consequence of such disturbance of the peace, and such person may be convicted of manslaughter.[8]

(4) When Death Occurs Within Three Years and a Day After the Initial Stroke or Cause of Death Administered

In the computation of such time, the whole of the day on which the act was done shall be considered the first day. (194 PC) Originally the time was one year and one day, but due to the advances of medical science and the ability of doctors to keep a person technically alive for years, the law was changed. In 1997 the law was changed to allow prosecution when the victim dies after three years and one day, however, the prosecutor has the burden of proof to show that the death was in fact the result of the initial assault. If the prosecutor fails to do this, the charge would be assault with a deadly weapon, or assault with intent to commit murder.

Mitigating Circumstances

If the prosecution proves the elements of homicide, excluding manslaughter and lawful homicide, and the defendant claims mitigating circumstances, the burden of proof for the mitigating circumstances is on the defendant. (1195 PC)

10.0:2 Breakdown of Homicide in California

(A) Unlawful Homicide (Felonious)
  (1) Murder
    (a) First Degree
    (b) Second Degree
  (2) Manslaughter
    (a) Voluntary
    (b) Involuntary
    (c) Vehicular

(B) Lawful Homicide
  (1) Excusable
  (2) Justifiable
    (a) In General
    (b) Peace Officers

10.1:0 UNLAWFUL HOMICIDE

10.1:1 Murder (187 PC)

Murder is the unlawful killing of a human being, or a fetus, with malice aforethought.

Malice (188 PC)

Malice may be expressed or implied. It is expressed when there is manifested a deliberate intention unlawfully to take away the life of a fellow creature; it is implied when no considerable provocation appears, or when the circumstances attending the killing show an abandoned and malignant heart. It can be assumed from the action.

Malice is shown when an act is accomplished in an unlawful and felonious way, intentionally and without legal reason. When a person intentionally commits an unlawful act and knows or should know that the act endangers the life of another, and it does result in someone's death without extenuating circumstances, provocation, or sudden passion, malice is presumed.[9] Malice may be present, without hatred or personal ill-will toward the victim. It does not imply deliberation. It does denote a purpose and design, not accident or misfortune.

The malice in first degree murder is expressed. In second degree murder it is implied. It is sometimes difficult for juries to determine from the facts whether the malice was expressed or implied.

Types of Acts Necessary for Murder

There are three:
(1) Willful, deliberate, and premeditated killing
(2) Statutory violations where the intent to kill is not required.
(3) Wanton and irresponsible acts

10.1:2 First Degree Murder

Fourteen conditions make murder first degree. Thirteen are statutory; one is conditional and debatable in court. Murder is first degree when it is perpetrated during, or by means of:
(1) Willful deliberation and premeditation.
(2) Explosives, a destructive device, or armor penetrating ammunition.
(3) Torture.
(4) Poison.
(5) Lying in wait.

This is one of the oldest known conditions for first degree murder. The Old Testament, (Exodus 21:14) states, "If a man kill his neighbor on set purpose, and by lying in wait for him; thou shalt take him away from my altar that he may die."

Felony Murder Rule

Murder is also first degree when the death results during the commission or attempt to commit one of the following crimes:
  (1) Mayhem
  (2) Drive-by shooting
  (3) Carjacking
  (4) Train wrecking
  (5) Selected sex offenses (261, 286, 288, 288a and 289 PC.)
  (6) Burglary
  (7) Arson
  (8) Robbery
  (9) Kidnapping

When the killing results from one of the statutory offenses, there need not be the intent to kill. It can be an accident.

It must be remembered that a crime, such as robbery, is not over when the victim is held up. Fleeing the scene is still part of the crime, and if the perpetrators hit and kill someone in a crosswalk while fleeing the scene, it still comes within the scope of the crime, and would be first degree murder.[10] There are two memory keys that will assist in remembering these fourteen points:

PET POLY

P — Premeditated
E — Explosives
T — Torture
Po — Poison
Ly — Lying in wait

MaD CaTS BARK

Ma — Mayhem
D — Drive-by shooting
Ca — Carjacking
T — Train wrecking
S — Selected sex offenses
(261, 286, 288,etc.)
B — Burglary
A — Arson
R — Robbery
K — Kidnapping

Definitions:

(1) **Willful:** means a purpose or willingness to commit the act or to omit the required act. It does not mean that the person intended to violate any law or to injure another.

(2) **Deliberate:** means that the purpose was formed or arrived at as a result of careful thought and the weighing of the various considerations. It is sometimes considered synonymous with premeditation.

(3) **Premeditation:** To think about and resolve in one's mind before doing. The length of time is not as important as the intent.

Killing Operator of Paid Transportation (190.25 PC)

When someone kills the driver of paid transportation for hire, or a ticket or station agent for the organization when he should reasonably know that the victim worked in such capacity, the punishment is life without parole.

The "Right To Die" Law (7189-7194 H & S)

This law allows persons to execute a directive to any doctor stating that life sustaining devices are to be withheld when the person has no chance of recovery without such devices. This document is good for five years or until revoked by the person originating the document. As with any legal document, it must be written when the person is of sound mind. Falsifying such a directive against the wishes of the patient, makes the person falsifying the document subject to prosecution for unlawful homicide if life sustaining devices are withheld.

10.1:3 Second Degree Murder

Murder in the second degree is distinguishable from murder in the first degree in that, while the element of malice aforethought is present in both degrees, the killing is not premeditated and is without considerable provocation. The malice in first degree is expressed; in second degree it is implied. (See malice, Page 236) If the killing is committed during a felony not listed under first degree, it is at least second degree murder. For example, a death resulting from an illegal abortion.

Inherently Dangerous Misdemeanors

If a wanton act is intentionally performed, and the natural consequences of that act would be dangerous to human life, any death resulting from such an act is murder in the second degree, even if the unlawful act is only a misdemeanor.[11] In order for the misdemeanor to qualify, it must be one that is inherently dangerous to human life.

Example:

If a parent were to abandon a very young child on a busy freeway at night it would be a violation of 271 PC or 273a PC, both misdemeanors. If, in panic, the child were to run out into the traffic and be killed, the parent would then be guilty of murder in the second degree because the misdemeanor was inherently dangerous.

If it is an act that involves consequences dangerous to life, and the person performing the act knows that this conduct endangers life, the act need not be unlawful for any resulting death to be classed as second degree murder.[12] An example would be dropping pennies from a tall building onto the sidewalk below where people are passing, not intending to hit anyone, but by accident hitting and killing a pedestrian.

Although most deaths resulting from drunken driving are classed as vehicular manslaughter, they can be classed as second degree murder. In the People v. Wallace[13] the death of a pedestrian was the result of the defendant driving an automobile while intoxicated. The courts affirmed that this could be classed as second degree murder. It also applies to deaths that result from the irresponsible driving of a stolen vehicle.[14]

The malice needed for second degree murder may be shown by the severity and the extent of injuries inflicted upon the victim. It could also be shown by the condition in which the victim was left by the perpetrator.[15]

If an adult administers narcotics to a minor, and the minor dies, it is second degree murder since it involves a felony.[16]

10.1:4 Manslaughter (192 PC)

Manslaughter is the unlawful killing of a human being without malice aforethought. There are three types of Manslaughter.

Voluntary Manslaughter (192(a) PC)

In voluntary manslaughter, there is the intent to kill, but it is brought on by sufficient provocation. This provocation is called "Heat of Passion."

"Voluntary manslaughter is a willful act, characterized by the presence of an intent to kill, engendered by sufficient provocation and the absence of premeditation, deliberation, and malice aforethought." "To be sufficient to reduce a homicide to manslaughter, the heat of passion must be such as would naturally be aroused in the mind of an ordinary, reasonable person, under the given facts and circumstances or in the mind of a person of ordinary self control."[17] The heat of passion which will reduce a killing to manslaughter may be generated by words of abuse or reproach.[18]

The classic "textbook" example of voluntary manslaughter is where a husband goes hunting, but for some reason, returns home early. When he enters the house, gun in hand, he finds his wife in bed with the next-door neighbor. He loses his temper and shoots either his wife or the neighbor.

This is a "textbook" example because the jury will nearly always find the defendant guilty of voluntary manslaughter, even in cases where it appears that the shooting might not have involved heat of passion. The jury feel they are carrying the moral standards of the  community on their shoulders. If they find the defendant guilty of second or first degree murder, they are in effect saying that finding your wife in bed with another man is really not that serious, and that a man should not lose his temper in such a situation.

Those who argue against the death penalty often argue that most murders are done in the heat of passion where the person does not have time to think about the penalty. Whether a person supports the death penalty or not , any student of law should know that killing another under these circumstances would be classed as voluntary manslaughter. No state has death as a punishment for voluntary manslaughter, only first degree murder.

Involuntary Manslaughter (192(b) PC)

There are three conditions that could cause a death to come under the classification of involuntary manslaughter. The three are:

(1) in the commission of a misdemeanor
(2) in the commission of a lawful act which might produce death in an unlawful manner, or without due caution and circumspection
(3) failure to perform a legal duty (this is not listed in the code, but is listed in case law; it is the "omission" side of #1)

In involuntary manslaughter there is no intent to kill. The law also states that none of these subdivisions shall apply to acts committed in the driving of a vehicle.

Examples:

(1) **In the commission of a misdemeanor:**
Clyde Crashcup gets mad at Homer Hashbrown and punches him in the nose while they are working at a construction site. Homer loses his balance and falls back into a piece of reinforcing rod that is sticking out of the cement wall. It punctures a vital organ and Homer dies. There is no intent to kill, but the proximate cause of the death is the misdemeanor Clyde committed by punching Homer in the nose.

(2) **In the commission of a lawful act, but in an unlawful manner without due caution:**
Bernard Boozer goes hunting with his new high powered rifle. He stays up late the first night playing cards and "hitting the bottle." The next morning he goes out hunting. After an hour of seeing nothing, he notices some movement in a clump of bushes. He aims his rifle and fires. Out rolls another hunter, shot through the head.
Bernard was performing a legal act. He had a license from the state of California authorizing him to hunt. However, he did this act without due caution and circumspection.

SORRY. I LOST MY HEAD!

(3) **Failure to perform a legal duty:** Millie Mashpott has an illegitimate son. She finds his presence painful, so she locks him up in the attic. Because she finds it psychologically unpleasant, she often forgets to feed him. As a result, he finally dies from malnutrition. Section 270 of the Penal Code makes it a legal duty for parents to feed their children.

Vehicular Manslaughter (192(c) & 192.5 PC)

In Vehicular Manslaughter, there is no intent to kill. It is similar to Involuntary Manslaughter except it involves a vehicle or vessel. If the act involves gross negligence, the punishment is greater.

The following acts do not involve driving or operating while under the influence.

(1) In the commission of a misdemeanor and involving gross negligence.

Example: Arvin drives 60 miles an hour in a residential area, skids around a corner on two wheels, then hits and kills a child in the street

(2) In the commission of a lawful act which might produce death in an unlawful manner with gross negliigence.

Example: Fred has a driver's license and is driving under the speed limit. A carload of girls comes alongside of Fred's car. They invite his passenger, Larry, to join them. Fred tells Larry to lean out the window and he will move closer to their car so Larry can climb over. As Fred moves his car closer to the other car, Larry skips and falls half out of the car. Fred drives too close and Larry is crushed between the two cars.

(3) In the commission of a misdemeanor, but without gross negligence.

Example: Sam is driving 35 MPH in a 25 MPH zone, and hits a young child who runs into the street.

(3) In the commission of a lawful act which might produce death in an unlawful manner, but without gross negligence.

Example: Henry has a driver's license and always drives under the speed limit. He is giving some friends a lift home from the local high school and the car is full. Mike, another friend, asks for a lift also, but since the car is full, Henry tells Mike that he will have to ride on the hood of the car. Mike hops on the hood and Henry takes off driving about 20 MPH. As Henry drives down the street, a car pulls out of a driveway and Henry slams on the brakes. Mike flies off the hood into the path of the other car and is killed.

Gross Vehicular Manslaughter While Intoxicated (191.5 PC)

Gross vehicular manslaughter while intoxicated is the unlawful killing of a human being without malice aforethought while driving a vehicle in violation of 23140, 23152, or 23153 CVC, or operating a vessel in violation of 655 H & N Code (under the influence) and the killing was the proximate result of:

(1) Commission of a misdemeanor (apart from driving under the influence) with gross negligence.

Example: Tom has been drinking and is intoxicated. As he is driving home he stops at a red light next to a friend. He challenges the friend to race him to the next light. When the light turn green Tom accelerates quickly to a very high speed. Near the end of the block an elderly man steps out from behind a parked car and is hit by Tom's car. He dies.

(2) The same as (1), but without gross negligence.

Example: Tom is driving while under the influence and is doing 30 MPH in a 25 MPH zone. He hits and kills a woman in a crosswalk.

(3) Commission of a lawful act (apart from driving under the influence) which might produce death in an unlawful manner and with gross negligence.

Example: Al is driving while under the influence of alcohol. He has a license and is driving just under the speed limit. He is so drunk that he drives onto the curb, hits a group of people standing at a bus stop, and kills two of them.

(4) The same as (3), but without gross negligence.

Example: Al is driving while under the influence of alcohol. He has a driver's license and is driving just under the speed limit. He hits and kills a woman crossing the street.

Proximate Cause:

Section 192(c)3 PC states that in Vehicular Manslaughter the death must be a proximate cause of committing the unlawful act, or lawful act which might produce death.

Gross Negligence:

The term "Gross Negligence" is a question of fact for the jury to decide. It has been described as "throwing all caution to the wind," "a complete lack of diligence," or "a complete indifference to safety." The term shall not prohibit a charge of murder when facts show wantonness and a conscious disregard for life supporting a finding of implied malice, or other evidence of malice.[19]

Examples:

Driving 80 miles an hour on a two lane road;[20] drag racing on a city street;[21] hitting a person in a clearly marked safety zone when visibility is good.[22]

10.2:0 LAWFUL HOMICIDE

10.2:1 Excusable Homicide (195 PC)

There are three things we look for in classifying a death as excusable homicide:

(1) There is no intent to kill
(2) No law is violated (lawful homicide)
(3) The person is using due caution.

The key words to excusable homicide are accident and misfortune. There are two sets of conditions that make a death excusable homicide:

(1) Committed by accident and misfortune when doing any lawful act by lawful means with usual and ordinary caution, without unlawful intent. OR

(2) When committed by accident and misfortune in the heat of passion upon any sudden or sufficient provocation. OR

Committed by accident and misfortune upon a sudden combat when no undue advantage is taken nor any dangerous weapon used when the killing is not done in a cruel manner and when the killing is not done in an unusual manner.

Examples:

(1) **(a)** A father has told his son not to shoot his BB gun in the back yard when other kids are present. He looks out the window and sees him doing just that. He calls him in and tells him since he did not obey, he is going to get two good swats on his rear end. The father gives his son one good swat and the boy feels he has had enough. He wiggles loose from his father's grip, falls against the stove and hits his head, causing a bad concussion that kills him.

   (b) Officer Smith is cleaning his gun on the kitchen table. When he is finished, he reloads it and starts to put it back into his holster. It slips out of his hands and falls to the floor on the hammer, causing the gun to fire. The bullet goes through the kitchen wall into the bedroom and kills Officer Smith's sleeping baby.

(2) **(a)** Fred Farkle is walking down the main street in town with his wife. As they pass one store, there is a group of "hard dudes" loitering around the front. One of them lifts up the back of Fred's wife's dress with a long bamboo cane as she passes and makes some obscene remark. Fred blows his top and punches him in the nose. He falls back and trips so his head hits the bumper of a parked car. The blow to his head causes a concussion that kills him.

Explanation;

The death was not intentional. It was by accident and misfortune. The proximate cause was the punch in the nose, brought about by heat of passion. It was incited by an act that is certainly both sudden and of sufficient provocation. No undue advantage was taken. No dangerous weapons were used, and the killing was not done in a cruel or unusual manner.

   (b) Arvin Ardvark is sitting in a bar when all of a sudden a big fight starts, and everyone joins in. Some "scum bag" approaches Arvin and takes a swing. Arvin jumps up and punches him in the nose. He falls backwards and hits his head against the brass rail at the bar. It causes a concussion which kills him. This situation would fit all the elements.

10.2:2 Justifiable Homicide (197 PC)
(There is the intent to kill or injure)

There are two classifications of justifiable homicide: Justifiable homicide by public officers, and justifiable homicide in general. Justifiable homicide is a lawful homicide for which there is no criminal punishment. (199 PC)

(A) Justifiable Homicide By Public Officers (196 PC)

(1) In obedience to any judgment of a competent court. (execution)

(2) Overcoming resistance to execution of some legal process or duty. (This section seems unnecessary since every example given in any law book falls under another classification such as self-defense.)

(3) In
   (a) Retaking escaped felons, or
   (b) Arresting fleeing felons, or
   (c) Arresting felons who are resisting arrest.

It must be remembered that the law does not allow the killing of a suspect or prisoner when the offense involved is just a misdemeanor. The feeling of the courts in this matter is that it is better that a misdemeanant escape than be killed.[23]

The theory behind justifiable homicide is not punishment. It is protection of the individual. Some would argue that an execution is indeed punishment. In California, however, it was never administered except when the defendant was a person whom the juries and courts felt did not belong in society (even including prison society). It also protects society as a whole.

This theory is being further developed by many departments who are enforcing departmental regulations that peace officers use deadly force only to save their own lives, or the lives of others. The Penal Code provisions regarding the killing of another under justifiable homicide are broad, but this does not prevent local agencies from further restricting the use of deadly force. It does not violate preemption.

Peterson v. City of Long Beach

The California Appellate Court, in Peterson v. City of Long Beach et al, ruled that the shooting of a fleeing burglary suspect was not justified because the suspect was running away from the officer, apparently not armed, and presented no fear of great bodily harm to the officer. This decision seems to give burglars a license to run. Most important is that it overrules the statutory law.

(B) Justifiable Homicide Generally

(1) When resisting any attempt at murder or a felony, or to do great bodily injury upon any person.

Since murder is a felony, it need not have been included in this section. It was put there as an example.

The part on an "attempt to do great bodily injury upon any person" is debatable. What action would amount to an attempt at great bodily injury? It must be remembered that the other party in this situation is now dead and cannot testify. Usually this section applies when a person comes to the aid of another person who is being victimized. The testimony of the victim is also important.

(2) Defense of habitation, property or person, against one who:
    (a) Manifestly intends by
        (i) violence or
        (ii) surprise
    (b) To enter the habitation of another
    (c) To commit a felony

OR:
    (a) Manifestly intends in a violent, riotous, or tumultuous manner
    (b) To enter the habitation of another
    (c) For the purpose of offering violence to any person inside

The second part needs little explanation. If a person tries to violently enter a house, his actions would in themselves justify both fear and self-defense.

The key words in the first part are "manifestly," "surprise," and "to commit a felony." (Violence is covered in part 2) Manifestly means the perpetrator does some act that leaves no doubt as to his intent. For example, cutting the screen outside the bedroom window so the person could then jimmy the window open, using some device such as a jimmy on the outside door, or turning the doorknob on a door entering the house.

Although there is not much case law in this matter, the California Supreme Court in People v. Flanagan[24] stated that, "The killing must be actually or apparently necessary." The term "apparently" leaves much room for interpretation, and since the other party is now dead, we have only the word of the person doing the killing.

A woman shoots her husband coming in the house late at night. She tells the police that she thought it was a burglar, and that her husband told her that he was not coming home for another day or two. Even if she murdered him, it would be almost impossible to obtain a conviction in court, especially if she was a good actor and shed many tears for her "dear, beloved husband."

The term "surprise" means that the perpetrator performed the manifest act in such a way as to avoid detection, or to commit the manifest act without being heard.

The term "to commit a felony" is much more difficult. The courts seem to allow a certain amount of conjecture. Why did the person try to enter the house in a surreptitious manner if it was not for the purpose of a felony? Even if it was for the purpose of stealing some small item, it would still be burglary because the entry was for the purpose of theft. Since burglary is a felony, it could be said that the entry was for the purpose of committing a felony.

Occasionally a householder will kill someone entering the house at night by accident and misfortune. For example, a woman who lived alone heard a noise like someone opening a window in the middle of the night. She got a gun and went to the bedroom that used to belong to her son. She opened the door and saw a dark figure coming through the window. She shot and killed the suspect. It turned out to be her son who was in the Navy. His ship had come in for repairs and he was given a special last-minute leave. He arrived home so late that he did not want to wake up his mother, so he tried to get into his own bedroom through the window.

Why wouldn't this be classed as excusable homicide? It was by misfortune. The answer is that the woman did intend to either kill or injure the person she shot. In excusable homicide, there is no intent to kill or injure.

Killing of Trespassers

There seems to be a common misunderstanding among the general public regarding the killing of trespassers. Trespassing is a misdemeanor. Unless the trespasser makes some manifest act that would indicate that he intends to enter the habitation, he is just a misdemeanor trespasser. He may be arrested, and that force used necessary to effect the arrest, but no deadly force may be used based solely on the fact that he is trespassing.[25] Any person killing another for trespassing alone is guilty of felonious homicide.[26]

Warnings to Intruder in Defense of Habitation

When a person feels that the intruders might be armed and dangerous, he is under no obligation to give warnings before shooting.[27]

(3) Self-Defense (and defense of certain others)

Section 197 PC states that self-defense is lawful when there are reasonable grounds to apprehend a design to do some great bodily injury, and imminent danger of such design being accomplished. In order for self-defense to be legal, it must appear to the person who is fearful of attack, as a reasonable person, not only that there is reason to believe he or she is in danger of receiving great bodily harm, but the actual belief that this will in fact happen.[28] In other words, there needs to be some evidence that the danger actually exists.

Bare Fear

Section 198 PC states that bare fear alone cannot justify a killing. There has to be some circumstance or overt act that is apart from this fear. Otherwise many people would be killed unjustly based only on a perception. For example, a little old lady is walking down the street. She looks around and sees a young man approaching her from behind. She sincerely believes that he is going to attack her. As he comes closer to her, she pulls out a gun and shoots him. The killing is not justified.

The fear, along with some overt act, must not be based on subjective feelings. Rather it must be fear that would be aroused in the average person in the same circumstances.

Previous Threats

Previous threats alone, when not accompanied by some hostile act, do not justify a homicide.[29]

Sam Snerd tells Freddie Farkle in front of 100 witnesses that the next time he sees him he is going to kill him. The next day, Sam comes to Freddie's house and knocks on the door. Freddie cannot shoot Sam when he opens the door. Sam must first commit some overt act (however slight) that would cause a reasonable person to feel he was about to commit great bodily harm. Reaching into his coat would be an example. The law does not require that a person wait until an assailant actually pulls out a gun, points it at him and starts to pull the trigger before he can act.[30]

Overt Acts Cannot be Created by The Slayer

The law does not allow the slayer to create a situation where the person slain is goaded into losing his temper or challenged into a fight, and during this altercation make some overt act that might justify self-defense.[31]

Amount of Force Limited to Circumstances

Obviously the defense must be against great bodily harm and not just simple battery. Again, the justification must be based on that of a reasonable person. The force used must be reasonable.[32]

There Is No Duty to Retreat in California

In some states and in many countries, it is required that when a person is attacked, that person must take one step backward to show that he or she does not wish to fight. That is not the case in California, where persons may not only stand their ground and defend themselves, but may pursue the assailant until they have secured themselves from danger.[33] Of course, it is to the slayer's advantage if it can be shown that he or she did in fact retreat, and that the attacker continued the assault. It would help remove any doubt that the slayer acted hastily.

When Danger Passes, So Does Justification

Once the danger from great bodily injury has passed, so does the justification of using deadly force against the attacker. The right of self-defense exists only as long as the danger itself exists.[34]

An exception would be if the assailant is retreating to procure better armaments. In this situation, the danger has not ceased but threatens to become greater. If Horace Hickle attacks Lester Lump with an axe handle which Lester is able to dodge, and Horace runs off stating "I'm going into the house to get a shotgun and really finish you off," the danger has not ceased, but increased. Lester will have a difficult time dodging a shotgun. At this point, although Horace seems to be retreating, Lester can use deadly force in self-defense.

Instigator Loses the Right to Self Defense

The person who starts the fight cannot use the excuse of self-defense. It would be too difficult to determine whether the fight was started for the purpose of creating a situation where the instigator could kill the other person.

For example, Percy Puke comes into a bar looking for a fight. He sees Arnold Ardvark sitting at the bar having a beer. Arnold is smaller than he is, so he approaches him and knocks his beer over. Arnold objects and Percy tells him to come outside or he will "deck" him right there. They go outside and the fight begins. Arnold turns out to be a better fighter than Percy thought. In fact he is cutting Percy to ribbons. Percy then becomes fearful that Arnold will cause him great bodily injury, so he pulls out a knife and stabs Arnold. Arnold dies. Percy claims self-defense and uses the doctor's report to show how badly Arnold had beaten him. Percy has no defense since he instigated the fight.

Exceptions:

(a) A peace officer never loses the right to self-defense (835a PC)

(b) If the instigator of a fight gives up, but the fight continues, he can regain the right to self-defense.[35]

(c) Private persons making legal arrests.

The reason that peace officers never lose the right to self-defense, even though they may be the instigators, is because when they are the instigators they are acting in behalf of the state, and law and order. There are times when they must instigate the action. A person is placed under arrest, and that person refuses to go. The officers first try to talk the prisoner into going along peacefully, but there comes a time when they must lay hands on the prisoner and forcibly restrain him or her. (Also private person's arrest)

When a private person is the instigator of a fight, and then gives up, this is, in effect, ending the first fight. Percy is getting the worst of the fight that he started, so he tells Arnold, "You're a better man than I thought; I give up." Technically the first fight is now ended. Arnold replies "You might have given up, but I just got started" and continues to fight. Percy can now legally use self-defense.

Mutual Combat or Duels (115 PC)

There is a difference between a duel and mutual combat. A duel is any combat with deadly weapons, fought between two or more persons, by previous agreement, or upon previous quarrel. Mutual combat is simply physical combat with or without weapons that has been agreed upon by all parties involved. In mutual combat, both parties

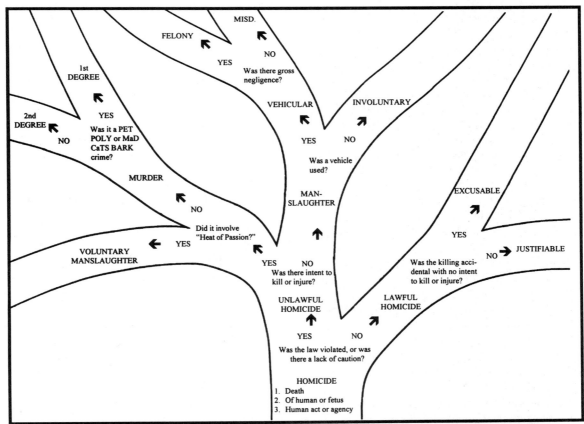

Fig. 10-1; Homicide Tree — By asking the above questions, the type or classification of a particular homicide can be determined.

Chapter Ten

are considered instigators so both parties lose the right to self-defense, unless one of them gives up. Killing another in mutual combat is murder.[36]

For example, A and B are drinking in a bar and start arguing. They agree, mutually, to go outside and fight. This would be a mutual combat.

(4) When Apprehending a Felon, Lawfully Suppressing Any Riot, or Lawfully Keeping and Preserving the Peace, When Done by Lawful Ways and Means

The legislative intent of this section is to encourage citizens to assist in the preservation of peace. This does not allow citizens to grab a shotgun, go to a riot and start shooting people. There must be an apparent or real imminent danger.[37] At many riots, however, there is this danger.

Today it is very doubtful that the police would welcome a group of irate, trigger-happy citizens at the scene of a riot. They have enough trouble on their hands as it is.

10.3:0 KIDNAPPING (207 & 209 PC)

In California there are two types of kidnapping. Regular kidnapping and ransom kidnapping.

10.3:1 Regular Kidnapping (207 PC) (Also called Simple Kidnapping)

In the Penal Code, the description of Kidnapping takes half a page. This is because the legislature gave examples for clarification. In this book, the law has been briefed to make it easier to understand without leaving out important elements.

In 1990, the legislature made an important change. Before this time the law only covered the moving of a victim. Now it covers the moving, holding or detaining of a person. This broadens the law considerably, and has an even more important effect on 209 PC as will be covered later.

207 PC does not require a specific intent. It need not be proved in court that the victim was moved for a particular reason as it does in 209 PC.

The elements of regular kidnapping are:
(1) The unlawful moving, holding or detaining of a person (Either asportation or detention)
(2) Against his or her will
(3) By force or any other means of instilling fear.

Exceptions:
(1) When the victim is a child under 14 and the taking is to protect the child from danger of imminent harm.
(2) The victim is taken under 834, 837 PC (legal arrest)

This law now applies to victims kidnapped in another state and brought into California.

Definitions:
(1) **Movement:** The courts require that the movement be "substantial" and not just "trivial." There is no simple formula regarding the term "substantial." The courts will judge each case based on the totality of the circumstances. If the distance moved would place the victim in a more dangerous situation regarding their personal safety or chances of rescue, the distance would be considered substantial. In view of the new element of "holding or detaining," the problem of defining "substantial" might be a moot question. The prosecutor will now charge the suspect(s) with just "detention" if the slightest detention can be shown .
(2) **Detention:** Restricting a person's free movement.

Against his or her will:

This term is all inclusive. It denotes a lack of consent on the part of the person being moved. A child or a mentally ill or deficient person is not capable of giving consent. However, in cases of this sort, an illegal purpose or intent must be shown.[38] This intent or purpose need not be shown in other kidnappings.

Consent by fraud:
(Consent by fraud is no consent.)

If a person gets into an automobile voluntarily, but later the driver takes this person to a place where he or she does not want to go, and against his or her will, it is kidnapping.[39] Obtaining the permission of the victim through threats or coercion is the same as having no permission. The permission has not been given freely.[40]

Kidnapping Occurs as Part of Another Crime

When the kidnapping is incidental to, and a means of accomplishing, another crime, only the more serious crime can be charged.[41] Also see Penal Code Section 654.

When kidnapping is part of another crime, kidnapping cannot become an additional charge unless the movement involved is substantial and not "incidental."[42] It must be above and beyond that needed to commit the other crime.

If simple kidnapping is part of another offense, the law does not require that the victim suffer increased risk of harm to also charge the defendant with kidnapping. This is required under 209 PC.[43]

False imprisonment can be a lesser offense to the crime of simple kidnapping.[44] Moving a person under the age of 14 from one place to another for the purpose of Lewd and Lascivious acts is also kidnapping. (207 PC).

The problem in multiple offenses is determining when the kidnapping is a separate offense from the other crime. If someone held up a gas station and took the attendant hostage to better effect an escape, this would be part of the robbery. There is, however, a distance where the escape would have been accomplished and the taking of the attendant any further would be a separate crime of kidnapping. The high court stated that each case of this sort must be judged by itself on it's own merit.

10.3:2 Ransom Kidnapping (209 PC) Also called the Little Lindbergh Law.

This crime involves two different offenses. The first is seizing OR kidnapping for ransom or extortion. The second is kidnapping for the purpose of robbery and selected sex offenses.

Briefed elements of ransom kidnapping:
(1) The seizing, enticing or kidnapping of another
(2) For the purpose of
   (a) ransom or
   (b) extortion. OR
(1) Kidnapping another
(2) for the purpose of robbery.

The high court has ruled that in order to charge Kidnapping for purposes of Robbery under 209 PC, the definition for "Kidnapping" will be the same as for 207 PC, simple kidnapping. The only difference is that, in 209 PC, the victim must have been placed in substantial risk of increased harm by the extended movement.

When robbery occurs during a kidnapping, the crime becomes "kidnapping for robbery," whether or not the kidnapper originally intended to rob the victim.[45]

Punishment for 209 PC
(1) Victim suffers no bodily harm:
   Life Imprisonment (Possible parole)
(2) Victim suffers bodily harm:
   Life Imprisonment
(3) Victim dies:
   Death penalty
(4) Victim confined in a dangerous manner:
   Life Imprisonment
(5) Probation:
   Minimum 12 months in county jail.

The Definition of the Term "Bodily Harm"

In the famous case of People v. Chessman,[46] the high court stated that the term means "any touching of the person of another against his will and with physical force in an intentional, hostile and aggravated manner of the projection of such force against his person." In this definition the word "intentional" is used. The law itself merely states that the victim must "suffer bodily harm."

Self-inflicted injuries suffered when escaping are NOT examples of bodily harm.[47] However, if the injuries occur as a result of the victim jumping out of a moving car after the kidnapper threatens rape, the courts hold that the threats are the proximate cause of the injuries and the law applies.[48]

Extortion by Posing as the Kidnapper (210 PC)

This section covers the person who, though he did not commit the kidnapping, tries to "cash in" on the offense by posing as the kidnapper and demanding ransom.

10.4:0 ASSAULT (240 PC)

The three elements to the crime of assault are:
(1) An unlawful attempt (to commit battery)
(2) coupled with the present ability
(3) to commit a violent injury upon the person of another

The term "simple assault" is often used interchangeably with the term "assault," and has been given recognition by the Appellate Court in the People v. Evan.[49]

The words used in the elements of assault are very important. The way the high courts have inter-preted these words has a great bearing on what actually comes under the classification of assault. The four most important terms are:

(1) Unlawful
Certain assaults are lawful—athletic events like boxing or football, medical operations, self-defense, and force used in making lawful arrests.

(2) Attempt
It must be remembered that this offense is an attempt and not the completion of the attempted offense. There need be no contact with the victim. The victim need suffer no injury.

(3) Present Ability
Present ability simply means that the act attempted is capable of being completed by the assailant. The key is the ability of the person attempting the unlawful act, and not the fact that some condition not controlled by the assailant prevents the intended injury from being inflicted.

If a person fired at police officers through a roof at a point where he believed them to be, but the officers were not hit because they had moved, that assailant would be guilty of unlawful assault.[50]

On the other hand, if the assailant were to point an empty revolver at another person who was a short distance away, it would not be classed as an assault because it is physically impossible for that gun to fire. There is no present ability.[51]

If there was ammunition in the clip, but no shell in the chamber of the gun, and the gun was pointed at another person, there would still be an assault because the present ability was there. All that was needed was to work the mechanism very quickly, and a shell would have been in the chamber ready to fire.[52]

If the assailant throws a rock or some heavy object at the victim, the distance can be very important. If the victim is far enough away that the assailant could not throw that far, there would be no "present ability" to complete the act, and therefore no crime of assault. This would be true even though there were present both act and intent.[53] In borderline cases, the defense attorney will use the lack of present ability as a defense.

(4) Violent Injury

The words "violent injury" are misleading. It sounds like something very severe. From a legal standpoint, it can be something quite simple and minor in nature. In the People v. Bradbury,[54] the court stated. "The kind of physical force is immaterial; it may consist in the taking of indecent liberties with a woman or laying hold of her and kissing her against her will."

The term "violent injury" as used in the section on assault merely means the unlawful application of physical force upon the person of another.

If Herbert Hickup took a swing at Clyde Crashcup and missed him, it would be classed as an assault. Threatening to kill persons, and then pointing a loaded gun at them would be classed as assault.[55] Spitting at a person and missing would be the attempt to make an unlawful application of force upon the person of another, and would be classed as an assault.

10.5:0 BATTERY (242 PC)

Battery is any willful and unlawful use of force upon the person of another. Battery is often called a completed assault.

If Harvey Hinkle swings at Mervin Mushmuscle and misses, it is assault. If he connects with Mervin's nose, it is battery.

Since battery is a completed assault, and since assault can be a very minor thing, battery can be very minor. Examples are:
  (a) grabbing a person's coat sleeve
  (b) pushing another person out of the way
  (c) pouring water on a person
  (d) spitting at a person and hitting him
  (e) setting a dog on another when the dog bites or touches him.
  (f) forcing another car off of the road
  (g) turning a water hose on someone

There can be no battery without also having an assault. Assault is a lesser offense of battery. If a jury believes that Harvey Hinkle did in fact take a swing at Mervin Mushmuscle, but that he really didn't touch him, they can find him guilty of the lesser offense of assault rather than the original charge of battery. There need be no injury nor infliction of pain in order for there to be a battery.

10.6:0 ASSAULT WITH A DEADLY WEAPON (245 PC)

Assault with a deadly weapon is more often referred to as "ADW" when used in the field by police officers. The elements are:
(1) Every person who commits an assault upon the person of another.
(2) With
  (a) a deadly weapon or
  (b) deadly instrument or
  (c) by any means of force likely to produce great bodily injury.

10.6:1 Definition of Deadly Weapon

A deadly weapon is any object, instrument, or weapon which, from the manner in which it is used, is capable and likely to produce death or great bodily injury.[56] For this section, the definition depends not upon the purpose for which an instrument is made, but the manner in which it is used.[57]

Examples of Instruments Classed As Deadly Weapons:
  (1) A sock filled with salt[58]
  (2) An iron pipe or bar[59]
  (3) A broken bottle[60]
  (4) A nail file[61]
  (5) An automobile[62]

Hands As Deadly Weapons

Hands may be deadly weapons if it can be proved that a person was trained in such a way that his hands were truly dangerous. (E.g., karate expert) Burden of proof is on the state to prove this.

Patrol officers often receive ADW calls when a battery has actually occurred. They must be careful that after a while they do not associate the term ADW with "Battery" with a deadly weapon. If they do, they may handle a case that only involves an assault and no battery, and "kiss off" the case on the grounds that no battery had occurred.

Circumstantial Evidence

There are many times that an ADW will occur, but when the police arrive at the scene, the weapon has disappeared. Can an ADW be proved without the weapon? The answer is yes. It can be done through testimony of witnesses and through the wound itself. If the wound is severe, and such that it could only be made with a sharp deadly instrument, the courts have held that this circumstantial evidence will suffice.[63]

ADW Cases Where The Assailant Has No Weapon

We normally think of ADW as an assault where the assailant possesses some type of a deadly weapon. There can be cases of ADW where the victim receives great bodily injury but not from an assailant's weapon.[64]

Examples would be where the assailant pushed another person out of a window. The bodily injury would occur from the sidewalk, not from a weapon.[65] Banging another's head against a parking meter,[66] would be another example.

ADW Also Includes Battery With a Deadly Weapon

It was the feeling of legislators that assaulting a person with a deadly weapon was such a serious offense, that they did not legislate a more serious offense of Battery with a Deadly Weapon.

Cases Where an ADW Has Not Occurred

If a person were to fire a gun into the air to frighten another person, without any intent of injuring or killing him, he would be guilty of 417 PC, (Displaying a Weapon in a Threatening Manner) but not ADW.[67]

If during an argument, one person pulled out a gun and stated "Don't come any closer; your life is in danger," the purpose of this display of a gun is not to commit an assault, but to protect himself.[68]

10.6:2 Assault With a Deadly Weapon on a Peace Officer, Fire Fighter, Transportation Worker or Custodial Officer

(1) Committing an ADW on one of the following persons:
    (a) A peace officer.
    (b) A firefighter.
    (c) A transportation worker, or passenger. (Bus or Taxi driver)(Light rail operator).
    (d) A custodial officer.
(2) When the person knows or should reasonably know that the victim is one of the above.
(3) And the victim is actually engaged in the performance of his or her duty.

10.7:0 RAPE (261 PC)

10.7:1 Rape In General

Rape has four elements. Three of them are always constant, and the fourth one varies according to how the rape was accomplished. The elements are:
(1) An act of sexual intercourse.
(2) Accomplished with a person.
(3) Not the spouse of the perpetrator.
(4) Under any of the following circumstances:
    (i) A person is incapable because of mental disease, defect, or disorder, or because of physical disability, of giving legal consent, and this condition is known or should be reasonably known to the perpetrator.
    (ii) It is accomplished against the person's will by means of force or fear of immediate and unlawful bodily injury on the person or another.
    (iii) Where the person is prevented from resisting by threats of great and immediate bodily harm, accompanied by apparent power of execution, or by any intoxicating narcotic, or anesthetic substance, and this condition was known or reasonably should have been known by the accused.
    (iv) Where the person is at the time unconscious of the nature of the act, and this is known to the accused. The following conditions apply to this subsection:
       1. was unconscious or asleep,
       2. was not aware, knowing, perceiving, or cognizant
          a. that the act occurred, or
          b. of the essential characteristics of the act due to the perpetrator's fraud in fact.
    (v) Where a person submits under the belief that the person committing the act is the victim's spouse, and this belief is induced by any artifice, pretense, or concealment practiced by the accused, with intent to induce belief.

(vi) Where the act is accomplished against the victim's will by threatening to retaliate in the future against the victim or any other person, and there is a reasonable possibility that the perpetrator will execute the threat.

As used in this paragraph, "threatening to retaliate" means a threat to kidnap or falsely imprison, or to inflict extreme pain, serious bodily injury, or death.

(vii) Accomplished by threat to use authority of a public official to
1. incarcerate,
2. arrest, or
3. deport,

the victim or another, and the victim has reasonable belief that the perpetrator is a public official.

Penetration (263 PC)

The essential guilt of rape consists in the outrage to the person and feelings of the victim of the rape. Any sexual penetration, however slight, is sufficient to complete the crime. The element of penetration in a rape case can be proved by both circumstantial and direct evidence.[69]

A conviction may be had for rape solely on the testimony of the victim. There need be no corroboration required.[70] This is unusual in criminal law. It is the feeling of legislators that the crime is a very severe one, and it is the type of a crime where there is often little evidence that could be used as corroboration. It must be understood, however, that the jury must be convinced beyond a reasonable doubt that the victim is telling the truth. They do not have to believe her, and the defense attorney will certainly put the victim through a very difficult cross examination.

Rape is an unusual crime in that it is often falsely reported, yet studies show that it is reported only about half of the time it occurs. It seems that many rape victims are so embarrassed at having been so personally violated, they refuse to report it, especially when the report will be taken by a male police officer most of the time.

Since the crime is so often falsely reported, the investigating officer must be very careful in questioning the victim and in obtaining vital information. The sooner the rape is reported, the more likely will the testimony of the victim be accepted in court. There was one case where the complaint was received three weeks after the rape occurred; the courts stated it was not made within a reasonable time, and ruled the complaint inadmissible.[71]

Element #1, Proof of Penetration

The first step investigating officers should take is to transport victims to a hospital where a doctor may examine them and determine if there is evidence of sexual penetration. If the doctor can find evidence of sperm or semen, it is good prima facie evidence of penetration, but not proof positive. It could have been put there by the victim's husband or boyfriend. When a doctor finds sperm or semen evidence, officers should ask victims in a confidential way if they have recently had intercourse with anyone else. If they say yes, the blood type of that person should be obtained. Then a special request should be sent to the crime lab to obtain the blood type from the semen. If it is different, it would block the defense in court that the semen belonged, not to the defendant, but to the victim's boyfriend or husband.

Other ways in which penetration can be corroborated is when the victim has become pregnant or contracted a venereal disease. In some cases, the fact that the victim has received physical injury such as scrapes and bruises is corroboration.

Element #2, Accomplished With a Person

This means that the victim must be a human being and not an animal. It also means that a woman can now legally commit rape on a male.

Element #3, Not the Spouse of the Perpetrator

Under section 261 PC, a spouse cannot rape another spouse. Rape of a spouse is covered under section 262 PC.

The "Principal" Concept of Rape

If a person assists another to commit rape, under the California classifications of "Principals," that person, male or female, would be just as guilty as the person who physically committed the rape. This could create an exception to 261 PC in that a husband could be guilty of the rape of his wife if he assisted another man to rape his wife. (Apart from section 262 PC)

Element #4, Subsections
(1) Where the Victim is of Unsound Mind

Legal consent requires that the victim have an intelligence capable of understanding the act, its nature and its possible consequences.[72] This can be difficult to determine in some cases. Technically this subsection covers persons under the mental age of 18, just as the crime of "Unlawful Intercourse" (Old Statutory Rape) covers persons under the chronological age of 18. However, the measuring of mental age is not a precise science, and any defense attorney can bring experts to show that test results can vary by as much as five years.

To play it safe, the District Attorney will want the victim to have a very observable lack of mental age, one that all the members of the jury will easily be able to detect by observing her on the stand. Because of this, the prosecutor will often want to personally talk to the victim in cases of this nature.

(2) Where it is accomplished by force or fear

This is the most commonly reported and prosecuted type of rape. It is also a class of rape that is often falsely reported, so officers should be most careful in their investigation of this type of offense.

Consent

The major defense in a rape of this type is that the victim gave consent and later changed his or her mind. People are legally entitled to give consent for each act of sexual intercourse. The fact that the victim was of unchaste character has no legal effect. In fact the victim could have had sex with the accused in the past. If consent was not given for the act in question, it is rape. The victim could even be a prostitute and it would be rape if permission was not given. To show lack of consent, the victim must either verbally or in a physical manner, make non-consent obvious (manifest).

Resistance

Unlike the old common law rule, resistance need not be "to the utmost." The resistance needs to be made manifest so that an ordinary reasonable person would be aware of the degree of feeling. Resistance need only last until penetration, when the crime becomes complete. Lack of resistance after that time is no defense.

(3) The Victim is Prevented From Resisting by Threats or Drugs

This now includes threats to do harm in the future, not only to the victim, but to another person.

Where the rapist held a knife against the victim's throat and told her that he would cut her throat if she cried out, the court held that she was in no way required to resist under such circumstances.[73]

Where the rapist had a knife, and threatened to kill her child, and where she was allowed to use a contraceptive device to avoid pregnancy, the court held that she was not required to resist.[74]

Threats as used in this subsection need not be expressed in words or through the exhibition of a weapon, but may be expressed by other acts and conduct.[75]

Rape through the use of drugs may be proved by circumstantial evidence.[76]

Where the victim and the defendant have consumed intoxicants, and she was later seen lying unconscious with the defendant nearby, and she later discovered physical evidence that someone had sexual intercourse with her, the courts held that this evidence along with other evidence was enough for a conviction.[77]

When a person reasonably determines that resistance will result in peril to his or her life or the safety of others, no further resistance is required.[78]

(4) Where Victim is Unconscious of the Nature of the Act

There is little in California case law in this area. There have been a number of convictions for this section, but none have been contested to higher courts where they could have interpretative rulings. One of the earliest cases, Regina v. Flattery, occurred in England in 1887. The victim thought that she was submitting to a surgical operation. Instead the doctor took advantage of the situation and made sexual penetration of her vagina.

Consent Obtained by Fraud

An earlier case occurred in the United States in 1872. In Don Moran v. People of Michigan, a doctor fraudulently induced a female patient to believe that sexual intercourse was essential to her medical treatment. She believed and submitted to sex. The court held that the consent was obtained by fraud, and a conviction was sustained.

Inducing Illegal Sex by Fraud (266c PC)

In 1986 this section was added to existing case law to make it clear that inducing sex by fraud was illegal. It also covers cases where the consent is obtained by fear.

Every person who induces another, other than the spouse of the perpetrator, to engage in

    (a) sexual intercourse,

    (b) oral copulation or

    (c) sodomy,

when the consent is obtained by fraud or with the intent to create fear (in a reasonable person) of unlawful physical injury or death to the victim or a relative, and which does in fact induce that fear, and causes the victim to act contrary to his or her free will, is guilty of a wobbler.

(5) Where the Victim Believed that the Perpetrator was Her Spouse

There are two common types of cases where this occurs. One is where the perpetrator sneaks into the bedroom of a woman whose husband is away. She is asleep, but senses someone sitting on the bed and getting undressed. He then gets into bed, and the woman, assuming it is her husband, allows the act of penetration to take place. When she discovers it is not her husband, the penetration has been made and the act of rape is complete.

The other type of case is where the perpetrator goes through a fraudulent or sham marriage with the victim, and she, believing it to be a legitimate marriage, allows the perpetrator to have sexual intercourse with her.[79] This type of offense could also be a violation of 266 PC.

Definitions:

Duress:

(1) A direct or implied threat of force, violence, danger, hardship, or retribution, or

(2) To coerce a reasonable person of ordinary susceptibilities to perform an act which otherwise would not have been performed, or

(3) Agree to an act to which one would not normally submit.

Further Corroboration: The circumstances of the situation, including the victim's age and his or her relationship to the defendant are factors to consider in determining the existence of duress.

Menace: any threat, declaration or act which shows an intention to inflict injury upon another.

Consent: For sections 261, 286, 288a, or 289 PC, a positive cooperation in an act or attitude involving the use of free will. The victim must not only act freely and voluntarily, but know the nature of the act. A current or previous dating relationship shall not be sufficient to prove consent. Neither admissibility of evidence nor burden of proof is affected by this definition. (261.1 PC).

Consent in Sex Offenses (261.7 PC)

(1) In prosecutions under sections 261, 286, 288a, or 289 PC,

(2) In which consent is an issue of defense,

(3) Evidence that the victim suggested, requested, or otherwise communicated to the defendant that he use a condom or birth control device,

(4) Without additional evidence of consent,

(5) Is not sufficient to constitute consent.

10.7:2 Rape Of Spouse (262 PC)

(1) An act of sexual intercourse

(2) With one who is the spouse of the perpetrator.

(3) By means of:

(a) force, violence, duress, menace, or fear of immediate and unlawful bodily injury to victim or another. (261.2 PC)

(b) Resistance prevented by intoxicating or anaesthetic substance. (261.3 PC)

(c) victim is unconscious of nature of act. (261.4 PC)

(d) by threat to retaliate in future against victim or another (261.6 PC)

(e) by threat of using public authority to incarcerate, arrest, or deport victim or another, and victim believes perpetrator is a public official. (261.7 PC)

(4) When

(a) a report is made to listed authorities within one year, or

(b) there is corroborating evidence beside the victim's testimony.

10.7:3 Unlawful Intercourse (261.5 PC)

Unlawful intercourse is the same as the old "Statutory Rape." It has been given a new name to remove it from the rape category since it never was really rape. It still has the same elements as "Statutory Rape." They are:

(1) An act of sexual intercourse

(2) Accomplished with a person

(3) Not the spouse of the perpetrator

(4) When the victim is under the age of 18 years.

Punishment

(1) Victim not more than three years older than perpetrator–misdemeanor

(2) Victim not more than three years younger than perpetrator–misdemeanor

(3) Victim more than three years younger than perpetrator–wobbler

(4) Victim under 16; perpetrator over 21–wobbler

Under the old law, if the girl was under 18 years of age, the defendant was guilty. There were no extenuating circumstances. Today there is one. If the "victim" appears to be over 18, the jury or judge can determine by observing the girl, as a "Question of Fact," whether she does appear to be over 18. If they feel she does, it removes the element of criminal intent, and the defendant may be found not guilty.[80] A person may be guilty of unlawful intercourse even if the victim is a married woman.[81] It is no defense if the perpetrator is younger than the victim and she was the aggressor.[81 Ibid] The victim could even have children. If she were under the age of 18, the law still applies.

10.8:0 ROBBERY (211 PC)

The term "robbery" is often misused by the general public. They will often say that they were robbed when they were really victims of theft or burglary. The newspapers are no help in this matter, since they constantly misuse the word. Will the real "robbery" please stand up?

10.8:1 The Elements of Robbery

(1) The felonious taking (asportation)

(2) Of the personal property of another

(3) From their person or immediate presence

(4) Against their will

(5) Accomplished by means of force or fear

Explanation of Elements

(1) The Felonious taking or asportation

The key to the term asportation, which means movement, is that the property was moved and not how far it was moved. The movement must be under the control or direction of the criminal.

In one case the victim was ordered by the robber to throw his wallet on the ground. The robber was arrested before he could pick up the wallet and was convicted in court of armed robbery. He contested the conviction on the grounds that the first element of asportation was not completed, as he did not move the wallet one inch. The Appellate Court held that the movement of the money from the victim's pocket to the floor was at the robber's command, and was thus asportation.[82]

(2) The Personal Property of Another

The property taken need not belong to the victim. In the case of a gas station robbery, the money does not belong to the attendant. The important fact is that the money does not belong to the robber.[83]

If the person taking the property happens to own it or have legal title to that property, his taking the property cannot be robbery. If a piece of property was owned by one person, but in the possession of another who refused to give it to the owner, and the owner retrieved the property by means of force or fear, it would not be classed as robbery because the second element of robbery "Of the personal property of another" would be missing.[84]

Even if the property did not belong to the person taking it, if he had a reasonable faith that it did belong to him, he could avoid a charge of robbery by using the defense of Mistake of Fact.[85]

(3) From Their Person or Immediate Presence

Normally this element would not need interpretation. "From his person" would be from his body or something worn. "From his immediate presence" would be from an area where he has immediate access to the property, for example: a briefcase. There have been situations, however, where the courts have held that the term "immediate presence" can be wider in definition. For example, if the robber were to force the victim into another room and tie him up and then return to where the money was kept and take it without the victim being present, it would still be considered to be from his immediate presence.[86]

This also applies where the perpetrator scares the victim into running off and leaving his property.[87] It would be robbery and not theft if the perpetrator pointed a gun at the cashier of a movie theater, and she ran out the back door of the booth, and he then entered and took the money. Removing the victim from the money and then taking it is the same as taking the money from the victim.

(4) Against His Will

This is the major difference between robbery and extortion. Sometimes it might appear that the victim is going along with the robbery, but he is doing so out of force or fear. He may be given the choice of "your money or your life." If it can be shown in court that the taking was not against the will of the victim, it is a good defense because this is an essential element.

An unusual conviction of robbery occurred after the defendant forced the victim at gun-point to participate in a dice game in which he lost all of his money.[88] It was considered against his will.

(5) Accomplished by Means of Force or Fear

The word "or" is very important. It means that there is a choice of the two. Both of them are not necessary for this element to be completed.[89]

Force

In order for force to be a valid element, it must be more force than is needed to carry off the property. This rule is important, especially in the common crime of "Purse Snatch." The mere fact that the perpetrator took the purse from the victim does not necessarily mean that force was used.

If the person were to sneak up on the victim, and then slip the purse off her arm so quickly that she did not have time to grab it and hold on to it, or for that matter, give it up voluntarily out of fear, the element of force would not apply. The only force used in this case would be that needed to carry off the purse.

Now let's change the situation a bit. Harry Hashbrown sneaks up on Tilly Tiddlywink with the intent of grabbing her purse. She hears him coming and guesses that he is after her purse. When he grabs for the purse, she holds on for dear life. He pulls very hard and she holds on all the tighter. A tug-of-war results. Finally Harry gives a strong pull and gets the purse loose and runs off with it. This is robbery because the force used was more than that needed just to carry off the purse.

In police work, the term "Strong Arm Robbery" is the term used for a robbery where the property is taken from the victim by force.

Fear

Section 212 of the Penal Code states that the fear mentioned in section 211 PC may be either:

(a) The fear of an unlawful injury to the person or property of the person robbed, or of any relative or member of his or her family.

(b) The fear of immediate and unlawful injury to the person or property of any one in the company of the victim at the time of the robbery.

Defense attorneys will often try to shame victims into stating they really weren't afraid of the robber. If this neat little trick is accomplished, it is of no avail. In the People v. Borra,[90] the Appellate Court noted that the circumstances can supply the proof of fear even though the victim might state that he wasn't afraid. In the case of People v. Callihan,[91] the court stated that "intimidation" is the same as "fear" in the crime of robbery.

Let's go back to Harry Hashbrown and Tilly Tiddlywink. If Harry told Tilly that she had better give up her purse or else, the element of fear would be present and we would have a robbery.

Robbery can be proved by circumstantial evidence. So can the degrees of robbery. For example; Bill is seen with John. A short time later John is found unconscious with his money missing. This can be enough to convict Bill.[92]

10.8:2 Degrees Of Robbery (there are two)

(A) First Degree Robbery (212.5 PC)
(1) Robbery of
   (a) An inhabited dwelling (etc.).
   (b) An inhabited vessel (21 H & N Code)
   (c) An inhabited trailer coach, or
   (d) An operator of paid transportation.
   (e) An inhabited floating home (18075.55 H & S)
   (f) A person using an ATM machine, or in the vicinity of an ATM machine after having used it.
(2) is first degree robbery. (3,4 or 6 years prison)

(B) Second Degree Robbery
All other robberies are second degree robbery.

10.8:3 Robbery of a Pharmacy
Whenever the robbery is of a pharmacy or a pharmacist, or other person in control of narcotics (controlled substances) and the purpose of the robbery is to obtain narcotics, the judge must give the longer of the three optional sentences.

10.8:4 Robbery and Extortion
Although robbery and extortion are found a considerable distance apart in the Penal Code, they are so similar in many respects that it is best to cover them consecutively so that the similarities can be discussed. The slightest change in one element can require that a suspect be charged with extortion rather than with robbery. The student of criminal law should know these differences.

10.9:0 EXTORTION (518 PC)

Extortion is often referred to as "blackmail." The key between robbery and extortion is that in extortion the victim parts with his property willingly. In other words, he gives his consent to the operation. It is a very broad crime, and can be used when robbery would not apply. Look below and compare the conditions of "fear." An example will be given for illustration.

Harrison Dunkenheimer and his girlfriend, Kitty Krump, are walking down the street. Mervin Maggot approaches them and tells Harrison that if he does not give Mervin $10, tomorrow he will cut off one of Kitty's ears. Harrison believes Mervin and gives him the $10. Is it robbery or extortion?

It must be extortion for two reasons:

(1) Under the crime of robbery, a girl friend does not come under the "any relative" category.

(2) Under the crime of robbery, anyone in the victim's company must be subjected to an immediate possibility of injury. Not tomorrow, as was the case here.

In the crime of extortion, a "third person" can be the object of the threat, and the threat can be carried out at any time.

Other Differences

(1) There need be no asportation or taking on the part of the perpetrator. The money could be sent in the mail. It could be sent to a third party, or it could be deposited in a bank account.

(2) What is obtained can be the official act of a public officer rather than just personal property of another as in robbery.
    For example: On the day that the city council votes for a raise in police salaries, an officer in the vice detail calls Councilman Larry Lillywaiver, and tells him that if he does not vote for the police raise, he will tell everyone that Larry was arrested in Kansas City for indecent exposure.

(3) The fear can be fear of secrets being exposed.

In midwestern and eastern cities, organized crime uses the "shakedown" or "payoff" type of extortion where a person pays the organization a certain amount of money to stay in business, or his place will "accidentally" burn down.

Today a borderline type of extortion is practiced by militant political groups and some labor organizations. They will boycott and picket certain businesses for the purpose of getting them to change certain procedures or in some cases to "donate" to their particular cause.

Example: You attend a football game, and park your car on the street. You are approached by a tough looking juvenile who states that for two dollars he will watch your car and see that your tires are not slashed. If you give him the money, what is the offense? It would most likely be extortion because you are in effect going along with the scheme. It is borderline because he has not actually made a threat. It is implied.

Comparison of the Corpus Delicti of Robbery (211 PC) and Extortion (518 PC)

Robbery
(1) The felonious taking (asportation)
(2) Of the personal property of another
(3) From the victim's person or immediate presence
(4) **Against his or her will**
(5) By means of force or fear

Fear in Robbery Can Be
(1) Threat of unlawful injury (at any time) to
    (a) the victim, or
    (b) the victim's property, or
    (c) any relative of the victim; OR
(2) The fear of immediate & unlawful injury to:
    (a) the victim, or
    (b) the victim's property, or
    (c) anyone in the victim's company

Extortion
(1) The obtaining (not necessarily taking)
(2) Of
    (a) the personal property of another, or
    (b) an official act of a public officer
(3) **With his or her consent**
(4) Induced by wrongful use of force or fear

Fear in Extortion Can Be
(1) Threat of unlawful injury (at any time) to:
    (a) the victim, or
    (b) the victim's property, or
    (c) any relative of the victim, or
    (d) <u>a third person</u>; OR
(2) Fear of being accused of a crime (victim or relative); OR
(3) Fear of deformity, disgrace, or crime being exposed; OR
(4) Fear of any secret being exposed

10.10:0 DISTURBING THE PEACE (415 PC)

Any of the following actions are punishable:
(1) Any person who unlawfully fights in a public place OR challenges another person, in a public place, to fight, or:
(2) Any person who maliciously and willfully disturbs another person by loud and unreasonable noise (not in a public place), or:
(3) Anyone who uses offensive words in a public place which are inherently likely to provoke an immediate violent reaction.

The law is very broad because some of the words are subject to interpretation. What is the meaning of the word unreasonable? Today, many officers carry audiometers that measure the decibels of any sound. This holds up in court very well.

10.11:0 BURGLARY (459 PC)

The three elements of burglary are:
(1) The entry
(2) Of a building, or one of the following:
    (a) Tent
    (b) Vessel (21 H & N)
    (c) Floating Home (18075.55 H & S)
    (d) Railroad Car
    (e) Trailer Coach (635 CVC)
    (f) House Car (362 CVC)
    (g) Inhabited Camper (243 CVC)
    (h) Locked Vehicle
    (i) Sealed Cargo Container (458 PC)
    (j) Aircraft (21012 PUC)
    (k) Mine or any underground part of mine.
(3) With the intent to:
    (a) Commit a theft, or
    (b) Commit a felony

Definitions

(a) **Vessel** (21 H & N Code) The word "vessel" includes ships of all kinds, steamboats, canalboats, barges, and every structure adapted to be navigated from place to place for the transportation of merchandise or persons.

(b) **Trailer Coach** (635 CVC) A "trailer coach" is a vehicle, other than a motor vehicle, designed for human habitation, or human occupancy for industrial, professional commercial purposes, for carrying persons and property on its own structure, and for being drawn by a motor vehicle.

(c) **Vehicle** (670 CVC) A "vehicle" is a device by which any person or property may be propelled, moved, or drawn upon a highway, excepting a device moved by human power or used exclusively upon stationary rails or tracks.

(d) **Aircraft** (21012 PUC) An "aircraft" includes any contrivance used or designed for flying except a parachute or other contrivance used primarily for safety.

(e) **House Car** (362 CVC) A motor vehicle originally designed, or permanently altered, and equipped for human habitation, or to which a camper has been permanently attached.

(f) **Camper** (243 CVC) A structure designed to be mounted upon a motor vehicle and to provide facilities for human habitation.

Meanings of the Elements of the Corpus Delicti for Burglary

(1) Entry:

There are two types of entry.

    (a) Actual
    (b) Constructive

Unlike other states and the military, forced entry is not required in California; any entry is sufficient.[93] The perpetrator could even be invited in.

(a) Actual Entry

This occurs when any part of the body enters the building or room. In most cases it is the whole body, but it can be any part of the body such as a hand reaching inside to steal something.[94]

(b) Constructive Entry

This occurs when the perpetrator does not actually enter the building, but uses some other person or a device that is under his control. An example would be the use of a trained monkey to make entry and look for valuables. It could also be a small child or even a device such as a fishing pole.[95]

(2) Of a building
    (or another place mentioned in the code)

The definition of a building is a structure with walls on all sides and covered by a roof.[96]

This definition is important, for it does not list a set number of walls (such as four). Therefore it can include a round house, or an octagon house. It can also include a cave that has a wall constructed at its entrance.[97]

Not only does it have to have walls on all sides, but one wall can be substituted with a door, as in a garage. Not only that, but the door does not have to be closed as long as it is in working condition.[98]

The building does not have to be intended for human habitation. A chicken house can be a building for the purposes of burglary.[99]

An old-style telephone booth can also be considered a building because it has walls on all sides and a roof, and a door substitutes one wall.[100]

For a vehicle to be the subject of burglary, the doors must be locked. If the doors are locked and the truck is locked, and a tire is taken from the locked trunk, it is burglary.[101]

However, if a semi-trailer is attached to a cab, and the semi-trailer is sealed, breaking into the semi-trailer would be burglary even though the cab was not locked.[102]

An old passenger bus that has been put on cement blocks, and is used as an office, can also be the subject of burglary.[103]

(3) With Intent to Commit Theft or a Felony

No crime need occur once entry is made with specific intent. Entry of a building with intent to commit murder or felonious assault is classed as burglary even if the intended victim is not there.[104]

Proving Intent

Proving intent can be a difficult task at times. Good attorneys have books of excuses on why a person might be in a building apart from being there to commit a theft or a felony.

In some California cases, convictions were sustained with very little circumstantial evidence.

- When a man was found inside a building where he had no permission to be, it was held to be prima facie evidence that he entered with the intent to commit a theft or a felony.[105]

- A man ran when hailed by the occupant of a building in which he had no legitimate business; this was held to be prima facie evidence of intent.[106]

Despite the cases cited, it is most difficult to obtain a conviction for burglary when there is a lack of good evidence to show intent. Some cases involving a stronger case of intent are:

- A defendant removed his shoes and entered an apartment where he had no legal business, and then ran when the owner saw him. It was held that there was sufficient evidence of the specific intent to steal.[107]
- In one case it was shown in court that the defendant had already arranged for the disposal of property that was to be taken in the burglary, before the burglary occurred.[108]
- Where the defendants used a "short change" scheme or trick that involved a lot of practice and skill, it was held that this was proof that they entered the food market with the intent to commit theft.

10.11:2 Shoplifting as Burglary

In the People v. Lowen,[109] it was held that if a person entered a building, and while inside, developed the intent to steal, and did then steal something, that it would not be burglary because he did not enter with that intent.

If it can be shown that a person did enter with the specific intent to steal, then it would be burglary. For example, if the defendant were to enter a store with a "booster box" (a device with a hidden spring trap door on the bottom in which stolen items may be hidden), entry of the store with that device would make the person guilty of burglary.[110] A special belt made for the concealing of merchandise would also make one guilty of burglary if it was taken into a department store.[111]

Persons who have no money when arrested for shoplifting did not necessarily enter the store to shoplift. They may have been passing time while waiting for the next bus, and formed the intent while inside the store.

10.11:3 Degrees of Burglary (460 PC)

(1) Burglary of the First Degree

Burglary is of the first degree when it is of an inhabited:

(a) Dwelling house, or
(b) Trailer coach (as per CVC), or
(c) Portion of any other building, or
(d) Vessel designed for habitation
(e) Floating home (18075.55 H & S)

(2) Burglary of the Second Degree

All other burglaries are burglaries of the second degree.

Definition:

Inhabited: When a building is normally used as a dwelling house, it is considered inhabited even if no one is there at the time.[112] The key is whether or not they return.[113] Includes places unoccupied due to disaster.

10.12:0 THEFT (484 PC)

There are three legal elements for theft. There is sometimes a fourth element, but it is not a legal one, and is assumed in most cases.

(1) The unlawful taking (or asportation),
(2) Of the personal property of another,
(3) With the specific intent of permanently depriving the owner

The sometimes assumed fourth element is:

(4) Without the owner's permission

This element becomes important later in the discussion of embezzlement and 532 PC (fraud). It is assumed, in cases of theft, that it is against the owner's will because consent is a defense to theft. However, since the prosecution need not prove this, it is not an element of the corpus delicti. If it is used as a defense, the burden of proof rests on the defendant. It must be remembered that, in cases of fraud (a type of theft), the victim voluntarily gives up the property.

Discussion Of The Elements
(1) Asportation

As with robbery, the key to asportation is some movement, not how far. One inch is enough. If, for example, a man were to grasp the handle of a suitcase, and was then arrested, there would be no theft because there was no movement or asportation. If, however, the perpetrator were to lift the suitcase four inches in a vertical direction, there would be movement, and theft could be charged.[114]

(2) The Personal Property of Another

This does not mean that the victim must own the property. It merely means that the property is not owned by the thief. If the victim has rightful possession, the property need not belong to him or her.[115] However, this rule would apply even if the victim had stolen the property. The key is that the perpetrator has no legal right to the property.[116]

In order for the property to be the subject of theft, it must have some legal value. Thus an illegal lottery or betting ticket would be contraband, and would have no legal value. Theft of such an item would not be theft from a legal standpoint.[117]

(3) With the Specific Intent of Permanently Depriving the Owner

Although it is not written into the code, intent must exist in the mind of the perpetrator at the time of the theft.118 It is obviously a difficult thing to prove what was in someone's mind. We must rely upon circumstantial evidence. In one case the Appellate Court affirmed a conviction of grand theft auto because the suspect had purchased sixteen gallons of gasoline after stealing the car, and this was held to be a significant act toward proving the intent to permanently deprive the owner.

(4) Consent

One of the best defenses in a theft case is consent. If the defense can convince just one member of the jury that the defendant was given permission to take the property, the trial will at least end in a hung jury. Remember that the prosecution does not have to prove lack of consent.[119]

10.12:1 Degrees Of Theft (486 PC)

In California, there are two degrees of theft, Grand Theft (section 497, felony) and Petty Theft (section 488, misdemeanor). Grand Theft is a complicated classification due to the many conditions under which a person can be guilty. Major considerations in determining Grand Theft are:
(1) What was the value of that taken?
(2) What was the particular item taken?
   (a) Certain items can come under Grand Theft at a reduced value. (e.g., Olives)
   (b) Certain items come under Grand Theft regardless of their value.
(3) Over what period of time? (e.g., small thefts over a period of less than one year)
(4) Was it taken from the person of another?
(5) What was the purpose of the theft? (E.g., stealing animals for the purpose of research)

10.12:2 Grand Theft (487 PC)

(1) When the money, labor or property taken is:
   (a) Of a value exceeding four hundred dollars ($400), or:
   (b) Of a value exceeding one hundred dollars ($100) AND the item taken is one of the following:
      (i) Domestic fowls
      (ii) Farm crops (fruits, vegetables, olives)
      (iii) Aquacultural products: (fish, shellfish, kelp, mollusks, crustaceans, algae), or:
   (c) The money, labor or property is taken by a servant, agent, or employee from their principal or employer, and the amount aggregates to four hundred dollars ($400) or more in any consecutive 12 month period. OR:

(2) When the property is taken from the person of another. OR:
(3) When the property taken is:
   (a) A firearm
   (b) A member of the horse, cow, goat, sheep or pig family. (Briefed) (The names used in the Penal Code are horse, mare, gelding, any bovine animal, any caprine animal, mule, jack, jenny, sheep, lamb, hog, sow, boar, gilt, barrow, or pig.)

10.12:3 Other Grand Theft Classifications

Grand Theft Of Real Estate (487c PC)
(1) Every person who converts $100 or more of real estate
(2) Into personal property
(3) By severance from the realty of another
(4) With felonious intent
(5) Is guilty of Grand Theft

Petty Theft Of Real Estate (487c PC)
(1) Every person who commits the above elements, but under $100.
(2) Is guilty of Petty Theft.

Grand Theft At A Mine (487d PC)
(1) Every person who feloniously steals, takes, or attempts to take
(2) From any
   (a) mining claim,
   (b) tunnel,
   (c) sluice,
   (d) undercurrent,
   (e) riffle box, or
   (f) sulfurate machine,
(3) Another's
   (a) gold dust,
   (b) amalgam, or
   (c) quicksilver
(4) Is guilty of Grand Theft.

Definition: Amalgam is an alloy of silver mixed with another metal.

Theft of Animals for Special Purposes (487e PC)

(1) Every person who feloniously steals or takes an animal belonging to another person. ("Feloniously" means with criminal intent)

(2) For the purpose of either:
    (a) Sale
    (b) Medical research, or
    (c) Commercial uses

(3) Is guilty of Grand Theft.

Note: Theft of animals with a value of over $400 is Grand Theft no matter what the purpose.

10.12:4 Petty Theft (488 PC)

All other thefts are Petty Thefts (misd.).

10.13:0 VANDALISM (594 PC)

Vandalism (Wobbler)

(1) Who does one of the following:
    (a) Sprays, scratches, writes, or otherwise defaces, or
    (b) Damages, or
    (c) Destroys

(2) Real or personal property not his or her own

(3) Is guilty of vandalism.

Punishment

(a) If value is less than $1,000,
    (Misdemeanor–6 months and/or $1,000 fine)

(b) If value is between $1,000 and $5,000
    (Misdemeanor–1 year and/or $5,000 fine)

(c) If value is between $5,000 and $50,000
    (Wobbler–1 year and/or $10,000 fine)

(d) If value is $50,000 or more
    (Wobbler–1 year and/or $50,000 fine)

Local jurisdictions may pass ordinances controlling the sale of aerosol paint containers.

A court may require, as a condition of probation, that a person guilty of this violation wash, paint, or repair the defaced property or otherwise make restitution to the property owner.

(728 W & I) Requires a juvenile to restore damage if given probation

(594.3 PC) Vandalism of a place of worship. (felony)

Liability Limits for Vandalism (1714.1 Civil Code)

The liability of parents for damage committed by their children is limited to $10,000. (Property or injury) (per child, per act). If damage is to school property, limit is $10,000 (Ed Code 48910).

REFERENCES FOR CHAPTER X

(1) People v. Scott (176 Cal. App. 2d 458)
(2) People v. Smith (59 Cal. 3d 751)
(3) People v. Cord (157 Cal. 562)
(4) People v. Moan (65 Cal. 532)
(5) People v. Freudenberg (121 Cal. App. 2d 564)
(6) People v. Fowler (178 Cal. 657)
(7) People v. Dallen (21 Cal. App. 770)
    People v. Lewis (124 Cal. 551)
(8) People v. Studern (59 Cal. App. 547)
(9) People v. Semone (140 Cal. App. 318)
(10) People v. Chavez (37 Cal. 2d 656)
(11) People v. Copley (32 Cal. App 2d 74)
(12) People v. Phillips (64 A.C. 629)
(13) People v. Wallace (2 Cal. App. 2d 238)
(14) People v. Pulley (225 Cal. App. 2d 366)
(15) People v. Taylor (189 Cal. App. 2d 490)
(16) People v. Poindexter (51 Cal. 2d 142)
(17) People v. Bridgehouse (47 Cal. 2d 406)
(18) People v. Valentine (28 Cal. 2d 121)
(19) People v. Watson (30 Cal. 3d 290)
(20) People v. Markham (153 Cal. App. 2d 260)
(21) People v. Kemp (150 Cal. App. 2d 654)
(22) People v. Flores (83 Cal. App. 2d 11)
(23) People v. Post (107 Cal. App. 550)
(24) People v. Flanagan (50 Cal. 2)
(25) People v. Corlett (67 Cal. App. 2d 33)
(26) People v. Doyell (48 Cal. 85)
(27) Nakashima v. Takara (8 Cal. App. 2d 35)
(28) People v. Head (105 Cal. App. 331)
(29) People v. Lynch (101 Cal. 229)
(30) People v. Hatchett (63 Cal. App. 2d 144)
(31) People v. Finall (31 Cal. App. 479)
(32) People v. Morine (61 Cal. 371)
(33) People v. Zuckerman (56 Cal. App. 2d 366)
(34) People v. Keys (62 Cal. App. 2d 903)
(35) People v. Hoover (107 Cal. App. 635)
(36) People v. Bush (65 Cal. 129)
(37) People v. Roe (189 Cal. 548)
(38) People v. Oliver (55 Cal. 2d 761)
(39) People v. Trawick (78 Cal. App. 2d 604)
(40) People v. Dagampat (167 Cal. App. 2d 492)
(41) People v. Nelson (233 Cal. App. 2d 440)
(42) In re Earley (120 Cal. Rptr. 887)
(43) People v. Williams (269 Cal. Rptr. 705)
(44) People v. Magana (281 Cal. Rptr. 338)
(45) People v. Brown (29 Cal. 555)
(46) People v. Chessman (38 Cal. 2d 166)
(47) People v. Gilbert (63 Cal. 2d 690)
(48) People v. Monk (56 Cal. 2d 288)
(49) People v. Evan (91 Cal. App. 44)
(50) People v. Lee Kong (95 Cal. 666)

(51) People v. Bennett (37 Cal. App. 324)
(52) People v. Simpson (134 Cal. App. 646)
(53) People v. Yslas (27 Cal. 630)
(54) People v. Bradbury (151 Cal. 675)
(55) People v. Montgomery (15 Cal. App. 315)
(56) People v. Franklin (70 Cal. 641)
(57) People v. Robertson (217 Cal. 671)
(58) People v. Valliere (123 Cal. 576)
(59) People v. Car (131 Cal. App. 664)
(60) People v. Sampson (75 Cal. App. 2d 571)
(61) People v. Russell (59 Cal. App. 2d 660)
(62) People v. Claborn (224 Cal. App. 2d 38)
(63) People v. Stevens (15 Cal. App. 294)
(64) People v. Tallman (27 Cal. 2d 209)
(65) People v. Emmons (61 Cal. 487)
(66) People v. Conley (110 Cal. App. 2d 731)
(67) People v. McGee (31 Cal. 2d 229)
(68) People v. Diamond (33 Cal. App. 2d 518)
(69) People v. Vicencio (71 Cal. App. 2d 36)
(70) People v. Frye (117 Cal. App. 2d 101)
(71) People v. Corey (8 Cal. App. 720)
(72) People v. Griffin (117 Cal. App. 583)
(73) People v. Trapps (152 Cal. App. 2d 413)
(74) People v. Blandership (171 Cal. App. 2d 66)
(75) People v. Flores (62 Cal. App. 2d 700)
(76) People v. Crosby (17 Cal. App. 518)
(77) People v. O'Brien (130 Cal. 1)
(78) People v. Nazworth (152 Cal. App. 2d 780)
(79) People v. McCoy (58 Cal. App. 534)
(80) People v. Hernandez (61 Cal 2d 537)
(81) People v. Derbert (138 Cal. 467)
(82) People v. Wellman (141 Cal. App. 2d 101)
(83) People v. Downs (114 Cal. App. 2d 758)
(84) People v. Vice (21 Cal. 334)
(85) People v. Sheasby (83 Cal. App. 459)
(86) People v. Dean (66 Cal. App. 602)
(87) People v. Sylvis (72 Cal. App. 632)
(88) People v. Unipeg (118 Cal. App. 485)
(89) People v. Ferrara (31 Cal. App. 1)
(90) People v. Borra (123 Cal. App. 482)
(91) People v. Callihan (81 Cal. App. 2d 928)
(92) People v. Hubbler (102 Cal. App. 2d 689)
(93) People v. Ferns (27 Cal. App. 285)
(94) People v. Pettinger (94 Cal. App. 297)
(95) People v. Allison (200 Cal. 404)
(96) People v. Stickman (34 Cal. 242)
(97) People v. Buyle (22 Cal. App. 2d 143)
(98) People v. Picaroni (131 Cal. App. 2d 612)
(99) Brooks v. Sessagisimo (139 Cal. App. 679)
(100) People v. Miller (95 Cal. App. 2d 631)
(101) People v. Toomes (148 Cal. App. 2d 465)

(102) People v. Massie (241 Cal. App. 2d 1023)
(103) People v. McLaughlin (156 Cal. App. 291)
(104) People v. Schwab (136 Cal. App. 2d 280)
(105) People v. Swenson (28 Cal. App. 2d 636)
(106) People v. Noon (1 Cal. App. 44)
(107) People v. Franklin (153 Cal. App. 2d 795)
(108) People v. Morris (143 Cal. App. 2d 344)
(109) People v. Lowen (109 Cal. 381)
(110) People v. De Nava (119 Cal. App. 2d 82)

(111) People v. Coral (60 Cal. App. 2d 66)
(112) People v. Allard (99 Cal. App. 591)
(113) People v. Lewis (274 Cal. App. 2d 912)
(114) People v. Davis (76 Cal. App. 2d 701)
(115) People v. Hayes (72 Cal. App. 292)
(116) People v. Beach (62 Cal. App. 2d 803)
(117) People v. Gonzales (62 Cal. App. 2d 274)
(118) People v. Jersey (18 Cal. 337)
(119) People v. Davis (97 Cal. 194)

STUDY QUESTIONS

CHAPTER X

(1)   In order for a death to be classed as a homicide, the victim must die within what time?
_____

(2)   The penal code section for murder is _____ PC.

(3)   In first degree murder, the malice aforethought is expressed. In second degree murder, the malice is _____.

(4)   Percy Puke poisons his wife Priscilla. Percy is guilty of what class of homicide?
_____ _____ _____

(5)   The "Ca" in "MaD CaTS BARK" stands for _____.

(6)   All deaths that result from the commission of a felony are classed as at least _____ _____ murder.

(7)   In voluntary manslaughter, there is the intent to kill.   T or F

(8)   Vehicular manslaughter is classed as a felony when it can be shown that there was _____ _____ on the part of the driver.

(9)   Phil Phrump is executed in the gas chamber for murder. What class of homicide is this?
_____ _____

(10)   Killing another during mutual combat is considered to be a class of murder.   T or F

(11)   A peace officer on duty never loses the right to self-defense.   T or F

(12)   The Penal Code section for simple kidnapping is _____ PC.

(13)   The term "asportation" means _____.

(14)   In kidnapping for robbery, there has to be some movement.   T or F

(15)   The Penal Code section for robbery is _____ PC.

(16)   In the crime of robbery, there must be some asportation.   T or F

(17)   In order for robbery to be a crime, the money must be taken from the victim's person and not from near him.   T or F

(18)   In robbery, both force and fear are necessary elements.   T or F

(19)   In policework, there is a term used for the type of robbery where the perpetrator robs the victim by using force rather than through the use of fear. It is called _____ _____ robbery.

(20)   Some assaults are lawful.   T or F

(21)   The term "violent injury" as used in the crime of assault, indicates that an injury be severe or at least leave a visible mark.   T or F

(22)   Kissing a woman against her will is a form of battery.   T or F

(23)   A battery is just a completed assault.   T or F

(24)   Spitting at a person and missing is an example of assault.   T or F

(25)   The Penal Code section for assault is _____ PC.

(26)   The Penal Code section for battery is _____ PC.

(27)   The Penal Code section for rape is _____ PC.

(28)   In order to have the crime of rape, any sexual penetration, however slight, is sufficient.   T or F

(29)   According to California law, a woman can rape a man.   T or F

(30)   Millie Mashpott is a single 23-year-old woman. She has the mental age of 13. She is legally entitled to consent to an act of sexual intercourse under California law.   T or F

(31)   Harriet Hooker is a streetwalker. She agrees to have sex with a customer for $20. At her room, he refuses to pay her and then forcibly has sex with her. This is legally a rape.   T or F

(32)   The crime of unlawful intercourse refers to sexual relations with a person who is under the age of _____.

(33)   The Penal Code section for disturbing the peace is _____ PC.

(34)   In order for the law on disturbing the peace to be violated, the peace of two or more persons must be disturbed.   T or F

(35)   The Penal Code section for burglary is _____ PC.

(36)   The entry in the crime of burglary must be a forced entry.   T or F

(37)   In order for the "entry" element of burglary to be complete, the whole body must be inside the building.   T or F

(38)   For a vehicle to be the subject of burglary, the doors must be locked.   T or F

(39)   Percy Puke burglarizes a warehouse at 12 midnight. This is classed as _____ degree burglary.

(40)   A garage can be the subject of burglary when the door is closed and capable of being locked.   T or F

(41)   A person's labor can be the subject of theft.   T or F

(42)   Asportation is one of the elements of theft.   T or F

(43)   Consent is a defense to the crime of theft, though not an element.   T or F

(44)   Prunella Porkpickle takes $400 from a wallet on a beach blanket while the owner is swimming. What classification of theft would this be?

_____   _____

(45)   Marvin Middlewiff steals $152 worth of ducks from a farm. He is guilty of a felony.   T or F

(46)   Sam Slurp reaches into Arvin Ardvark's pocket and steals a nickel. He is guilty of what crime and degree? _____   _____

(47)   Claud Clunk steals a car that is worth only $50. He is guilty of what crime and degree?

_____   _____

(48)   The value of quicksilver taken from a mine must amount to _____ in order for it to be a felony.

(49)   Stealing a gun worth $10 is classed as what crime? _____

_____

(50)   It is illegal to steal amalgam from a mine. What is "amalgam"? _____

_____

CHAPTER XI

TITLE 15
CALIFORNIA CODE OF REGULATIONS
CORRECTIONS

11.0   INTRODUCTION

11.1   RULES AND REGULATIONS OF THE DIRECTOR
        OF CORRECTIONS

11.2   INMATE RESOURCES

11.3   INMATE ACTIVITIES

11.4   GENERAL INSTITUTION REGULATIONS

11.5   OFFENSES BY PRISONERS

11.6   ESCAPES AND RESCUES

11.7   UNAUTHORIZED COMMUNICATIONS

11.0:0 INTRODUCTION

This chapter is an abbreviation of Title 15 — California Code of Regulations — Corrections. The authors have summarized key areas of the policy that a student majoring in corrections at one of the California Community Colleges would want to know. The authors want to emphasize that this is an abridged version of Title 15. Students who wish to do more research in this area or learn the content of the omitted sections should obtain a copy of Title 15. This chapter and the one following have also been approved by C-P.O.S.T. as providing adequate coverage of correctional law and policy in their recommended course, Introduction to Law.

Title 15– Department of Corrections

Title 15 is the comprehensive set of rules and regulations, which governs how all of the Department of Correction facilities will be run. It is divided into subchapters and articles, which spell out clearly what is expected from every inmate in the institution.

Areas covered in Title 15 are numerous and diverse. The authors have chosen to begin by covering selected Articles from Chapter 1.

11.1:0 RULES AND REGULATIONS OF THE DIRECTOR OF COR-RECTIONS.

This section covers the following policy topics:
- Behavior
- State-Issued Inmate Clothing and Linen
- Work and Education
- Credits
- Food Services
- Personal Cleanliness
- Camp Assignment
- Alternative Sentencing Program
- Intake, Release and Discharge of Inmates
- Furloughs and Temporary Leave
- Appeals.

The following pages summarize the content of Title 15, covering the areas which are most needed by a student studying toward the Associate of Arts in Corrections.

11.1:1 Article 1 — Behavior

This article identifies crimes that frequently occur in an institution, and the sanctions, which the director can impose. This article also addresses "gang activity."

11.1:2 Article 3.5 — Credits

Inmates can earn credit, which is essentially time reduced from their sentence. They can be granted pre-sentence credit for time served in jail prior to sentencing. In addition, Section 2931 PC states that all inmates serving a determinate term of imprisonment for a crime committed before January 1, 1983, who have not waived the time credit provisions, shall be credited with a one-fourth reduction on their term of imprisonment. An inmate can lose all or part of these credits as the result of disciplinary action in the amounts listed in Section 3323 CCR.

The same is true for inmates sentenced under Section 190 PC to an indeterminate term of 15 years-to-life or 25 years-to-life and received by the CDC on or after May 27, 1987. They are credited with a one-fourth reduction on their minimum eligible parole date, unless all or part of such good behavior credit is denied or forfeited as a result of disciplinary action in the amounts listed in Section 3323 CCR.

Waivers

Inmates may elect to waive their right to receive behavior and participation credit in favor of worktime credits in the amount provided for in Section 3043 CCR. In other words, an inmate cannot earn credits for both. An exception to this waiver is that inmates serving an indeterminate term of imprisonment of 15 years to life or 25 years to life shall not be entitled to waive behavior and participation credits to earn Section 2933 PC worktime credits to reduce their minimum eligible parole dates.

Loss of Participation Credit

Inmates can forfeit or be denied participation credit by refusing to work as assigned or for any serious disciplinary offense committed while participating in prison work. Various levels of seriousness of the offense cause the inmate to lose credits in graduated amounts. Inmates who refuse to accept a full-time qualifying assignment, or who are placed on non-credit earning status (Work Group "C") by a classification committee for frequent work/training violations shall not receive a work-time credit reduction from their sentence.

Credit-Earning Special Assignments

The following are examples of inmate special assignments which earn work-time credit:

- Inmate Advisory Council
- Pre-release Program
- Medical/Psychiatric inpatient hospitalization.
- Inmate Work and Training Incentive Groups.

Full-time work/training assignments normally mean eight (8) hours per day on a five-day/week basis, exclusive of meals. Half-time work/training assignments normally mean four (4) hours/day on a five day/week basis, exclusive of meals.

Work Group Assignments

Classification Committees assign inmates to one of four Work Groups A-1, A-2, B, or C.

(1) **Work Group A-1 – Full-time work/training assignment:** Inmates are eligible to earn Penal Code Section 2933 work time credits for each 6 months of full-time performance. Attendance at a full time education/training program will also qualify

(2) **Work Group A-2 – Involuntary Unassigned:** An inmate willing but unable to work in a full-time assignment shall receive three months credit for each six months served, in the following status:

  (a) The inmate is placed on a waiting list pending availability of a full-time work/training assignment

  (b) An unassigned inmate awaiting adverse transfer to another institution.

(3) **Work Group B – Half-time work/training assignment:** Half-time programs shall normally consist of a work/training assignment of four hours/day, excluding meals, five days per week, or full-time enrollment in college consisting of 12 units in credit courses leading to an AA or BA. The workday shall be no less then three hours and the workweek no less than 15 hours.

(4) **Work Group C – Voluntary Unassigned; Zero credit:** An inmate who refuses to accept or perform in a work/training assignment, or who is placed on a non-credit earning status by a classification committee for frequent work/training violations. The inmate must request in writing to be removed from Work Group C. The classification committee will hold a hearing within 30 days.

(5) **Work Group D-1 – Indeterminate lockup status:** An inmate assigned to a segregated housing program shall be awarded 3 months credit for each 6 months served. Segregated housing is defined as:

  (a) Administrative Segregation (ADSEG) and

  (b) Security Housing Unit (SHU)

(6) **Work Group D-2:** Serving SHU term or voluntarily unassigned in SHU or Protective Housing Unit (PHU).

(7) **Work Group U – Unclassified:** An inmate undergoing reception center processing is in this status from the date of their reception until classified at their assigned institution.

Privilege Groups

In addition to Work Group placement, inmates are assigned to Privilege Groups. Privileges for each work/training incentive group shall be those privileges earned by the inmate. Inmate privileges are governed by an inmates' behavior, custody classification and assignment.

The Privilege Groups follow the same classification scheme as the Work Groups — A, B, C, D and U. The range of privileges using A, the most liberal, and U, the most restrictive, as examples, gives you an idea as to what B, C and D contain :

Group A:

- Family visits limited only by institutional resources.
- Visits during non-work/training hours limited only by space available.
- Maximum canteen draw allowed.
- Telephone access limited only by phone resources

Group U:

  Reception Center inmates being processed.

- No privilege card
- No family visitation
- Telephone for emergency use only
- Yard access limited
- No accrual of excused time
- No canteen
- No special packages

11.1:3   Article 8 — Appeals

Any inmate or parolee under the department's jurisdiction may appeal any departmental decision, action, condition or policy perceived by those individuals as adversely affecting their welfare, except decisions of the Departmental Review Board. Decisions of the Department Review Board are final.

Levels of Appeal Review and Disposition

Informal – The appellant and staff involved attempt to resolve the appeal informally. Most appeals must be handled informally before going to the formal process.

Formal – The formal process involves three levels and is screened by an appeals coordinator.

11.2:0 INMATE RESOURCES

11.2:1 Article 4 – Mail

Disapproval of Mail

Staff shall not permit an inmate to send or receive mail which, in their judgment, has any of the characteristics listed in Section 3006 CCR:

- Any matter of a character tending to incite murder; arson; riot; or any form of violence or physical harm to any person, or any ethnic, gender, racial, religious, or other group.
- Blackmail or extortion.
- Contraband, or sending or receiving contraband.
- Plans to escape or assist in an escape.
- Plans to disrupt the order, or breach the security of any facility.
- Plans for activities which violate the law, these regulations, or local procedures.
- Coded messages.
- A description of the making of any weapon, explosive, poison or destructive device.
- Illustrations, explanations, and/or description of how to sabotage or disrupt computers, communications, or electronics.
- Diskettes.
- Maps of area within 10-mile radius of facility.

Appeals Relating to Mail

Inmates and the correspondents of inmates may appeal department rules, regulations, policies, approved facility procedures and the application of it, relating to mail and correspondence.

Confidential Mail and Inspection

Inmates may send confidential mail, if addressed to certain persons or approved offices. However, to determine the possible presence of contraband, all incoming confidential mail is inspected prior to delivery.

11.2:2 Article 7 – Visiting

The value of visiting as a means to establish and maintain meaningful family and community relationship has always been recognized as a means to promote goodwill. The California Department of Corrections's policy is to allow visiting in as accommodating a manner as is possible in keeping with the need to maintain order.

Family Visits

Some inmates are forbidden to have family visits. Inmates who were convicted of violent crimes against family members or designated sex crimes fall into this category. In addition, inmates who are in any of the following categories are denied:

- Life with parole
- Life with a parole date established by the Board of Prison Terms

- Designated close A or B custody
- Designated a condemned inmate
- Assigned to a reception center
- Assigned to an administrative segregation unit
- Assigned to a security housing unit
- Designated "C" status
- Guilty of one or more Division A or B offenses within the last 12 months
- Guilty of narcotics trafficking while in state prison.

11.3:0 INMATE ACTIVITIES

11.3:1 Article 3 – Inmate Councils, Committees and Activity Groups.

Wardens are tasked with establishing inmate advisory councils which are representative of that facility's inmate ethnic groups. These inmate advisory councils are tasked with communicating with the warden and other staff those matters of common interest and concern to the inmate general population.

11.4:0 GENERAL INSTITUTION REGULATIONS

11.4:1 Article 1 – Public Information and Community Relations.

Authorized Released of Information

Only an employee of the CDC designated by the institution head will inform the media regarding a facility incident or newsworthy event. There are strict regulations regarding what information can be released to the media regarding an inmate. Below is listed the data which may be released to the media:

- Name
- Age
- Birthplace
- Place of previous residence
- Commitment information obtained from the adult probation officer's report
- Facility assignments and behavior
- General State of Health
- Cause of death
- Nature of critical illness or injury (except aids)
- Sentencing and release actions

11.4:2 Article 2 – Security

The purpose of the correctional institutions is to protect the public by insuring inmate remain incarcerated an to provide the inmate with rehabilitative activities. Security is the most important goal.

The most reliable way to ensure security is by inmate count. Every institution head is tasked with maintaining a system to account at all times for inmates. In the CDC, a physical count will be taken at least 4 times daily. The following are the types of counts which correctional officers take:

Standing Count

At least one count will be a standing count wherein the inmates stand at their cell doors.

Emergency Count

If the staff determines that an inmate may be missing, they will conduct an emergency count.

Inmate Movement

Each facility will establish a schedule of routine inmate movement from activities

11.4:3   Article 7 – Administrative Segregation

Administrative segregation is the term used to identify those inmates who have been confined in a designated segregation unit or, in an emergency, to any single cell unit capable of providing secure segregation. An inmate's placement in temporary segregation is reviewed by the Institutional Classification Committee (ICC) within 10 days of receipt in the unit. The ICC will act to retain the inmate in temporary segregation or release to the general population. The ICC reviews the inmate's case at least every 30 days thereafter until the inmate is removed from temporary segregation.

Segregated Program Housing Units

Special housing units are designated for extended term programming of inmates not suited for the general population. Placement into and release from these units requires approval by a Classification Staff Representative (CSR).

Protective Housing Unit (PHU)

An inmate whose safety would be endangered by general population placement may be placed in the PHU provided that certain criteria are met:

- The inmate does not require specialized housing for any reason other than protection;
- The inmate does not have a serious psychiatric or medical condition;
- The inmate is not documented as a member or affiliate of a prison gang;
- The inmate does not pose a threat to the safety or security of other inmates in the PHU;
- The inmate has specific, verified enemies identified on CDC Form 812;
- The inmate's notoriety may result in great bodily harm;
- There is no alternative placement
- There is verifiable certainty that the inmate is in present danger of great bodily harm.

Psychiatric Management Unit (PMU)

An inmate with a diagnosed psychiatric disorder not requiring inpatient hospital care, whose conduct threatens the safety of the inmate or others, may be housed in a PMU. However, the inmate must be capable of participating in the unit's activities without undue risk to the safety of the inmate or others in the unit.

Security Housing Unit (SHU)

An inmate whose conduct endangers the safety of others or the security of the institution will be housed in a SHU. The SHU is the most secure confinement in the institution. The inmate has no contact with other inmates. The general criteria that places an inmate in the SHU is he has been found guilty of an offense for which a determinate term of confinement has been assessed or is deemed to be a threat to the safety of others or the security of the institution. Confinement to a SHU can be for an indeterminate or fixed period of time.

An inmate confined for an indeterminate period is reviewed by a classification committee at least every 180 days for consideration of release to the general inmate population. Determinate periods are for inmates found guilty of a serious offense listed in section 3315 of the Title 15 Regulations. The term is set by the Institutional Classification Committee (ICC) using the standards in Section 3315 CCR, including the SHU Term Assessment Chart (see page 269).

Factors in Mitigation of SHU Term

The SHU Term will be set at the expected range unless a classification committee finds factors exist which warrant the imposition of a lesser or greater period of confinement. The total period of confinement assessed will be no less than nor greater than the lowest or highest months listed for each offense in the SHU Term Assessment Chart. When setting the term, the committee will determine the base offense. If the term being assessed includes multiple offenses, the offense which provides for the longest period of confinement will be the base offense. Lesser offenses may be used to increase the period beyond the expected range. After determining the base offense, the committee will review the circumstances of the disciplinary offense and the inmate's institutional behavior history using the factors below. The committee will then determine that either no unusual factors exist or find that specific aggravating or mitigating factors do exist and specify a greater or lesser range. The reasons for deviation from the expected range are documented on the SHU Term Assessment Worksheet, a copy of which is provided to the inmate.

SHU Term Assessment Chart
(Fixing of Determinate Confinement)

OFFENSE	Low	Expected	High	OFFENSE	Low	Expected	High
(A) Homicide:				**(E) Trafficking in Drugs:**			
1. Murder, attempted murder, solicitation of murder, or voluntary manslaughter of a non-inmate.	(36	48	60)	Distributing controlled substances in an institution or camp or causing controlled substances to be brought into an institution or camp for the purpose of distribution.	(06	09	12)
2. Murder, attempted murder, solicitation of murder, or voluntary manslaughter of an inmate.	(15	26	36)				
				(F) Escape With Force or Attempted Escape With Force.	(09	16	24)
(B) Violence Against Persons:				**(G) Disturbance, Riot, or Strike:**			
1. Assault on a non-inmate with a weapon or physical force capable of causing mortal or serious injury	(09	28	48)	1. Leading a disturbance, riot, or strike.	(06	12	18)
2. Assault on an inmate with a weapon or physical force capable of causing mortal or serious injury.	(06	15	24)	2. Active participation in, or attempting to cause conditions likely to threaten institution security.	(02	04	06)
3. Assault on a non-inmate with physical force insufficient to cause serious injury.	(06	12	18)				
4. Assault on an inmate with physical force insufficient to cause serious injury.	(02	03	06)	**(H) Harassment of another person, group, or entity either directly or indirectly through the use of the mail or other means.**	(06	12	18)
5. Throwing a caustic substance on a non-inmate.	(02	03	04)				
(C) Threat to Kill or Assault Persons:				**(I) Arson, Theft, Destruction of Property**			
1. Use of non-inmate as hostage.	(18	27	36)	Theft or destruction of State property where the loss or potential loss exceeds $10,000 or threatens the safety of others.	(02	08	12)
2. Threat to a non-inmate.	(02	05	09)				
3. Threat to an inmate.	(02	03	04)				
(D) Possession of a Weapon:				**(J) Extortion and Bribery:**			
				Extortion or bribery of a non-inmate.	(02	06	09)
1. Possession of a firearm or explosive device.	(18	27	36)	**(K) Except as otherwise specified in this section, proven attempts to commit any of the above listed offenses shall receive one-half (½) of the term specified for that offense.**			
2. Possession of a weapon, other than a firearm or explosive device which has been manufactured or modified so as to have the obvious intent or capability of inflicting traumatic injury, and which is under the immediate or identifiable control of the inmate.	(06	10	15)	**(L) Any inmate who conspires to commit any of the above offenses shall receive the term specified for that offense.**			

Fig. XI-1: SHU Term Assessment Chart

Factors in Mitigation

- The inmate has a minor or no prior disciplinary history
- The inmate has not been involved in prior acts of the same or of a similar nature.
- The misconduct was situational and spontaneous as opposed to planned.
- The inmate was influenced by others to commit the offense.
- The misconduct resulted, in part, from the inmate's fear for safety.

Factors in Aggravation

- The inmate's prior disciplinary record includes acts of misconduct of the same or similar nature.
- The misconduct was planned and executed as opposed to situational or spontaneous.
- The misconduct for which a SHU term is being assessed resulted in a finding of guilty for more than one offense.
- The inmate influenced others to commit serious disciplinary infractions during the time of the offense.

11.4:4   Article 10 – Classification

The Classification of inmates takes into consideration the inmate's needs, interests and desires in keeping with the facility's needs; the inmate's behavior, performance and classification score; and the effect on the inmate, other inmates, staff, security of the facility, and public safety. A classification committee composed of staff knowledgeable in the classification process determine the inmate's placement within a facility, transfer between facilities, program participation, privilege groups or custody designation.

The classification of felon inmates will include the classification score system as established. Below are the classification score ranges:

- An inmate with a classification score of 0 through 18 will be paced in a Level I facility.
- An inmate with a classification score of 19 through 27 will be placed in a Level II facility.
- An inmate with a classification score of 28 through 51 will be placed in a Level III facility.
- An inmate with a classification score 52 and above will be placed in a Level IV facility.

A lower classification score indicates lesser security control needs and a higher score indicates greater security control needs.

TITLE 5 OFFENSES RELATING TO PRISONS AND PRISONERS

11.5:0   CHAPTER 1 – OFFENSES BY PRISONERS

115:1   Assaults With Deadly Weapon by Life Prisoner (4500 PC)
(1) Every person, who, while serving a life sentence
(2) With malice aforethought, commits an assault upon another
(3) Within or without the walls of the prison
(4) With either
    (a) a deadly weapon or instrument, or
    (b) by any means of force likely to produce great bodily injury
(5) Is punishable by either
    (a) death, or
    (b) life without possibility of parole (If the victim does not die within a year and a day as the proximate result of the assault.)

11.5:2   Assaults with a Deadly Weapon by Prisoner Not Serving Life (4501 PC)
(1) Every prisoner, not serving life,
(2) Who commits an assault upon another
(3) With either
    (a) a deadly weapon or instrument, or
    (b) by means of force likely to produce great bodily harm
(4) Shall serve an additional two, four, or six years consecutively

11.5:3   Battery by Gassing by Prison Inmate (4501.1 PC)
(1) Every person who is confined to a state prison
(2) Who commits a battery upon the person of any officer or employee of the prison
(3) By means of "gassing"
(4) Shall serve an additional two, three, or four years consecutively .

Definition:

The term "gassing" means intentionally placing or throwing, or causing to be placed or thrown, upon the person of another, any mixture of human excrement or other bodily fluids or substances.

Followup:

If a gassing occurs, the prisoner responsible shall be tested for communicable diseases and the results given to the officer or employee. The Department of Corrections shall compile a special report for the Legislature on the number of offenses committed in state prisons. The Department shall also make a special effort to protect its officers through such steps as training and the use of protective clothing and goggles.

11.5:4   Battery Upon a Person Who is Not a Prisoner (4501.5 PC)

Every prisoner who commits a battery upon another person who is not a prisoner, shall serve an additional two, three or four years consecutively.

11.5:5 Possession of Deadly Weapons by Prisoner (4502 PC)

(1) Every prisoner who, while
   (a) confined to a penal institution, or
   (b) being transported to or from an institution
   (c) under the custody of an officer or prison employee
(2) Possess or has under his or her control, any tear gas or weapons listed under 12020 PC
(3) Or who, while in prison, manufactures or attempts to manufacture any of these weapons
(4) Shall serve an additional 16 months, two or three years consecutively

11.5:6 Holding a Hostage Within a Prison (4503 PC)

(1) Any prisoner confined to a state prison or facility
(2) Who, within the institution,
(3) Either
   (a) holds any person hostage, or
   (b) by force or threats, holds any person against their will in defiance of official orders
(4) Shall serve an additional three, five or seven years consecutively.

11.6:0 CHAPTER 2 – ESCAPES AND RESCUES

11.6:1 Escape or Attempt to Escape From Prison (4530 PC)

A

(1) Every prisoner who
   (a) while confined to a state prison, camp or facility (including adults from CYA's Deuel Vocational Institution 4530.5 PC)
   (b) being transported to or from such institution
   (c) under the custody or control of a prison official, or
   (d) engaged in a program involving work outside the prison
(2) And by force or violence
(3) Escapes or attempts escape
(4) Is guilty of escape (2, 4 or 6 yrs)

B

If the escape is accomplished without force or violence, the punishment is 16 months, 2 or 3 yrs)

C

(1) Every prisoner who while confined to a state prison, camp or facilty
(2) Is temporarily released under sections 2690, 2910, 6254 or 3306 W & I
(3) For either a work or educational release program
(4) And fails to return at the designated time
(5) Is guilty of escape (16 mo., 2 or 3 years)

11.6:2 Escape or Attempted Escape from County or City Correctional Facility (4532 PC)

(1) Every person who:
   (a) is arrested and booked for a crime
   (b) is charged with a crime, or
   (c) has been convicted of a crime
(2) And is
   (a) confined in a city or county jail or jail farm or camp etc.
   (b) confined as an inebriate (5654, 5656 or 5677 W & I)
   (c) under the control or in lawful custody of an officer or person of authority
   (d) released on a work or educational furlough
   (e) released under a home detention program (1203.016 PC), or
   (f) being transported from one institution to another
(3) And thereafter
   (a) escapes or attempts to escape, or
   (b) being under a furlough program, fails to return at the required time, or
   (c) being in a home detention program, leaves his or her home without authorization
(4) Is guilty of escape

Punishment:

   (a) If crime was misdemeanor: (1 yr & 1 day, state prison ,or up to 1 yr in county jail)
   (b) If crime was felony (16 mo., 2 or 3 yrs , state prison, or up to 1 yr in county jail)
   (c) If the escape was by means of force or violence, punishment is: 2, 4, or 6yrs prison or 1 yr jail)
   (d) All sentences shall be consecutive
   (e) If the court grants probation, the reasons must be stated in court record.

11.6:3　Officers Aiding Escape (4533 PC)

(1) Every keeper of a prison, sheriff, deputy sheriff or jailer, or person employed as a guard
(2) Fraudulently contrives, procures, aids, connives at, or voluntarily permits a prisoner's escape
(3) Is guilty of a felony.

11.6:4　Assisting Escape or Attempted Escape by Prisoner Whose Parole is Revoked (4534 PC)

(1) When a person's parole has been revoked
(2) Whether that person is incarcerated or in custody of an officer
(3) And anyone willfully assists that person to escape
(4) That person assisting is guilty of a felony

11.6:5　Carrying Article Useful for Escape Into Prison or Jail (4535 PC)

(1) Any person who carries or sends into a prison or jail
(2) Anything useful to aid a prisoner in making an escape
(3) With the specific intent to help that prisoner escape
(4) Is guilty of a felony

11.6:6　Escape by Mentally Disordered Sex Offender (4536 PC)

(1) Every person committed to a state hospital or other public or private mental health facility
(2) As a mentally disordered sex offender
(3) And
　　(a) escapes from that institution, or
　　(b) escapes while being transported to or from such institution or facility
(4) Is guilty of a wobbler.

Mentally Disordered Sex Offender (6300 W & I)

(1) Who, by reason of mental defect, disease, or disorder,
(2) Is predisposed to the commission of sexual offenses
(3) To such a degree that he is dangerous to the health and safety of others.

Duties of Medical Director (4536(b) PC)

(1) When a mentally disordered sex offender escapes from an institution or facility, the medical director shall promptly notify the chief of police or sheriff of local jurisdiction, and shall request assistance in the apprehension of that person.
(2) Within <u>48 hours</u> of an escape, the medical director shall <u>orally</u> notify the following agencies of the escape:
　　(a) The court that made the commitment
　　(b) The prosecutor in the case
　　(c) The Department of Justice

11.6:7　Notification of Law Enforcement of Escape From Secure Detention Facility (4537 PC)

(1) When a person has escaped from a <u>secure detention facility</u> (e.g., Prison, jail, juvenile hall, CYA institution)
(2) The person in charge of that facility shall promptly notify the chief of police or sheriff of local jurisdiction of that escape
(3) If the facility is under the Department of Corrections or the CYA, the person in charge must provide law enforcement agencies with the name and description of the escapee and other information that can help in the apprehension or protect the public from harm.
(4) If the escape was accomplished by means of force or violence, and the escapee is a felon, local TV and newspapers must be promptly given a description and photograph of the escapee.

11.6:8　Rescue or Attempted Rescue (4550 PC)

Rescue is the taking of a prisoner from lawful custody.

(1) Every person who rescues or attempts to rescue or aids another to rescue
(2) Any prisoner from a prison, prison road camp or jail or county road camp
(3) Or from any officer or person having him in lawful custody
(4) Is guilty of the crime of rescue
Punishment:
　　(a) If the prisoner was convicted of a felony punishable by death, 2, 3 or 4 yrs in prison
　　(b) In all other cases it is a wobbler

11.7:0 CHAPTER 3 – UNAUTHORIZED COMMUNICATIONS WITH PRISONERS

11.7:1 Taking From or Bringing in Letters to Prisons (4570 PC)

(1) Every person who
 (a) communicates with, or
 (b) brings or takes any letter, writing, literature or reading matter to or from
(2) A prisoner
 (a) detained in a prison or prison associated camp or farm
 (b) in custody of a prison official, officer, or employee, or
 (c) in any jail or county road camp in this state
(3) Without the permission of the warden or officer in charge
(4) Is guilty of a misdemeanor

SO I GOT THIS LETTER FROM THE WIFE SMUGGLED IN BY MY BROTHER. THE LETTER SAYS "DEAR JOHN," BUT MY NAME'S HOWARD!

11.7:2 Unauthorized Communication With a Prisoner in Transport (4570.1 PC)

(1) Any person who delivers or receives a written communication
(2) To or from a prisoner
 (a) being transported in a prison vehicle, or
 (b) Being escorted to or from such vehicle
(3) Without permission of the peace officer or corrections officer in charge
(4) Is guilty of a misdemeanor

11.7:3 Using False Identification to Secure Admission to Prison or Camp (4570.5 PC)

(1) Every person who would not otherwise qualify for admission as a visitor to a state prison
(2) Who presents to prison officials false identification either
 (a) verbally, or
 (b) through false papers
(3) With the intent to gain entry to the premises or grounds
(4) Is guilty of a misdemanor

11.7:4 Unauthorized Entry on Prison or Jail Grounds by an Ex-Convict (4571 PC)

(1) Every person who having previously served time in a state prison
(2) Either
 (a) enters upon the grounds of a state prison, camp or farm, jail or county work camp (etc.), or
 (b) enters lands belonging to or adjacent to such facility
(3) Without the consent of the warden or official in charge
(4) Is guilty of a felony

11.7:5 Smuggling Controlled Substances Into Prison or Jail (4573 PC)

(1) Every person who knowingly
 (a) brings or sends into, or
 (b) assists in bringing or sending into
(2) Any prison, jail or place where prisoners are located or under the control of officers or officials
(3) Any
 (a) controlled substance (Division 10 H & S Code), or
 (b) any device or instrument for the illegal injection or consumption of narcotics
(4) Except when
 (a) authorized by the person in charge, or
 (b) authorized by law (e.g., Medical personnel)
(5) When signs have been posted at or around the prohibited location
(6) Violation is a felony (2, 3, or 4 years)

11.7:6 Bringing Drugs or Alcoholic Beverages Into Penal Institutions or Jails (4573.5 PC)

(1) Any person who knowingly brings into any prison, jail or associated camp or farm or place where prisoners are under the control of officers or officials.
(2) Any
 (a) alcoholic beverage, drug or controlled substance (in any form or shape), or
 (b) any device or instrument used for the unlawful injection or consumption of narcotics
(3) Without having authority to do so under Department of Corrections rules
(4) Or without specific authorization from the warden or official in charge
(5) When signs have been posted at or around the prohibited location

11.7:7 Possession of Controlled Substances Where Prisoners are Kept (4573.6 PC)

(1) Every person who knowingly has in his or her possession any:
   (a) controlled substance (Div. 10, 11000 H & S Code), or
   (b) any device or instrument for use with narcotics
(2) In any prison or jail or on a corrections camp or farm, or while in custody of an officer or official
(3) Without being legally authorized to possess such items by Dept. of Corrections rules (e.g., diabetics)
(4) When signs have been posted at or around the prohibited location
(5) That person is guilty of a felony (2, 3 or 4 years consecutive)

11.7:8 Possession of Alcoholic Beverages, Drugs etc. in Prison, Camp or Jail (4573.8 PC)

This section is the same as 4547.6 PC except that it covers drugs and alcohol instead of controlled substances

11.7:9 Selling, Furnishing, Controlled Substances in Prison, Camp or Jail (4573.9 PC)

(1) Any person, other than one held in custody
(2) Who sells, furnishes, administers, or gives away (or offers to do any of these)
(3) To any person:
   (a) in custody in a DOC institution, camp or farm, or under official control, or
   (b) in custody of a county or city jail, road camp or farm, or under official control
(4) Any controlled substance (11000 H & s Code)
(5) Unless authorized by the warden etc. or by the rules of the DOC or county or city jail regulations

(6) When warning signs have been prominently posted in or around the prohibited area.
(7) Is guilty of a felony (2, 4 or 6 years)

11.7:10 Smuggling Firearms, Deadly Weapons, or Tear Gas Into a Prison or Jail (4574 PC)

(1) Every person who knowing brings or sends (or assists such acts) into:
   (a) a state prison, camp or farm, or where prisoners are under official control of an officer, or
   (b) a county or city jail, camp or farm or place where prisoners are under official control
(2) Any firearm, deadly weapon, explosive, tear gas or tear gas weapon
(3) Or who, while lawfully confined, possesses such weapon or device
(4) Unless authorized by law or by permission of the warden or person in charge
(5) Is guilty of a felony (2, 3 or 4 years) (tear gas and tear gas weapons can be a wobbler if they are not discharged.

11.7:11 Damaging or Injuring a Prison or Jail (4600 PC)

(1) Any person who willfully and intentionally breaks down, destroys or injures
(2) Any jail or prison or public property in that facility
(3) Is guilty of a wobbler (If damage is $400 or less it is a misdemeanor; $401 and over is a felony)

STUDY QUESTIONS

Chapter XI

(1) Section 2931PC states that all inmates serving a determinate term of imprisonment for a crime committed before January 1, 1983, who have not waived the time credit provisions, will be credited with a one-fourth reduction on their term of imprisonment.　T or F

(2) Inmates may waive their right to receive behavior and participation credit in favor of work-time credits in the amount provided for in Section 3043 PC.　T or F

(3) The three credit earning special assignments are _____, _____, and _____.

(4) Work Group A-1 is full-time work/training assignment.　T or F

(5) Work Group U means the inmate is unemployed and awaiting an assignment.　T or F

(6) An informal appeal is one during which the appellant and involved staff attempt to resolve the problem.　T or F

(7) Inmate mail cannot be intercepted for any reason.　T or F

(8) Inmates who have been convicted of violent crimes against family members or designated sex crimes are forbidden to have family visits.　T or F

(9) Any correctional officer may release information to the press regarding a facility incident or newsworthy event.　T or F

(10) When security comes into question in a facility, there are three types of counts. These three counts are _____, _____, and _____.

(11) Administrative Segregation (ADSEG) is the term used to identify those inmates who have been confined in a designated segregation unit, or, in an emergency, to any single cell unit capable of providing secure segregation.　T or F

(12) Segregated Program Housing Units (SPHU) are special housing units where "honor inmates" are allowed to live with sepcial privileges.　T or F

(13) Placement into and release from the SPHUs requires approval from:

    (A) ____Institutional Classification Committee (ICC)
    (B) ____Inmate Advisory Council (IAC)
    (C) ____Classification Staff Representative (CSR)
    (D) ____All of the above

(14) An inmate whose safety would be endangered by general population placement may be placed in the Protective Housing Unit (PHU), provided certain conditions are met.　T or F

(15) An inmate whose conduct endangers the safety of others or the security of the institution will be housed in a :

    (A) ____Security Housing Unit (SHU)
    (B) ____Protective Housing Unit (PHU)
    (C) ____Psychiatric Housing Unit (PMU)
    (D) ____Maximum Security Unit (MSU)

(16) Assignment to a SHU can be either _____, or _____ .

(17) An inmate confined to the SHU for an indeterminate period is reviewed by the ICC at least every:

(A) ____90 days   (B) ____120 days
(C) ____150 days   (D) ____180 days

(18) When determining the determinate SHU term, the ICC uses the SHU Term Assessment Chart. If there are no mitigating or aggravating circumstances, the offender inmate will receive:

(A) ____the "low" months   (B) ____the "expected" months
(C) ____the "high" months   (D) ____none of the above

(19) If the inmate has one or more "factors in mitigation," he will most likely receive the _____ months

(20) An inmate with a classification score of 0-18 will be placed in:

(A) ____Level II facility   (B) ____Level III facility
(C) ____Level IV facility   (D) ____Level I facility

(21) A "lifer" can be sentenced to death for an assault with a deadly weapon inside a prison.   T or F

(22) What is the term used for the act of throwing human body fluids on a corrections officer?

(A) ____Barfing   (B) ____Gassing
(C) ____Launching   (D) ____Lobbing

(23) A prisoner who possesses an illegal manufactured weapon (4502 PC) must serve the extra   T or F
punishment as a consecutive sentence.

(24) Escape from a state prison (4530 PC) also includes escape from a California Youth Authority   T or F
institution.

(25) A person confined as an "inebriate" is covered by the laws on escape (4532 PC). **What does**
the term "inebriate" mean?

(A) ____Repeat offender   (B) ____**Habitual drunk**
(C) ____A person on probation   (D) ____**Convicted sex offender**

(26) A convicted person is sentenced to a home detention program. His probation officer drops by   T or F
and finds that the person is not at home. He can be charged with the crime of escape.

(27) The word "incarcerated" as used in 45343 PC, means:

(A) ____Stripped of citizenship   (B) ____Taken off **probation**
(C) ____Put into solitary confinement   (D) ____Placed in **prison or jail**

(28) When a "Mentally Disordered Sex Offender" escapes, the medical director of the institution must promptly notify the police or sheriff, and orally notify the court making the commitment within how many hours?

(A) ____24   (B) ____72
(C) ____48   (D) ____12

(29) The term "Secure Detention Facility" (4537 PC) does not include a juvenile hall facility.   T or F

(30) When a felon escapes from a "Secure Detention Facility" (4537 PC), the press must be promptly given a description and photo of the escapee, only when?

(A) ____The escape is accomplished by force or violence
(B) ____The escapee received assistance from an outsider
(C) ____The escapee has escaped on prior occasion
(D) ____The escapee has made threats of retaliation against witnesses.

(31)   What is the legal term for helping a person in custody to escape? (4550 PC)

      (A) ____Subornation   (B) ____Lynching
      (C) ____Anti-carceration   (D) ____Rescue

(32)   It is a misdemeanor to give a written communication to a prisoner who is in transit to or from a prison. (4570.1 PC)   T or F

(33)   Fred Farkle is an ex-convict and not allowed to visit San Quentin prison. He obtains false identification and uses this to gain entry as a visitor. This is a felony.   T or F

(34)   Mervin Mushmuscle was just released from Folsom prison. A week after his release, he gets drunk and goes to a position just outside the main gate. He stands there and gives the "finger" to all of the corrections officers who pass the gate. This is a felony under 4571 PC.   T or F

(35)   Arvin Ardvark smuggles 2 ounces of marijuana into Solidad prison during visiting hours. Since it is under 3 ounces, there is no violation.   T or F

(36)   Larry Lump has been sentenced to a prison forest camp. While working in the forest he comes across a marijuana plant growing wild. He picks the bush clean and gives portions to four fellow prisoners. Since he did not charge them anything he has not violated 4573.9 PC.   T or F

(37)   Section 4573 PC refers to a "controlled substance" that comes under section 11000. Under what code would 11000 be found?

      (A) ____Business & Professions Code   (B) ____Health & Safety Code
      (C) ____Penal Code   (D) ____Welfare & Institutions Code

CHAPTER XII

CORRECTIONS, THE COURTS, & INMATE RIGHTS

12.1   INTRODUCTION

12.2   INMATES AND LITIGATION

12.3   ACCESS TO THE COURTS

12.4   INMATE FREEDOMS AND INSTITUTIONAL SECURITY

12.5   THE BILL OF RIGHTS AND INMATE RIGHTS

12.6   INMATE SUICIDE

12.7   LEGAL ASPECTS OF THE USE OF FORCE

12.8   AMERICANS WITH DISABILITIES ACT (ADA)

12.1:0 INTRODUCTION

It is interesting to note that 19th and 20th Century corrections had a similar progression to law enforcement. Until the 1960's, law enforcement enjoyed a fairly unencumbered rule of the streets. The law was what the officer on the street said it was. Oftentimes police officers got away with violations of constitutional law because the courts did not want to restrict police officers in their war against crime. This ended with the Warren Court era of the late 1950s and 1960s.

There was similar evolution in corrections. Although some state courts responded to some inmate claims in the late 19th and early 20th centuries, this has been the exception.

Until the 1960s, there was a decidedly laissez faire period when courts chose not to respond to inmate claims. Judges in many courts were quite reluctant to take action because they did not know anything about managing a correctional facility. It was much easier to defer to the decisions of wardens or other officials. As for federal courts, they were reluctant to overrule decisions of state courts for fear of accusations of federalism. Moreover, the feeling of judges was one of "prisoners do not have the same rights as the free citizen." This attitude was first voiced by a Virginia judge in Ruffin v. Commonwealth (1871):

> The prisoner has, as a consequence of his crime, not only forfeited his liberty, but all his personal rights, except those which the law in its humanity accords him. He is for the time being the slave of the state.[1]

Consequently, wardens had tremendous power as did the correctional officer in the cell block. They were the ultimate authority in the correctional systems, just as the police officer was on the beat.

The End of the Laissez Faire Period.

The end of the laissez faire period is generally put at 1964. In 1964 the U.S. Supreme Court decided Cooper v. Pate.[2] The justices stated that prisoners in state and local institutions are entitled to the protections of the Civil rights Act of 1871. The ruling allowed a prisoner to sue a warden or other official under Title 42 of the United States Code, section 1983. This section, which is often used, imposes civil liability on anyone who deprives another of constitutional rights:

> Every person who, under color of any statute, ordinance, regulation, custom, or usage, of any state or territory, subjects, or causes to be subject, any citizen of the United States or other person within the jurisdiction thereof to the deprivation of any rights, privileges, or immunities secured by the Constitution and laws, shall be liable to the party injured in an action at law, suit in equity, or other proper proceeding for redress.

This case clearly ended the attitude that prisoners were "slaves of the state," and set the stage for a spate of litigation over the next 25 years. (Specific cases will be discussed throughout this chapter).

The Regulations Period (1964-1978)

The sudden change in policy by the courts caused reaction by the correctional administrators. The first cases to be decided were directed at ending some of the deplorable conditions in prisons. Prior to the 1960s the qualifications for entry-level correctional officer were low. Many state prison systems did not require even a high school diploma. Poor and insufficient training compounded this statistic. This combination of low education and poor training was bound to result in abuses that would cause the courts to act.

The courts responded to these excesses in the 1960s by saying, "enough is enough," immediately taking aim at ending some of the substandard conditions that had prevailed for years. One of the areas of concern by the Federal Government was the lack of education and training required for correctional officers. The Federal Government felt it was time to invest in the criminal justice system — both Federal and states. In July of 1965 President Lyndon Johnson established the Commission on Law Enforcement and the Administration of Justice. The task of this Commission was to study the criminal justice systems and propose changes to improve its functions. By 1967 the Commission had published its report, The Challenge of Crime in a Free Society. Among the many recommendations was the creation of a Federal agency to oversee improvements in the criminal justice systems. This agency was created and called the Law Enforcement Assistance Administration (LEAA). LEAA began to pour millions of dollars into both police and correctional training and education. From 1968-1981 LEAA gave millions of dollars to improve both correctional personnel and facilities.

At the same time, the Supreme Court was invading the sanctuary of correctional policy and administration. In the opinion of the courts, this intervention was long overdue; in the opinion of the correctional administrators, it was overreaction. Because correctional law as a separate area of legal concern was invested around 1970, there were no court precedents. The natural result of no precedents was a flurry of new rights which we shall discuss in this chapter.

Exercise is a good example of how the courts dove head-first into regulation. The courts went from requiring outdoor exercise for death row inmates to requiring outdoor exercise for jail inmates. Another court addressed the "fundamental" right to exercise.[3] The courts, however, began to contradict themselves on the issue of how much exercise was sufficient. The U.S. Supreme Court attempted to resolve the issue with two decisions on conditions of confinement.[4] The contention of the court regarding the adequacy of conditions was the effect that they had on inmates. Their conclusion, as with any condition or practice, was that it must be shown to have a serious effect on inmates before it may be unconstitutional.[5]

The Period of Vacillation (1978-Present)

In the 1970s, more conservative judges were replacing the "Warren Court". The case that set the more conservative tone with regard to correctional issues was Bell v. Wolfish.[6] Decided in 1979, Bell signaled the change back to a more conservative approach, tempered with an occasional "slap on the hand" when the courts felt that inmates' rights were being trampled on once again.

Bell was a crowding/conditions of confinement case that involved a new Federal jail in Manhattan. The court ruled that there was no "one inmate-per-cell rule" in the Constitution. The court emphasized that factors such as time out of the cell and activities available to the inmates were more important than cell occupancy. The court sent a strong message to the lower courts to stay out of the fine details of correctional administration.

12.2:0 INMATES AND LITIGATION

The vast majority of lawsuits filed by inmates falls into one of three categories:
(1) civil rights actions, in which inmates claim a constitutional violation based on a condition or practice in the institution,
(2) habeas corpus actions, in which the inmate asks for release, and
(3) tort suits, in which the inmate claims a personal injury or damages as a result of the negligence of someone.

12.2:1 The Civil Rights Act

The Civil Rights Act, 42 United States Code 1983 (cited above), was passed by Congress in 1871. It was intended to give Congress the power to force southern states to comply with the Emancipation Proclamation. During the renewed civil rights movement of the 50s and 60s, protestors and civil rights groups found it to be a useful tool in lawsuits against government in general. This was true for both state and federal courts.

Even though Section 1983 was designed to punish the person directly responsible for the constitutional violation, it is often applied where management or supervisory personnel fail to supervise others properly or training falls short of minimum levels.

Relief Granted Under the Civil Rights Act
Injunctions:
These are orders from a court to a defendant to stop (or start) doing something. "Start allowing inmates more access to the courts." Failure to comply with the injunction subjects the defendant to potential sanctions.
Damages:
Monetary damages are available under 1983.
Attorney's Fees:
The prevailing party in a civil rights case are entitled to attorneys' fees.
Direct federal court access:
1983 allows a petitioner to bypass the state courts and go directly to the federal court system.
Civil Rights of Institutionalized Persons Act (CRIPA):
This act gave the U.S. Justice Department the power to bring lawsuits on behalf of persons in prisons or jails. Nevertheless, it is very seldom used.
Torts:
A tort is a civil action which arises when there is a violation of some duty that the defendant owes the plaintiff. The plaintiff can receive monetary damages only from the defendant, but there are no jail or prison sentences. Torts actions common in corrections include negligent loss of property, failure to protect inmates from harm, medical malpractice, or breaches of other duties of reasonable care that correctional staff may owe inmates or others. Improper or inadequate training, supervision or assignment of staff can also be the basis of a claim against a supervisor.
Habeas Corpus:
Habeas Corpus is Latin and means, "you have the body." The petitioner (inmate) claims that he or she is being held in custody illegally in violation of some constitutional right. Generally a habeas corpus petition does not challenge actions by the correctional staff, rather it goes after the court or

agency responsible for the individual being in custody. Habeas Corpus petitions always name the custodian (warden) as the defendant. For example, in the landmark case of Gideon v. Wainwright,[7] Gideon filed a habeas corpus action listing Wainwright, the warden of the State of Florida prison in which Gideon was confined, as defendant.

12.3:0 ACCESS TO THE COURTS

For the law-abiding citizen, access to the courts is generally not a problem. Filing a lawsuit means either hiring a lawyer to assist you, or deciphering how to complete the legal paperwork and then representing yourself once in court.

For those in custody, however, the right of access is not so easy because the facility may erect barriers. In 1941 the U.S. Supreme Court took its first step to ensure access for inmates. In Ex Parte Hull[8] the court declared that the "state" and its officers may not abridge or impair an inmate's right to apply to a Federal court for a writ of habeas corpus. The Supreme Court heard this case because of a State of Michigan policy requiring inmates to have their suits approved for form by the lawyer for the state parole board. The Court made it clear that this policy was unconstitutional. It would seem that the Hull decision was the "turning point" for the Court from Laissez-faire to Regulation. Hull was clearly an inmate-positive decision, but it would be 23 years before another inmate "victory" (Cooper v. Pate).

In 1969 in Johnson v. Avery,[9] the U.S. Supreme Court ruled on "jailhouse lawyers " (e.g., Jerry Rosenberg, Michael Costello, and Richard Demarest, all serving time for murder. Costello's efforts resulted in the Florida Department of Corrections investing $500 million in new facilities and $7 million in legal fees to fight his suits in court). They held that the prison may impose certain reasonable limitations and regulations on one inmate assisting another, but cannot prohibit this activity, unless the prison provides reasonable alternative forms of assistance.

In 1974 the U.S. Supreme Court decided Wolff v. McDonnell.[10] Although this case was about inmate disciplinary hearings, the court looked at whether the right of access to the courts was limited to habeas corpus petitions or whether it should include civil rights cases brought under 42 U.S.C. 1983. The court decreed that it included both.

The most important Supreme Court case in the area of court access came in 1977 with Bounds v. Smith.[11] This case announced that the state had an affirmative duty to assist inmates:

> …the fundamental constitutional right of access to the courts requires prison authorities to assist inmates in the preparation and filing of meaningful legal papers by providing prisoners with adequate law libraries or adequate assistance from persons trained in the law…[12]

This requirement for "meaningful assistance" includes jails, although assistance in a jail is probably not so extensive, considering the shorter time in custody.

In 1996 the Supreme Court revisited access to the courts in Lewis v. Casey.[13] The court reaffirmed Bounds, with a caveat that prisoners could not sue for denial of access unless they could prove harm as a result of inadequate resources. The end result of all these cases is that most states have opted for a law library. Some of these law libraries, however, do not meet the Bounds standards because their adequacy has not been challenged.

12.4:0 INMATE FREEDOMS AND IN-STITUTIONAL SECURITY

What happens when the legitimate interest of inmates conflicts with prison policy? For example, does a prison have to make special religious accommodations for a group which the prison determines is unreasonable and violative of their security interests.

In the case of O'lone v. Estate of Shabazz,[14] a group of Black Muslim inmates wanted to be released from a work detail to return to the institution for a religious ceremony. The institution argued that providing this service would cause security problems. The court agreed and set up a four step process that was to be followed to determine the issue of "reasonably related to legitimate penological interests." The test has the following four points:

- Is there a valid, rational connection between the restriction and legitimate interests of the institution?
- Are their other ways the inmate has of exercising the right in question?
- If the right is accommodated, what impact will that have on staff, other inmates, and on institution resources? Will there be a "ripple effect" on others?
- Finally, the reasonableness of a restriction tends to be shown if there are no ready (obvious, easy) alternatives that would accommodate the inmates' interest at a minimal cost to the institution. In the Shabazz case, which dealt with religious practices, the Court could see no such alternatives.

Shabazz was one of two 1987 Supreme Court cases in which the Court applied this test. In the second case, Turner v. Safley,[15] regulations prohibiting inmate-to-inmate mail and virtually prohibiting inmate marriages were challenged. The Court used the four-step approach above and upheld the mail restrictions, but overturned the marriage rule.

The Turner decision has now become the Turner "test" with regard to the four-step evaluation. In early 1990, in the case of Washington v. Harper,16 the issue of involuntarily medicating mentally ill inmates arouse under the due process clause of the Fourteenth Amendment. The Court applied the Turner test in ruling in favor of the state and said Turner applied, no matter what Constitutional Amendment under which the inmate was suing, and even if not all four steps fit. Thus, the Turner test governs First Amendment issues (religious practice questions or publication rejection), Fourth Amendment (searches), Eighth Amendment (cruel and unusual punishment) and the Fourteenth Amendment (due process), if the right the inmate is claiming conflicts with the interests of the institution (security, safety, and rehabilitation).

The Turner test has resulted in tipping the "balancing of the scale" somewhat in favor of the institution. Even though the institution still must convince a reviewing court that a restriction it is imposing furthers a legitimate penological interest, that burden will not be so difficult. The deference will go to the prison officials.

12.5:0 THE BILL OF RIGHTS AND INMATE RIGHTS

Having introduced the Turner test and its application to the Bill of Rights affecting corrections, we shall in this section discuss in depth each of the Amendments.

This section looks at the First, Fourth, Eighth, and Fourteenth Amendments as they apply to inmates. Clearly the inmate's rights under these amendments are less than that enjoyed by the average citizen. Too often we hear, however, that a convicted felon gives up all of his Constitutional rights. Is this true? The answer is no, but he or she certainly gives up significant parts of these rights.

12.5:1 The First Amendment: Religion, Mail, Publications, Visiting, and Expression
The First Amendment to the U.S. Constitution provides freedom of religion, of speech, and of the press.

Congress shall make no law respecting an establishment of religion, or prohibiting the free exercise thereof, or abridging the freedom of speech, or of the press; or the right of the people peaceably to assemble, and to petition the government for a redress of grievances.[17]

The First Amendment may be the most cherished of all the rights in the Constitution. It is often seen as the one distinguishing factor that separates a truly free nation from one that is tyrannical. It is the fabric of which our democratic freedoms and beliefs are based. But even the First Amendment has its limitations. It would not be a First Amendment freedom to stand up in a theater and falsely shout, "fire, fire" to satisfy some morbid desire to see others panic. The government must show, however, a "clear and present danger" to restrict any form of speech. Moreover, prior restraint is not favored either. In other words, the law demands that a person be given the freedom express oneself; action is taken if the behavior is deemed unlawful.

With this said, the burden to restrict First Amendment rights inside a correctional institution is not this great because the government's legitimate need is to be able to run a safe, secure facility. This means that the incarcerated enjoy substantially fewer rights.

The courts have held that the concepts of least restrictive methods,[18] compelling state interest,[19] and clear and present danger[20] establish the boundaries between protected and unprotected speech. Consequently, when correctional officials have shown that the speech, assembly or religion poses a threat, courts have supported rules restricting the rights.[21]

The Religious Freedom Restoration Act
In the previous section we discussed the Turner decision. The Turner decision gave the advantage to the correctional official's judgment by using the "legitimate penological interest" test. As of late 1993, the Turner test no longer applies to religious claims. Instead, courts review such claims under the Religious Freedom Restoration Act (RFRA).[22] Under RFRA, if a prison or jail imposes a "substantial burden" on an inmate's exercise of religion, then to justify that burden, the government must show that
(1) the restriction or burden "is in furtherance of a compelling governmental interest," and
(2) that it is the "least restrictive means" of furthering that interest.[23]

Here again, as with many Supreme Court decisions, the guidelines given are not objective, causing the institution to act as best they can, knowing the courts will decide after the fact using the guidelines as they interpret them. So far the courts have continued to defer to correctional officials' assertion of security concerns under RFRA much as they did when applying the Turner test.

What is a Religion?

A vexing problem for correctional officials is defining religion. If they determine that the practice is not a religion, then they do not have to apply the RFRA. For example, the Universal Life Church has for years bestowed religious titles for free by mail for the purpose of tax evasion. Is it a religion? The courts have said no.[24] For many years prison administrators refused to accept the Black Muslims as a legitimate religion, preferring to see them as a criminal conspiracy disguised as a religion. This, of course, has changed.

Mail and Publications

As a form of speech, mail falls under the First Amendment. Even though the use of the mail system is a right, case law has mandated that correctional officials can place reasonable restrictions on prisoners if there is a "clear and present danger" or "compelling state need." Recent court decisions have found that most censorship of communications between inmates and their lawyers is unconstitutional;[25] and this concept is generally extended to communications with the news media.[26] As we discussed earlier in the Turner decision, mail sent from one inmate to another is preventable. In addition the courts have upheld restrictions on incoming newspapers and magazines that would permit receipt of such mail if "only the publisher" is the sender.[27] This is to prevent contraband being sent by relatives concealed inside a publication of this nature.

Because prison administrators realize that contact with the outside world is very important to the inmate's mental health and stability, many have eased restrictions on the mails.

Due Process and Mail

To ensure that correctional officials make rejection decisions fairly, the Supreme Court requires the following guidelines be followed:

- The inmate is given notice of the rejection (regardless of whether the inmate was the sender or intended recipient of the letter).
- The author of the letter is given an opportunity to protest the censorship decision to an official other than the person who made the original decision to reflect the correspondence. This obviously requires that notice of the rejections also be given to the sender of the letter, if the sender is not an inmate.[28]

Visitation

As mentioned above, visitation privileges are very important to both the inmate and the correctional staff. There is still debate as to whether visitation is a right or a privilege. Certainly correctional administrators can and do put limits on the times when visitation can occur and the number of visitations that each inmate may have over any given period of time. However, limitations on visiting hours, restricted visitor lists, overcrowded visiting rooms, and the constant presence of guards all contribute to the inmate's difficulty in maintaining ties with family and the outside world. When deprived of basic social contacts, inmates turn to the other inmates and the inmate subculture and gangs for solace.[29] With this in mind, correctional officials have been liberal in this area, even to the degree of allowing so-called conjugal visits (a conjugal visit allows a wife to stay overnight with the prisoner) and home furlough.

12.5:2   The Fourth Amendment: Searches and Seizures within the Institution

The Fourth Amendment states:

The right of the people to be secure in their persons, houses, papers, and effects, against unreasonable searches and seizures, shall not be violated, and no Warrant shall issue, but upon probable cause, supported by oath or affirmation, and particularly describing the person or place to be search and the things to be seized.[30]

As with the First Amendment correctional officers and officials are not under the same constraints that police officers would be when faced with Fourth Amendment issues. Search warrants are virtually never required for the searches that might be made in a prison or jail by the facility staff.

When looking at whether to approve a search or not, the courts use a balancing test: Is the greater safety of society more important than the right to privacy of one or several individuals? If the answer is yes, then the courts will approve the searches and seizures. "Reasonable suspicion" is another term that the courts accept. The suspicion usually must be focused on the person to be searched, and there must be a specific fact, combined with the reasonable inferences that can be drawn from experience. Police officers are frequently faced with this dilemma when trying to decide if they can search or not.

Searches in Prison and Jails

The need for security necessitates that searches in prisons and jails be done frequently and without delay or notice.

Cell Searches

The courts have not been active in extending Fourth Amendment protections to prisoners; for example, the decision in Hudson v. Palmer[31] sanctioned the right of officials to search cells and confiscate any materials found there. In addition, inmates have no right to be present when their cells are being searched.[32] This does not mean that correctional officers may ransack a cell and leave it in a mess for the inmate to clean up. This could very easily lead to court intervention.

Patdown searches

The courts also have generally given their blessing to patdown searches being done randomly. The key here is not using the patdown search to harass certain inmates.

Strip searches

If there has been any area of doubt on the part of the courts it has been with the strip searches. Nevertheless, they have approved strip searches following an inmate's exposure to the opportunity to obtain contraband, such as after a contact visit or trip to a hospital.[33] The Courts have also approved strip searching inmates when they leave segregation unit cells because of the greater security concerns present in these types of cells.[34] Institutions should have a policy defining exactly when strip searches can be done.

Strip searches in jails presents another matter altogether. Without exception, courts across the country have held that automatic strip searches of persons arrested and booked for minor offenses are unreasonable and violate the Fourth Amendment.

The courts have consistently said that reasonable suspicion is required to strip search arrestees. Jail personnel could base this on the arrestee's behavior or on the specific charge. If the person were arrested for a drug or violent offense, the courts, for the most part, have upheld a strip search. The fact that the offense is a felony does not automatically justify a strip search.

Body Cavity Probe Searches

These searches are the most intrusive of all. For this reason, there must be some articulable suspicion that a particular inmate is hiding contraband in a body cavity.[35] These searches should be done by medical staff and done in a manner and place that respects the inmate's dignity and privacy as much as is reasonably possible. As with strip searches, there should be clear facility policy addressing the circumstances in which body cavity probe searches may be done.

Visitor searches

Obviously visitors are entitled to greater protections from searches than inmates. But visitors give up some of their expectations of privacy on entering the prison or jail. Visitors are subject to routine patdowns, searches of purses and briefcases, and magnometer searches; the courts have approved these.

12.5:3 The Eighth Amendment and Cruel and Unusual Punishment

The Eight Amendment addresses bails, fines and punishments:

Excessive bail shall not be required, nor excessive fines imposed, nor cruel and unusual punishment inflicted.[36]

Because the Eighth Amendment does not normally attach until after a person has been convicted, it is the one amendment that is unique to corrections. The "cruel and unusual punishment" clause has been used for many inmate claims of mistreatment: use of excessive force, adequacy of medical care and protection afforded an inmate.

What Exactly is Cruel and Unusual Punishment?

Among the phrases or "tests" the Supreme Court has developed over the years to clarify this nebulous phrase "cruel and unusual punishment" are:

(1) Shocks the conscience of the Court
(2) Violates the evolving standards of decency of a civilized society.
(3) Punishment disproportionate to the offense.
(4) Involves the wanton and unnecessary infliction of pain.

The Courts have also used the term "deliberate indifference", saying that the defendant must have shown some "deliberate indifference" to some significant basic human need of the inmate, such as medical care. The Supreme Court first introduced the term "deliberate indifference" in 1976 in the case of Estelle v. Gamble.[37] In this case, the Court said that deliberate indifference to an inmate's medical need violated the Eighth Amendment It was not until 1994 in the case of Farmer v. Brennan[38] that the Supreme Court actually defined what "deliberate indifference" is.

In this case a transsexual inmate was raped after being placed in the general population of a federal penitentiary. The Court stated that, to be deliberately indifferent, an official must have actual knowledge that an inmate faces a substantial risk of serious harm and then must disregard that risk by failing to take reasonable steps to abate it.

Conditions of Confinement

Often referred to as overcrowding cases, the courts have found one or more prisons in almost every state to be overcrowded and thus unconstitutional under the Fourteenth Amendment. As of January 1, 1995, thirty-nine states plus the District of Columbia, Puerto Rico and the Virgin Islands were under court order or consent decrees to limit their prison populations and/or improve conditions. In seven states the entire prison system was under court order and only three states (Minnesota, New Jersey, and North Dakota) have never been under court order. In addition hundreds of jails have been under similar orders over the years because the conditions of the jails is expected to be the same as in the prisons.[39]

Cases and Standards

The landmark decision in confinement cases was Bell v. Wolfish (cited earlier), which stated there was no one-man, one-cell rule. Bell added that it was the effects of crowding and not simply the fact of crowding that was the main issue.

In Wilson v. Seiter[40] the Supreme Court added a new factor that had to be shown to prevail in an Eighth Amendment suit: the inmates must prove the defendants were "deliberately indifferent" to conditions that denied inmates "the minimal civilized measure of life's necessities." So post-Wilson there are two separate factors that must be shown to prevail:

(1) The conditions must be very bad, failing to adequately provide inmates with one or more basic human needs, and

(2) The defendants knew of the serious problems and failed to take any sort of meaningful corrective action.

Wilson forced correctional personnel to consider conditions separately rather than the totality of conditions. The Wilson test deals with the basic needs of inmates:

- Food
- Clothing
- Shelter
- Sanitation
- Medical care
- Personal safety
- Exercise

What Happens When an Institution Comes Under Court Order

There are basically two avenues of approach the courts can take to bring "relief" in conditions cases. First, the Court can order an injunction (fix problem), or a consent decree (fix problem by mutual consent).

Some problems are so complex it can take years to fix the problem. The Texas Department of Corrections faced just such a problem from 1980-1990. The Supreme Court case that set the stage for the court-imposed supervision was Estelle v. Ruiz.[41] A federal judge for the Eastern District of Texas issued a sweeping decree. He ordered prison officials to address a host of unconstitutional conditions, including over-crowding, unnecessary use of force by personnel, inadequate numbers of guards, poor health care practices, and a building-tender system that allowed some inmates to control other inmates. Ironically, there is a "domino effect" to these court ordered caps, as was the case with the Texas Department of Corrections. Jails in Texas began to experience overcrowding because they could not send convicted felons on to the state prisons.

This in turn can effect police arrest practices, charging policies of prosecutors, and judge's decisions regarding bail and sentencing. When a court order affects conditions (rather than population caps), the court must have someone oversee the progress that the institution is making. These overseers are most often referred to as "special masters." The courts appoint a special master who reports to the court on the progress being made.

The Prison Litigation Reform Act (PLRA)

By 1996 the U.S. Congress was weary of the control the federal courts had over the operation of the state correctional systems such as that discussed above in Estelle v. Ruiz. Attached as an amendment to the 1994 Crime Bill, the Prison Litigation Reform Act of 1996[42] was passed and set new, more restrictive rules on the federal courts. Below are the salient points of this Act.

- Injunctions should go no further than is minimally necessary to correct constitutional violations.
- Population caps should be imposed only after other methods of correction have been tried and failed.
- A single judge cannot impose a cap; only a specially convened 3-judge court can now impose caps.
- Terminating injunctive orders is easier.
- The powers of special masters have been diminished.

Individual Eighth Amendment Issues
Medical Care
Individual inmates can bring suit against the medical staff and the institution where one or both show "deliberate indifference to serious medical needs."
Smoking
Courts have denied inmate claims that they had a constitutionally protected right to smoke, thus approving smoke-free institutions.
Tort suits
Inadequate medical care could also be the basis for a tort suit. These would be brought in state court rather than federal court.

12.5:4 The Fourteenth Amendment: Due Process and Equal Protection
The Fourteenth Amendment to the U.S. Constitution reads, in part:

> ...*nor shall any state deprive any person of life, liberty, or property, without due process of law; nor deny to any person within its jurisdiction the equal protection of the laws.*[43]

This amendment was added shortly after the Civil War to have the strength of a Constitutional Amendment to prosecute those who were still discriminating and prosecuting against the newly emancipated Black citizens. The Amendment does not say that there cannot ever be deprivation of life, liberty or property; it does say that in order for this to be legal, there must be a process that is due the person. This process is the criminal justice system. In order to treat people or groups differently, the government must justify the unequal treatment.

Procedural Due Process
Procedural due process is concerned with the steps the state goes through to arrive at a decision more so than the actual decision itself. Of course the ultimate goal to be achieved is fairness, and by requiring the government to go through certain steps, the following can be better determined:

- If the facts really are as the government claims them to be (For example, did the inmate really violate the disciplinary rule as accused, or did a parolee really violate a condition of parole?)
- If the government has the legal authority to make the deprivation it proposes to make. (For example, does the institution have the right to censor mail?)

Are There Certain Occasions When "Process" is Due?
The question the court must ask when faced with a procedural due process issue is "Does the Fourteenth Amendment apply to a particular type of decision which affects an inmate? How serious must the deprivation of liberty or property be that the Fourteenth Amendment requires that it be accompanied by some degree of procedural protections? It is clear that in disciplinary issues due process protections must be followed. But what about administrative segregation, removing an inmate from a program, or transferring an inmate to another institution?

Prior to 1995, the courts used a complicated rule to determine whether an inmate was entitled to Fourteenth Amendment due process protections. Basically, the courts said that if the institution had limited its ability to act by the language in its policy, then the inmate was granted due process protections. Under this test, the seriousness of the loss of liberty or property was not relevant; only the language of the rule or policy governing the decision. Understandably, with this rule in force, institutional policy makers were reluctant to place any restrictions of their ability to act.

In 1995 the Supreme Court finally abandoned their "language-focused test" in the case of Sandin v. Conner.[44] The Court replaced the language-focused test with the "atypical and significant deprivation" test. This test, too, is somewhat confusing, but it allowed administrators to return to making logical policy decisions.

The Practical Application of Due Process
Discipline is the most important consideration for custodial personnel. Therefore, taking away an inmate's liberty as a result of disciplinary problems is the one area that requires limited due process. In Wolff v. McDonnel[45] the Court ruled that where state law created a right to good time and that where good time could be forfeited only for serious misbehavior, some due process protections were necessary "to ensure that the state-created right is not arbitrarily abrogated."

In Wolff, the Court laid out the following guidelines where disciplinary procedures would result in loss of good time.
- A Hearing at which the inmate has the right to be present.
- Advance Written Notice Of The Charges, given to the inmate at least twenty-four hours in advance of the hearing.
- The Opportunity For The Inmate To Call Witnesses And Present Evidence On His Or Her Own Behalf, except when it can be shown that to allow this would, "be unduly hazardous to constitutional safety or correctional goals."

- The Right To Assistance (occasionally). Inmates do not, under any circumstances, have a right to a lawyer in a disciplinary hearing, even if criminal charges may be pending against the inmate. Limited circumstances where there may be an exception is where the inmate may be illiterate or where the complexity of the issues makes it unlikely that the inmate will be able to properly represent him or herself.
- Impartial tribunal. No institutional personnel may serve on the tribunal, if he/she was a witness or otherwise involved.
- Written Decision. There must be a written statement by the tribunal "as to the evidence relied on and reasons.[46]

For actions short of loss of good time, the deprivation would have to be serious to warrant the application of Wolff. Administrative segregation for a term of at least a year or more would be required before Wolff would attach.

Confidential Informants

Many times the members of the disciplinary hearing rely on inmate informants to gather the information they need to make a decision. Because of the possibility of abuse of this investigative method, the confidential informant must pass two tests: reliability and credibility. Reliability means that the hearing officer must be convinced the informant is trustworthy. He may do this in a number of ways, but the most common is to show that he has given accurate information in the past.

The credibility test means that the information is corroborated by other information and thus believable.

Alternatives to Litigation

Civil litigation by inmates is costly and diverts correctional officials from their more important task of overseeing the day-to-day operations of the institution. There are other "side effects" as well: decline in staff morale, officer stress, reluctant by correctional staff to take action, and staff-inmate alienation. In a search for alternatives to litigation, four basic approaches have been proposed: grievance boards, inmate grievance procedures, ombudsman, and mediators.[47]

Grievance Board

Usually staffed by institutional employees, or an occasional concerned citizen, to accept and investigate inmate complaints and propose solutions.

Inmate Grievance

Similar to the grievance board, except that inmates are selected to serve as part of the grievance committee. Understandably this is not popular with correctional managers as it gives a great deal of power to the inmates.

Ombudsman

A public official who investigates complaints against correctional personnel, practices, policies, and customs and who is empowered to recommend corrective solutions and measures.

Mediators

A new concept in corrections. They represent a third party skilled in correctional work who agree to hear differences and to render a decision to remedy the condition that would be binding on both parties.

The final section of Chapter XII addresses three areas of corrections that have legal implications for correctional institutions. These three areas are inmate suicides, correctional officer use of force, and the Americans with Disabilities Act (ADA).

12.6:0 SUICIDE

Suicide is always a concern for correctional personnel. The problem is more acute in jails than it is in prisons. Also, correctional personnel can be expected to be sued as a result of both completed and attempted suicide.

12.6:1 Liability Theories: Why Inmates Must Be Protected From Themselves

Anyone using logic would probably say that if an inmate wants to commit suicide, he/she will and this should not be a basis for a lawsuit against the institution. However, this is not the case. Correctional staff do have a responsibility to protect inmates — even from themselves. This duty to protect is found in the Constitution also.[48]

Negligence on the part of the institutional staff is not sufficient for a successful tort suit. As with our past discussion, the "deliberate indifference" test is the measure by which the institution will be judged. As a matter of fact, the degree of significant indifference seems to be growing rather then shrinking. In Patridge v. Two Unknown Police Officers,[49] the majority of Justices emphasized that to state a claim under a deliberate indifference theory, there must be a failure to take action when there is a strong likelihood, not a mere possibility, that injury will occur.

12.6:2 Categories of Factual Allegations

There are three areas, when suicide is involved, that the plaintiff will focus on to build a "deliberate indifference" case:

Failure to Identify

This is the most common claim. The family of the deceased will attempt to show that the police or correctional facility did not heed or observe the indicators of suicide: scarred wrists, bizarre behavior, previous recorded attempts at suicide.

Failure to Monitor

Here the claim is that the facility did not regularly check on the inmate, either in person by keeping regular rounds or by remote, visual monitoring.

Failure to Respond

Here the jail staff will be evaluated by their quick and proper action. Did the jail staff apply life saving techniques—usually CPR—, and were they properly trained in its use.

12.7:0 LEGAL ASPECTS OF THE USE OF FORCE

Correctional officers are legally permitted to use deadly force under very carefully and legally drawn circumstances. Of course this also means that they may use physical force, if the particular situation justifies the use of force according to policy. Using force means that there is the possibility of suits either as torts or as civil rights actions.

12.7:1 When Can Force Be Justified?

The best "rule of thumb" is that force can be used when a reasonable correctional officer believes he has no other alternative. The following are some of the most common situations:

- In self-defense
- To protect others or to protect property
- To enforce prison rules and discipline
- To prevent a crime, including escapes

12.7:2 Deadly Force

Deadly force requires a special circumstance or circumstances for its use. The general rule is that deadly force may be used in self-defense and in the protection of others from death or serious bodily harm, and, in some cases, in the prevention of escape. An example of the proper use of deadly force is where two inmates are fighting in the exercise yard and one has a fabricated knife and is lunging at the opponent. The gun-tower officer sees this and gives warning to the inmates and particularly the armed inmate. The fight continues. The tower officer shoots the armed inmate. Clearly he is using deadly force to prevent serious bodily harm to another inmate.

12.7:3 Excessive Force

Even when force of any kind is justified, it does not allow the correctional officer to use "excessive force." In other words, when the inmate has been subdued or submits, force is no longer necessary. The officer can no longer justify using deadly force. Most excessive force litigation looks at the following basic questions:

(1) Was there a need for force in the first place?
(2) If some force was appropriate, was the amount used appropriate?
(3) If force was not appropriate and/or the amount used was excessive, was the amount used so excessive as to violate the Constitution or state law?[50]

In the case of Hudson v. McMillan,[51] the Supreme Court established a set of rules to determine if the correctional officer acted irresponsibly and inflicted "wanton and unnecessary pain." These five rules are listed below:

(1) Was there a need to use any force?
(2) What was he amount of force used?
(3) What injuries were inflicted, if any?
(4) What was the threat perceived by responsible correctional officials?
(5) What efforts to temper the use of force were made?

12.7:4 Restraints

Restraints cannot be left on prisoners indefinitely or as "punishment." When this has occurred, the courts have intervened. Areas of concern regarding the use of restraints include:

(1) the decision to place an inmate in restraints: who makes it, and in accordance with what criteria?
(2) the types of restraints used,
(3) how long an inmate remains in restraints, and
(4) monitoring both to determine if the need remains for restraints and of the inmate's general safety, comfort, hygiene, and medical/mental health condition.

The key to avoiding litigation in this area is having a sound policy, which addresses these factors and provides guidance for the line and staff personnel.

12.7:5 Documentation of Excessive Force

The key to being prepared to successfully defend against excessive use of force suits is documentation. As a general rule, there are four different types of reports that are useful.

Incident Reports

Proper documentation is the critical ingredient of every report. The safest way for correctional officers to protect against excessive use o force complaints is to properly document their actions, knowing that they have adhered to the policies of the institution.

Videotapes

Where possible, always videotape an incident because this is conclusive proof of what actually happened.

Medical Records

It is important to have the inmate taken immediately to medical personnel after the use of force. This serves two purposes:

(1) the inmate gets treatment and cannot bring suit for "depraved indifference," and

(2) an accurate record of the injuries or lack of them is recorded for posterity.

Training Records

Finally regular, updated training in the use and application of force demonstrates that the institution is expending the effort to insure that their correctional officers know when and how to use force. Records of these training sessions provides the records for proof in court or to an investigating agency.

12.8:0 THE AMERICANS WITH DISABILITIES ACT (ADA)

The ADA prohibits discrimination, isolation, and political powerlessness in:
- employment,
- public services and transportation,
- public accommodations, and
- telecommunications services[52]

This all-encompassing act grew out of the civil rights legislation of the 1960s and 1970s in regard to civil rights in general and vocational rehabilitation in particular. Its impact was not foreseen when Congress passed it in 1990 and certainly the correctional field cannot predict what the future impact will be for corrections. It may very well create some major problems to fully implement its provisions in corrections. For example, of the five titles contained in the ADA, Titles I and II have a direct effect on corrections. These two titles deal with employment practices and access to public-sector services. The following are some implications of Title I and II:

- In corrections, three distinct groups are protected under the ADA: staff, inmates, and public, both visitors and volunteers. Each group must be considered in the design of inmate programs and the space in which programs take place.

- By definition, an individual with a disability has a physical or mental impairment that substantially limits one or more major life activities, has a record of such impairment, or is regarded as having such an impairment.

- The aging offender population, the debilitating effects of alcohol and drug abuse, and injuries sustained through the violent behavior of inmates mean that corrections will be responsible for an increasing number of disabled offenders. Simultaneously, as the individuals with disabilities begin to feel empowered by the ADA to enter the corrections profession, corrections will find that an increasing number of staff and volunteers also will be disabled.[53]

The ADA is the law of the land and must be complied with by correctional leaders. It will most certainly cause correctional leaders to constrain their budgets even more in anticipation of having to meet the mandates of the ADA.

REFERENCES FOR CHAPTER XII

(1) Ruffin v. Commonwealth, 62 Va. 790 (1871)
(2) 378 U.S. 546 (1964)
(3) Rheem v. Malcolm, 371 F. Supp. 594 (S.D.N.Y., 1974)
(4) Bell v. Wolfish, 441 U.S. 529 (1979) and Rhodes v. Chapman, 452 U.S. 337 (1981)
(5) Ibid Bell
(6) 441 U.S. 529 (1979)
(7) 372 U.S. 335 (1963)
(8) 312 U.S. 546 (1941)
(9) 393 U.S. 483 (1969)
(10) 418 U.S. 539 (1974)
(11) 430 U.S. 817 (1977)
(12) Bounds v. Smith, 430 U.S. 817 (1977)
(13) 116 S.Ct. 2174 (1996)
(14) 107 S.Ct. 2400 (1987)
(15) 107 S.Ct. 2254 (1987)
(16) 449 U.S. 210 (1990)
(17) U.S. Constitution, Article V, Amendment Number One
(18) Means of ensuring a legitimate state interest (such as security) that impose fewer limits to prisoners' First Amendment rights than alternative means of securing that end.
(19) An interest of the state that must take precedence over rights guaranteed by the First Amendment.
(20) Any threat to security or to the safety of individuals that is so obvious and compelling that the need to counter it overrides the guarantees of the First Amendment.
(21) Todd R. Clear and George F. Cole, American Corrections, 4th ed., Wadsworth Publishing Co. (1997), p. 393
(22) 42 U.S. Code, Section 2000bb(b)(1)
(23) William C. Collins, Correctional Law for the Correctional Officer, 2nd ed., American Correctional Association (1997), p. 49
(24) Jones v. Bradley, 590 F. 2d. 294 (9th Cir., 1979)
(25) Palmigiano v. Travisono, 317 F. Supp. 776 (D.R.I. 1970)
(26) Harry E. Allen and Clifford E. Simonsen, Corrections in America, 8th ed., Prentice-Hall, Inc. (1995), p. 379
(27) Guajardo v. Estelle, 580 F. 2d. 748 (5th Cir. 1978)
(28) Procunier v. Martinez, 94 S.Ct. 1800 (1974)
(29) Allen and Simonsen, Corrections in America, p. 378
(30) U.S. Constitution, Article V, Amendment Number Four
(31) Hudson v. Palmer, 52 L.W. 5052 (1984)
(32) Block v. Rutherford, 104 S.Ct. 3227 (1984)
(33) Collins, Correctional Law for the Correctional Officer, p. 63
(34) Ibid.
(35) Vaughn v. Ricketts, 663 F. Supp. 410 (D. Ariz., 1987)
(36) U.S. Constitution, Article V, Amendment Number Eight.
(37) 429 U.S. 97 (1976)
(38) 114 S.Ct. 1970 (1994)
(39) Collins, Correctional Law for the Correctional Officer, p. 73
(40) 111 S.Ct. 2321 (1991)
(41) Ruiz v. Estelle, 503 F. Supp. 1265 (S.D. Tex 1980)
(42) PLRA, 28 U.S. Code 3626
(43) U.S. Constitution, Article V, Amendment Number Fourteen
(44) 115 S. Ct. 2293 (1995)
(45) 418 U.S. 539 (1974)
(46) Ibid.
(47) Allen and Simonsen, Corrections in America, p. 386
(48) 751 F. 2d. 1448 (5th Cir., 1985)
(49) Ibid.
(50) Collins, Correctional Law for the Correctional Officer, p. 98
(51) 112 S. Ct. 995 (1992)
(52) Allen and Simonsen, Corrections in America, p. 387
(53) Ibid

STUDY QUESTIONS

CHAPTER XII

(1)   "The prisoner has, as a consequence of his crime, not only forfeited his liberty, but all of his personal rights, except those which the law in its humanity accords him." The case that decided this was policy, and generally set the tone of prisoners as "slaves of the state" was:

        (A) ____Cooper v. Pate   (B) ____Ruffin v. Commonwealth
        (C) ____Bell v. Wolfish   (D) ____Estelle v. Ruiz

(2)   The case that began the "Regulations Period" and assured inmates protection under the Civil rights Act of 1871 was:

        (A) ____Bell v. Wolfish   (B) ____Turner v. Safley
        (C) ____Ex parte Hull   (D) ____Cooper v. Pate

(3)   Relief granted under the Civil Rights Act of 1871, 42 USC 1983, occurs in four aspects. What are these four?

     _____, _____
     _____, and _____ .

(4)   "Habeas Corpus" means:

        (A) ____you've found a dead body
        (B) ____a prisoner in federal prison
        (C) ____you have the body
        (D) ____release the warden from a 42 USC 1983 suit.

(5)   The case that decided that "jailhouse lawyers" could not be prohibited from assisting other inmates was:

        (A) ____Ex parte Hull   (B) ____Johnson v. Avery
        (C) ____Lewis v. Casey   (D) ____Washington v. Harper

(6)   In the case of O'lone v. Estate of Shabazz, the Supreme Court set up a four step approach for correctional officials to use to decide if a restriction was "reasonably related to legitimate penological interests." List these four below:

     _____
     _____
     _____
     _____

(7)   Penal institutions (jails included) must now provide assistance to inmates in preparing and filing legal papers by either providing adequate law libraries or adequate assistance from persons trained in the law. Which case established this right?

        (A) ____Bounds v. Smith   (B) ____Wolff v. McDonnel
        (C) ____Hudson v. Palmer   (D) ____Sandin v. Conner

(8)   The First Amendment guarantees the right to freedom of_____, freedom of _____, and the freedom to _____ .

(9)   Unless it is legal mail (from attorney or attorneys), incoming correspondence may be routinely opened and searched by correctional officers and administrators.   T or F

(10)   Under the "Turner test", religious practices can be restricted by legitimate correctional interests.   T or F

(11) Under the Religious Freedom Restoration Act (RFRA), restrictions on inmates' religious freedoms will be valid only if the institution can show that the restrictions serve a

_____.

(12) The right of inmates to receive printed matter from outside the facility is more protected than their right to publish and distribute their own printed matter.   T or F

(13) Which of the following Amendments protects people against unreasonable searches and seizures?

    (A) ____The First Amendment
    (B) ____The Fourth Amendment
    (C) ____The Eight Amendment
    (D) ____The Fourteenth Amendment

(14) Cells may be searched only in the presence of the inmates who live in them.   T or F

(15) Strip searches of convicted inmates may be conducted only when there is probable cause to believe that the inmate is concealing contraband.   T or F

(16) In Bell v. Wolfish, the Supreme Court decreed that courts should look at the _____ of the crowding situation, rather than _____, to determine whether constitutional violations exist.

(17) The Court's decision in Wilson v. Seiter approved the "totality of conditions" approach to evaluation of conditions-of-confinement cases.   T or F

(18) In the blanks below, list the six basic human needs the courts will generally look at when deciding conditions-of-confinement cases.

_____, _____,
_____, _____,
_____, and _____.

(19) Even though they are not trained medical staff, correctional officers can be sued for "deliberate indifference to a serious medical need."   T or F

(20) An inmate believes that the force used on him by a correctional officer was excessive. He may initiate a civil case for improper or unjustified use of force either as a _____ action or as a _____ case.

Topical Index

A

Access to the Courts 283
Accessories 171
   after the fact 171
   examples 172
   having knowledge (knowingly) 171
   no exceptions to law in California 173
   Scienter 171
Accomplices
   corroboration 174
   feigned 174
   People v. Plascile 174
   who is an accomplice in California? 174
   who is not an accomplice? 174
ADA
   See: Americans with Disabilities Act
Adam and Eve 5
Adams, John 44
Administrative Segregation 266, 268
Admissions 113
The Adversary System 103
   American Bar System 104
   California Bar Examination 105
   California Peace Officer's Association 106
   guilty persons, ethics of defending 104
   In re Gault 105
   inadequate counsel for the poor 105
   judge, function of 103
   The Juvenile Court System 104
   Miranda v. Arizona 105
   plea bargaining 105
   poor, inadequate counsel for the 105
   questions of fact 104
   questions of law 104
Agents
   ammunition 168
   children 168
   innocent 168
   mail-carriers 168
   mechanical device 168
   telephone 168
   trained animals 168
All Crimes Are Crimes Against the State 115
Allegations, Factual 290
Alternatives to Litigation
   See: Litigation, Alternatives to
Amendment 1
   Branzburg v. Hayes 44
   Clear and Present Danger Doctrine 44
   Due Process and Mail 285
   establishment of religion 42

   free exercise of religion 43
   freedom of expression 43
   freedom of radio and television 44
   freedom of speech 43
   freedom of the press 44
   Mail and Publications 285
   Religious Freedom Restoration Act 284
   right of people peaceably to assemble 45
   right to petition for redress of grievances ..45
   Universal Life Church 285
   Visitation 285
   What is a Religion 285
Amendment 2 45
   Dangerous Weapons Control Law 46
   militia 45
   National Guard 45
   National Rifle Association 46
   right to keep and bear arms 45
   Supreme Court decisions 46
   U.S. v. Cruikshank 46
   U.S. v. Miller 46
Amendment 4 ....46, 285
   Body Cavity Probe Searches 286
   Cell Searches 286
   Exclusionary Rule 46, 47
   Illegally seized evidence 46
   Mapp v. Ohio 47
   Patdown Searches 286
   probable cause 47
   search and seizure 46
   Searches in Prison and Jails 286
   Strip Searches 286
   Unreasonable search and seizure 47
   Visitor Searches 286
   warrants 46
   Weeks v. United States 46
Amendment 5 ....47, 220
   Blackstone, Sir William 48
   capital crimes 47
   criminal complaint 47
   double jeopardy 47, 48
   due process of law 49
   eminent domain 47, 50
   grand jury 47
   Hurtado v. California 55
   indictment 47
   infamous crimes 47
   Miranda decision 49
   Peine Forte et Dure 48
   presentment 47
   proper and fair trial 47

self-incrimination................................47, 48
Solesbee v. Balkcom..............................49
third degree 48
true bill 47
Amendment 6 50
Acts XXV:16 52
arraignment 51
cross-examination 52
due process..108
dying declarations 52
Federal Speedy Trial Act 50
impartial jury......................................51
jurisdiction 51
jury selection 51
plea bargaining...................................50
process of obtaining witnesses.............52
right to a public trial...........................51
right to a speedy trial...........................50
right to a trial where
          crime was committed.................51
right to be confronted with witnesses 52
right to be informed of the accusation 51
right to have assistance of counsel.............52
speedy and public trial 50
Star Chamber 51
subpoena 52
venue 51
Amendment 7..52
Amendment 8..52, 286
Conditions of Confinement...................287
cruel and unusual punishment............53, 286
the death penalty 53
excessive bail 52
excessive fines 53
Furman v. Georgia 53
Magna Charta......................................53
Medical Care.......................................288
Prison Litigation Reform Act 287
Smoking...288
special masters 287
Tort suits 288
Trop v. Dulles 53
When an Institution Comes
          Under Court Order....................287
Wilson test 287
Amendment 9..53
Amendment 10......................................54, 150
grant of power......................................54
limitations on power 54
state charter 54
systems of police protection.................54
Amendment 14......................................54, 288
Adamson v. California..........................55
Application of Due Process 288
Brown v. Board of Education 56

Civil Rights Acts.................................56
Confidential Informants......................289
due process of law................................56, 288
equal protection of the laws 56, 288
Grievance Board 289
Griffin v. California.............................55
Hurtado v. California 55
Inmate Grievance................................289
Jim Crow laws 56
Litigation, Alternatives to 289
Mediators 289
NAACP...56
Ombudsman 289
Plessy v. Ferguson 56
Procedural Due Process 288
reverse discrimination........................56
the separate but equal doctrine...........56
sex discrimination 56
shorthand doctrine..............................55
women's rights 56
American Bar Association 104
American Law Institute.........................60
Americans With Disabilities Act 291
Americans with Disabilities Act 289
Ancient Laws, Effect on American Law...........7
Appeals..266
court of last resort 79
Levels of Appeal.................................266
Aquinas, St. Thomas 211
Areopagus, Great Court of....................11
Aristotle...5
Assault...245
Assault with a Deadly Weapon...............246
by Life Prisoner 270
by Prisoner Not Serving Life................270
deadly weapon, definition of...............246
on a peace officer...............................245
Athens 15, 16
Attempts 196
abandonment of..................................201
California law......................................196
due to intervention,
          crime is not completed..............200
elements of..197
          discussion...............................197
inability in law to commit a crime 199
last proximate act...............................197
method reasonably capable
          of completing crime..................201
overt act..197
          examples 197
point of no return 197
Rex v. Scofield.....................................196
Sayre, Law Professor at Harvard 196
specific intent......................................199

Stephen, Sir James 196
toward a crime legally capable
    of completion 198
Attorney General Opinions 97
    formal opinions 98
    informal opinions 98
    types of opinions 98
    weight and effect of 97

B

Babylon 7, 14
    Black Head People 8
    juvenile laws 10
    legal concepts 10
    sabattu 13
    Sun-God Shamash...................8
    witnesses 9
Bastinado.......................................11
Battery..246
    Battery by Gassing by Prison Inmate.......270
    Battery Upon a Person
        Who is Not a Prisoner.......................270
Behavior in a correctional institution
    gang activity................................265
Behavior in correctional institution.................265
Bill of Rights 42, 55
    Acts XXV:16 52
    Amendment 1 ....42, 284
    Amendment 4 285
    Amendment 8 286
    arraignment 51
    Branzburg v. Hayes....................44
    capital crimes 47
    Clear and Present Danger Doctrine...........44
    criminal complaint 47
    cross-examination 52
    cruel and unusual punishment....................53
    Dangerous Weapons Control Law 46
    the death penalty 53
    double jeopardy.....................47, 48
    due process of law....................49
    dying declarations 52
    eminent domain.....................47, 50
    establishment of religion,
        no law respecting 42
    excessive bail 52
    excessive fines 53
    Exclusionary Rule.................46, 47
    Federal Speedy Trial Act 50
    freedom of radio and television 44
    freedom of religion 43
    freedom of speech 43
    freedom of the press....................44
    The Fundamental Rights Theory 55
    Furman v. Georgia 53

grand jury....................................47
grant of power..............................54
Illegally seized evidence 46
impartial jury..............................51
indictment 47
infamous crimes...........................47
Inmate Rights.............................284
jurisdiction 51
jury selection...............................51
limitations on power 54
Mapp v. Ohio..............................47
militia..45
Miranda decision..........................49
National Guard.............................45
National Rifle Association...............46
Peine Forte et Dure 48
plea bargaining............................50
presentment 47
probable cause.............................47
process of obtaining witnesses..................52
proper and fair trial 47
Religious Freedom Restoration Act........284
reversal trend...............................55
right of people peaceably to assemble 45
right to a public trial......................51
right to a speedy trial.....................50
right to a trial where
    crime was committed......................51
right to be confronted with witnesses 52
right to be informed of the accusation 51
right to have assistance of counsel............52
right to keep and bear arms......................45
right to petition for
    reddress of grievances......................45
self-incrimination.....................47, 48
Solesbee v. Balkcom......................49
Star Chamber 51
subpoena 52
systems of police protection.....................54
third degree 48
Trop v. Dulles 53
true bill......................................47
U.S. v. Miller 46
Unreasonable search and seizure 46, 47
venue..51
Bills of Attainder.......................40, 111
Black Head People 8
Black's Law Dictionary.................145
Blackstone, Sir William 23, 48, 59, 76, 139
Body of the Crime
    See: Corpus Delicti
Bringing Drugs or Alcoholic Beverages
    Into Penal Institutions or Jails 273
Burden of Proof.........................114
    insanity.................................114

Burglary 253
    degrees of...255
    shoplifting 255
Burke, Edmund 133

C

Cain 5
California Bar Examination 105
California Code of Regulations
    Title 15 265
California Code of Regulations Sections
    3006 CCR 267
    3043 CCR 265
    3315 CCR 268
    3323 CCR 265
California Constitution..............................60
California Peace Officer's Association 106
California Penal Code 139
California Vehicle Code Sections
    243 CVC 253, 254
    362 CVC 253, 254
    635 CVC 253, 254
    670 CVC 254
Capital Crimes.......................................47
Capital Punishment 53
    Furman v. Georgia 53
Case Citations 79
    explanation of a case..........................80
    Opinions of the Attorney General.............80
    reporters 80
Cases Cited
    Adamson v. California 55
    Bias v. United States 146
    Branzburg v. Hayes...............................44
    Brown v. Board of Education 56
    Fletcher v. Peck...................................76
    Furman v. Georgia 53
    Gault, In re 105
    Griffin v. California 55
    Hurtado v. California 55
    Hutchins v. County Clerk
        of Merced County....................98
    In re Gault 79, 105
    In re Iverson 110
    Jackson v. Commonwealth 145
    Kelly v. United States 187
    Lupo v. Superior Court 96
    Mapp v. Ohio......................................47
    Marbury v. Madison.........................75, 76
    Miranda v. Arizona 49, 76, 79, 105
    Mountain View Union High School Dist. v.
        City Council of City of Sunnyvale 98
    People by McCullough v. Shearer 97
    People v. Barranza 218
    People v. Borra....................................252

People v. Bradbury...............................246
People v. Callihan 252
People v. Chapman 219
People v. Chessman 245
People v. Drew....................................214
People v. Evan 245
People v. Flanagan 241
People v. Hanselman.............................218
People v. Hernandez 76, 96
People v. Lowen...................................255
People v. Macintire 218
People v. Meyers...................................96
People v. Moran 191
People v. Moss.....................................96
People v. Nicolaus 214
People v. Parker 96
People v. Pierre 218
People v. Plascile 174
People v. Robey 150
People v. Rojas 96
People v. Sheffield................................76
People v. Silverstein 218
People v. Wallace.................................237
People v. Weber...................................116
People v. Werner..................................186
Peterson v. City of Long Beach 241
Plessy v. Ferguson 56
Powell v. Texas...................................142
Rex v. Higgins 185
Rex v. Scofield....................................196
Sauer v. United States 106
Solesbee v. Balkcom..............................49
State v. Miller 148
State v. Whitfield 144
Stehr v. State 148
Trop v. Dulles 53
U.S. v. Cruikshank 46
U.S. v. Miller 46
United States v. Watson.........................107
Weeks v. United States 46
Young v. Superior Court.........................96
The Cause and Effect Relationship.................153
    causation 153
        direct..154
        indirect 154
    cause in fact....................................154
    contributing causes.............................155
    doctrine of proximate cause.............153, 155
    the "domino reaction"..........................157
    elements needed for criminal causation...154
    improbability of outcome.......................157
    increased risk 157
    indirect causation 155
    physical cause 157
    proximate cause 157

sole causes 155
   the substantial factor rule 155
   the "but for" rule 154
Chain of Causation 197
Charlemagne 19
   Holy Roman Emperor 19
Charlemagne's Capitularies 19
Checks and Balances 40
   President's veto 40
Civil and Criminal Law
   differences between 127
Civil Code Sections
   1714.1 CC 257
Civil Offenses 127
   torts 127
Civil rights Act of 1871 281
Civil Rights Acts 56, 281, 282
Civil Rights of Institutionalized
   Persons Act 282
Classification of Offenses by Punishment 128
   felonies 128
   graduated offenses 128
   misdemeanors 128
   wobblers 128
Classification of Offenses by Purpose 128
   adjective law 128
   procedural law...128
   substantive law..128
Classification of Offenses by Seriousness 127
   Mala In Se 127
   Mala Prohibita...127
Classification of Offenses by Type of Law 127
   civil offenses 127
   crimes..127
   differences between civil
      and criminal law 127
   torts 127
Clear and Present Danger Doctrine..................44
The Code Napoleon 20
   eminent domain.......................................50
   Japan 20
   The Justinian Code...................................20
Code of Hammurabi...................8, 9, 14, 17
   eye for an eye 9
   Law of Multiple Retaliation........................9
   law of retaliation......................................9
   Lex Talionis 9
   Louvre Museum 8
   Rosicrucian Museum 8
The Code of Solon 15, 16, 106
   Archon..15
   Solon 15
Coke, Sir Edward 23
Commission on Law Enforcement
   and the Administration of Justice................281

Common Law 21, 58, 130
Compounding a Crime 173
   compromise, exceptions to.........................173
   examples 173
   misdemeanors, compromising of.............173
Conditions of Confinement 287
   Prison Litigation Reform Act 287
   special masters 287
   When an Institution Comes
      Under Court Order......................287
   Wilson test 287
Confessions 113
Confidential Informants 289
Confinement, conditions of..........................287
Congress....................................40, 41, 57, 60
   House of Representatives...............40, 57, 60
   Senate....................................40, 57, 60
Conspiracy 188
   criticism of conspiracy laws....................192
   dangers of...188
   defenses that remove specific intent 191
   definition..189
   does not merge 193
   elements of...189
   Federal Criminal Code.............................196
   lawful purpose by unlawful means 191
   The Model Penal Code.................194, 195
   overt act beyond mere agreement 192
   partnership aspects 193
   People v. Moran.......................................191
   proof of..194
   proximate cause 193
   scope of..194
   Stephen, Sir James 188
   two or more persons................................190
   unlawful purpose.....................................191
   when one person can be tried...................190
   withdrawal from......................................194
Constitutional Law
   the father of..75
Constructive Knowledge
   See: Presumed Knowledge
Controlled Substances Act 220
Cooley, Chief Justice 150
   People v. Robey.......................................150
Corporation Code Sections
   25354 CC 220
Corpus Delicti 112
   how are the elements proved?.................113
   Prima Facie proof....................................114
Corpus Juris Civilis....................................18, 130
Corrections
   See also: Offenses by Prisoners
   4571 PC...273
   Access to the Courts................................283

Administrative Segregation 266
Allegations, Factual 290
Amendment 1..284
Amendment 4..285
Amendment 8..286
Amendment 14......................................288
Americans With Disabilities Act 291
Appeals 266
Appeals Relating to Mail 267
Application of Due Process 288
Assisting Escape or Attempted Escape by
    Prisoner Whose Parole is Revoked...272
Behavior...265
Bil of Rights...284
Body Cavity Probe Searches...................286
Bringing Drugs or Alcoholic Beverages
    Into Penal Institutions or Jails...........273
Bringing in Letters to Prisons 273
Carrying Article Useful for Escape Into
    Prison or Jail 272
Cell Searches..286
Civil Rights Act 282
Civil rights Act of 1871 281
Civil Rights of Institutionalized
    Persons Act......................................282
Classification 270
Commission on Law Enforcement and
    the Administration of Justice 281
Conditions of Confinement.....................287
Confidential Informants..........................289
Confidential Mail and Inspection.............267
Credit-Earning Special Assignments 266
Credits...264
Cruel and Unusual Punishment...............286
Damaging or Injuring a Prison or Jail 274
Due Process..288
Due Process and Mail 285
Equal Protection....................................288
Escape by Mentally Disordered
    Sex Offender....................................272
Escapes and Rescues.............................271
Excessive Force 290
    documentation of 291
Force, Deadly..291
Force, Legal Aspects of Use...................291
Force, when justified?............................291
gang activity...265
General Institution Regulations 267
Grievance Board 289
Habeas Corpus 282
Inmate activities....................................267
Inmate Councils 267
Inmate Freedoms and
    Institutional Security.........................283
Inmate Grievance 289

Inmate resources 267
Inmate Rights.......................................284
Inmates and Litigation 282
laissez faire period 281
Law Enforcement Assistance
    Administration 281
Liability Theories..................................289
Litigation...282
    Alternatives to..................................289
Loss of Participation Credit 265
Mail...267
    Publications......................................285
Mediators 289
Medical Care...288
Notification of Law Enforcement of Escape
    From Secure Detention Facility.......272
Ombudsman..289
one inmate-per-cell rule 282
Patdown Searches 286
Period of Vacillation..............................282
Possession of Controlled Substances
    Where Prisoners are Kept 274
Prison Litigation Reform Act 287
Privilege Groups 265
Procedural Due Process 288
Protective Housing Unit.........................268
Psychiatric Management Unit..................268
Public Information 267
Regulations Period................................281
Religious Freedom Restoration Act.........283
Rescue or Attempted Rescue 272
Restraints 290
Searches in Prison and Jails 286
Security 267
Security Housing Unit 266, 268
Selling, Furnishing, Controlled Substances
    in Prison, Camp or Jail.....................274
Smoking...288
Smuggling Firearms, Deadly Weapons,
    or Tear Gas Into a Prison or Jail.......274
special masters 287
Strip Searches.......................................286
Suicide 289
Tort suits 282, 288
Turner test 284
Unauthorized Communication
    With a Prisoner in Transport.............273
Unauthorized Communications 273
United States Code, section 1983 281
Universal Life Church............................285
Using False Identification to Secure
    Admission to Prison or Camp...........273
Visitation...285
Visiting..267
Visitor Searches 286

Waivers 265
Warren Court 282
When an Institution Comes
    Under Court Order.......................287
Wilson test 287
Work Group Assignments...................266
Corroboration 174
    why is it needed?.............................175
Corruption of Blood 41
Court of Appeals 40
Court of Last Resort 79
Court Trials 115
C-P.O.S.T...265
Credit for good behavior
    Loss of Participation Credit 265
Credits for good behavior 265
    Waivers 265
Crime
    15 PC..139
    20 PC..139
    Blackstone, Sir William 139
    California Penal Code Definition.......139
    definition of.....................................139
    elements needed to constitute 139
    Perkins, Rollin M. 139
    triangle of..139
Crimen Falsi..117
Crimes 127
Crimes and Punishment Act (1850).................167
Crimes Without Victims 133
    Burke, Edmund 133
Criminal Complaint..................................47
Criminal Conduct 139
    Amendment 14.................................141
    constructive acts..............................140
    continuing acts 141
    failure to act 140
    illegal possession or transportation..........140
    important cases regarding status 142
    passive participation.........................140
    Powell v. Texas 142
    status as an act.................................141
    supreme court...................................141
    types of..140
    unconstitutional status acts 141
    unconstitutionality 141
    verbal conduct.................................140
        directive or instructive 141
        indecent language, use of................141
        soliciting or procuring.....................140
    voluntary acts 140
Criminal Law, Purpose of
    See: The Purpose of Criminal Law
Criminal Negligence 147
    chain of causation 148

example 149
moral obligations 148
recklessness...150
rules on...149
State v. Miller 148
Stehr v. State 148
Cross-Examination....................................52
Cruel and Unusual Punishment................53, 286
    the death penalty 53
    Trop v. Dulles 53
Customs and Taboos 6

D

Damaging or Injuring a Prison or Jail 274
Dangerous Weapons Control Law 46, 97, 153
    section 12020 97
Dark Ages 18
Deadly Force 290
The Death Penalty
    See: Capital Punishment
Declaration of Independence 45
Defenses Against Criminal Prosecution
    See also: Defenses Based on
        Constitutional Protection
    See also: Defenses Based on Lack of Intent
    See also: Defenses Involving Limited
        Mental Capacity
    See also: Defenses, Other
    See also: Illegal Defenses
    California defenses under Section 26 PC.212
    common law defenses.........................281
    diminished capacity 212
    mental impairment 212
    Stephen, Sir James 223
Defenses Based on Constitutional Protection .217
    See also: Statute of Limitations
    consent 221
    contract immunity 221
        turning "state's evidence" 221
    diplomatic immunity.........................221
    entrapment..218
    former jeopardy.................................217
    immunity 220
        contract 221
        turning "state's evidence" 221
        diplomatic 221
        feigned accomplice 221
        statutory 220
    legislative intent...............................222
    People v. Barranza 218
    People v. Chapman 219
    People v. Hanselman..........................218
    People v. Macintire...........................218
    People v. Pierre 218
    People v. Silverstein 218

prior offense 217
self-defense 221
spirit of the law 222
status 221
statute of limitations:
    Ex Post Facto application 220
statutory immunity.........................220
    feigned accomplice 221
when jeopardy does attach..............217
when jeopardy does not attach..........217
Defenses Based on Lack of Intent.................222
accident and misfortune....................222
acts under force, threat, or duress 223
innocent agents................................222
mistake of fact.................................222
mistake of law 222
Defenses Involving Limited Mental Capacity
children ages 7 – 14 213
children under 7 212
delirium from fever or medication..........216
The Durham Test 215
evidence of insanity 215
evidence of insanity that is
    not acceptable 215
idiocy 213
infancy.......................................212
injuries to the head......................216
the insanity defense in California 214
involuntary intoxication..................216
The Irresistible Impulse Test 215
The M'Naghten Rule...........................214
not guilty by reason of insanity...............214
Peel, Sir Robert..............................214
People v. Drew................................214
People v. Nicolaus 214
persons unconscious of the act.................216
sleepwalking 216
somnambulism 216
The Substantial Capacity Test 215
voluntary intoxication 216
Defenses, Other....................................223
necessity as a defense.........................223
physical impossibility 224
Stephen, Sir James 223
Definition of Crime 139
15 PC..139
20 PC..139
Blackstone, Sir William.......................139
California Penal Code definition 139
Perkins, Rollin M. 139
The Development of Law 5
District Courts 40
Disturbing the Peace 253
The Doctrine of Proximate Cause...........153, 155
Double Jeopardy 47, 48, 217

Draco...15
The Draconian Code 15
Due Process and Mail 285
Due Process of Law 49, 56, 108, 288
Application of 288
petition of right (English, 1628) 49
Procedural Due Process 288
Solesbee v. Balkcom...........................49
Dying Declarations 52

E

Ebla 7
Ecclesiastical Courts 18
Educational Code Sections
48910 Ed Code................................257
Egypt...10
Acts of the Apostles.........................10
bastinado.....................................11
Cleopatra.....................................12
courts...11
feather of Maat...............................11
importance of Egyptian law to the U.S......12
judgment 11
Maat 11
Medjay 11
Menes...11
Moses 10, 12
police...11
polygamy 12
punishment...................................10
seat of wisdom 10
selected laws 12
Solon..11
wisdom of the Egyptians.....................10
Elements Needed to Constitute a Crime 139
criminal conduct.............................139
criminal conduct, types of....................140
law 139
the mental element...........................142
the triangle of crime.........................139
Eminent Domain 47, 50
Code Napoleon..............................50
Magna Charta................................50
England
Alfred the Great 21
Angles and Saxons...........................20
Anglo-Saxons................................20
Blackstone, Sir William.......................23
Canute 21
Coke, Sir Edward............................23
Common Law of England....................21
compurgation 21
Edward I......................................22
Edward the Confessor.......................21
English Justinian 22

Frankpledge.................................20
Habeas Corpus amendment act..................22
Hue and Cry................................20
jurists of note 23
The Justinian Code.........................21
King Aethelbert............................21
King John..................................22
Law of Edward the Confessor................21
Lord Avonmore..............................23
The Magna Charta...........................22
Normans....................................21
petition of right 23
Precedence 24
Reform Act of 1832.........................23
Rules of Equity 23
Runnymede 22
Sheriff 21
Stare Decisis..........................21, 24
Stephen Langdon 22
the Inns of Court 22
Tithings 20
trial by duel 21
trial by jury..............................21
trials 21
William the Conqueror 21
English Common Law 58, 114
Entrapment............................187, 218
Equal Protection..........................288
Equal Protection Clause 56
reverse discrimination.............56
sex discrimination 56
women's rights 56
Equal Protection of the Laws 56
Escape 272
Assisting Escape or Attempted Escape by
Prisoner Whose Parole is Revoked..272
Notification of Law Enforcement of Escape
From Secure Detention Facility.......272
Officers Aiding Escape 272
Escape by Mentally Disordered Sex Offender
Duties of Medical Director 272
Escape from County or City
Correctional Facility....................271
Escape From Prison 271
Escapes and Rescues....................271
Ethics of Defending Guilty Persons.............104
Europe 18
See also: England
See also: Feudal Law
See also: France
See also: Spain
Charlemagne's Capitularies.............19
Ex Post Facto Laws....................40, 110
Excessive Bail 52
Excessive Fines 53

Excessive Force...........................290
documentation of 291
Exclusionary Rule 46, 47
Executive Branch of Government.............40
Extortion.................................252
Extradition, rules of.......................41
Eye for an eye 9, 14

F

Factual Allegations
See: Allegations, Factual
False Identification........................273
Family Rules of Order.........................5
Family Visits..............................267
FCC (Federal Communictions Commission)....44
The Federal Bureau of Investigation (FBI).......57
Federal Communications Commission (FCC)..44
Federal Criminal Code 188, 196
The Federalist Papers 39, 75
Hamilton, Alexander...................75
Felony....................................128
Feudal Law................................18
See also: Common Law
dark ages 18
feudal lord 18
serfs 18
Final Classification of Crime 130
Force, Deadly 290
Force, Excessive..........................290
documentation of 291
Force, Legal Aspects of Use 290
Deadly Force..............................290
Excessive Force 290
documentation of 291
Restraints 290
When can force be justified?..............290
Force, when justified? 290
Former Jeopardy 217
France
See also: The Code Napoleon
Bonaparte, Napoleon...................20
Cambaceres............................20
Freedom of Radio and Television...............44
Freedom of the Press......................44
Branzburg v. Hayes....................44
The Fundamental Rights Theory...............55

G

gang activity in a correctional facility.............265
Good Samaritan Laws.........................9
Government Code Sections
9410 GC.................................220
9608 GC.................................111
12519 GC.................................97

12550 GC...97
12560 GC...97
27491.3 GC...235
Graduated Offenses.............................128
Grand Jury...47
   indictment 47
   true bill 47
Grant of Power 54
The Great Court of Areopagus...........11, 16
   Acropolis...16
   Athens 16
   Hill of Mars..16
Greece 15
   See also: The Code of Solon
   See also: The Draconian Code
   See also: The Great Court of Areopagus
   Acropolis...16
   Athens 15, 16
   Draco...15
   Solon 15, 106
   Sparta 15
Grievance Board 289
Guilty Persons
   ethics of defending..........................104

H

Habeas Corpus 22, 282
   writ of...40
Hamilton, Alexander........................39, 75
Hammurabi...8
   See also: Code of Hammurabi
   Judgment of Righteousness 8
Hand, Justice Learned 143
Harbor and Navigation Code Sections
   21 H & N.......................................253, 254
Health and Safety Code Sections
   7181 H & S 235
   7189 - 7194 H & S 237
   11000 H & S 274
   11367 H & S 220
   18075.55 H & S 252, 255
Holmes, Oliver Wendell 44
Homicide...235
   See also: Lawful Homicide
   See also: Unlawful Homicide
   death occurs within three years
      and a day...................................236
   death, definition of...........................235
   elements 235
   proximate cause 235
   right to search bodies (police officers).....235
   transplanting body parts..................235
House of Representatives......................40

How Laws Are Made 60
   assembly bill (AB)..............................62
   bills 61
   codes 61
   congress..60
   house of representatives...................60
   The Legislative Counsel 64
   procedures involved in the
      making of new law....................61
   senate..60
   senate bill (SB)...................................61
   state assembly 60
   state legislature.................................60
   state senate 60
   statutes 61
   through a referendum 64
   through an initiative 64
How Laws Are Made – Formal Organization
   The Highway Patrol Pay Initiative.............64
   The Jarvis-Gann Tax Initiative 64
How Laws Are Made – Informal Organization
   The Marijuana Referendum 64
Hughes, Chief Justice...........................76

I

Illegal Defenses
   alibi as a defense 225
   contributory negligence 226
   custom as a defense..........................225
   irresistible impulse...........................226
   matters of honor as a defense.................225
   moral insanity 226
   religion as a defense.........................225
   sexual deviance 226
   uncontrollable impulse....................226
Illegally Seized Evidence.......................46
Immunity..220
   contract..221
      turning "state's evidence" 221
   Controlled Substances Act......................220
   diplomatic 221
   statutory 220
      feigned accomplice 221
   turning "state's evidence"..................221
Impartial Jury 51
   change of venue 51
   Voir Dire 51
Inadequate Counsel for the Poor.............105
   California Bar.....................................105
Inchoate Offenses................................185
   See also: Attempts
   See also: Conspiracy
   See also: Solicitation
Indeterminate Sentencing....................130
Indictment 47

Infamous Crimes 47
Informants, Confidential 289
Infraction 129
Initiative
    proposing a new amendment 64
    proposing a new law 64
Inmate Councils 267
Inmate Freedoms and Institutional Security ...283
    Turner test 284
Inmate Grievance 289
    Mediators 289
Inmate Rights 284
    Amendment 1 284
    Amendment 4 285
    Amendment 8 286
    Amendment 14 288
    Americans With Disabilities Act 291
    Application of Due Process 288
    Body Cavity Probe Searches 286
    Cell Searches 286
    Conditions of Confinement 287
    Confidential Informants 289
    Cruel and Unusual Punishment 286
    Due Process 288
    Due Process and Mail 285
    Equal Protection 288
    Excessive Force 290
        documentation of 291
    Force, Deadly 290
    Force, Legal Aspects of Use 290
    Force, when justified? 290
    Grievance Board 289
    Inmate Grievance 289
    Litigation, Alternatives to 289
    Mail and Publications 285
    Mediators 289
    Medical Care 288
    Ombudsman 289
    Patdown Searches 286
    Prison Litigation Reform Act 287
    Procedural Due Process 288
    Religious Freedom Restoration Act 284
    Restraints 290
    Searches in Prison and Jails 286
    Smoking 288
    special masters 287
    Strip Searches 286
    Tort suits 288
    Visitation 285
    Visitor Searches 286
    When an Institution Comes
        Under Court Order 287
    Wilson test 287
Inmates and Litigation 282
Insanity 114

Intent 142
    constructive 144
    definition of 142
    general 143
    specific 143
    transferred 144
Israel 12
    See also: The Mosaic Code
    See also: Moses

J

Jay, John 39
Jefferson, Thomas 54
Jim Crow Laws 56
Joint Relationship Between Act and Intent 153
Judgement of Righteousness
    See: Code of Hammurabi
Judicial Branch of Government 41
    Independent Judiciary 41
Judicial Review 75
    The Federalist Papers 75
    Fletcher v. Peck 76
    Hamilton, Alexander 75
    Hughes, Chief Justice 76
    The Judiciary Act of 1789 75
    lower court decisions 76
    Marbury v. Madison 75, 76
    Marshall, John 75
    The Miranda Decision 76
    U.S. Constitution, Article 3, Section 2 76
    United States Reports 76
Jury Selection 51
    challenge for cause 51
    peremptory challenges 51
    Voir Dire 51
Jury Trials 115
The Justinian Code 17, 19, 20, 21, 130
    Corpus Juris Civilis 18
    Tribonianus 17
The Juvenile Court System 104
    In re Gault 105
    Miranda v. Arizona 105

K

Kidnapping 244
    as part of another crime 244
    bodily harm, definition of 245
    extortion by posing as kidnapper 245
    Little Lindbergh Law 245
    ransom 245
    regular 244
    simple 244
King Hammurabi
    See: Hammurabi

King Henry VIII...44
King Naram-Sin 7

L

Language and Construction of Penal Codes
    conflict at the same level
        of government....................................110
Language and Construction
    of Penal Statutes 108
    all California law is statutory...................108
    Bills of Attainder 111
    breaking down a crime by its elements....113
    conflict between different
        levels of governme.........................109
    conflict between statutes 109
    Corpus Delicti 112
    Ex Post Facto laws 110
    In re Iverson 110
    interpretation of the law..........................111
    The Letter of the Law 111
    new law found, in part,
        unconstitutional.............................110
    no statute will be too vague 108
    pre-emption 109
    repeal of existing laws 111
    The Spirit of the Law 111
    the statute must be in English 108
    when laws are considered to be
        in effect 110
Las Siete Partidas 20
Law Enforcement Assistance
    Administration...281
Law Library, Use of...80
    See also: Locating Particular Cases
    Annotated California Codes......................85
    California Blue and White Book...............86
    California Digest.......................................85
    California Reporter 86
    case citations, cross references for............86
    Cumulative Annual Pocket Parts 85
    general areas of law 85
    other information in the codes 85
    Shepardizing a case..................................86
    Shepard's Citations..................................86
Law of Multiple Retribution 9
Law of Retaliation...9
The Law of the Twelve Tables 17
    The Code of Solon 17
    Hermodorus...17
    Lex Talionis 17
    maxims..17
    patricians and plebes 17
    Temple of Jupiter 17
    vendetta..17

Lawful Homicide 240
    See also: Self-Defense, Exceptions to
    defense of habitation 241
    excusable homicide..................................240
    justifiable homicide.................................240
    killing of trespassers 242
    no duty to retreat in California.................242
    self-defense 242
    trespassers, killing of 242
    when apprehending a felon 244
Laws of Reciprocity 41
LEAA
    See: Law Enforcement Assistance
        Administration
The Legal Brief...95
    parts of the case brief...............................95
    three good rules in briefing a case 95
    writing a case brief...................................95
Legal Requirements for Citizen Action 116
    California Labor Code 116
    misprision of treason...............................116
    People v. Weber.......................................116
    Posse Comitatus 116
    Workman's Compensation 116
Legal Research
    computerized research 75
    LEXIS computer system 75
    ramifications of..75
Legislative Branch of Government
    See: Congress
Legislative Intent..111
Lesser Degrees of Crime.................................132
Lesser Offenses 132
The Letter of the Law......................................111
Lex Talionis **9, 14, 17**
LEXIS Computer System.................................**75**
Liability Theories..**289**
Limitations on Power **54**
Litigation..**282**
Litigation, Alternatives to **289**
    Grievance Board **289**
    Ombudsman **289**
Locating Particular Cases................................**80**
    Annotated California Codes......................**85**
    California Blue and White Book...............**86**
    California Digest.......................................**85**
    California Reporter **86**
    case citations, cross references for............**86**
    Cumulative Annual Pocket Parts **85**
    general areas of law **85**
    other information in the codes **85**
    searcher has name of appellant only **84**
    searcher has the actual case citation..........**84**
    searcher knows a special condition
        of offense **85**

searcher knows type of offense only..........84
Shepardizing a case.....................................86
Shepard's Citations.....................................86
Locke, John..108

M

Maat...11
    Chamber of Maat....................................12
    the God of Justice...................................11
MAD CATS BARK.....................................237
Madison, James...39
Magna Charta.......................................48, 53
    eminent domain.......................................50
Mail in correctional facility
    Appeals relating to.................................267
    Disapproval of Mail...............................267
Mala In Se..............................127, 142, 143, 150
Mala Prohibita..................................127, 150
Malice...116, 145
    Bias v. United States...............................146
    Black's Law Dictionary............................145
    definition of...145
    express...146
    implied..146
    in murder...146
Manslaughter
    See: Unlawful Homicide
Marshall, John...75
Meanings of Terms.....................................116
    book...117
    bribe..117
    corruptly..116
    county..116
    Crimen Falsi...117
    daytime..117
    deposition...116
    feloniously...117
    gender..116
    infamous crime.......................................117
    knowingly..117
    magistrate..117
    malice..116
    mark..116
    month..117
    moral turpitude......................................117
    neglect...116
    nighttime...117
    number..116
    oath..116
    peace officer..117
    person..116
    personal property....................................117
    process...117
    property..117
    real property...117

    seal..117
    section..117
    state...117
    tense..116
    testify..116
    vessel..117
    wantonly..117
    will..117
    willful...116
    writ...117
    writing...116
Mediators..289
Medical Care...288
Medjay...11
Menes..11
Mens Rea...142, 211
The Mental Element
    See also: Criminal Negligence
    See also: malice
    See also: Presumed Knowledge
    See also: Presumptive Laws
    constructive intent..................................144
    general intent...143
    intent...142
        constructive......................................144
        definition of.....................................142
        general...143
        specific..143
        transferred.......................................144
    Jackson v. Commonwealth.......................145
    Justice Learned Hand..............................143
    mens rea..142
    motive...146
    specific intent..143
    State v. Whitfield....................................144
    Stephen, Sir James..................................143
    transferred intent...................................144
    trespass ab initio....................................145
Mentally Disordered Sex Offender..............272
Mesopotamia..7
Michelangelo..13
Military and Veteran's Code
    National Guardsman................................14
Military and Veteran's Code Sections
    393 M & V..14
Miranda Decision..................40, 49, 52, 76, 79
Misdemeanor..128
Misprision of Treason................................116
Model Penal Code............60, 185, 187, 194, 195
    The American Law Institute.......................60
Moors...19
Moral Turpitude..117
mores..6
Morris, M.F..8

Mosaic Code 12, 24
    Deuteronomy...14
    examples of Mosaic law.............................13
    eye for an eye...14
    Ezekiel...13
    Ezra...14
    Five Books of Moses 13
    Joshua..13
    Leviticus...13, 14
    Lex Talionis 14
    Luke 14
    multiple retribution 14
    Pentateuch 13
    sabbatical year...13
    The Talmud..14
    The Torah...13
    Zacchaeus..14
Moses 10, 12
    examples of Mosaic law.............................13
    Five Books of Moses 13
    the Lawgiver 13
    Michelangelo...13
    Mosaic Code 12
    Pentateuch...13
    The Torah...13
Motive...146
Multiple Retribution.....................................14
Murder
    See: Unlawful Homicide

N

Naram-Sin, King 7
National Rifle Association (NRA)....................46
Neglect 116
Negligence
    See: Criminal Negligence
Nixon, Richard M. 40

O

Offenses by Prisoners
    Carrying Article Useful for Escape
        Into Prison or Jail 272
    Damaging or Injuring a Prison or Jail 274
    Escape by Mentally Disordered
        Sex Offender....................................272
    Holding a Hostage Within a Prison 271
    Possession of Alcoholic Beverages, Drugs
        etc. in Prison, Camp or Jail...............274
    Possession of Deadly Weapons
        by Prisoner 271
Ombudsman 289
one inmate-per-cell rule 282
Ordinances 129

P

P.O.S.T.
    C-P.O.S.T...265
Paine, Thomas 5
Parties to a Crime...167
    See also: Accessories
    See also: Agents
    See also: Compounding a Crime
    abet: definition 168
    actual presence 168
    aid: definition.......................................168
    California System, advantages of 167
    constructive presence 168
    Crimes and Punishment Act 167
    must have specific intent.........................168
    principals...167
    several persons pursue
        a common design 169
    sympathy alone not sufficient 169
    those who advise and encourage..............170
    those who aid and abet............................168
    those who compel another
        to commit a crime 170
    under common law...................................175
Parts of the Crime
    See: Corpus Delicti
Peel, Sir Robert 214
Peeping Tom 59
Peine Forte et Dure 48
Penal Code Sections
    4 PC..111, 222
    7 PC...116
    15 PC...139
    17 PC...128
    19.6 PC..129
    19.7 PC..129
    20 PC..97, 139
    21 PC...214
    25a PC...214
    25b PC...214
    25c PC...214
    26 PC...212, 214
    27 PC...167
    28a PC...214
    31 PC...167, 170
    32 PC...171
    38 PC...116
    115 PC...243
    127(c) PC 186
    150 PC...116, 224
    153 PC...173
    182 PC...189, 191
    184 PC...189
    187 PC...218, 236

188 PC	236
190 PC	265
190.25 PC	237
191.5 PC	240
192(a) PC	238
192(b) PC	238
192(c) PC	239
192(c)3 PC	239
195 PC	240
196 PC	240
197 PC	221, 240, 242
198 PC	221, 242
199 PC	240
207 PC	244, 245
209 PC	244, 245
210 PC	245
211 PC	250, 252
212 PC	252
240 PC	197, 200, 245
242 PC	200, 245
245 PC	245
261 PC	217, 219, 236, 247, 250
261.1 PC	217, 250
261.2 PC	217, 250
261.3 PC	250
261.4 PC	250
261.5 PC	250
261.6 PC	250
261.7 PC	250
262 PC	248, 250
263 PC	248
266 PC	249
266(h) PC	186
266c PC	249
270 PC	43, 147, 239
271 PC	237
273.5 PC	128
273a PC	237
285 PC	199
286 PC	219, 236, 250
288 PC	219, 236
288.5 PC	219
288a PC	219, 223, 236, 250
289 PC	113, 219, 236, 250
415 PC	253
417 PC	221
451 PC	196
458 PC	253
459 PC	253
484 PC	114, 255
486 PC	256
487 PC	256
487c PC	256
487d PC	256
487e PC	257
488 PC	256, 257
496 PC	96
496(4) PC	14
497 PC	256
518 PC	252
532 PC	255
594 PC	257
594.3 PC	257
647(a) PC	186
647(b) PC	186
653f PC	185, 186
654 PC	244
656 PC	217
663 PC	196
664 PC	96, 196
687 PC	217
793 PC	217
794 PC	217
799 PC	219, 220
800 PC	219
801 PC	219
801.5 PC	219
802 PC	220
802(a) PC	219
802(b) PC	219
803 PC	219
804 PC	219
805 PC	219
834 PC	244
835a PC	243
837 PC	244
995 PC	96
1026 PC	214
1027 PC	214
1096 PC	114
1099 PC	218
1100 PC	218
1111 PC	174, 213
1140 PC	217
1141 PC	217
1203.016 PC	271
1238(a) PC	96
1324 PC	220
1324.1 PC	221
1377 PC	173
1378 PC	173
1379 PC	173
1429.5 PC	212
2931 PC	265
2933 PC	265
4500 PC	270
4501 PC	270
4501.1 PC	270
4501.5 PC	270
4502 PC	271

4503 PC..271
4530 PC..271
4530.5 PC...271
4532 PC..271
4533 PC..272
4534 PC..272
4535 PC..272
4536 PC..272
4536(b) PC..272
4537 PC..272
4550 PC..272
4570 PC..273
4570.1 PC...273
4570.5 PC...273
4571 PC..273
4573 PC..273
4573.5 PC...273
4573.6 PC...274
4573.8 PC...274
4573.9 PC...274
4574 PC..274
4600 PC..274
12003 PC..110
12021 PC..141
12025 PC..112
12091 PC..114
12420 PC..112
Period of Vacillation 282
Perkins, Rollin M. 139
PET POLY 237
Phoenicia...7
PHU
    See: Protective Housing Unit
Plea Bargaining.................................50, 105
    California Peace Officer's Association 106
PLRA
    See: Prison Litigation Reform Act
PMU
    See: Psychiatric Management Unit
Police Power and its Limits 60
Poor, inadequate counsel for the 105
Posse Comitatus 116
Possession of Controlled Substances
    Where Prisoners are Kept....................274
Precedence 24, 76
    appeal, basis for 79
    Blackstone, Sir William.........................76
    case law and its uses 79
    People v. Hernandez 76
    Words and Phrases................................79
Pre-emption..109
    In re Iverson 110
Pre-emption, rule of 42
Presentment..47
President's veto..40

Presumed Knowledge 150
    Amendment 10....................................150
    constructive knowledge 151
    Cooley, Chief Justice 150
    criminal acts coerced by employer 152
    People v. Robey 150
    strict liability crimes 150
        justification for...............................150
        legality of......................................150
    the principal-agent rule 152
Presumptions of Guilt 114
Presumptive Laws....................................152
    examples 153
Prima Facie Proof....................................114
Prison Litigation Reform Act....................287
Prisoners
    Unauthorized Communications with.........273
Privilege Groups
    Group A 266
    Group U 266
Probable Cause..47
Process of Obtaining Witnesses....................52
    subpoena 52
Prohibition..7
Proper and Fair Trial.................................47
Public Offenses 129
    infractions 129
    ordinances 129
Public Utilities Code Sections
    21012 PUC..................................253, 254
Punishment
    enhancements.....................................131
        limit on..131
    good-time credit..................................131
    parole..131
    probation 131
    procedure in sentencing 131
    suspended sentences............................131
Puritan Theocracy 42
The Purpose of Criminal Law 106
    The Code of Solon 106
    establishing predictability 107
    establishment of peace and order.............106
    Locke, John..108
    preservation of freedom and liberty.........107
    preserving morals and social behavior.....107
    prevention of anarchy 108
    prevention of crime..............................107
    protection of life and property 106
    punishment..108
    resolving problems in a fair
        and just manner...............................107
    Sauer v. United States 106
    Solon...106
    Stephen, Sir James 108

U.S. Constitution.................................106
United States v. Watson.........................107
vengeance...108
Putting someone in Coventry......................59

Q

Questions of Fact 104, 115
Questions of Law 104, 115

R

Rape 247
   accomplished by force or fear.................249
   inducing illegal sex by fraud................249
   of spouse 250
   penetration...................................248
   privity, definition of.......................249
   the "principal" concept of rape 248
   unlawful intercourse.........................250
   victim believed perpetrator was spouse ...249
   victim is of unsound mind 248
   victim is prevented from resisting...........249
   victim unconscious
      of the nature of the act 249
Reasonable Doubt 114
Reciprocity, Laws of..............................41
Referendum
   changing existing law 64
   changing the state constitution...............64
Regulations Period 281
Religious Freedom Restoration Act................284
   Universal Life Church........................285
Repeal of Existing Laws 111
Republican form of government 41
Res Gestae..171
Rescue or Attempted Rescue 272
Restraints..290
Reverse Discrimination............................56
RFRA
   See: Religious Freedom Restoration Act
Right of People Peaceably to Assemble 45
Right of the People to Keep and Bear Arms.....45
   National Rifle Association...................46
Right to a Public Trial...........................51
   Star Chamber 51
Right to a Speedy Trial 50
   Federal Speedy Trial Act 50
Right to a Trial Where
   Crime Was Committed 51
   jurisdiction 51
   venue 51
Right to be Confronted with Witnesses 52
Right to be Confronted With Witnesses
   cross-examination 52
   dying declarations 52

Right to be Informed of the Accusation...........51
   arraignment 51
Right to Have Assistance of Counsel...............52
   Public Defender's Office.....................52
Right to petition for redress of grievances 45
Robbery...250
   degrees 252
   elements of..................................250
   pharmacy.....................................252
Roman Law 19
   Ecclesiastical Courts 18
   role of the church in preserving 18
   University of Bologna........................18
Rome 17
   See also: The Justinian Code
   See also: The Law of the Twelve Tables
   See also: Roman Law
   fall of......................................18
   The Judices..................................17
   patricians and plebes 17
   sabbatical leave 13
Rule of pre-emption 42
Rules Controlling Conviction 114
   all crimes are crimes against the state......115
   burden of proof 114
   court trials 115
   Insanity.....................................114
   jury trials 115
   presumptions of guilt 114
   questions of fact............................115
   questions of law 115
   reasonable doubt 114
   unanimous verdicts 115
Rules of Extradition 41

S

Sayre, Law Professor at Harvard 196
Scienter..171
Searches in Prison and Jails 286
   Body Cavity Probe Searches...................286
   Cell Searches................................286
   Patdown Searches 286
   Strip Searches...............................286
   Visitor Searches 286
Seat of Wisdom
   See: Egypt
Security 267
   Emergency Count..............................268
   Inmate Freedoms..............................283
   Inmate Movement 268
   Protective Housing Unit......................268
   Psychiatric Management Unit..................268
   Segregated Program Housing Units.........268
   Standing Count 268
   Turner test 284

Security Housing Unit.....................................266
    Factors in Mitigation of SHU Term.........268
Security Housing Unit Term
    Factors in Aggravation............................269
    Factors in Mitigation..............................269
Self-Defense, Exceptions to
    See also: Unlawful Homicide
    bare fear 242
    duels 243
    mutual combat...243
    previous threats 242
Self-Incrimination 47
    protection against....................................48
Selling, Furnishing, Controlled Substances
    in Prison, Camp or Jail 274
Senate 40
The Separate but Equal Doctrine 56
    Brown v. Board of Education 56
    Civil Rights Acts.....................................56
    Jim Crow laws 56
    NAACP..56
    Plessy v. Ferguson 56
Sex Discrimination.......................................56
Shamash 8
SHU
    See: Security Housing Unit
Smoking 288
Smuggling Controlled Substances
    Into Prison or Jail....................................273
Smuggling Firearms, Deadly Weapons,
    or Tear Gas Into a Prison or Jail.................274
Solicitation 185
    Federal Criminal Code............................188
    The Model Penal Code.............................187
    Rex v. Higgins 185
Soliciting
    corroboration for 187
    dangers of..187
    elements of..186
    entrapment...187
    Kelly v. United States 187
    merging and 187
Solon 11, 15, 16, 106
Source of Law 56
Sources of Law
    appellate court decisions 58
    Blackstone's Commentaries 59
    congress...57
    custom and mores 59
    English Common Law 58
    executive agency rules 59
    federal legislature....................................57
    historical and cultural background.............58
    house of representatives............................57
    public corporations...................................58

religion and morality....................................59
social control through
    custom and mores 59
    state constitutions....................................57
    state legislatures......................................58
    U.S. Constitution.....................................57
Spain...19
    Las Siete Partidas....................................20
    Moors 19
    University of Bologna...............................20
    Visigoths 19
Sparta 15
special masters 287
Special Penalties 130
    See also: Punishment
Speedy and Public Trial 50
The Spirit of the Law 111
St. Augustine 211
St. Thomas Aquinas 211
Star Chamber...51
Stare Decisis...21, 24
    See also: Precedent
State Legislature
    assembly..60
    senate..60
Statute of Limitations...................................219
    commencement of prosecution 219
    determining length of sentence 219
    Ex Post Facto application 220
    felonies in general..................................219
        exceptions 219
    misdemeanor offenses.............................219
        exceptions 219
    offenses for which there is none 219
    serious felonies.......................................219
    tolling the time 219
Statutory Law 130
Stephen, Sir James 108, 143, 188, 196, 223
Strict Liability Crimes
    See: Presumed Knowledge
Subpoena..52
Suicide...289
    Allegations, Factual 290
    Liability Theories....................................289
Supreme Court 40, 41, 54, 141
    Decisions re. Amendment 2......................46
    Holmes, Oliver Wendell 44
    justices, nomination of.............................40
    Mapp v. Ohio 47
    Miranda decision.....................................49
    U.S. v. Miller 46
    Warren Court 40
    Warren, Earl..49
Susa 8

Systems of Law 130
    common law....................................130
    statutory law..................................130

T

The Model Penal Code.........................174
Theft..255
    degrees of..256
    grand theft......................................256
    grand theft at a mine 256
    grand theft, other classifications 256
    petty theft 257
    theft of an animal 257
Third Degree 48
Title 15 – California Code of Regulations 265
    Article 1 ....265, 267
    Article 2 267
    Article 3 267
    Article 3.5 265
    Article 4 267
    Article 7 ....267, 268
    Article 8 266
    Article 10 270
Tort suits 288
Torts 127, 282
Trespass Ab Initio 145
Trial by Duel 21
Trial by Jury 21, 41
    Jury of Knights................................22
The Triangle of Crime.........................139
    the cause and effect relationship 153
    criminal conduct.............................139
    joint relationship between
        act and intent.........................153
    law 139
    the mental element 142
True Bill 47
    indictment 47
Turner test 284
Types of Sentencing....................130, 131
    See also: Punishment
    concurrent sentencing 131
    consecutive sentencing...................131
    indeterminate sentencing 130

U

U.S. Constitution..........................57, 215
    See also: Bill of Rights
    Amendments to 42
    Article 1 40
    Article 2 ....40, 44
    Article 3 ....41, 76
    Article 4 41
    Article 5 42

Article 6 ....42, 76, 109
    criminal law, purpose of 106
    fountainhead of American law...........57
    The U.S. Constitution in Development......39
U.S. Supreme Court 75
    court of last resort 79
    Hughes, Chief Justice.......................76
    Marshall, John..................................75
Unanimous Verdicts............................115
Unauthorized Communication 273
Unauthorized Communications
    Selling, Furnishing, Controlled Substances
      in Prison, Camp or Jail.....................274
    Smuggling Controlled Substances
      Into Prison or Jail.............................273
    Smuggling Firearms, Deadly Weapons,
      or Tear Gas Into a Prison or Jail.......274
    Unauthorized Entry on Prison or Jail
      Grounds by an Ex-Convict 273
    Using False Identification to Secure
      Admission to Prison or Camp...........273
The United States 24
    Adams, John......................................26
    Articles of Confederation..................28
    Colony of Rhode Island & Providence
      Plantation 26
    The Declaration of Independence 26
    Declaration of Rights 26
    English mismanagement
      of the colonies................................26
    Franklin, Benjamin 26
    Henry, Patrick 26
    Independent Judiciary 28
    Intolerable Acts.................................26
    Jamestown..24
    Jefferson, Thomas 26
    King James I 24
    Law in Post-Revolutionary Times 28
    Massachusetts Bay Colony 24
    Paine, Thomas..................................28
    Pre-Revolution Colonies...................24
    puritans..24
    The Rights of Man 28
    Second Continental Congress 26
    States' Rights.............................24, 28
    theocracy 24
    Virginia Company.............................24
    Williams, Roger 26
    Winthrop John..................................24
United States Code, section 1983 281
United States Reports............................76
Universal Life Church..........................285
University of Bologna.....................18, 20
Unlawful Assembly...............................45

Unlawful Homicide..................................236
    bare fear 242
    duels 243
    felony murder rule................................236
        (MAD CATS BARK)....................237
        (PET POLY)................................237
    first degree murder................................236
    inherently dangerous misdemeanors........237
    involuntary manslaughter........................238
    killing of trespassers 242
    MAD CATS BARK...............................237
    malice..236
    Manslaughter..238
        involuntary...................................238
        vehicular 237, 239
        voluntary.....................................238
    misdemeanors, inherently dangerous.......237
    murder..236
        first degree 236
        second degree..............................237
    mutual combat......................................243
    PET POLY 237
    previous threats 242
    second degree murder 237
    The "Right to Die" Law.........................237
    trespassers, killing of 242
    vehicular manslaughter...................237, 239
    voluntary manslaughter.........................238
Unreasonable Search and Seizure.............46, 47

V

Vandalism 257
    defacing property 257
    liability limits.......................................257
veto 40
Victimless Crimes...................................133
    Burke, Edmund 133
Visigoths 19

W

Warren Court..282
Watergate
    cover-up 40
Webster, Noah...130
Weld, William F..39
Welfare & Institutions Code Sections
    300 W & I 43
    728 W & I 257
    2690 W & I 271
    2910 W & I 271
    3306 W & I 271
    5654 W & I 271
    5656 W & I 271
    5677 W & I 271
    6254 W & I 271
    6300 W & I 272
    14014 W & I 186
What Makes a Good Law?...........................7
When an Institution Comes
    Under Court Order.................................287
Wilson test...287
Winthrop, Governor 48
Wobbler...128
Women's Rights 56
Words and Phrases 79
Work Group Assignments
    Work Group A-1 266
    Work Group A-2 266
    Work Group B..266
    Work Group C..266
    Work Group D-1 266
    Work Group D-2 266
    Work Group U 266
Wormser, Rene A......................................39
Written Laws, Codes, and Ordinances...............6

Penal Code Sections Referenced

Section	Topic	Page
4 PC	Spirit of the Law	111, 222
7 PC	Definitions of Specialized Terms	116
15 PC	Definition of Crime	139
17 PC	Definitions: Felony, Misdemeanor, Infraction	128
19.6 PC	Infractions	129
19.7 PC	Handling Infractions	129
20 PC	Need for Act and Intent	97, 139
21 PC	Admissibility of Mental State	214
25a PC	Diminished Capacity	214
25b PC	Evidence for Diminished Capacity	214
25c PC	Diminished Capacity at Sentencing	214
26 PC	Persons Capable of Committing Crimes	212, 214
27 PC	Persons Punishable for Crimes	167
28a PC	Evidence of Mental Disease	214
31 PC	Who are Principals in California	167, 170
32 PC	Who are Accessories in California	171
38 PC	Misprision of Treason	116
115 PC	Forged Instruments	243
127 PC	Subornation of Perjury	186
150 PC	Refusing to Assist Officers	116, 224
153 PC	Compounding Crimes	173
182 PC	Conspiracy	189, 191
184 PC	Overt Act Needed in Conspiracy	189
187 PC	Murder Defined	218, 236
188 PC	Malice Defined	236
190 PC	Punishment for Murder	265
190.25 PC	Murder of Transportation Worker	237
191.5 PC	Gross Vehicular Manslaughter	239
192(a) PC	Voluntary Manslaughter	238
192(b) PC	Involuntary Manslaughter	238
192(c) PC	Vehicular Manslaughter	239
192(c)3 PC	Vehicular Manslaughter	239
195 PC	Excusable Homicide	240
196 PC	Justifiable Homicide by Officers	240
197 PC	Justifiable Homicide in General	221, 240, 242
198 PC	Bare Fear in Homicide	221, 242
199 PC	Justifiable and Excusable Homicide, Not Punishable	240
207 PC	Simple Kidnapping	244, 245
209 PC	Ransom Kidnapping	244, 245
210 PC	Posing as a Kidnapper	245
211 PC	Robbery Defined	250, 252
212 PC	Fear as Used in Robbery	252
240 PC	Assault Defined	197, 200, 245
242 PC	Battery Defined	200, 246
245 PC	Assault With a Deadly Weapon	246

Section	Topic	Page
261 PC	Rape	217, 219, 236, 247, 250
261.1 PC	Rape of Mentally Deficient Persons	217, 250
261.2 PC	Rape by Force	217, 250
261.3 PC	Rape by Use of Intoxicants	250
261.4 PC	Rape When Victim is Unconscious	250
261.5 PC	Rape by Fraud	250
261.6 PC	Rape by Threat	250
261.7 PC	Rape by Threat to Retaliate	250
262 PC	Spousal Rape	248, 250
263 PC	Penetration in Rape	248
266 PC	Procuring Females for Prostitution	249
266(h) PC	Pimping	186
266c PC	Inducing Consent by Fraud	249
270 PC	Failure to Provide for Child	43, 147, 239
271 PC	Desertion of Child	237
273.5 PC	Injury Upon Spouse or Cohabitant	128
273a PC	Cruelty to Child	237
285 PC	Incest	199
286 PC	Sodomy	219, 236, 250
288 PC	Child Molesting	219, 236
288.5 PC	Continuous Child Molesting	219
288a PC	Oral Copulation	219, 223, 236, 250
289 PC	Penetration by Foreign Object	113, 219, 236, 250
415 PC	Disturbing the Peace	253
417 PC	Brandishing a Weapon	221
451 PC	Arson Punishment	196
458 PC	Burglary of Cargo Container	253
459 PC	Burglary	253
484 PC	Theft	114, 255
486 PC	Degrees of Theft	256
487 PC	Grand Theft	256
487c PC	Grand Theft of Real Estate	256
487d PC	Grand Theft of Silver From Mine	256
487e PC	Grand Theft of Dogs	257
488 PC	Petty Theft	256, 257
496 PC	Receiving Stolen Property	96
496(4) PC	Receiving Stolen Property	14
497 PC	Bringing Stolen Property into State	256
518 PC	Extortion	252
532 PC	Fraud	255
594 PC	Vandalism	257
594.3 PC	Vandalism of Place of Worship	257
647(a) PC	Soliciting Lewd Acts	186
647(b) PC	Soliciting Prostitution	186
653f PC	Soliciting Listed Crimes	185, 186
654 PC	Double Jeopardy	244
656 PC	Double Jeopardy – Foreign Acquittals	217
663 PC	Attempts to Commit Crime	196

Section	Topic	Page
664 PC	Attempts to Commit Crime – Punishment	96, 196
687 PC	Double Jeopardy	217
793 PC	Double Jeopardy – Conviction or Acquittal in Another State	217
794 PC	Double Jeopardy – Conviction or Acquittal in Another Court	217
799 PC	Statute of Limitations	219, 220
800 PC	Statute of Limitations	219
801 PC	Statute of Limitations for Felonies	219
801.5 PC	Statute of Limitations – False Insurance Claims	219
802 PC	Statute of Limitations – Misdemeanors	220
802(a) PC	Statute of Limitations – Misdemeanors, Exceptions	219
802(b) PC	Statute of Limitations – Exceptions	219
803 PC	Tolling or Extension of Statute of Limitations	219
804 PC	Commencement of Prosecution – Statute of Limitations	219
805 PC	Limitations Determined by Maximum Punishment Listed	219
834 PC	Arrest Defined	244
835a PC	Reasonable Force	243
837 PC	Arrest by Private Persons	244
995 PC	Indictments	96
1026 PC	Plea of Insanity	214
1027 PC	Examination by Psychiatrist	214
1096 PC	Presumption of Innocence	114
1099 PC	Turning State's Evidence	218
1100 PC	Turning State's Evidence	218
1111 PC	Corroboration of an Accomplice	174, 213
1140 PC	Discharge of Juries	217
1141 PC	Hung Juries	217
1203.016 PC	Home Detention Program	271
1238(a) PC	Appeals	96
1324 PC	Compelling Witness Testimony – Felonies	220
1324.1 PC	Compelling Witness Testimonies – Misdemeanors	221
1377 PC	Compromising Crimes	173
1378 PC	Compromising Crimes	173
1379 PC	Compromising Crimes	173
1429.5 PC	Pleas of Insanity – Misdemeanors	214
2931 PC	Reduction of Sentence for Good Behavior	265
2933 PC	Work-time Credit	265
4500 PC	Aggravated Assault by Life Prisoner	270
4501 PC	Aggravated Assault by Non-Life Prisoner	270
4501.1 PC	"Gassing" by Inmate	270
4501.5 PC	Battery by Prisoner on Non-Prisoner	270
4502 PC	Possession of Weapons by Prisoner	271
4503 PC	Holding Hostage in Prison	271
4530 PC	Escape or Attempted Escape	271
4530.5 PC	Escape From Dual Vocational Institution	271
4532 PC	Escape From County or City Jail	271
4533 PC	Officers Who Aid Escape	272
4534 PC	Assisting Escapee With Revoked Parole	272
4535 PC	Bringing Escape Articles Into Prison or Jail	272

Section	Topic	Page
4536 PC	Escape by Sex Offender	272
4536(b) PC	Duties of Prison Medical Director Upon Escape by Sex Offender	272
4537 PC	Duties Upon Escape From Secure Detention Facility	272
4550 PC	Rescue	272
4570 PC	Smuggling Letters Into Prisons	273
4570.1 PC	Unauthorized Communication With Prisoner in Transport	273
4570.5 PC	Securing Admission to Prison With False I.D.	273
4571 PC	Unauthorized Entry by Ex-Convict	273
4573 PC	Smuggling Controlled Substances Into Prison or Jail	273
4573.5 PC	Bringing Drugs or Alcohol Into Prison or Jail	273
4573.6 PC	Possession of Controlled Substances Where Prisoners Are Kept	274
4573.8 PC	Possession of Alcohol in Prison Camp or Jail	274
4573.9 PC	Selling Controlled Substances in Prison or Jail	274
4574 PC	Smuggling Deadly Weapons Into Prison or Jail	274
4600 PC	Damaging Prison or Jail	274
12021 PC	Possession of Illegal Weapons	141
12025 PC	Carrying Concealed Weapons	112
12091 PC	Tampering With Firearm Identification	114
12420 PC	Sale of Firearms	112

Cases Cited in Body of Text

Adamson v. California 55
Bias v. United States 146
Branzburg v. Hayes.......................................44
Brown v. Board of Education 56
Fletcher v. Peck.......................................76
Furman v. Georgia 53
Griffin v. California 55
Hurtado v. California 52
Hutchins v. County Clerk
    of Merced County 98
In re Gault 79, 105
In re Iverson 110
Jackson v. Commonwealth 145
Kelly v. United States 187
Lupo v. Superior Court 96
Mapp v. Ohio 47
Marbury v. Madison.......................................75, 76
Miranda v. Arizona 49, 76, 79, 105
Mountain View Union High School District v.
    City Council Of City Of Sunnyvale...........98
People by McCullough v. Shearer 97
People v. Barranza 218
People v. Borra.......................................252
People v. Bradbury.......................................246
People v. Callihan 252
People v. Chapman 219
People v. Chessman 245
People v. Drew.......................................214
People v. Evan.......................................245
People v. Flanagan 241
People v. Hanselman.......................................218
People v. Hernandez 76, 96

People v. Lowen.......................................255
People v. Macintire 218
People v. Meyers.......................................96
People v. Moran 191
People v. Moss 96
People v. Nicolaus.......................................214
People v. Parker 96
People v. Pierre 218
People v. Plascile 174
People v. Robey 150
People v. Rojas.......................................96
People v. Sheffield 76
People v. Silverstein.......................................218
People v. Wallace.......................................237
People v. Weber 116
People v. Werner.......................................186
Peterson v. City of Long Beach 241
Plessy v. Ferguson.......................................56
Powell v. Texas 142
Rex v. Higgins.......................................185
Rex v. Scofield.......................................196
Sauer v. United States 106
Solesbee v. Balkcom 49
State v. Miller.......................................148
State v. Whitfield 144
Stehr v. State 148
Trop v. Dulles 53
U.S. v. Cruikshank 46
U.S. v. Miller.......................................46
United States v. Watson 107
Weeks v. United States 46
Young v. Superior Court.......................................96